LANGUAGE HISTORY

Volume 191

Andrew L. Sihler

Language History
An introduction

LANGUAGE HISTORY

AN INTRODUCTION

ANDREW L. SIHLER
University of Wisconsin, Madison

JOHN BENJAMINS PUBLISHING COMPANY
AMSTERDAM/PHILADELPHIA

The paper used in this publication meets the minimum requirements of American National Standard for Information Sciences — Permanence of Paper for Printed Library Materials, ANSI Z39.48-1984.

Cover design:Françoise Berserik

Library of Congress Cataloging-in-Publication Data

Sihler, Andrew L.
     Language history : an introduction / Andrew L. Sihler.
          p.   cm. -- (Amsterdam studies in the theory and history of linguistic science. Series IV,
Current issues in linguistic theory, ISSN 0304-0763 ; v. 191)
     Includes bibliographical references and index.
     1. Historical linguistics. 2. Linguistic change. I. Title. II. Series.
P140.S53   2000
417'.7--dc21   99-049417
ISBN 90 272 3697 6 (Eur.) / 1 55619 968 6 (US) (Hb; alk. paper)   CIP
ISBN 90 272 3698 4 (Eur.) / 1 55619 969 4 (US) (Pb; alk. paper)

John Benjamins Publishing Co. • P.O.Box 75577 • 1070 AN Amsterdam • The Netherlands
John Benjamins North America • P.O.Box 27519 • Philadelphia PA 19118-0519 • USA

IN MEMORY OF

Valdis Juris Zeps

1932 – 1996

PREFACE

THIS WORK STARTED OUT as a revision and expansion of the remarks about historical linguistics, titled 'Some general features of linguistic history', that occupy 37 pages of Carl Darling Buck's *Comparative Grammar of Greek and Latin* (1933: University of Chicago), now out of print. My revision of the comparative grammar itself resulted in a work so large that it seemed prudent to publish separately what had grown into a whole course in the whys and hows of historical and comparative linguistics.

Published separately, moreover, it would be not only a companion volume to the *New Comparative Grammar of Greek and Latin;* it should be a useful guide for anyone unfamiliar with linguistics who was trying to study of the history of any language, and perhaps even those who are enrolled in courses devoted to reading texts in old languages (Old English, Old Church Slavic, Middle French, Gothic, e.g.), since the way most such courses are taught, some portion of them is devoted to the history of the language.

Conversations with colleagues who regularly teach such courses confirmed two things. Very few of their students have any idea of why or how languages change, or what proto-forms actually are, or how they are arrived at (never mind why). In an ideal world, students would take a couple of semesters of descriptive and historical linguistics as prerequisites, but that is an unrealistic expectation. Of course, some students, presented with the findings of historical linguistics, seem to be able to infer by induction at least some of the principles involved. But even the apt and interested would learn more (as well as more accurately and in less time) given a systematic survey, however compendious.

In fact, compendiousness would be a prime virtue. There are several superb introductions to historical and comparative linguistics available now, such as Bynon 1977, Anttila 1988, Hock 1985, Hock and Joseph 1996; but their excellence is due in part to their thoroughness and technical rigor. These very qualities unsuit them for the purpose at hand. They amount to full semester (if not full year) courses of study. There are, or have been, briefer and simpler treatments available, but in my opinion they are marred by serious technical and even factual errors. Virtually all general introductory linguistic textbooks have a chapter on historical linguistics; but they are superficial (comparative linguistics is rarely more than mentioned, for example) and worse, they usually are inaccurate and flawed technically in all sorts of ways large and small—misused terms, incorrectly cited forms, and just plain mistakes (a best-selling introductory text now in its 5th edition lists *orthography* as an example of a loan word from Latin, and *verdict* as a borrowing from French).

This work aspires to be a brief but technically and factually accurate exposition of linguistic description and history. Whether studied as a thing in itself at the beginning of the term, or 'backgrounded' while the prime subject matter is tackled, it should help students understand the assumptions and reasoning that underlie the contents of their handbooks and etymological dictionaries. And while the facts and theories set forth here are prevailingly what might be called the Industry Standard, no claim is made for certified *communis opinio* status of any particular assertion. Some widely-held views, furthermore, are simply disregarded as being too fallacious to bother with, wide belief to the contrary notwithstanding (for example, the proposition that loan words are 'immune' to phonological rules, or the fictitious phonetic features known as *tense* and *lax*).

The heart of the book is the brief chapter on linguistic reconstruction (which traditionally goes by the odd name of 'the comparative method'). Leading up to it are some discussions of how languages change through time. Taken as a whole, this sequence of chapters explains where the teachings of handbooks regarding unrecorded language change come from.

Following the discussion and demonstration of linguistic reconstruction there are chapters on the interpretation of written records, the language-external aspects of language change (dialects, for example), and then finally, almost as an appendix, a systematic discussion of articulatory phonetics. There is a glossary of terms.

Although as stated above Buck's introductory section to his *Comparative Grammar* formed the basis for this work, even in the early stages of reworking the material it was both much enlarged and very much transformed. Subsequently, as the prospect of publishing a free-standing volume became more palpable, I have actually undertaken to free the work from specific indebtedness to Buck, retaining at most a few of his examples, though here and there a phrase may have survived verbatim.

ACKNOWLEDGEMENTS

I am indebted to classroom tests of earlier versions of this work by Jeffrey Wills and Rob Howell, of the University of Wisconsin – Madison, and to their good-natured students. Brent Vine contributed useful comments when the work was still encysted in the *New Comparative Grammar,* and also has used a draft of *Language Change* in a course of his at UCLA. I have been fortunate to be able to take advantage of the acute and useful suggestions provided by Michael Job and a second (anonymous) reader for John Benjamins. Thomas Purnell was kind enough to look over the Appendix, and to respond helpfully to many inquiries on phonetic matters, both articulatory and acoustic. Friends and former students, most notably John Winston, Benjamin Moore, and Ted Voth, have contributed valuable observations and corrections. Of course, whatever faults remain are on my head alone.

Apart from functioning occasionally as a native-speaker sounding-board, John Tallman made no technical contribution to this work; but without his encouragement and support, you would not be reading these lines.

As I buckled down to work on this book, I consulted profitably with my colleague Valdis Zeps on a numberless variety of matters of both form and content. I looked forward with relish to his inspection of the completed text—for the pleasure it probably would have given him; for the praise I smugly anticipated; and, most of all, for the valuable criticism he would have certainly offered. I am cheated of his pleasure; the reader is cheated of his wisdom and knowledge.

A.L.S.
MADISON, OCTOBER 1999

CONTENTS

A NOTE ON NOTATION

For the values of phonetic symbols and definitions of phonetic terms see the Appendix on phonetics (p. 209) and the charts on pp. 230 ff.

All forms cited or mentioned (rather than used) are printed in *italics*.

Glosses or translations are presented between 'single quotes'.

For emphasis, words in running text are printed in SMALL CAPS.

Square brackets [ ] enclose phonetic symbols, virgules / / enclose phonemic transcriptions, thus: NE *span* /spæn/ [sp˭æˀn].

A few times, the standard notation ⟨ ⟩ is used to enclose letters qua letters, as ⟨s⟩ = 'the letter *s*', though usually italics serve the same purpose.

The symbol > means 'becomes, gives'; < means 'comes from'.

An asterisk (*) marks forms unattested as such, usually because they are reconstructed. For example: PIE *dek̑m̥t* 'ten' > PGmc *tehun* > OE *tíen* 'ten', where both the Proto-Indo-European and Proto-Germanic forms are hypothetical.

If the form is unattested because it is thought never to have existed, it is marked thus: NE ˣ*wenten*.

Modern languages are cited in standard native orthography, occasionally with phonetic or phonemic notes.

Latin forms are cited in normalized native orthography, with the addition of indications of vowel length by macrons, *ā ē* and so on.

Greek is transliterated from normalized native orthography into Latin characters following the usual conventions (φ θ χ = *ph th kh*, ξ ψ = *ks ps*, ἁ ῆ οῦ = *â ê oû*, ἁ ἡ ὑ = *ha, hē, hu,* and so on).

Gothic: *e o* are long vowels corresponding to short *ai, au;* and *ei* is a high front long vowel corresponding to short *i* (see **131** for further discussion of Gothic vowels). *þ* is a voiceless apical slit fricative, and *h* is a consonant in all positions.

Old English: forms are usually cited in a normalized West Saxon orthography. Fricatives (*f þ s*) are voiced between vowels and voiceless elsewhere; *sc* /š/ is always voiceless, and *h* is pronounced in all positions (probably as [χ] in some of them, as still in present-day Scots).

The letter *c* stands for /k/ but occasionally for /č/ or possibly /k̯/, in which case it will be spelled *ċ*, as in *ċinn* 'chin'. The letter *g* has the value /y/ before a front vowel: *giest* /yiest/ 'guest', *geoc* /yok/ 'yoke'. After a front vowel it has the value [y̯]; between back vowels, [ɣ]: OE *dæg* [dæy̯] 'day', *dagas* nom.pl. [daɣas]. The letter *y* stands for a high front rounded vowel: *cynn* /künn/ 'kinsman'. Long vowels are indicated with an acute accent: *á* = /ā/.

Indic (Vedic and Sanskrit) forms are cited according to a widely-used system of transliteration. Retroflex (apico-domal) consonants are rendered *ṭ ṭh ḍ ḍh ṇ ṣ*. Stop symbols with a following *h* (e.g. *th dh bh*) are phonemes, distinguished from plain stops by an aspirated release. (The sounds written *gh ḍh dh bh* and *h* are usually called *voiced aspirated* but are more likely to have been *murmured*.) The letters *c j* represent palatal stops; *ś* is a palatal fricative. The short vowels of Indic are *a i u;* the letters *e o* are officially diphthongs, reflecting PInIr. **ai *au*, but from an early time were phonetically [e· o·]. Other long vowels are written with macrons. The symbol *ṛ* represents a syllabic liquid.

Old Irish orthography is complicated and all cited forms will be accompanied by phonemic transcriptions. Long vowels are indicated by an acute accent.

In transcription, Irish consonants are indicated as follows. Palatalized consonants are indicated by a following ᵞ. Plain consonants are written in Latin letters, lenited consonants are indicated by letters from the Greek alphabet, as follows:

plain: /t k b d g m n r l/
lenited: /θ χ β δ γ μ ν ρ λ/

Examples: *fer* nom.sg. 'man' /feρ/; *fir* gen.sg. /fiρ ᵞ/; *siur* 'sister' /s ᵞiuρ/; *én* 'bird' /ēn/; *cóic* 'five' /kōg ᵞ/; *in tain* 'when' /intav ᵞ/; *teng(a)e* 'tongue' /t ᵞeŋge/.

ABBREVIATIONS

acc. accusative
Av. Avestan
f. feminine
Fi. Finnish
Fr. French
gen. genitive
Gk Greek
Go. Gothic
Hebr. Hebrew
Hu. Hungarian
It. Italian
Ital. Italic
Lat. Latin
Lith. Lithuanian
LLat. Late Latin
m. masculine
ME Middle English
n. neuter
NE Modern English
NHG Modern (High) German
nom. nominative
OCS Old Church Slavic
OE Old Engish
OFr. Old French
OHG Old High German

OIr. Old Irish
OLat. Old Latin
ON Old Norse
OPr. Old Prussian
OS Old Saxon
PFiUg. Proto-Finno-Ugric
PGk Proto-Greek
PGmc Proto-Germanic
PIE Proto-Indo-European
PInIr. Proto-Indo-Iranian
PItal. Proto-Italic
pl. plural
Port. Portuguese
PreRom. PreRomance
PRom. Proto-Romance
PWGmc Proto-West-Germanic
PWRom. Proto-Western Romance
Rom. Romanian
Ru. Russian
sg. singular
Skt Sanskrit
Sp. Spanish
Ukr. Ukrainian
Ved. Vedic
W Welsh

INTRODUCTION

1. What is historical linguistics? (And why?)

All languages used with any regularity for framing fresh communications change continuously. These changes will occur in all realms of linguistic organization: the pronunciation, the sound system, the morphology, the lexicon, the semantics, the syntax. Presumably the only components of language truly immune to change are *language universals*, that is, those structural properties which are indispensable to human language. The identification of specific traits which can claim to be truly universal has hitherto resisted consensus; but that is no real problem for us, since the concern of historical linguistics is those traits of human language which are LANGUAGE-SPECIFIC, not universal: by definition, truly universal traits can tell us nothing about the specific history of specific languages.

> **a.** The description 'framing fresh communications' applies to languages used routinely in a speech community, obviously; but less obviously also to languages cultivated by a subset of the population for written use, exclusively or primarily. Thus, the Latin used in communications issued by the Roman Catholic Church in 1990 will be seen to be different, in various consistent ways, from the Latin used in such communications in 1880 or 1660. The same thing applies to Classical Arabic as currently written or spoken, compared to the language of the same name used several centuries ago. Part of the reason for the requirement is to exclude texts which are transmitted only in faithfully (re)copied and reproduced forms. What are called linguistic monuments—the text of a speech by Cicero, say, or a play by Kālidāsa, bookkeeping records of Mycenaean accountants, the novels of Trollope—will alter only by error or by editorial decision, changes quite unlike the changes discussed in this book.

Historical (diachronic) linguistics is the study of the principles of language change, and this book is nothing more than a survey of the implications of the first sentence of this chapter. In particular, we are concerned with the fact that a language can change so much as to become a different language, or (quite commonly) evolve into several different languages—which make up what is known as a *language family*. An example of this is the family of Romance languages (French, Italian, Portuguese, and many others).

This has an interesting implication, namely, that it might be possible, theoretically, to tell when different languages are the products of such an evolution, even when it took place prehistorically. That is, different languages can be proved to have been THE SAME LANGUAGE at some time in the past, when the known principles of language change allow us to *reconstruct* the features of such a *proto-language,* as it is called. The body of reasoning and principles for turning the linguistic clock back, so to say, is known as the *comparative method*—an odd term, but the standard one. The comparative method is discussed and demonstrated in 94-103.

    b. It is important to remember that it is now the case, and always has been so, that the great majority of the world's languages are known only in spoken form, being written down only—if ever—by scholars as objects of study. Such study, incidentally, though largely a modern phenomenon, does have antecedents. In Istanbul in the late 16th century the Flemish merchant-diplomat Ogier Ghiselin van Busbecq invited two speakers of the Germanic language we now call Crimean Gothic to dinner, and performed some rough and ready field work on the spot. Doubtless the same sort of thing has happened from time to time the world over, though largely lost to history.

2. Innovations

Changes in language, or *innovations*, are interesting chiefly when they become general in a community, but obviously innovations cannot originate collectively. All must have modest beginnings; in fact they presumably have to be uttered for the first time by a single speaker. Some of these novelties will be imitated by other speakers, and then imitated by still others. If the process is sustained, the innovation will spread through the whole speech community, though commonly it spreads only to a greater or lesser fraction of the community, resulting in linguistic discontinuities in the community.[1]

---

[1] It is not of course an absolute requirement that innovations originate with a 'single speaker'. Obvious ones might well occur to different speakers independently, for example the reinterpretation of adverbial genitives like *Mondays* and *nights* (as in *Closed Mondays* or *Fred doesn't mind working nights*) as plurals, whence *closed on Mondays*. It is unlikely that this happened only once in the history of English.

    See 112-4 and 116 regarding the origin of dialects, and of dialect continua.)

At first, since most innovations are matters of minor detail when compared to the profuse complexity of language as a whole, they largely escape notice; but with the passage of time, differences accumulate to the point that native speakers are conscious of them, if only impressionistically—Americans will readily say that someone has 'a southern accent', for example, without having any grasp of the objective facts that lead them to that impression; and without knowing—or caring—that they lump together a multitude of distinct regional forms of speech under the term 'southern accent'.

With the passage of enough time, however, and the steady accumulation of innovations, inevitably the language used in different speech communities will become too different for there to be much hope of successful communication between speakers of the different varieties. 'Communication' between a monolingual speaker of English and a monolingual German, if it takes place at all, will be largely by gesture, physical context, and guess-work. It makes no difference that English and German were the same language at some point in the not very distant past; and even though there are still extensive similarities between them, and of a highly systematic nature besides. As wholes they are simply too different for a speaker of one to understand a speaker of the other, without special training.

From the point of view of such special training—learning a foreign language, as it is commonly put—it is probably no easier for a speaker of English to learn German than Latin, and arguably harder than learning Chinese. But owing to their histories, an objective and systematic COMPARISON of the features of English and German will yield very different results from such a comparison of the features of English and Latin, or English and Chinese. Upon inspection, the similarities in structure between English and German will be observed to be closer and very much more numerous than between English and Latin or English and Chinese. This is because English and German were the same language as recently as 2200 years ago, whereas English and Latin were the same language some 7000 years ago. (In both cases the dating is mostly a guess, but the difference in magnitude is trustworthy.) The innovations which created ever-greater differences between originally identical languages have been accumulating for something like four times as long between English and Latin as between English and

German. And if English and Chinese were ever the same language in the first place, it was so long ago that the fact itself cannot be demonstrated, though there is no reason to think it impossible.

    a. There are serious conceptual challenges involved in any discussion of language change. In a very real sense, French is 'the same language' as Latin. At least, it's 'the same language' in exactly the way that French spoken 100 years ago and modern French are 'the same language'. Put differently, Latin is not a dead language, as it's often called: it's alive and well, only we CALL it French. (By contrast, a language like Gothic, a Germanic language, is truly 'dead': it has not only ceased being spoken in the form known to Bishop Wulfilas and his friends; it has ceased being spoken in any form whatever.)

    At the same time, however, if we think of French as just Latin by a different name, that presents us with the problem of Italian, Sardo, Romanian, and the other Romance languages: they too are just Latin by a different name. But there is no question that all these ARE different languages. This, then, is the paradox: that a pair of languages like French and Spanish are from one perspective 'the same language by different names', and from another perspective they are unquestionably 'different languages'; and, similarly, from one perspective a language like Latin 'has no native speakers', that is, it is 'dead'; while from another it is very much alive, being spoken by many millions of speakers of Romance languages.

    Parenthetically, Latin occupies yet another niche, that of a *classical language*, that is, a language with no native speakers which has some sort of specialized use, often contemporaneously with its own 'descendants'. Sanskrit and (genuine) Classical Arabic are in this category; Old Church Slavic used to be, but no longer is.

3. Pervasiveness of Change

As stated above, if one looks at the changes that take place in a given language through time one will find great and small changes in all components of the language. To take Old English (ca. 10th century AD) and Modern English as an example, consider the following.

Changes in phonology:

Old English	Modern English
gós /gōs/	goose /guws/
gés /gēs/	geese /giys/
hús /hūs/	house /haws/
furh /furχ/	furrow /fərow/

mýs /mūs/	mice /mays/
þynne /θünne/	thin /θin/
nama /nama/	name /neym/
wulfas /wulfas/	wolves /wulvz/
cniht /kniχt/	knight /nayt/
on lífe /on līfe/	alive /əlayv/
hafoc /hafok/	hawk /hɔk/
hring /hring/	ring /riŋ/ (finger)

Changes in morphology:

Old English	Modern English
(tó) climban(ne) /tō klimban(ne)/	to climb /klaym/
iċ climbe /ič klimbe/	I climb
þú climbest /θū klimbest/	you climb
hé, héo, hit climbeþ /hē, hēə, hit klimbeθ/	he, she, it climbs
wé climbaþ /wē klimbaθ/	we climb
gé climbaþ /yē klimbaθ/	you climb
híe climbaþ /hīə klimbaθ/	they climb
iċ clamb /ič klamb/	I climbed /klaymd/
þú clumbe /θū klumbe/	you climbed
hé, héo, hit clamb /hē, hēə, hit klamb/	he, she, it climbed
wé clumbon /wē klumbon/	we climbed
gé clumbon /yē klumbon/	you climbed
híe clumbon /hīə klumbon/	they climbed
climbend /klimbend/	climbing /klaymiŋ/

4. **Changes in the verb system** involve two separate but interrelated matters, the subject pronouns and the forms of the verbs themselves.

   The changes in the forms of *iċ, hé, héo, hit,* and *wé* are largely phonological (with contamination (51) in the case of NE *she* for expected— and dialectal—*sho*).

   The second person singular has been lost in standard English altogether. Where it is found, in religious and poetic texts (that is, in archaic and archaizing texts), both the pronoun and the verb forms are transmitted faithfully: *thou comest.*

   What is etymologically the objective case of the 2nd person plural, *you,* has displaced the subject form *ye.* The process of replacement (accompanied by much confusion) is well under way as early as the King James Bible, which has only a statistical preference for *ye* over *you* as subject. The old pronoun is fossilized in *looky (here), thankee,* and in various versions of the home-call in the game of hide and seek (the one I grew up with was the nonsensical *all-ee all-ee in come free*).

NE *they* is not from OE *híe;* it is a loan from a Scandinavian source.

With regard to the verb forms themselves, one of the more obvious changes is seen in the preterite (past tense). In Old English, many classes of common verbs (such as the one *climban* belongs to) had two different stems in the preterite: one just for the first and third persons singular indicative, and a different one for the remaining forms, including the subjunctive. With the sole exception of the verb *be,* and its past tense forms *was* and *were* (which—by chance—has exactly the same distribution as in Old English), all verbs now have a single past tense stem.

The person-marking endings of verbs in Old English had already undergone considerable reduction and simplification from still earlier states; the plural persons, for example, had had three distinct endings in both the present and the preterite (cf. Go. *bairam, bairiþ, bairand* 'we, ye, they carry'). Nevertheless, all finite verbs in Old English had a person-marking ending, whereas Modern English has only one, the 3sg. in *-s.* And ironically this does not actually continue the ending *-þ* seen above. It is an ending proper to northern dialects, and competed with the inherited ending (*goeth, cometh,* and so on) well into Early Modern English. The ending *-s* is etymologically the original form of the SECOND person singular ending (cf. Go. *þu bairis* 'you carry')—a shift in function found also in the North Germanic branch.

The absence of 2sg. *-st* in Modern English is not the loss of an ending, but the loss of the whole category of second person singular; that is, *you climb* is the old second person plural, and a replacement of *thou climbest,* not an evolution from it.

The loss of the 1sg. *-e* would be phonologically regular, that is, it is one example of the general loss of word-final vowels; but the dropping of the infinitive marker, and of the plural endings (both present and preterite), must be a STRUCTURAL change, to judge by the preservation of similar shapes in forms like *token, chosen, golden, oxen,* and the 3sg.

forms *cometh* and the like mentioned above. The plural ending survived longest in *doth* (a word both short and very frequent), which is attested as a plural verb (all persons) as late as the 16th century.

The history of the present-day form *climbing* is uncertain, beyond the observation that *-ing* cannot reflect OE *climbend*. Forms in *-and* (which do) survived in Scots until very recently; and informal/colloquial forms of the *climbin'* type, though late attested in southerly dialects of English, are probably also reflexes of the Old English form.[1]

5. Nouns

So much has changed in the structure of English nouns that it would be misleading to try to compare the morphology of Old and Modern English directly. An earlier system has simply been swept away, replaced by a very different system. A fragment of the replacement process may be glimpsed in a comparison of NE *(the) wound*, pl. *(the) wounds* (no cases and no gender concord) with its Old English source, one of several feminine-concord noun types (and one of some ten or a dozen paradigmatic noun types in three different genders).

The noun paradigm (with the feminine definite article) runs thus:

	singular	*plural*
nominative	séo wund	þá wunda
genitive	þǽre wunde	þára wunda
dative	þǽre wunde	þǽm wundum
accusative	þá wunde	þá wunda

6. Remarks on the noun forms

The loss of case-marked nouns was partly a matter of phonology, as by Early Modern English all of the cases consisting of a final vowel

---

[1] That is, the ending in *comin'* has not in fact 'dropped a *g*' but never had it in the first place. The similar alternation seen in *nothin'* vs *nothing* is then either a parallel and unrelated development, or else is somehow a secondary development growing out of the competition between gerunds with and without the 'dropped *g*'. (In Modern English, of course, the competition between /n/ and /ŋ/ as the final consonant of e.g. *coming* is not a matter of 'dropping' anything, but a matter of a change in point of articulation (A12). The 'dropping' business is based on spelling.)

would have fallen off of the ends of the words by regular sound laws (30). The loss of the dative plural *-um* must have been a morphological innovation, however, since the ending should have been preserved, and is actually seen in *seldom* and the now uncommon form *whilom* 'former(ly)' < OE *hwílum*, the dative plural of *hwíl* 'time(span)' (NE *while*). (But *-om* is not straight from *-um;* see p. 25 fn.)

Note that Modern English nouns do not have a possessive (better: genitive) case. The old genitive case as seen in OE *wulfes* 'wolf's' is the SOURCE of present-day 'apostrophe *-s*', but the form itself is now an enclitic—as distinct from a suffix—and therefore is no longer a feature of noun morphology. This may be seen in such commonplace utterances as *I can't find that painter who called yesterday's phone number,* or: *What's the car in back of mine's license number?* The process of detaching the ending may have started in situations where a genitive noun is modified by a prepositional phrase, as in *Duke of Norfolk:* exactly how the Duke of Norfolk could possess something was debated several hundred years ago, some grammarians condemning an expression like *The Duke of Norfolk's horse* as illogical and ungrammatical.[1] Once it prevailed, however, it led to the modern English situation as demonstrated above, namely, that the genitive relation is marked not by a suffix but by a particle which is enclitic upon whatever the last word of a noun phrase happens to be. That this is in fact usually a noun is only incidental (it's often the wrong noun in any case).

By one interpretation pronouns have an actual genitive case, but in fact the pronouns of English fit into the structure of nouns and adjectives so badly overall that it's a non-trivial problem how to analyze the morphosyntax of the various forms.

---

[1] The notion that the ending *-s* was a contraction of *his* accounts for the convention of spelling the form with an apostrophe (and for the occasional writing-out, in earlier times, of the supposed full form: *the king his ministers*). This misprision led in turn to puristical quandaries over the supposedly oxymoronic nature of phrases like *mother's milk* or *Queen's favourite*, which by such reasoning should be *mother her milk* and *Queen her favourite*. Some grammarians and usage arbiters actually plumped for such forms.

7. Changes in English syntax

Until a few hundred years ago the normal English syntax for questions and denials in sentences with simple verbs were of the type *What says she?* and *He gave not his reasons.* That is, they were formed the same way as present-day *Where is she?* and *He was not happy.* This syntax was replaced by structures containing a form of the verb *do*, which brings no meaning to the utterance; it serves the morphosyntactic function of carrying the tense-marker: the present-day equivalents of the given sentences would be *He didn't give his reasons* (parallel to *He hasn't given his reasons*) and *What does she say?* (parallel to *What would she say?*). That is, the syntax of negatives and denials in clauses containing simple verbs has been assimilated to the syntax of phrasal verbs, by using *do* as a dummy auxiliary. The process is still continuing in a small way: older speakers of American English, and speakers of British English generally, prefer *Have you the time?* and *They haven't any children* to the now commonplace American *Do you have the time?* and *They don't have any children.*[1]

A very recent development in English is seen in sentences like *The problem is is that the payment always arrives late.* The innovation seems to consist of redefining *The problem is* as a sentence, which is the subject of the matrix sentence ...*is that the payment always arrives late.* This may somehow be traceable to structures like *What the problem is is still unclear,* where the syntax is transparent.

8. Changes in meaning

Semantic change is so ubiquitous that hardly a word in the dictionary lacks earlier meanings more or less different from the present-day sense(s). These matters are discussed more fully in **56-92**. For now consider the following samples. *Sacrilege* in Early Modern English meant 'stealing from a church', but now it means 'any serious affront to re-

---

[1] Even in the conservative dialects, *do you have* does occur, but with a different meaning from *have you.* This may be seen in the response of an Englishwoman when asked *Do you have children?* by an American. She said, *Yes, from time to time.* Note that in both American and British English, but to a greater extent in the latter, *have got* has become a virtual synonym of *have,* thus *Have you got enough money?* or, even more informally, *Got the time?*

ligious teaching or sensibility'; *effeminate* formerly meant 'given to the company and pleasures of women', now 'like a woman; lacking manly traits' (prominently including by implication the manly trait of a preference for the opposite sex). Lat. *meticulōsus* 'fearful', i.e. both 'timid' and 'intimidating' was borrowed into English in the 16th century as *meticulous* with the meaning 'timid'; it would be more than three hundred years before the first appearance of the present-day meaning. OE *spillan* meant 'kill, put to death' (and commonly contrasted with 'spare'), then 'demolish, spoil' (an unrelated word), 'render useless' (AD 1124: *six men [wæron] spilde of here æʒon & of here stanes,* i.e. they were blinded and castrated), then 'waste, squander' whence the present-day sense (which is not always negative: cf. *spillway,* and letting wind out of a sail is called *spilling.*) As recently as a hundred years ago the normal meaning of *versatile* was 'changeable, opportunistic, fickle'. The modal auxiliaries have played a kind of semantic Musical Chairs: *may* formerly meant 'is able' (whence the original meaning of *dismay* 'deprive of courage, neutralize'); *can* meant 'knows how to'; *shall* meant 'must'; *will* meant 'wants to'; *wants* meant 'is lacking'. (The case of *wants* differs from the other examples in that the earlier meaning is still at least somewhat accessible.)

9. Changes in English lexicon

Changes in lexicon are common in languages generally, but are abundant in the recent history of English. A single column in a standard glossary to the Old English poem *Béowulf* consists of the thirteen items on the facing page.

Many of these forms, including most of those lost in modern English, appear to have been poetical words in any case. But some in this category, like *gamol* 'old', have well-attested non-poetic cognates in both ancient and modern Germanic languages.

Truly, only *galga, gán,* and *-tréow* 'gallows, go, tree' have survived into present times unchanged apart from the regular action of sound laws and the usual morphological adjustments (with the additional detail of the conversion of *galga* into a plural noun; and the dialectal and old-fashioned terms *galluses* and *gallus* 'suspenders, braces' are the same word).

gád 'lack, want'
gædeling 'kinsman, companion'
gæst, gest 'visitor, stranger'
gǽst, gást 'spirit, soul'
galan 'to sing; to sound'
g(e)aldor 'sound; incantation'
galga 'gallows'
galgmód 'gloomy, depressed'
galgtréow 'gallows-tree'
gamen, gomen 'mirth; amusement, sport'
gamol 'old'
gamolfeax 'grey-haired'
gán 'to go, to walk'

Some have survived in form but have undergone changes in meaning. *Gamen/gomen* survives in NE *game* (all senses, including animal quarry); *gǽst/gást* survives in NE *ghost* with a bogus -*h*- and a substantial change in meaning;[1] the root element of *galan* survives—etymologically only—in the old compound *nightingale*. (NE *yell* reflects OE *giellan*, the same root but a different stem.) *Gædeling* lasted into Early Modern English, and is said to survive in dialects, as *gadling* 'hanger-on, young punk; vagabond'; its root verb maintains a precarious existence in standard English *to gad about* 'to be busy with foolish or suspect errands'.[2] NE *guest*—the Frenchified spelling is bogus—with its intial /g/, is not directly from OE *giest* /yiest/ (to cite it in its West Saxon form). The modern word is a borrowing from or influenced by a Scandinavian source, as are a large number of basic English words.

In sum, what we see here is considerable lexical mortality. We also see that the items which survive formally have usually undergone considerable (if generally straightforward) changes in sense. Finally, some items are maintained in the current lexicon but only in out-of-the-way places (*nightingale*) or in very narrow usage (*gad about*).

---

[1] The Old English sense occurs in a few fixed collocations: *Holy Ghost* (common), *ghostly advice* 'advice on spiritual matters' (and similar phrases; rare). Pockets of obsolete semantics in a lexicon are normal, as we shall see (59a).

[2] *Gadfly* is unrelated: the first element is cognate with *goad*, OE *gád* 'spear, stabbing instrument'.

Taking the modern English GLOSSES of the Old English forms listed above as reasonable approximations of the current lexicon, it will be seen that some of the lost or semantically displaced items have been replaced by words of foreign origin (*stranger, companion, visitor, depressed, spirit, amusement, sound, sport*). Others—fewer—have been replaced by native elements in a sort of lexical reshuffling, a process more formally (if rather oddly) known as *internal borrowing*. In some such cases there is little change in meaning involved; for example, the Old English antecedents of *want* 'lack', *sing*, and *soul*, meant much what they mean today. But we also have here one example of a typical English puzzle, namely *lack:* this is not an Old English item and, while there are several possible sources in other Germanic languages for a borrowing, the form is without satisfactory etymology even in the languages that might be sources for the borrowing. The example is not exceptional. Both the Old English and present-day lexicons, like most lexicons actually, contain a large number of words of basic meaning, like *lack*, which have doubtful or unknown etymologies.

An example of a somewhat more extensive shuffling of the semantics is OE *bearn* 'child'. Its replacement by *child* involved a substantial semantic change for OE *čild* '(male) offspring of high birth, scion'.

This classification is traditional; but from the point of view of lexicon per se, a lexical loss is a lexical loss. It is hard to see what insight is gained by making a distinction between lexical replacement via external and 'internal' borrowing.

10. Words of high frequency of occurrence

The survival rate of lexical items is very different if we look at Old English poetic vocabulary from the point of view of frequency of occurrence. The survival rate for the twenty most frequent words and paradigms is 80%; and in the case of all four lexical replacements, the new form is a native English element.

In order of declining frequency, the commonest Old English forms and paradigms in poetry are listed on the facing page.

Now, first, in the case of the big complicated paradigms (the personal pronouns, the definite article, the verb 'be', and the modals), not all of the actual forms in the paradigms have survived, of course; *that* (both the pronoun and the conjunction) and *the* are the only rem-

iċ, þú, hé *personal pronouns,*
  'I, thou, he' &c.
sé, séo, þæt *definite article and*
  demonstrative pronoun 'the;
   that'
and 'and'
on/in 'on, at, in'
wesan, bíon 'be'
ne/né 'not'
tó 'at, to; too'
þá 'then, when'
eall 'all'

magan 'be able, can'
swá 'so'
dryhten 'lord'
mid 'with'
god 'God'
mann 'human (Mensch); man
  (adult male)'
willan 'want to'
þǽr 'there, where, if'
þanne (*rarely* þan) 'then, when'
weorþan 'become'
án, nán 'one, none'

nants of an Old English paradigm containing well over a dozen different forms. But the lexical items themselves have survived in a very real sense. Second, a number of FORMS have survived even though the associated MEANING has changed, just as in the first list: *magan* 'can' is the ancestor of *may*, and *willan* 'want to' is the ancestor of *will* (the modal auxiliary).

What can we say about the fallen soldiers?

The genuine mortalities are *þá* 'then', *dryhten* 'lord', *mid* 'with', and *weorþan* 'become'. Of these, *dryhten* 'lord' is in a sense an intruder. It is in this list only because it is frequent in heroic poetry specifically, besides being a common metonym for 'God'. Of course, it might well have been pretty frequent in certain conversational settings, as when the (temporal) *dryhten* himself or his cronies were present, but otherwise probably not. (Cognate forms are alive and well in Scandinavian languages, incidentally.)

The reflex of OE *þá*, usually written *tho*, survived until the 17th century in conservative speech and later in dialects (the OED cites late 19th century evidence).

The loss of so basic an item as *mid* 'with' is less strange than it may look. 'With' is a somewhat fragile element, lexically; there is no Indo-European item reconstructable for 'with', for example, because each branch has its own form. Part of the problem is that notions like 'up against', 'along side', 'near', 'together', and so on, so readily encroach on and eventually replace earlier forms meaning 'with'. In any case, *mid* does survive encapsulated in one word, *midwife*.

Finally, the ancient form reflected in *weorþan* 'become'—its etymon,

PIE *wert- 'turn', is attested in most branches of Indo-European—is lost in modern English.[1]

    a. It is hard to know how to score *ne/né* (the word scans with both short and long vowels). It does not survive as an actual word in English, but it lives on in *not* and *naught,* the atonic and tonic outcomes, respectively, of *ne wiht* 'not a thing'. (*Naught* is now dialectal or literary, but its derivative *naughty* is alive and well.)

11. Lexical change on a smaller time scale

Accurate observation of this is difficult, because notice of changes under such circumstances is practically limited to ADDITIONS to lexicon. Loss is going on at the same time, of course, but the loss of a lexical item or of a shade of meaning is likely to be gradual and over a long period. It usually means that fewer and fewer members of a speech community are using a form, rather than everyone in a community using it less and less often, which makes it particularly hard to be sure, in the short term, when an item is actually quite gone.

The following run of fifteen entries in the 'new words' section of the Merriam-Webster *New International Dictionary of the English Language,* 2nd ed., 1927 printing, will give an idea of short-term lexical change. It is from a supplement listing new words, and new meanings of existing forms, noted in the 16 years since 1909 (the publication date of the dictionary proper). Lemmata entered in italics, below, give NEW SENSES for previously-listed FORMS.

The items are shown exactly as they stand in the source (including the baffling language under *drag*) except that Greek forms have been transliterated.

A casual glance at the following is all that is called for, though closer study would have its rewards.

draftee, *n.* One who has been drafted, as for military service.
drag, n. Aeronautics. The component parallel to the relative wind of the total force on an airfoil or aircraft due to the air through which it moves. It the case of an airplane, that part of the drag which is due to the wings is called *wing resistance;* that due to the rest of the airplane is called *structural,* or *parasite, resistance.*

---

[1] It is doubtful that many English speakers who encounter *Woe worth the day* in Ezekiel xxx.2 have any clear idea what it means.

dragon balloon A kite balloon: —a misnomer due to mistranslation of Ger. *Drache* a dragon, also, a kite.

draw step. *Dancing.* A step in which the foot is drawn back or aside, as before the dip in the one-step.

dreadnought, n. **a** [*cap.*] A British battleship, completed 1906-07, having an armament of ten 12-inch guns, and twenty-four 12-pound quick-fire guns for protection against torpedo boats. This was the first battleship of the type characterized by a main armament of big guns all of the same caliber. She had a displacement of 17,900 tons at load draft, and a speed of 21 knots. **b** Hence, any battleship having its main armament entirely of big guns all of one caliber. Since the *Dreadnought* was built, the caliber of the heaviest guns has increased from 12 in. to 13¼ in., 14 in., 15 in., or more, and the displacement of the largest battleships from 18,000 to 35,000 tons and upwards. The term *superdreadnought* is popularly applied to battleships of the greater displacement and gun caliber.

drift, n. *Aeronautics.* **a** The lateral velocity of an aircraft, due to air currents or other causes. **b** = DRIFT ANGLE. **c** Drag;—a former use.

drift angle. *Aeronautics.* The angular deviation from a set course due to cross currents of wind; leeway.

drifter, n. Specif., a boat engaged in, or of a type used in, drift fishing (see DRIFT *n.* II b). Many drifters and other fishing boats were used during the World War in the British coast defense as against U-boats.

drift meter. *Aeronautics.* An instrument for measuring or indicating the drift angle.

drip band or **flap.** A strip of fabric attached by one edge to the envelope of a balloon or airship in such a way that rain will run off its free edge instead of dripping into the basket or car. The drip flap also helps to keep the ropes by which the car is suspended dry and nonconducting.

drive, n. **1.** An attack, as in military operations, in which a push forward is made with very great force and violence. **2.** A vigorous effort, as by a committee, to raise money within a limited time, as for a charitable or patriotic purpose, to enlist new members for an organization, or the like. **3.** In an automobile, the apparatus collectively by means of which the propulsion of the vehicle is controlled and directed; also, the place where the operator sits to drive.

drome, n. Short for AIRDROME. *Slang.*

Drosophila, n. [New Latin, from Gr. *drósos* dew, moisture, liquid + *phílos* loving.] *Zoöl.* A genus containing the common fruit fly (*D. melanogaster*, syn. *D. ampelophila*), members of which inhabit chiefly fermenting fruits, and liquids, as wine, beer, and cider. The genus has been used extensively in breeding experiments for the study of inheritance of characters.

drumfire, n. The firing of, or discharge of projectiles from, a machine gun or machine guns.

dry, a. Marked by, concerned with, or advocating laws, or the enforcement of laws, prohibiting the manufacture, sale, etc., of intoxicating liquor; as *dry* sentiment. *Colloq.,* U.S.

Note the prominence of items related to new technologies (aeronautics, automobiles); in more recent times there has been a similar growth in terms relating to electronics of all kinds, and the application of such terms figuratively. Second, note that some items (*dragon balloon, drome, drive* in the sense of 'the place in an automobile where the driver sits') have since disappeared from usage, though the last is arguably seen in *right- (left-)hand drive;* others (*dreadnought*) are surely rare, while *drumfire* is nowadays journalistic and mainly (only?) figurative (*a drumfire of hostile criticism* and the like), a sense which was not noticed in 1927. On the other hand, many of these words, novelties as of 1927, are secure in current usage and standard.

Two remarks about *drifter*. It is likely that the term as defined above was not new at all, but emerged from waterman vocabulary into general use in connection with specific events in World War I, as mentioned in the encyclopedic entry. Second, the 1927 Webster's contains no notice of a now common word, *drifter* 'a person (usually male) without career or long-term employment who moves planlessly from place to place pursuing employment, recreation, or adventure'.

12. Phonological change

The only type of language change with any degree of system and pattern is phonological change. These uniquely valuable properties stem from the basic nature of phonologies: they are highly patterned, full of detail, and abstract.

The importance of the abstractness of phonology requires a little comment. All components of language except the speech sounds that make it up have function (meaning). Function by itself influences change in an infinity of ad hoc (and therefore unpredictable) ways. It is no accident that the first discovery of the true principles of language change and language relatedness (25, 95) were made through study of the sound systems of languages; morphology had little to do with it, and syntax and semantics figured not at all.

It must be added that the overall morphosyntax of a language is pretty persistent through time, so that one expects even remotely-related languages to have general similarities of structure (prefixal person-marking on verbs, say). At the same time, morphosyntax is without question subject to influence from other languages spoken in the area, and it is commonplace to find languages of diverse ancestry in the same geographic area showing a high degree of structural congruence. These two factors taken together explain why the languages of Europe, as various as they are, have such a high level of structural similarity. In the first place, most of them have a common source (Proto-Indo-European), and in addition their mutual proximity has always tended to reinforce the inherited similarities, as well as foster the spread of non-inherited ones, such as the use of *be* and *have* as auxiliary verbs. In any case, the readiness with which morphology and syntax can be influenced by other languages is evident in Finnish, a NON-Indo-European language of Europe which has grown to resemble its Germanic neighbors to a striking degree, an example that goes far to undercut the proposition that for historical purposes morphology and syntax might be more reliable indices of relatedness than phonology.

A point which cannot be too strongly imphasized is that phonological patterning is not merely handy: it is the sovereign analytical tool in historical linguistics, and is the foundation upon which every other aspect of historical linguistics is built. Unless and until formal (phonological) connections can be established between meaning-bearing forms (words or affixes), it is not possible apart from mere guessing to speak of 'relatedness', of semantic or morphological or lexical changes, of etymology or borrowing, or indeed of any aspect of historical linguistics at all.

SUGGESTIONS FOR FURTHER READING

Most of the general works in the Bibliography have introductory chapters covering similar ground. A work of lasting value despite its date is **Bloomfield 1933**, whose chapters 17 to 27 are a rich source (overwhelming, in fact) of examples and analysis. Also of interest would be **Anttila 1988** chapters 1 and 3, and **Hock & Joseph 1996** chapter 1. **Campbell 1999** chapter 1 is an approach to the subject which is interestingly different from the usual.

CHANGES IN PRONUNCIATION

Readers who are harassed by a feeling that the following two
chapters are heavy going may want to refresh their phonetics
by glancing at the Appendix, pp. 209-37.

13. Phonetic and phonological change

Some types of changes in pronunciation are so commonly encountered that there are technical terms for them. These terms come under
two headings: those that describe the relationship between the starting
point of a change and its outcome from the standpoint of the PHO-
NETICS (15-24), and those that describe this relationship from the
standpoint of the changes (if any) in the STRUCTURAL ROLE (26-9) the
phones play in their sound systems qua systems. The terminology for
the former is both older and more elaborate than the terminology for
the latter. They will be taken up in order, below.

TECHNICAL TERMS
DESCRIBING PHONETIC CHANGE

The following technical terms will be discussed in this chapter:

Assimilation – Segments become more alike
Dissimilation – Segments become less alike

Addition of segments:
    Anaptyxis – vowel added between segments
    Gemination – lengthening of a consonant
    Prothesis – addition at the beginning of a word
    Excrescence – consonant added between segments or finally

Loss:
    Syncope – from between segments
    Apocope – from end of word
    Aphaeresis – from beginning of word
    Haplology – loss of a sequence of segments

Metathesis – transposition of segments

Compensatory Lengthening – lengthening of a segment when another segment is lost

Fusion (blending) – two segments become one with some of the features of both

Palatalization – development of coarticulated high front tongue body (and the consequences of such a development)

Spirantization – occlusives become spirants

14. Explanation vs. description; ease of pronunciation

We say that *assimilation* and *dissimilation* are changes that result in an increase or decrease, respectively, in the degree of phonetic similarity between two segments. It is tempting to think that such changes in the one segment are somehow CAUSED BY the phonetics of the other, and for generations that is actually how the matter has usually been presented. It is easy to see why: it seems only natural to speak of the phonetics of a segment as 'triggering' an assimilatory or dissimilatory change in another segment—attracting or repelling it, phonetically. But this is a confusion of cause and effect. It is true that the EFFECT of the change is a net increase/decrease of similarity between two segments, but it is begging the question (to say the least) to assume that the degree of similarity is also somehow the CAUSE of the change. The fact is that very little is known of the actual mechanisms of these changes, commonplace as they are. The extreme preponderance of certain types of such changes—phonetic anticipation is very much the rule; and, whereas assimilations usually involve contiguous segments, dissimilations usually involve noncontiguous segments—are presumably clues to the actuating mechanisms, but only clues.

An ancient notion which reinflates itself no matter how often it is punctured—it is even found in present-day introductory textbooks—is that there is a correlation between the number of articulatory shifts from one segment to the next and 'ease of pronunciation', such that sheer laziness is an efficient cause of assimilation. This is yet another example of telescoping cause and effect, as mentioned above; but in fact unless and until some means is found of actually quantifying and measuring articulatory effort, the claim itself (as in pointed out in 41) is totally untestable. Besides, it is likely that auditory factors interact with purely articulatory ones. This is—perhaps—part of the explanation of why the points of articulation of nasal consonants assimilate in consonant clusters very readily, whereas the points of articulation of obstruents are very much more stable. That is, it might well be that the real catalyst (or lubricant) in a change like /strenθ/ > /strenθ/ *strength* is the slenderness of the auditory difference between the two renditions, and has nothing to do with 'saving' articulatory 'effort'. A correspondent points out that the identifying letters for Minnesota Public Radio, MPR, are under many conditions indistinguishable from the letters for National Public Radio. By contrast, a change like that of Latin *septem* 'seven' into Italian *sette* is acoustically very obvious.

There is no reason to expect the effective mechanisms to be very simple in any case, given how much is going on in normal articulated speech: at a conversational tempo, a native speaker of English makes the fine and exact adjustments in mouth and throat necessary to get from one segment to the next at a rate of around twenty segments per second (and English is only about average as such things go). For now, we can simply say that it is essential to think of what follows as descriptive, and without any pretentions to explanation.

ASSIMILATION

15. Assimilation

Assimilation is a development whereby a phone becomes phonetically more like a nearby phone. This is an extremely common phenomenon, but not all types of assimilation are equally frequent.

The segment that undergoes the phonetic change may be either adjacent to the reference phone, or at a distance; the former situation is immensely more common. The phone that changes may either precede or follow the reference segment; the former is very much more common than the latter.

The traditional terms for the two directions of influence are *regressive* for the type *ns > ss,* and *progressive* for the type *ns > nn.* These terms are confusing in part because they can easily be taken to mean the opposite of what they are supposed to mean. Perhaps clearer terms are *anticipatory* assimilation (*ns > ss*) and *lag* assimilation (*ns > nn*). These terms will be used here.

Anticipatory assimilation to an adjacent segment is far more common than the three other varieties together, and unlike them, is usually a regular matter, i.e., the subject of a sound law (see 16a, p. 25).

Total assimilation is the copying of ALL the originally different phonetic features of the reference phone, as in a change like *ns* > *ss*. Partial assimilation, that is, where the altered segment retains at least one feature which is different from the reference phone, is more common. (In any case, the distinction has little linguistic interest.)

ANTICIPATORY ASSIMILATION
TO AN ADJACENT SEGMENT

This is very much the most common type of assimilation:

Lat. *scrīptus* 'written' > It. *scritto*.
PIE *swepnos* > Lat. *somnus* 'dream'.
Lat. *maximus* [ks] 'biggest' > It. *massimo*.
PItal. *kom-leg-ō* 'collect' > Lat. *colligō*.
PIE *si-sd-ō* (thematized reduplicated present to root *sed-* 'sit') > Gk *hízō* i.e. [hízdo·] 'I seat, I place'.
OE *godsib(b)* 'god-parent' > NE *gossip* (in Shakespeare still 'chum, crony', and a term of address among old friends).

ANTICIPATORY ASSIMILATION
TO A NON-ADJACENT SEGMENT

OLat. *semul* 'at once' > Lat. *simul* (a mid vowel becomes high before a high vowel following).
PIE *swekrū́-* 'mother-in-law' > Ved. *śvaśrū́-* (for expected *svaśrū́-*).
PIE *s(w)eḱs* 'six' > Ved. *ṣáṭ* (for expected *sáṭ*).
OFr. *cercher* /sɛrčɛr/ (the source of NE *search*) > Fr. *chercher* /šɛrše/.

(Sibilants seem particularly liable to this kind of influence.)

Anticipatory assimilation of vocalics is called *umlaut*, and such developments are conspicuous in the histories of the Germanic languages. In West Germanic, for example, PGmc *u* > *o* before *a* in the following syllable (that is, a high vowel lowers to mid before a low vowel): PGmc *wulfaz 'wolf' > OHG uuolf. Similarly, *u > ü before *i in the following syllable (a back vowel fronts before a front vowel): PGmc *hulliz > OE hyll [hül·] 'hill'.[1] The Lat. simul example, above, is of course umlaut as well, as are the numerous raising and lowering developments in Old Irish: *wiros nom.sg. 'man' > PCelt. *wiras > *werah (*i lowers before *a in the following syllable) > OIr. fer; cf. PCelt. *wirī gen.sg. > *wiri > OIr. fir.

A very striking example of assimilation at a distance is seen in Italic and Celtic, where PIE *p ... kʷ- sequences become *kʷ ... kʷ-sequences: PIE *penkʷe 'five' > Ital. *kʷinkʷe > Lat. quīnque (-ī- for -ĭ- from the ordinal quīn(c)tus), OIr. cóic /kōgʸ/, W pimp (p < PCelt. *kʷ).

LAG ASSIMILATION
TO AN ADJACENT SEGMENT

PIE *kl̥-ni- 'hill' > Lat. collis, via *kolnis; an exact cognate is PGmc *hulliz, mentioned above.
PIE *tors-eye- 'make dry' > Lat. torreō.
Gk pénte /pente/ 'five' > NGk /pende/ ([n] is a voiced sound).

The assimilation of obstruent clusters containing a voiced aspirated stop in Sanskrit is known as Bartholomae's Law, which states that ANY such cluster becomes voiced aspirated throughout. Some such events entail lag assimilation: PIE *dhugh-tó- 'milked' > Ved. dugdhá- [gḍ].

LAG ASSIMILATION
TO A NON-ADJACENT PRECEDING SEGMENT

Very rare for consonants, less rare for vowels:

In Old English, posttonic vowels before -r are determined by the

---

[1] Note that in the traditional terminology of Germanists, various umlaut phenomena go by special names—*sinking, breaking, rounding,* and so on. These distinctions may be convenient; but phonetically they are distinctions without differences.

phonetic features of the preceding tonic vowel: the *-er* of *fœder* 'father' and the *-or* of *brōþor* 'brother' continue the selfsame Proto-Germanic vowel.

More generally, the phenomenon known as *vowel harmony* is the conditioning of vowels in affixes by the phonetics of vowels in stems. Finnish has two forms of the privative suffix, *-ttom-* and *-ttöm-*, whose occurrence is determined by whether the preceding vowel is back or front: *parrattom-* 'beardless' but *kengättöm-* /keŋŋættöm-/ 'shoeless'.

PIE *$\acute{k}$aso-* 'hare, rabbit' (the etymon of both NE *hare* and NHG *Haase*) > Skt *śaśa-* for expected *$\acute{s}asa$-*.

Gk *leírion* 'lily' was borrowed into Latin as *līlium*.

Some kinds of assimilation are double-edged: NE *Social Security* is widely to be heard pronounced ['sowsɯlsɯ'kyɹətiy]; it is unknown and unknowable whether the change of ['sowšɨl] to ['sowsɯl] is a case of anticipation or of lag.

DISSIMILATION

16. Dissimilation

Dissimilation is a change which results in a segment being phonetically less like a neighboring phone. Like assimilatory changes, dissimilatory changes in a segment much more often seem to refer to a following segment than a preceding one. Exactly UNLIKE assimilation, though, the two segments in question are usually not contiguous: dissimilation works mainly at a distance. And for the most part, it is an accident befalling a form, rather than a regular development.

ANTICIPATORY DISSIMILATION
FROM A CONTIGUOUS SEGMENT

Fairly rare: in Latin, *n > r before *m, as in *kan-$mn̥$ 'song' (cf. Lat. *canō*) > *$kanmen$ > Lat. *carmen*.

In Indic, a sibilant followed by another sibilant became a stop: PInIr. *$\acute{s}s$ becomes (via several intermediate stages) Indic *$kṣ$: *$wi\acute{s}$-su loc. pl. 'in homesteads' > Ved. *vikṣú*. Analogously, PInIr. *$s\acute{s}$ becomes *$t\acute{s}$, finally *c(c)h*: *-$s\acute{k}^{e}/_{o}$- (a present stem marker, as in Gk *-skō*, Lat. *-scō*) > Indic *-ccha-* (the phonetics of which are actually something like [k^{y}ś]).

In Modern Greek, ancient clusters of stops become fricative + stop: Att. *núx, nuktós* 'night' > NGk *núkhta* [niχta]; Att. *heptá* 'seven' > NGk *ephtá*. Conversely in the Proto-Germanic cluster **hs* (that is, [χs]), as seen in Go. *saihs* 'six', the first fricative becomes a stop in the West Germanic languages, thus OE *siex*, NE *six* [sɪks].

NE *etcetera* is often pronounced *eksetera* (original [t] shares a point of articulation with [s]; [k] does not). However, the spelling may have some role in this.[1]

ANTICIPATORY DISSIMILATION
FROM A NON-CONTIGUOUS SEGMENT

This is the most common sort of dissimilation by far:

PIE **temH̥sreH₂-* 'darkness' (pl. tant.) > PItal. **temaθrās* > Lat. *tenebrae* for expected **temebrae*.

Lat. *venēnum* 'poison' > It. *veleno*.

Lat. *quīnque* 'five' > PRom. **kīnque* > Fr. *cinq*, Sp. *cinco*, and the rest.

NE *February* pronounced *Febuary* [fɛbyuwɛri] (but see also **51a**).

An innovation known as Grassmann's Law is shared by Greek and Indo-Iranian; it entails the dissimilation of aspirate consonants: PreGk **tʰeykʰos* 'wall' > Gk *teîkhos*; **kʰe-kʰu-* (perfect stem of *khéō* 'pour') > *kékhu-*; PInIr. **dhadhāti* 'puts' > Ved. *dádhāti*.

LAG DISSIMILATION
FROM A CONTIGUOUS SEGMENT

This is exceedingly rare:

NE dial. *chimley* for standard *chimney*, from OFr. *cheminée* < LLat. *camīnāta* (cf. Lat. *camīnus* 'forge').

---

[1] At least, a suggestive misspelling of the abbreviation as *ect.* is not uncommon. But it has also been suggested that the sequence /ts/ may be at risk per se on account of its rarity in English except across clear morpheme boundaries (as in *cats* or *heart-sick*), whereas /ks/ is commonplace, particularly at the end of the first syllable of a word, as in *exception, excessive, extra* and the like; and NB the very common *excape*.

Sp. *nombre* 'name' < *nomre* < *nomne* < PRom. **nom(i)ne*, cf. Lat. *nōmen* (stem *nōmin-*). One is tempted to regard it as self-evident that the dissimilations seen here must have predated the syncope of the second syllable, that is, that they are examples of dissimilation at a distance. But the early Spanish textual evidence makes it clear that the dissimilation took place only after the nasals became contiguous.

The conversion of fricatives to stops after another fricative, a feature of the histories of many languages, belongs here: ME *fifth* > NE (nonstandard) *fift;* ON *slǿgþ* is the source of ME *slicht* > NE *sleight* (as in *sleight of hand*).

LAG DISSIMILATION FROM A NON-CONTIGUOUS SEGMENT

Lat. *arborem* acc.sg. 'tree' > Sp. *árbol*.

PItal. **flōsāsiā* neut.pl. 'festival of Flora' (cf. Osc. **fiuusasia-**, with fi- for presumed fl-) > **flōrāria* > Lat. *Flōrālia*. (This is the source of other festival names, *Rōbīgālia*, *Sāturnālia*, and so on.)

In early Middle English there was a sporadic dissimilation of *-n* to *-m* after an apical: NE *seldom* < *selden*, *venom* < OFr. *venin* cf. Lat. *venēnum*, *vellum* < OFr. *veelin* (the word is ultimately related to *veal*).[1]

It. *rado* 'sparse, rare' < PRom. *raru-* (Lat. *rārus;* cf. the Italian doublet *raro*). NE *cardamom* often written (and pronounced) *cardamon*.

a. Assimilation phenomena, particularly assimilations to a contiguous segment, are usually regular; in other words, they are sound laws. By contrast, assimilation at a distance, and both varieties of dissimilation, are usually sporadic developments: they are details of the history of a particular word, and present the historian with a puzzle to be solved, not with a key to history. Occasionally, however, as in the Germanic umlauts (assimilations at a distance), Grassmann's Law (dissimilation of aspirates), and the Sanskrit dissimilation of a sibilant before another sibilant (mentioned above), the developments are in fact regular, that is, they are sound laws.

---

[1] This is never seen in morphological categories (*golden, wool(l)en, linen; beaten, swollen; redden, whiten*) where leveling may have disturbed a regular outcome, but it fails to take place in some isolates as well, like *basin, sudden,* and *Helen*. Many apparent exceptions, like *pollen,* were not present in the language at the time of the change; some others continue different Old English shapes, like *midden* < *midding*.

b. Sometimes a segment in the neighborhood of a similar or (more usually) identical segment will disappear altogether, as in the Germanic and Italic reflexes of PIE *k^wetwr̥tos 'fourth', e.g. Lat. *quārtus* < *k^waortos* < *k^wawortos*, cf. OE *feorþa*. This is treated by many authorities as a special, if extreme, case of dissimilation. Such a classification is defensible, but the phenomenon is perhaps better considered a special case of haplology (p. 31).

ADDITION OF SEGMENTS

17. The general term for any development whereby a phonetic segment appears where none was before is *excrescence*. Some specific types are denoted by special terms, and the term excrescence itself may be reserved for specific types of added segments:

ANAPTYXIS

This term (Gk *anáptuxis* 'unfolding') is commonly applied to the evolution of a vowel out of certain consonant groups, mostly such as contain a liquid or nasal. Often it is an accident befalling a single word, as in the widely-encountered pronunciation of *athlete* in three syllables or *realtor* as *realator,* but anaptyxis can be a regular development, as in Ital. *$*pōklom$ 'cup' > Lat. *pōcolom, pōculum* and *$*sūθlom$ 'awl' > *sūbulum.* The phenomenon known as pleophony in East Slavic languages affecting liquids in coda is ubiquitous, with or without the syncope of the original syllabic: *$*gord$ 'town' (loanword from Germanic) > Ru. *gorod,* *$*moldos$ 'soft' > OCS *mladŭ.* In Old Irish, sound laws regularly stranded a resonant in word-final position after an obstruent; a vowel then grew between them: PCelt. *$*aratron$ 'plow' > *$*araθran$ > *$*araθr$ > OIr. *arathar* /apəθər/. The same thing, unwritten, occurs in NE /izəm/ < *-ism* in e.g. *prism* (a minimal pair with *prison*), *botulism,* and the like.

Note that the term anaptyxis has been also used for any segment that grows from nothing, vowel or consonant. See *excrescence,* below.

GEMINATION

The lengthening of a consonant is traditionally called *gemination* ('twinning')—from the doubling of the consonants as written. The actual phonetic change is an increase in the duration of the segment.

In many Indo-European languages at different times consonants became long before certain resonants. In West Germanic, all consonants (except *r*) lengthen between a short vowel and a following **j* ([y]): PGmc **sat-jana^n* 'to set' > PWGmc **settjan* > OE *settan*, OHG *sezzen* (NHG *setzen*), OS *settian*.

In Old English, but not in the other West Germanic languages, a similar process took place before *r*, even after a long vowel: **fōd-ra-* > OE *fóddor* (*-er*, *-ur*; NE *fodder*; cf. *fód* > *food*).

In Italian a sporadic development in similar environments accounts for many examples of lengthened consonants: It. *acqua* 'water' < Lat. *aqua*, *repubblica* < Lat. *rēs pūblica*, *labbro* 'lip' < Lat. *labrum*. (Still other cases seem to be spontaneous, as It. *leggere* < Lat. *legere* 'gather, read'.)

PROTHESIS

Prothesis is the sprouting of a sound (usually a vowel) at the beginning of a word. This is widely seen in the history of Greek, as in **lng^{w}hros* 'light' > Gk *elaphrós* 'light, nimble' (cf. Ved. *raghú-* 'light', OE *lungre*, Lat. *levis*). This development is sporadic in Greek before **w*, **l*, **m* and **n*, but before **r* it is regular. In West European dialects of the Romance languages, Lat. *sp-*, *st-*, *sc-* regularly grow an initial *e-*, as in Sp. *espero* 'I hope' < Lat. *spērō; estéril* 'sterile' < *sterilis; escoba* 'broom' < *scōpae*. (In French the *-s-* itself subsequently disappears in many words, leaving a very altered aspect: Lat. *spat(h)a* > Fr. *épée* 'sword'; *status* > *été* 'been'; *scutella* > *écuelle* 'bowl'.) In Welsh, a short vowel sprouts before a word-initial *n-* in a number of Latin loanwords: W *ynifer* [əníver] from Lat. *numerus* 'number'. Motu, a language of central New Guinea, adds a lateral to words previously beginning with a vowel: Motu *lau* 'I', *lahi* 'fire' < **au*, **api*. This is remarkable; much more typical are onglides before word-initial vowels, as in Ru. *vydra* 'otter' < **ūdr-* or NE *one* /wən/ < /ōn/ (cf. *only, alone,* and dial. *woke* for *oak*).

EXCRESCENCE

Since nowadays *anaptyxis* is usually restricted to inserted vowels, another term, *excrescence* is commonly used specifically for the insertion of a consonant.[1] Excrescent consonants typically arise between segments of markedly different phonetics, e.g. *sr* > *str* (PIE *srowmos 'flowing (thing)' > OE *stréam* 'stream'), *nr* > *ndr* (OE *þunor* > NE *thunder*, cf. NHG *Donner*), *ml* > *mbl* (Lat. *humilis* 'low, mean' is the source of NE *humble*), *mt* > *mpt* (Lat. *ēmptus* 'taken, bought' < **emtos;* cf. *emō* 'take, buy'); *ms* > *mps* (Lat. *ēmpsī*, perfect tense of *emō*).

These typical cases are traditionally traced to carelessness, as they mean a reduction in the number of articulatory shifts that must be executed simultaneously: in *mt* there are three simultaneous adjustments (voiced to voiceless, labial to apical point of articulation, and nasal to oral), while in *mpt* there are fewer shifts from one phonetic segment to the next (two and one, respectively). Here we see the commonplace confusion of effect and cause; in any case, even on its own terms such an analysis cannot be the whole story, as it does not compass many examples of excrescence:

In Slavic, *-l-* grows on palatalized labials, thus **m^y*, **p^y* > *ml^y*, *pl^y*.

In dialects of German there are such cases as *lš* > *ltš*, paralleled in American NE dialectal /elks/ and /elts/ < /els/ 'else'. It is hard to understand how a stop between two continuants is in any sense 'phonetically transitional'.

In Avestan (and other languages) a feature of nasality seems to condense on the dorsal fricative sound [χ], such as the Avestan sound law whereby *s > *ŋχ* before a back vowel: PInIr. *źanas-as gen.sg. 'race, people' > *zanaχaz > *zanaŋχō*.

A puzzling case, which has the regularity of a sound law, is the excrescent *-n-* in NE *messenger, passenger, porringer, St Leger* > *Sallenger* (cf. *message, porridge*, and the rest).

More puzzling still is *-mpn-* for *-mn-* which is found sporadically in late Old English, and regularly in Middle English: OE *nempnian* 'to name' for the more usual *nemnian*, Chaucer's consistent *solempnite, dampnacioun*. The same phenomenon is seen a millennium earlier in

---

[1] The *-t* which sporadically crops up on English genitive-case adverbs is an example of excrescence at the END of a word: *against, betwixt, amongst*, nonstandard /wənst/ for *once*. The same phenomenon is seen in a fair number of continental West Germanic forms, for example NHG *Palast* 'palace' and *Obst* 'fruit'.

epigraphic Latin of a type whose informality suggests a colloquial style, e.g. *contempnō* 'despise', *sompnus* 'sleep'.

LOSS OF SEGMENTS

18. The general term for any development whereby a segment or string of segments disappears from a form is *loss*. Word-final sounds are especially liable to loss, and a typical case is the dropping of all stops in word-final position in Greek: PIE **melit* 'honey' > Gk *méli* (the original stem form is still evident in gen. *mélitos*, and cf. Go. *miliþ*).

Several types of loss are known by particular names:

SYNCOPE

Syncope is the loss of any medial segment, such as the loss of /t/ in NE *nestle* and *soften* (cf. *nest, soft*), though the term by custom is now practically reserved for medial vowels, as in Gk *êlthon* for *éluthon* (aor. of *érkhomai* 'go'), Lat. *caldus* 'hot' < *calidus* and, with a regularity that amounts to a sound law, atonic **ro* > *r* as in **wiros* 'man' > **wirs* > Lat. *vir*, **alteros* '(the) other' > **alters* > *alter*. NE *every, evening*, and *chocolate* were formerly trisyllabic. Among ancient languages, the phenomenon is common in Latin, even more so in Oscan and Umbrian; similarly in the development of Germanic and Celtic languages. In all these groups it is to some degree regular, but of course in highly-inflected languages regular tendencies are subject to the disturbing influences of leveling.[1] It is also very general in the development of Romance languages from Proto-Romance, for example Lat. *anima* > Sp. *alma* 'soul', which shows two innovations at once, and Lat. *fēmina* > Fr. *femme*.

---

[1] Regular sound laws account for the development of PCelt. **an-kom-samalīs* nom.pl. 'dissimilar' into OIr. *écsamli* /ēgsəμλʸi/—the Greek letters are lenited consonants (see the Note on Notation, p. xiv). Among its adventures are a late syncope rule which deleted even-numbered medial vowels (counting from the left). That is, the Proto-Celtic form given above first underwent regular developments to become **eggossamali* whence, by the two regular syncopes, the attested form.

APOCOPE

Apocope is the loss of a vowel (or, in some uses of the term, any sound) in absolute final position, as in PIE *-si 2sg., *-ti 3sg. > Lat. -s, -t: venīs, venit 'you, he comes'; Lat. nec 'nor' < neque; Lat. animāl 'animal' < *anamāli. In Proto-Germanic, all PIE short vowels dropped in final position, as PIE *penkʷe 'five' > Go. fimf, OE fíf; *woyde 'knows' > Go. wait, OE wát. All posttonic vowels dropped in the evolution of French; many of the vowels thus affected were word-final. Thus Lat. mīlle /mílle/ 'thousand' > Fr. mille /mil/, Lat. venīre 'to come' > Fr. venir /vǝnir/.

In some languages, apocope is routine in prepositions and other particles, as in the Italian distinction between de 'from' before consonants but d' before vowels, or la f.sg. 'the' before consonants but l' before vowels; similarly the object pronouns in French: il m'a donné... 'he has given me...' vs. il me donne... 'he gives me...'.

APHAERESIS

The loss of an initial sound—it is usually a vowel, but can be any sound—is known as aphaeresis. It is virtually unknown in the ancient Indo-European languages but is widely encountered in Romance and in the development of modern Greek. Thus, in Italian, LLat. in illo 'in that' > It. nel 'in the', Lat. Honōra (the name) > Nora, historia 'narrative' > storia; Gk odónt- 'tooth' > NGk dónti; *ommátion 'eye' (the diminutive of Gk ómma; see 62) > máti.

The 'same' form with and without aphaeresis may continue side by side, usually with some difference in meaning, as in NE lone < alone,[1] special < especial, cute < acute, story < history, sport < disport. No such differentiation is obligatory: compare informal 'bout, 'possum, 'lectric and about, opossum, electric.

Glides (including—or particularly—[h]) are especially vulnerable to

---

[1] This particular item may be a morphosyntactic development in part, influenced by such pairs as alive predicate adj. next to live attributive adj. Etymologically, alone is a compound of all and one, and therefore unrelated to alive, aloft, apart, and others, which are in origin prepositional phrases with on.

aphaeresis. Latin initial *h-* was prone to loss in Classical Latin and even earlier, and had disappeared from Vulgar Latin (notwithstanding the anachronistic spelling of French). In Greek, /h/ (spiritus asper) was lost very early in some dialects, the so-called psilotic, or 'plain', dialects; and by the 4th cent. AD it was lost in all.

In Attic-Ionic, PGk **w-* dropped in word-initial position: **wanakts* 'prince' > Gk *ánax*, **woyde* 'knows' > *oîde*.

In Old Norse, all initial **j-* [y] dropped, as in ON *oc* 'yoke' < PGmc **juka^n*; the same thing happened in Old Irish, as in OIr. *óac* /oəg/ (two syllables) 'young' < PCelt. **yuwankos*.

Consonantal aphaeresis is seen in the loss of initial stops before palatal *l* in Spanish, as *llave* 'key' < *[kʎave] < Lat. *clavem*.

PIE **s-* dropped before nasals in both Greek and Latin: PIE **snig^{w}h-* 'snow' > Gk *nípha* acc. 'snowflake', Lat. *ninguit* 'it is snowing' (cf. OE *snieweþ*, Lith. *sniñga*).

a. Diachronic processes such as these must be kept distinct from the *substitution* of one pronunciation for another when words are borrowed. Finnish (like many languages) had no word-initial consonant sequences, such that loan-words from Indo-European languages of the Baltic and Germanic branches which originally began with consonant clusters were subject to what looks like a systematic aphaeresis: Fi. *ranta* 'shore' < **strand-*, *rengas* 'ring' < PGmc **hrengaz* (*h* = [χ]), *tarkku* 'exact' < PGmc **starkuz* 'stiff, strong'. But this is not a true diachronic process, any more than the general (and strange) substitution of English /ž/ for /ǰ/ in foreign words is a diachronic process (for example, *raja* often pronounced /ražə/, *Beijing* often /beyžiŋ/.

HAPLOLOGY

Haplology is the term for loss in a repeated sequence of segments in a word. The affected repetition is only very rarely exact:

Gk *eidōlo-latreía* 'idol-veneration' > NE *idolatry*; NE *probably* is commonly pronounced /prabliy/.

Hom. *amphi-phoreús* 'jar with two carrying handles' > *amphoreús* (NE *amphora*).

PreItal. **septm̥-mn̥s-ri-s* 'seven-month' > **septem-memb-ri-s* > **septem-bris* > Lat. *September*. (The changes **-ris* > **-rs* > **-ers* > *-er* are all regular.)

Fr. *sœur* 'sister' points to PRom. **sǫre* < **sorǫ́re* (Lat. *sorōrem*).
Lat. *stīpi-pendium* 'soldier's pay' usually *stīpendium*.
OE *Engla land* 'land of the Angles' > NE *England* (an example of the rare case where the original syllables were actually identical).

A single segment may be lost in a similar way. The first of two identical segments is lost in PIE **ti-sr-* fem. 'three' from ***tri-sr-* (Ved. *tisrás*, OIr. *téoir;* cf. Lat. *tri-* and NE *three*) and **swéḱuro-* 'husband's father' from ***swéḱru-ro-* (Av. *χvasura-*, OHG *suuehur*, Gk *hekurós*), a derivative of **swéḱru-* 'husband's mother', as in Ved. *śváśrū-;* NE *library* dial. *libary;* Fr. *faible* (the source of both NE *feeble* and *foible*) < Lat. *flē-bilis* 'pitiful, weak', originally 'causing weeping'. The second of two *r*'s is lost in Greek dial. *rhḗtā* 'compact, verbal agreement' < *rhḗtrā*.

METATHESIS

19. **Metathesis**
The transposition of segments is called *metathesis*.
PIE **kʷetwr̥-*, the compounding form of 'four' (e.g. **kʷetwr̥-ped-* 'four-footed, quadruped'), shows metathesis in Av. *čaθru-* and Lat. *quadru-*.
OE *þridda* > NE *third;* OE *beorht* > NE *bright;* OE *ácsian* > NE *ask* (but conservative dialects still have /æks/).[1] PIE **wepseH* > Lat. *vespa* 'wasp' (cf. OE *wæps;* NE *wasp* appears to be an independent reprise of the Latin metathesis). NE *comfortable* normally /kəmftərbəl/. LLat. *oblītāre* 'to forget' > Sp. *olvidar*.
The transposition usually involves contiguous segments, but examples of non-contiguous ones are also found:
NGk *armégō* '(I) milk' < Gk *amélgō;* Sp. *milagro* 'miracle' < Lat. *mīrāculum;* Gk *sképtomai* 'see' < PIE **speḱ-;* PItal. **oynodekem* 'eleven' > Lat. *ūndecim* for expected **ūndicem;* Lith. *kepù*, Latv. *cepu* 'fry' < **kʷep-* < **pekʷ-;* Gk *térēn* 'delicate, tender' but Lat. *tener*. As these exam-

---

[1] Old English has both *áscian* and *ácsian*. The former is not, however, the etymon of *ask:* attested dialectally (southwest and west midlands) are *esch(e), esse, asch(e), as(s)he*, etc., showing the expected development of *sc*, forestalling any suggestion that *ask* somehow escaped the sound laws. Curiously, comparative evidence makes it clear that, in Old English terms, *ácsian* shows the effects of metathesis.

ples suggest, sibilants and liquids play a prominent role in metathesis.

Metathesis is normally a sporadic innovation, as in all the examples given. Thus Italic and Greek metathesize PIE *$w\underset{.}{l}k^{w}o$- 'wolf' to *$luk^{w}o$-, but the same sequence is preserved intact in both languages in the reflexes of e.g. *$w\underset{.}{l}Hno$- 'wool'. Occasionally, however, metathesis does take the form of a sound law. In Greek, in clusters in which apical stops were originally followed by dorsals, there was a regular transposition: PIE *tek- 'beget', redup. pres. *ti-tk-$\bar{o}$ > Gk *tíktō*; PIE *$(H)\underset{.}{r}tko$- > Gk *árktos* 'bear'; PIE *$dh\acute{g}h\bar{o}m$ 'earth' > Gk *khthṓn*. In the history of Spanish, PRom. *-tl-* > *-ld-*: *capitulum* > *cabildo* 'council', *titulus* 'tittle' > *tilde*, and *date illōs* 2pl. imperative 'give them' > *dadlos* > *daldos*.

In the *quantitative metathesis* of Attic, another instance of a metathesis which is the subject of a sound law, the articulatory segments remain in the inherited order while the feature of LENGTH is transposed: thus Att. *póleōs* gen.sg. 'city' reflects earlier *pólēos*.

a. A metathetic RELATIONSHIP is not invariably the result of an actual metathetic EVENT. So Att. *baínō* 'I go' reflects PGk *$g^{w}any\bar{o}$, but it is unlikely in the extreme that the actual historical process was one of transposition. Rather, it was something like *any > *$añ\tilde{n}$ (long palatalized nasal) > *$a^{i}\tilde{n}(\tilde{n})$ whence, with depalatalization and shortening, [ayn]. Similarly, OLat. *facul* 'easily' < *$\theta akli$ actually involved a development along the lines of *li > *[$\underset{.}{l}$] (syllabic liquid) with the subsequent growth of a short vowel before the liquid (any short vowel would have resulted in attested *ul*). That is, here we have syncope (18) followed by anaptyxis (17), not metathesis.

A different issue is presented by Sp. *milagro* < *mīrāculum*, mentioned above, *peligroso* 'dangerous' < LLat. *perīculōsus*, and many similar forms. These look like metathesis but may be something different. That is, non-initial PRom. *l* and *r* seem to have been in almost free variation at some point in the history of Spanish, though subsequently the distribution of each became fixed—sometimes (more or less by accident, it seems) in agreement with the etymology of the word, sometimes with the 'wrong' liquid, as in e.g. *papel* 'paper'. Therefore it is possible that the transposed liquids in *milagro* and *peligroso* are actually cases of words with two liquids in which, when the confusion subsided, both liquids came out 'wrong'.

OTHER INTERACTIONS BETWEEN SEGMENTS

20. Compensatory lengthening

In any language with a contrast of vowel length, some long vowels through time become short, and some short vowels become long. Also, a contrast between long and short vowels may develop in a language that didn't have one in the first place. One source of new long vowels is particularly commonplace: a short vowel becomes long as the direct consequence of the loss of another phonetic segment. This is called *compensatory lengthening*.

The lost segment is almost invariably a following consonant which is also almost invariably contiguous with the affected vowel.

In Latin, *[z] before most consonants is lost, and any preceding short vowel becomes long: PIE *nisdos* 'nest' (*ni-sd-*, that is [nizd-], being *ni-* 'down' with the zero grade of *sed-* 'sit') > Lat. *nīdus*; Lat. *dislegō* 'select out, put aside' [dizlego·] > *dīligō* 'prize, esteem highly'.

In the late prehistory of Old Irish, a wholesale compensatory lengthening resulted from the loss of lenited stops followed by certain resonants, so *eθnah* 'bird' (PIE *petnos*) > OIr. *én*. PCelt. *kolignos* 'puppy' > *kuleɣnah* > OIr. *cuilén* /kuλʸēn/. (This development is structurally significant, since it restores long vowels to post-tonic syllables. By an earlier rule, all inherited post-tonic long vowels became short.)

In Germanic, *n droped before *χ, and the preceding vowel became long if it was originally short: PreGmc *branχ-tō* 'brought' > OE *bróhte*. In a parallel but much later development, Middle English /χ/ (spelled *gh*) drops after a front vowel, lengthening the vowel: ME *night* /niχt/ > late ME /nīt/ > NE *night* /nayt/. In Greek, short vowels become long before *ns* sequences arising from certain other developments: *pant-s* nom.sg.masc. 'all' > *pans* > Gk *pâs* /pās/.

The lost consonant, as mentioned above, is usually contiguous to the affected vowel, but there are exceptions. Pre-IE **ḱerd* nom./acc.sg. 'heart' (the bare stem) seems to have become PIE *ḱēr*, as seen in the old Greek nom.sg. *kêr*, Ved. *hā́rdi*, Hitt. HEART-*ir* nom./acc.sg., and OPr. *seyr*.[1] This is not solid evidence, however, as we might actually be dealing with the usual type of lengthening if the true history was a stepwise sequence like **ḱerd* > **ḱerr* > *ḱēr;* and some such scenario

---

[1] In *hā́rdi* the original form has been papered over with a restored *-d* (with the aid of prop-vowel *-i* < *-ə*). The Hittite form is attested written with a sign known to mean 'heart' followed by the phonogram *-ir;* the writing system is ambiguous, but this attestation is consistent with an interpretation /kēr/.

is strongly supported by the fact that Proto-Indo-European words seem not to have included long consonants even across morpheme boundaries. Clearer evidence for non-contiguous compensatory lengthening of short vowels is provided by the development of short vowels in Old English before Proto-West-Germanic *-$l\chi$- and *-$r\chi$- intervocalically: OE *sulh* 'plow', dat. *súle; feorh* 'life; body' gen. *féores*. No stepwise scenario will do for these forms (say, PGmc *$sul\chi\bar{a}$ > ˣ*sullœ* > OE *súle*), since -*ll*- is the regular Old English reflex of *-*ll*-: *fylle* f. 'fill, plenty', *ealles* gen.sg. 'all'. Differently, in West Slavic languages there was compensatory lengthening of vowels when a vowel was lost in the following syllable, thus OCS *vozŭ* 'wagon' > Polish *wóz* /vus/ but *vozu* /vozu/ gen. (The length distinction was later lost in Polish, but leaves its trace in the different qualities of the root vowels.)

   a. Some long consonants look like the results of compensatory lengthening, such as PGmc *kinn*- < *$\text{*}\acute{g}enw$*- 'chin', or Gk *állos* 'another' (< *$\text{*}a\widehat{l}los$) < *alyos*, or Fi. *hammas* 'tooth' < *hamβas* < *šampas* (cf. gen.sg. *hampaan* < *šampasen* or the like). But the term is usually reserved for vowel lengthening, and these consonantal phenomena are usually thought of as assimilations, like the unambiguous It. *sette* 'seven' < *septem*, or PGmc *þammai* < PIE *tosmōy* dat.pl. 'them'. In other cases, though, which might include one or another of the items above (*kinn*-, *állos*, *hammas*), the true story does seem to be a matter of lengthening before a consonant which is subsequently lost, as in the West Germanic Consonant Gemination, as seen in OE *settan* 'to set' < *settjan* < *satjana^n* < PIE *sodeyonom* (see 17, above).

   b. Compensatory lengthening may be seen as a CONSERVATIVE trait. When a segment drops without a trace, as when *soften* lost its [t], two separate changes are involved: the omission of certain articulatory gestures, and the shortening of the duration of the whole string of segments by however many milliseconds were occupied by the elided segment. These two factors, though intimately and routinely connected, are not invariably so: but if the timing of a sequence of segments is to remain unchanged when the articulatory gestures disappear, then some segment in the string must be prolonged.

21. Fusion

Fusion (or blending) occurs when a sequence of segments turns into a single segment with some of the phonetic properties of each of the ingredient elements, or some averaging of them (so to say). Thus *dw*- > Lat. *b*- as in *dwis* > *bis* 'twice' (cf. Gk *dís*, Ved. *dvís*); *ny* > *ñ* (innumerable examples); Lat. /ŋn/ as in *lignum* 'wood' /liŋnum/ > Western Romance *ñ* as in It. *legno* /leño/—that is, a sequence of a dorsal and an apical nasal becomes a single palatal segment. In certain casual styles of American English *sandwich* emerges as *sammage* /sæməĵ/.

22. Palatalization

Palatalization often (but not invariably) involves just such a fusion.[1] It frequently entails a shift of the point of articulation of apical or dorsal consonants to a dorso-palatal position, but sounds of ANY point of articulation may be palatalized in the articulatory sense of the word, as reviewed in the footnote below. Palatalization of apical or dorsal segments is often (but not invariably) attended by *affrication*, particularly *assibilation*, i.e. the development of sibilant features either preceding or following the original consonant. This affrication often (but not invariably) leads to further more or less significant developments, and some such chain of events is the real story behind such French sound laws as *ky > s* (PRom. *glacia* /glakya/ > *glace* /glas/ 'ice'); *by > ž* (PRom. *rabia* /rabya/ > *rage* /raž/); *my > (n)ž* (*simia* /simya/ > *singe* /sēž/ 'monkey').

The usual catalyst for palatalization is a following front vocalic. The higher the vocalic, the more potent the palatalizing influence, and glides palatalize more potently than syllabics. Palatalization may be a matter of a stray sound law here and there, but generally a phonology either undergoes extensive palatalization or else has little or none of it. Latin prior to the classical period has little to do with palatalization, but once palatalization kicks in it significantly changes the phonologies of most Romance languages, thus Lat. *centum* /kentum/ 'hundred' > It. *cento* /čento/, Sp. *ciento* /θiento/ or /siento/, Fr. *cent* /sã/, and so on.

A front vocalic is not indispensable for palatalization, however. In

---

[1] Terminological ambiguity easily leads to misunderstanding here. *Palatalized* is commonly used in two different ways. One describes the result of a diachronic PROCESS, the subject of this paragraph. The other refers to a type of PHONE which distinctively includes a coarticulation of a high front vocalic. Note also that in the phonetic sense of the word it is important not to confuse PALATALIZED consonants, as defined just now, and consonants of PALATAL POINT OF ARTICULATION (AI2).

Romance languages of Italy and Spain the *l of PRom. *pl, *kl, *fl becomes palatalized, spontaneously as it were. The matter stops there in Spain (apart from the loss of the obstruent before the palatalized liquid, e.g. Sp. llave 'key' < *klave); but in Portugal and most parts of Italy the palatalized *l loses the liquid articulation altogether, becoming a high front glide: *py, *ky, *fy. And the matter stops there in standard Italian: It. piombo 'lead' (the metal), chiamare /kya'mare/ 'call', and fiamma 'flame', from PRom. *plǫmbu, *klamare, and *flamma, respectively. But in Portuguese (and also in northern Italy) the obstruents themselves become palatalized by the following *y, and assibilated as well; hence corresponding to the above Italian words, Port. /'čumbo/, /ča'mar/, and /'čamma/; such a pronunciation is still found in northern dialects, but in standard Portuguese this /č/ became /š/. Cf. Sp. llamar and llama.[1]

Another case is NE dial. [gyardən], [kyar] for standard garden, car. This change of [k g] to [kʸ gʸ] before [a] has not developed assibilation, at least not yet, but a similar innovation in the history of French went as follows: PRom. *ka, *ga > *[kya], *[gya] > OFr. [ča], [ǰa]; and then later the consonants became Fr. [š] (written ch) and [ž] (written j or g), thus PRom. *kattu 'cat' > Fr. chat [ša], and *galbina 'yellow' > jaune [žon]. —Another Western Romance palatalization not dependent on front vocalics is the spontaneous development of *kt into *ķt, with assorted outcomes: PreRom. *ǫkto (Lat. octō) 'eight' > PWRom. *ǫ̨kto > Fr. huit [ẅi(t)], Sp. ocho [očo], Port. oito [uytu]. A similar development is seen in Slavic, e.g. OCS noští 'night' < *nokt- < PIE *nokʷt-.

Because palatalized consonants entail a coarticulated vocalic, they often influence the phonetics of adjacent vocalics, especially preceding ones. Accordingly, in the course of the Greek development mentioned in 19a, Pre-Greek *gʷan-yō 'I go' > PGk *gʷaňňō > Att. baínō. This process is sometimes known as epenthesis or penetration, as though the originally postconsonantal *-y- somehow leaked through the consonant and ended up in front of it. There is little to be said for the literal

---

[1] Spanish plomo 'lead' (Pb) shows traits of 'learned borrowing', that is, its formal details have been influenced by the Classical Latin word plumbum. The regular development of *pl- is seen in more basic vocabulary, for example Sp. llueve 'it is raining' < Lat. pluit.

truth of such a view, nor for the idea touched on in 19a that the process is one of metathesis. A concrete objection to either of these views for ancient Greek is that a front vocalic in such a situation did not evolve a diphthongal pronunciation but merely lengthened, as PGk *k^{wh}eññō 'kill' > Att. *theínō* /t^{h}ēnō/. Now, since Greek had the diphthong /ey/ in its inventory, a process which was genuinely metathetic must have resulted in ˣ/t^{h}eynō/, and a genuine epenthesis would likely have done so.

The phenomenon seen in these Greek examples and discussed earlier (19a) is better taken as *regressive* (or *anticipatory*) *palatalization*.

CHANGES IN MANNER OF ARTICULATION

23. Spirantization

Spirantization, or fricativization, is a process whereby occlusives (stops or affricates, A7-8) and, rarely, nasals, become spirants. If the input is a stop, spirantization entails the development of a spirant aperture at the point of articulation, either in addition to the occlusion or in place of it.

Affricates are already complex articulations, and for them 'spirantization' means the loss of the stop component of the affricate, i.e. [t^s] > [s] (examples below).

Thus, by two different processes of spirantization, original [t] might acquire a spirant release and become [t^s] or (more rarely) [t$^\theta$]; or else it might simply develop a spirant aperture and become [θ] or [s] directly.

PIE *p *t *ḱ and *k^w all became spirants in Proto-Germanic, unless they were immediately preceded by a spirant: PIE *p̥tér- 'father' > PGmc *faðar-; contrast PIE *sperH- 'kick' > PGmc *spern- (NE *spurn*), PIE *kap-tó-s 'seized, captive' > PGmc *haftas. In Proto-Italic the voiceless aspirated reflexes of PIE *bh *dh *ǵh and *g^wh early became *f *θ *χ and *χ^w.

In Greek a similar development of voiceless aspirated stops is seen, but starting almost a millennium later and strung out over eight hundred years or so (see pp. 56-7). In Avestan, voiceless stops became spirants when followed by non-syllabic continuants: *pro 'forth' > PInIr. *pra > Av. *fra;* PIE *twe-óm 'thee (emphatic)' > PInIr. *twām > Av.

θwǫm. In Middle English, OE *dr* > *ðr* after a stressed vowel: OE *fæder* > NE *father,* OE *weder* > NE *weather.*[1]

Starting with affricates, OFr. /č ǰ t^s/ > Fr. /š ž s/: OFr. *chambre* (cf. NE *chamber,* borrowed from French before the change) > /šābr/, *juge* (cf. NE *judge*) > /žüž/, *cent* /t^{s}ent/ 'hundred' > /sã/. In Greek, the likely history of e.g. **-k$^{(h)}$y-* > *-ss-* (as in **p^{h}ulak^{h}yō* 'I guard' > *phulássō*) is **k$^{(h)}$y* > **čč* > *(t)ts* (? or *tss*) > *ss.*

Note that the developments of PRom. **k* and **g* to Fr. /š/ and /ž/, given above, might be mistaken for the spirantization of a stop; in fact, in this case we know that the stops first became affricates, and only very much later (in a general development) all Old French affricates lost the occlusive component and thereby turned into spirants. A great number of words were borrowed from French into English at a time when the sounds in question were still affricates, however, hence the discrepancy between NE /č/ and Fr. /š/ in such words as NE *chamber* = Fr. *chambre* /šābr/, *chief* = *chef* /šεf/, *pouch* = *poche* /poš/. Since English from the earliest historical period had the phone [š], there can be no suspicion that speakers of English substituted /č/ for Fr. /š/. (Contrast the substitution of /š/ for Fr. *s,* pp. 192-3.)

24. Lenition and fortition

Lenition 'weakening' and *fortition* 'strengthening' of speech sounds are prescientific terms that are nevertheless still current. *Lenition* at least does have some valid technical applications, mainly as it applies to the development of postvocalic consonants in certain languages of the Celtic branch (and similar phenomena seen in other languages such as Berber). The problem is that the actual phonetic changes grouped under lenition and fortition have little in common. For example, in the development of Celtic languages, postvocalic voiceless stops (**t, *k*) become voiceless fricatives ([θ χ]) in Old Irish, but become voiced stops ([d g]) in Welsh. It seems vacuously impressionistic to see a common basis for a relaxation of occlusion (**t > θ*) and not switching off

---

[1] One way to tell whether a given English /ð/ before *r* continues OE *dr* or *þr* is to compare the German cognate, in which /t/ = OE *d,* /d/ = OE *þ,* thus: NHG *Wetter* 'weather', *Leder* 'leather' reveal that *weather* continues an OE *d* while *leather* continues OE *þ.* —For the split of OE *þ* into NE /θ/ and /ð/, see **29**.

the vocal cords (*t > d*), even without consideration of the physiolog-ical fact that the production of voiced stops, [g] in particular, requires MORE muscular effort on the part of the speaker than the production of voiceless ones.

Under lenition, as a pseudo-PHONETIC term, are included not only the two developments given above, but also such developments as the evolution of a consonantal into a glide, such as the development of OE *r* (presumably a tap or trill) into the present-day vocalic [ɹ], or the change of a whole range of Altaic consonants into Turkic /y/, or the commonplace change of [s] > [h]. Presumably other commonplaces like the deocclusion of affricates mentioned in 23 come under this head. But many of these developments are not usually specifically called 'lenition'.

Less common than lenition is *fortition* (so called), which is simply the opposite kind of development, e.g. the devoicing of voiced sib-ilants in the histories of Spanish and Sanskrit (not parallel beyond the fact of devoicing); the evolution of glides into fricatives, or of frica-tives into stops; or a change of plain stops into aspirates ([t] > [tʰ]). Sometimes such developments are surprising, as in the fortition of *w to *f* in Old Irish, as in *wiros* 'man' > OIr. *fer* (p. 22).

For some reason, scholars rarely refer to such banalities as devoic-ing in word-final position, or [w] > [v], or [ð] > [d], as 'fortition'.

a. Some authorities see a fundamental truth in what they call the prevalence of 'lenition' among sound changes, but the reasoning is circular. It goes like this: it is postulated that laziness, or anyhow a ceaseless yearning for less effort, is a given of human activity; it is observed that certain sound changes are extremely common (such as the voicing of fricatives between vowels); it is then guessed that that is because the outcomes of such changes are 'weaker' (less effortful) than their inputs. The voicing of intervocalic fricatives becomes therefore an example of 'weakening/lenition' (and the reverse change would be 'fortition').

This circle of reasoning adds nothing to the bare observation that some kinds of changes are very common and others are less so.

SUGGESTIONS FOR FURTHER READING

Not all historical treatments discuss these matters. Generally similar and good accounts albeit differently organized and with a somewhat different terminology will be found in **Hock 1985** chapters 5–7, **Hock & Joseph 1996** chapter 4 §5, **Crowley 1998** chapter 2, **Campbell 1999** chapter 2 §§5–6. A different approach will be found in **Lass 1997** chapter 7.

SOUND LAWS

25. Overview

As stated above (12), the most highly structured kind of language change is *phonological change,* and this structuring is what makes it the the primary tool in comparative linguistics.[1] Phonological change will be discussed below, 26-34. Forms change through time by other mechanisms as well, the most important of which is *analogical change,* which will be discussed in 46-53.

It is—usually—easy to tell which of the two classes of change we are dealing with. *Phonological changes* are those innovations which can be defined by a statement (or *sound law*) of inputs and conditions (if any) which specify SOUNDS ALONE. Put differently, sound laws act independently of the meaning-bearing functions of linguistic structure.

Analogical change is basically different: it is the influence of the pronunciation of one form (or class of forms) on the pronunciation of another form or class. Thus, any change that necessitates the naming of a specific form or class of forms is an analogical change. The catalyst for this analogical influence is *function* (more or less synonymous with *meaning*): something about the functions of two elements—words or endings or whatever—causes some sort of association which is strong enough to lead to one form undergoing alteration in the image of the other. (Occasionally the influence is mutual.)

The fact that phonological changes take place in an abstract system is the explanation for their 'mindlessly' systematic nature; by contrast, the lexicon-specific nature of analogical changes means that they are less systematic—and strikingly so as a rule. In fact, it is commonplace for an analogical change to affect a single form, and, even if its theater is a whole class, it will often affect appropriate forms one by one in a process that can extend over centuries—and even then leave a form or two unaltered. This incidentally is another crucial difference between phonological and analogical change: phonological changes take place

---

[1] For a review of phonetic terms and symbols, see the Appendix pp. 209-37.

at a certain time (to oversimplify a bit), and are manifested in the entire lexicon current at that time; and when the change is complete the process ceases.

Some authorities denigrate the appeal to analogy in historical linguistics as a patch-up device, one which is applied in an ad hoc rather than a theoretically justified way. There is a measure of truth in this. The unsystematic nature of analogy means that there are few objective measures of the value of a proposed analogical explanation. Some are 'obviously right', or appear to be; but once one departs even a little distance from 'obviously right', such accounts decline in cogency very rapidly, and truth, like beauty, is in the eye of the beholder.

Sporadic Changes (43-5, 51-3, 55). There are in addition to these two sorts of changes a number of sporadic and patternless accidents with various causes, e.g. spelling-pronunciation (43) and dialect borrowing (44). As in the case of analogy, their detection—since their operation is by nature sporadic and patternless—is more or less guess-work.

   a. We have been talking of 'phonological CHANGE', but it is crucial to bear in mind that ALL regular diachronic phonological relationships are sound laws. Thus, in the evolution of Greek, the statement *s > s/__# ('*s remains unchanged in word-final position') is just as much a sound law as *s > h/#__V ('*s changes to h in word-initial position before a vowel'). Historians and theorists may devote most of their attention to the kinds of rule that involve change, but in fact most details of a language stay the same, for long periods.

   Even though *analogy* and *analogical change* are interchangeable terms, sometimes analogy too maintains rather than alters a form. For example, *s from Proto-Indo-European normally drops between vowels in Greek, as PIE *ǵenesos 'of a clan' > Hom. *ǵéneos;* but when the *s is a marker of the aorist tense it normally survives as such. Since the crucial events are prehistoric, it remains a topic of debate whether this is a 'therapeutic analogy'—that is, an innovation that restored intervocalic *s after it was lost—or instead involved a continuous adjustment that prevented the consonant from being lost in the first place. (A clear example of a therapeutic analogy would be the English ordinals *fift, sixt, twelft,* in which phonologically regular, and attested, -*t* was replaced by -*th* on the analogy of the other ordinals.) See 50.

26. Diachronic phonology

In sections 13-24 we discussed phonetic changes. But as the SOUNDS of a language change, its PHONOLOGY necessarily changes pari passu. The following terms refer to the ways in which changes in pronunciation alter phonological systems. The specific terms designate the relationship between the new structure and the structure that preceded it.

The following technical terms will be discussed in this chapter:

Merger – unconditioned loss of contrast
Split – one phoneme becomes two or more
Sound law – a regular change in pronunciation which can be stated
    purely in terms of phonological inputs and conditions (see 30)

MERGER

27. Merger refers to the unconditioned disappearance of a phonological contrast. In the aftermath of a merger, there is no direct evidence of the earlier contrast, and often no evidence of any kind.

  PIE *r and *l merge completely in Indo-Iranian, as do PIE *e, *o, and *a. PIE *plneHti 'fills' > Ved. pṛṇáti; PIE *bhṛto- 'carried' > Ved. bhṛtá-; *me-mor-tHe 2sg. 'are dead' > mamartha; *kaso- 'hare' > Ved. śáśa-.

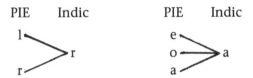

In Modern Greek, the earlier contrast of length has disappeared from the vowel system, with the wholesale falling together of previously distinct sounds. Thanks to this and other changes, eleven different Periclean syllabics end up as Modern Greek /i/.

In the evolution of Sardo from Proto-Romance, long and short vowel phonemes fell together pairwise; and in all varieties of Romance the original contrast of a and ā was lost without a trace. In standard German, MHG ei /ey/ and ī merge as the diphthong /ay/ (variously spelled, but most commonly ei): MHG mīn > NHG mein /mayn/ 'my', MHG bein 'leg; bone' > NHG Bein /bayn/ 'leg'.

Frequently-encountered synonyms for merger are *syncretism* and *falling together*; the verbs *merge* and *fall together* are also synonyms.

PRIMARY SPLIT

28. Primary split (also known as *conditioned merger*) results when an earlier sound merges with some other sound in certain explicitly stated environments only. The phonological history of most languages is a complex tangle of such conditioned mergers.

Proto-Italic had a contrast between **s* and **r*. However, in the history of both Latin and Umbrian, **s > r* between vowels, a phenomenon familiar to Roman grammarians and termed by them *rhotacism* (from Gr. *rhô*, the name for the letter corresponding to *r*). The two crucial factors for primary split are: the development is CONDITIONED, and the novel outcome of the split (in this case *r* coming from *s* between vowels) is a sound ALREADY PRESENT in the language.

Early   Classical
Latin   Latin

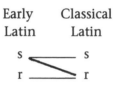

Examples: **dwen-āsom* gen.pl.fem. 'good' > *bonārum; *koys-ō* 'I care for' > *cūrō; *es-ti* 'is' > *est, *es-e-t(i)* 'will be' > *erit; *ges-ō* 'I do' > *gerō*, pple. **ges-tos > gestus; *mōs* 'custom' > *mōs*, acc. **mōs-em > mōrem*.

This has the following results:

(1) the total number of different sounds remains the same; but

(2) the frequency of the sounds is changed: as a consequence of the above split, there were in Latin more instances of /r/ than before, and fewer of /s/; and

(3) there is a *gap* in the distribution of the sound that undergoes the split. That is, there is an environment—in this case, between vowels—where Lat. *s* is not found at all.[1] (This state of affairs is often temporary. In this case, for example, /s/ was rather soon to be found once again between vowels in Latin, thanks to borrowing and the action of other sound laws.

---

[1] Except when followed by /r/, as in *miser* 'wretched'. See fn. on p. 51.

Sometimes the total phoneme inventory is REDUCED as the result of a primary split, so that in a sense result (1) does not hold. For example, the four Proto-Greek stops *p, *t, *k, *kᵂ are reflected in literary Greek as p, t, and k. This came about when Proto-Greek *kᵂ underwent a three way primary split, such that all the split products merged with another phoneme:

> *kᵂ > k when immediately following *w or adjacent to *ŭ;
> *kᵂ > t before front vowels otherwise; and
> *kᵂ > p elsewhere.

Proto-Greek   Attic

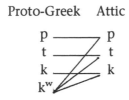

Examples: PIE *nokᵂt- 'night' > PGk *nukᵂt- > Gk nukt-; *kᵂis 'who' > tís, *penkᵂe 'five' > pénte; *kᵂoteros 'which (of two)' > póteros; *likᵂtos 'left (over)' > liptós.

In such a case, then, we see that ALL of the split products of *kᵂ fall together with some other sound already in the system. When such a thing happens, the total number of sound types in a language decreases. Note that if, say, PIE *k and *kᵂ had simply merged (which is what happened in early Old Irish), the overall phonological structure of Greek would look the same as it does—namely, in place of *p *t *k *kᵂ there would be only p t and k—but the relationship between the earlier and later systems, as expressed in the lexicon, would have been very different.

The development of NE /ð/ from OE /d/ before /r/ (34), is another case of primary split: Old English had two phonemes, /þ/ and /d/. By the process of *secondary split* (29, below), /þ/ became two phonemes, /θ/ (voiceless) and /ð/ (voiced). After the split of /d/, there were the same three phonemes, /d ð θ/, but in one specific environment what had been /d/ merged with /ð/.

SECONDARY SPLIT

29. Secondary split (also known as *phonologization*) likewise consists of a sound evolving into two or more different sounds, but in this case the split produces A NEW CONTRAST in the phonology. It is the explanation for a famous development in Indo-European languages, namely the appearance of palatalized consonants in Indo-Iranian: PIE *k^w for example split into Proto-Satem *$č$, when followed by a front vowel, and *k in all other cases. Thus PIE *$k^w i$-d 'what' > Ved. *cit* (an indefiniteness marker; *c* = something like [č]); *$k^w o$-*syo* gen.sg. 'whose' > *kásya;* *-$k^w e$ 'and' > *-ca;* *$penk^w e$ 'five' > *páñca;* *$k^w ṛmi$-* 'worm' > *kṛmi-;* *$k^w eyt$-e-ti 'notices' > PInIr. *$čaytati$ > *cétati,* and, from the same root, *$k^w oyt$-o-* 'intention' > PInIr. *$kayta$-* > *kéta-.*

The salient point here, as always with this type of change, is that the crucial environments for the split are not to be seen in Indo-Iranian itself: they belong to an earlier period in the language. The innovation in Indo-Iranian which turned *[k č] < */k^w/ into two separate phonemes was the merger of *e *o *a into PInIr. *a, and of *$ē$ *$ō$ *$ā$ into *$ā$. Put differently, the split of *k^w into InIr. *k and *$č$ was a sort of by-product of a quite independent change, namely, the merger of front and non-front vowels, so that *ka* and *ča* were in contrastive distribution:

    1. Pre-InIr.   *k > [č] before front vocalics
                    > [k] elsewhere
    2. PIE *e (a front vocalic), *o, and *a > PInIr. *a

Thus *ke > *$če$ > *ča*, while *ko, *ka > PInIr. *ka*.

A similarly sweeping secondary split in the history of English created a phonemic contrast between voiced and voiceless fricatives seen in the contrast system of present-day English. In Old English, [v z ð ɣ] were in complementary distribution with [f s θ χ], respectively. That is, [f] (for example) occurred only initially, finally, and adjacent to an obstruent, whereas [v] only occurred between resonants. (This statement of distribution is not complete, but will do for our purposes.)

wulf 'wolf'	[wulf]
wulfas nom.pl.	[wulvas]
līf 'life'	[li·f]
on līfe 'alive'	[onli·ve]
efne 'even'	[evne]
lifde 'lived'	[livde]

The rug was pulled out from under the complementation of voiced and voiceless fricatives when two unrelated things happened. The more important was the wholesale loss of posttonic vowels, such that e.g. [onli·ve] or [ali·ve] became [ali·v], with [v] in the same environment as [f] in nom.sg. *līf* [li·f]. (The Great Vowel Shift plus atonic vowel reduction give NE *alive* /əlayv/ and *life* /layf/.) Contributing to the new contrast, but less important than the loss of posttonic vowels, was the shortening of long—always voiceless—fricatives, whereby both voiceless and voiced fricatives were found between vowels, as in OE *hassuc* 'coarse tuft of grass' > *hassock* /hæsək/. The upshot is that each Old English spirant phoneme (except for /š/) split into two different phonemes, one voiced, one voiceless.

$$\text{OE /f/ [f, v]} \underbrace{\begin{matrix} \nearrow \text{ME /f/} \\ \searrow \text{ME /v/} \end{matrix}}$$

a. Two common errors are found in discussions of this and similar examples.

First, many sources misstate what has happened here, structurally: they say that when (for example) OE /f/ split, the result was 'a new phoneme, /v/'.

There is in fact a new CONTRAST; but once the split occurred, BOTH /f/ (always voiceless) AND /v/ (always voiced) were 'new phonemes'. The fact that the Old English element is written with the letter *f* doubtless fosters the confusion, since it (irrelevantly) invokes a feeling of voicelessness in the modern beholder. In fact, the feature [voice] was not part of the definition of OE /f/ at all. The addition of [voice] created TWO 'new' phonemes, one [+voice], the other [–voice].

The second questionable commonplace has to do with the fact that around the period that the contrast of voice was developing in Middle English, French already had a contrast between /f/ and /v/, and between /s/ and /z/. Since English was borrowing heavily from the French lexicon at the time, many authorities state as fact that borrowing from French was the source of the new voicing contrast in English. But as mentioned in 127, Romance [v] in initial position (or [s] in medial position) would have been literally unpronounceable in Old English or Early Middle English.

Attempts to borrow forms like Romance *verse* resulted, not in a new English contrast, but in OE *fers*, with a sound substitution of [f] for [v]. As soon as the voicing contrast was established, of course, alien forms with word-initial [v] or medial [s] were accurately borrowed—perhaps earlier still in texts showing heavy French influence, but how influential such texts were is debatable. In any case no French participation can be claimed for the parallel new contrast between /θ/ and /ð/ as in *wreath* and *wreathe*.

b. The same phonetic development may have different structural consequences. The incident in the evolution of Proto-Germanic known as Verner's Law grew out of the loss of the Proto-Indo-European accent. The original position of this accent determined which pre-Germanic voiceless fricatives became voiced and which stayed voiceless. In the case of Pre-Germanic **f *þ *χ* and **χ^w*, the phones **v* ([β]), **ð *γ* and **γ^w* were already present in the language (being the reflexes of PIE **bh *dh *gh*, and **g^wh*), so that here the effect of Verner's Law was Primary Split (28). In the case of **s > *s* and **z*, however, the exact same change under the exact same conditions resulted in Secondary Split, since a new contrast was the outcome:

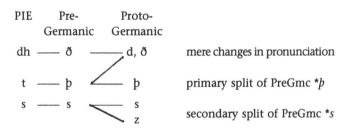

PIE	Pre-Germanic	Proto-Germanic	
dh — ð	—	d, ð	mere changes in pronunciation
t — þ		þ	primary split of PreGmc *þ
s — s		s	secondary split of PreGmc *s
		z	

c. Loss. It is not self-evident where to put the LOSS of a phoneme (as opposed to the merger of two phonemes) in this scheme. Since loss is sometimes unconditioned (albeit not commonly) and sometimes conditioned, it might be held to bear a resemblance to conditioned and unconditioned merger—in this case, merger with 'zero'. For those theorists for whom 'phonological zero' is a term without a referent (whether as a matter of principle or in this particular analysis), loss of a phone has to be set up as a separate category of event. Redefining the event as a loss of CONTRAST might be more palatable.

SOUND LAWS

As mentioned in 12, PHONOLOGY is the only component of language where innovation and conservation is sufficiently systematic, patterned, and observable to allow the formulation of testable diachronic hypotheses. Such hypotheses go under the name of *sound laws* (or less commonly, and less accurately, *sound changes*).

30. Sound laws

Sound laws are the formulation of the regular phonetic and phonological changes seen in the history of a language. The term, being reminiscent of 'laws of nature' or 'laws of physics', has been called a dangerous metaphor. There are no sound laws applicable to all languages
or to all periods of the history of a given language. To be sure, certain
phonetic developments are found repeatedly in different languages, or
in the same language at different periods; but no matter how commonplace a type of phonetic change is, it will never be remotely
universal. Sound laws, then, are purely empirical formulae describing
relationships, whether observed or hypothetical, between two chrono-
logically different stages of a given form of speech. Subsequent to the
given time, the change will cease. For reasons that will become clear
shortly, this limitation of sound laws to a specific time is an important
trait.

Finally, other things being equal, a given sound law will apply to
ALL FORMS PRESENT IN THE LANGUAGE AT THE TIME which satisfy the input conditions. (But see *lexical diffusion*, 32, below.) This includes fancy
words, plain words, loan-words, nursery words—everything. Even
onomatopoeia and expletives are not exempt: Modern Greek sheep say
/vi/, the phonologically regular outcome of Proto-Greek *bā: this regularly became Attic-Ionic [bæ·] and then koinē (Attic) Gk *bê* [bε·], and
then subsequently regular changes spirantized voiced stops and added
[ε·] to the crowd of syllabics that converged on Modern Greek /i/ (27).
The PIE cry of anguish, *aw, faithfully follows sound laws to become
Ved. *o* [o·] and OE *éa* [æ·ə] (and the latter may live on in NE *eek*). NE
/aw/ 'ow!' is therefore not an example of some sort of immunity on
the part of PIE *aw to the action of sound laws, but a new creation
which only replicates the PIE form.[1]

---

[1] A common misunderstanding of the slogan 'basic vocabulary is resistant to
change' takes it to mean 'resistant to the action of sound laws'. The 'changes' in the
slogan, however, have nothing to do with sound laws; at stake are LEXICAL RE-
PLACEMENT and ANALOGICAL REMODELING. As far as sound laws go, there is nothing
at all distinctive about basic vocabulary. Indeed, given their special resistance (not
immunity!) to analogical change, unusually common forms and even whole para-

At later dates, thanks to borrowing and the action of later sound laws, new forms conforming to the conditions for an earlier sound law may arise. SUCH FORMS WILL NOT SHOW THE EFFECTS OF THE ONCE-ACTIVE INNOVATION. For example, as we have already seen above (28) in the discussion of rhotacism, in the 4th century BC Lat. *s* > *r* between vowels. All cases of *s* present in the language at the time were thus altered.[1] What then are we to make of such Latin forms as *rosa* 'rose', *nisi* 'unless', and *causa* 'lawsuit; affair'?

The explanations differ in different cases, though the underlying cause is the same for all three (and many others like them: the formation did not exist in the lexicon at the time when intervocalic *-s-* became *-r-*:

Rosa is a loan-word. But it is crucial to note that this fact per se is not what accounts for the unchanged *-s-*: the nub of the explanation is that the word was borrowed after the rhotacism innovation had taken place. Hence *rosa* was unaffected by its action. Note that *pirum* 'pear' < *pisom* (= Gk *ápion*), also a loan-word, does show the effects of rhotacism. The difference between the treatments of **pisom* and **rosa* is entirely due to chronology: **pisom* was present in the Latin lexicon at the time when events leading to rhotacism were set in motion, and **rosa* was not. The same explanation accounts for why the numerous words borrowed by Germanic languages from Latin and Greek never show the effects of the Germanic Consonant Shift (Grimm's Law): they were borrowed after Grimm's Law had ceased altering the pronunciation of stops. The words do of course undergo all subsequent innovations: Lat. *cāseum* becomes NE *cheese* as the result of a good number of specifically Old and Middle English innovations, which affected loan words like *cheese* and native words alike.

---

digms are often odd ('irregular') precisely because they transmit the results of sound laws unaltered by leveling and other disturbances.

[1] For accuracy's sake, the sound law must be refined slightly. In four words, intervocalic *s* seems to remain unchanged: *miser* 'wretched', *caesaries* 'bushy-haired', *aser* 'blood' (archaic), and *diser(c)tus* 'eloquent'. But note that in all cases the consonant following the intervocalic *s* is an *r*. Though the data are few, there is a clear generalization here, and we must therefore revise our sound law: in the 4th century BC Lat. *s* > *r* between vowels unless the next following consonant is *r*.

Nisi 'unless' was still a phrase at the time of rhotacism, **ne sei;* that is, its *s* was prosodically word-initial at the time when Latin *s* medially between vowels was becoming *r*. (The coalescence of phrases into phonological words—a process known as *univerbation*—is of course commonplace: for example NE *alive, however, about, because, maybe;* NHG *vielleicht* 'perhaps', *umsonst* 'for nothing'; Fr. *beaucoup* 'much', *bienvenu* 'welcome'; Lat. *animadvertō* 'take [possibly critical] notice of'.)

Causa is the product of a 1st cent. BC sound law which shortened -*ss*- when it followed a diphthong or long vowel. That is, *causa* comes from *caussa < *kawssā (< *kawt-tā-)*; likewise *clausī* 'I shut' < *claussī < *klawt-sai*, perfect of *claudō*. In other words, at the time of the rhotacism of intervocalic *s, causa* and *clausī* did not have *s* between vowels, but rather *ss*.

31. Relative chronology

Lat. *causa, clausī*, above, and the numerous other forms of like shape, demonstrate an important principle. When it happens that two or more sound laws will give different results depending on what order they apply in, and only one ordering yields the observed forms, the fact that sound laws are fixed in real time allows us to speak of the *relative chronology* of the innovations. Consider the following sound laws in the history of Latin:

> (1) certain short vowels apocopated at the ends of
>   words, as PIE **lege-si* 'you gather' > **lege-s;*
> (2) *s > r* between vowels; and
> (3) *ss > s* immediately following a diphthong or long vowel.

The forms actually occurring in Latin show that these three changes must have taken place in the order given. If rhotacism had preceded apocope, **legesi* 'you gather' would have given Lat. *ˣleger*, not *legis*. If shortening of *ss* predated rhotacism, **kawssā* would have become *ˣcaura*, not *causa*.

The term *relative* makes explicit the lack of any connection between this kind of inference and real, or calendric, time. We do not know from such considerations the dates of any of the changes, or if much time or little elapsed between them. We only know that of the three innovations, the apocope of final vowels must have come first, then rhotacism, and last the shortening of *ss*. Note that in this example there is no relative chronological interplay between the first and third developments per se: their relative ordering is a purely logical consequence of their necessary ordering relative to the remaining change, rhotacism.

32. **Lexically-mediated sound laws** ('lexical diffusion')
The regularity of sound laws is an idealized concept. In reality, as has always been seen, the outcome of the regular application of a sound law is subject to various kinds of disturbance. First, there are the so-called *apparent exceptions,* treated in sections below: the results of dialect borrowing (44); spelling pronunciation (43); sporadic *phonetic* change such as haplology (pp. 31-2), metathesis (19), and dissimilation (16), and the action of analogy (46-53). Second, with the passage of time and the accumulated effects of subsequent sound laws, the conditions for a sound change, though perfectly regular at the time, become hard to figure out (if they can be figured out at all).[1]

In addition to these factors, it is now well known that some phonological innovations spread through a lexicon from word to word rather than applying to the whole lexicon uniformly. What the mechanism for this is is unknown—which at least puts it in the same category as 'regular' sound laws, whose mechanism is also unknown—but it is an indisputable fact. If such an innovation eventually spreads to all appropriate forms, its action is of course indistinguishable from a sound law as that term is usually conceived. If it runs out of steam be-

---

[1] As Verner's Law (29b) shows, sometimes it takes very little to create deep historical mysteries. Verner's Law determines when Proto-Indo-European voiceless obstruents become voiced fricatives in Germanic, and when voiceless: PIE **bhreHter-* 'brother' > Go. *broþar* but **pH̥ter-* > Go. *fadar* (*d* = [ð]). The clue to this mystery was provided by Vedic accentuation (here, Ved. *bhrā́tar-* vs *pitár-*), which revealed that pre-Germanic voiceless fricatives remain voiceless postvocalically when the tonic accent—the Proto-Indo-European tonic accent, note—lay on the immediately preceding vowel. But evidence for the original accent of Proto-Indo-European is confined to a few sources only; without them, no explanation of Verner phenomena is possible that is superior to mere guessing. See also pp. 159-61 for a discussion of the complexities of English vowel alternations of very recent date.

fore reaching that point, however, the result is an irregular and in many cases inexplicable patchwork of forms with changed and unchanged sounds.

An example of this from English is the distribution of /a/ and /æ/ in British English in words like *pass* /pas/ vs *passage* /pæsəĭ/, *mass* /mæs/ vs *master* /mastə/, or *can* /kæn/ vs *can't* /kant/. Which vowel is the innovation remains a matter for debate, but that is immaterial for our purposes—the point is the same either way, namely that in British English a new pronunciation (whichever one it is) has only partially replaced its predecessor.

Moreover, there are clear instances of such a change not merely faltering but actually receding and eventually disappearing, leaving behind perhaps a few doublets (such as NE *rile* vs *roil*, a souvenir of a failed merger of English /oy/ and /ay/).

It is probable that many forms whose pronunciation has traditionally been explained as dialect borrowing (44) are in fact instances of incomplete lexical spread. Good candidates for such an explanation are the sporadic appearance of *l* for *d* in Latin, and the inconsistent reflexes of *tn, *dn. In the former case, Latin has perhaps a dozen forms with *l* where a *d* surely stood originally, as *Capitōlium* (the name of one of the hills of Rome), which Roman antiquaries tell us was earlier *Capitodium;* and, within a single paradigm, *odor* 'a smell' vs *oleō* 'have a smell', cf. Gk *ódōde* 'smells'. In the case of the reflexes of apical stop followed by *n, PIE *atnos (or *Hetnos) 'year' (cf. Go. *aþna-* 'year') becomes Lat. *annus,* showing the expected assimilation of a sequence *t + nasal, parallel to *pn > mn (*somnus* 'dream' < *swepnos) and the like; but on the other hand *pandō* 'stretch out; throw open' is best explained as continuing *pat-n-, with the same root form as in *patēns* 'open', *patefaciō* 'throw open', and so on. There are a number of solid etymologies showing both metathesis and its lack, with no pattern of distribution.

Lexical diffusion, of course, is next to useless as a tool of historical linguistics: its nature makes it nearly impossible to tell the difference between a historically correct hypothesis of lexical diffusion and a vacuous guess. (The same caveat, and for the same reason, applies to dialect borrowing (44) as an explanation.) Furthermore, the secrets of many interesting sound laws would never have been worked out if the vogue in historical research were to dismiss all but the most obvious patterns of change as artifacts of haphazard lexical diffusion: persistently revisiting old problems can on occasion turn up elegant explanations for what had long been regarded as some kind of historical accident.

> a. It seems clear that not all sound changes spread by lexical diffusion, but it is not yet known what the relative importance of the different modes is. There is comparatively little clear evidence (even indirect evidence) for diffusion, but probably this is just because most lexically-mediated innovations, once they break out from the few source forms, progress very rapidly to the whole lexicon. Evidence from recent studies of innovations in progress attests just such a scenario, but it is too soon to tell whether it is any kind of NORM.

33. Sound shifts

Sound shifts are phonological changes which affect an entire natural class (A21) en bloc. As such, shifts would seem to be particularly good evidence for a theory of language change which holds—whatever the details of the actual mechanism—that something at the most ABSTRACT level of linguistic structure has altered a SERIES-GENERATING PHONETIC FEATURE. And this is the usual way of presenting prehistorical phenomena like the Germanic Consonant Shift (*Grimm's Law*). Where we have direct evidence, however, for the actual course of a change whose end point is a shift, the picture is often not consistent with any notion of a simple change in a series-generating feature.

Two examples are the spirantization of voiceless stops in Tuscan Italian (often called the *gorgia* ['guttural way of speaking'] *toscana*), and the similar spirantization of voiceless aspirated stops in Greek.

GORGIA TOSCANA

The earliest clear evidence for the phenomenon of stop sprirantization in Tuscan Italian is from the first quarter of the 16th century. Contemporaneous remarks about Tuscan dialect traits (and the *gorgia toscana* in particular), though varying in quality, are fairly copious; and the evidence is clear on the point that at this time only the intervocalic dorsal stop /k/ [k ~ χ] was involved.

The first definite mention of fricative pronunciation of the other two voiceless stops comes three hundred years later, from the first quarter of the 19th century, and then the writer specifically states that this trait is limited to Florence, and is not Tuscan as a whole. Authorities have doubted that the spirantization of *p* and *t* was literally confined to urban Florence even at that time, but take it as plausible that it was perhaps limited to the province of Firenze, more or less, whence it has spread only a little in modern times. As a result, today the region of Tuscany where original [k] is pronounced [χ] or [h] is more than twice as large as the area where [p] and [t] have also been replaced by spirants.

GREEK VOICELESS ASPIRATES

The history of Greek voiceless aspirates is similar in principle but different in detail. Evidence for [pʰ] (Greek Φ) > [f] is found in Pompeii in the first century AD, significantly earlier than evidence bearing on [tʰ] (Greek Θ) and [kʰ] (Greek X). As one might expect, evidence for [f] is spotty at first, and the use of Latin *f* to transliterate Greek Φ (125.1) does not become routine until the fourth century AD. Still, Wulfila consistently renders Φ with *f* in his third-century translation of the Bible into Gothic—in both names (*Aifaisium* dat.pl. 'to the Ephesians') and loanwords (*praufetes* 'prophet').[1] Evidence for spirant pronunciation of stops apart from *f* for Φ would be elusive in Latin sources in any case (125.1), but at least by the 3rd century there is evidence from Gothic again for the change of [tʰ] to [θ], for example Wulfila's rendition of the name *Thômas* in Gothic as *Þomas* /θōmas/.

Evidence that X was still a stop even at that period (and for several centuries more) comes from three sources.

First, Wulfila's Gothic represents Greek X with a special letter whose shape (X in effect) and location in the alphabet both look to Gk X.

---

[1] Curiously, the letter in the Gothic signary transliterated *f* has the shape of Latin F but its location in the Gothic alphabet corresponds to the location of Greek φ. There is no reason to doubt that it represents a fricative in Gothic; it is the letter used to write the sound corresponding to the *f* of English (and all other Germanic) words like *five* and *wolf*.

This is interesting, because it is likely that the sound represented by *h* in Gothic, e.g. *ufhlohjan* 'to provoke laughter' or *sloh* 'killed', was a voiceless fricative, that is, the very sound that the Greek sound represented by Χ evolved into, at some point. But in rendering the name rendered in Greek as Σεχενία(ς) 'Shechaniah' (in the Nehemiah fragment), Wulfila does not use the regular Gothic letter we transliterate as *h*; he wrote *Saixaineia* /se{?}enīa/ with the special Greek-based letter.

Second, in the Armenian alphabet (ca. 400 AD), the letters used to write the voiceless aspirated stops appear to be based on Greek Φ, Θ and Χ. The letter for the Armenian voiceless dorsal fricative is differently derived.

Third, four hundred years later, the earliest form of the Glagolitic alphabet for Church Slavic shows a similar pattern. The rarity of genuinely early texts written in this script enjoins caution, as does the fewness of attestations of the crucial character, but in the old monuments there are two different letters with, seemingly, the same value. One, the so-called spider-form *x*, occurs only a handful of times in early MSS and also in two Glagolitic abecedaria, and is not found later. Its shape is easily traced to the Gk Χ (though not necessarily directly), and there are other reasons as well for taking it as functionally equivalent. The letter which was used from the beginning to represent the Old Church Slavic sound [χ], as in *ěxŭ* [yæ·χʊ] loc.pl. 'they', is a sign not obviously based on any Greek letter (though antecents have been seen in the Coptic and Armenian signaries).

To summarize, the evidence is clear that the process of getting from uniform /pʰ tʰ kʰ/ to uniform /f θ χ/ in the evolution of Greek was not a coordinated shift achieved by applying a single rule to all voiceless aspirated segments. Rather, it proceeded stepwise: spirantization first appeared in the labial point of articulation, then pretty shortly thereafter in apical, and then finally, and only after a wide interval, the dorsal stop followed suit. Note too that dorsal spirantization, the last change in the evolution of Greek, was the first stage in the shift in Tuscan Italian.

a. Hungarian has what looks like an aborted consonant shift. Proto-Finno-Ugric **p* everywhere became Hu. /f/ initially and /v/ medially; PFiUg. **k* > Hu. /h/ but only before back vowels; and PFiUg. **t* undergoes no change initially, while becoming Hu. /z/ medially, except when preceded by a nasal consonant. Examples:

PFiUg. *p- in Hu. *fa* 'tree' (cf. Fi. *puu*), Hu. *fő* 'head' (cf. Fi. *pää*);
Hu. *hal* 'fish' (cf. Fi. *kala*) and *három* 'three' (cf. Fi. *kolme*) but Hu. *kéz* 'hand' (cf.
    Fi. *käte-*), Hu. *kő* 'stone' (cf. Fi. *kivi*);
Hu. *tél* 'winter' (cf. Fi. *talvi*), Hu. *tud-* 'know' (cf. Fi. *tunte-*);
for medial *t–not following a nasal–Hu. *víz* 'water' (cf. Fi. *vete-*), and Hu. *kéz*
    'hand', above.

In light of the above discussion, these ragged developments in Hungarian are readily understandable.

34. Understanding a sound law

When the formulation *X > Y describes an innovation, it must be viewed as a statement of a relationship rather than a specification of a process. To be sure, what used to be *X has somehow become Y, but when the complete facts are known, it is often the case that a sound change is far from a straight shot from the starting point to the outcome. A simple example of this is seen in a formula like PRom. *k/__a > Fr. *š* (that is: 'original and hypothetical k before original and hypothetical a becomes French *š*'). When this was discussed above (**22**), the point was made that between *k and *š* there are a number of steps, some hypothetical, some attested.

More dramatically, the formula PIE *pH̥tér- > NE *father* /faðər/ looks like, but is not, a statement that PIE *t underwent voicing and spirantization to become NE /ð/ The actual history was a whole procession of specific developments: *t > *t^h > *θ > *ð > d > ð. That is, in sequence:

    1. aspiration (*t > *t^h);
    2. spirantization (*t^h > *θ);
    3. voicing (PGmc *fadēr, where *d is [ð]);
    4. occlusion (OE *fæder*, where d = [d]);
    5. spirantization before r (d > ð, a second round, totally unlike
        the first one and unconnected to it).

(In some dialects of English there is yet a sixth development that changes the last /ð/ back to /d/, hence non-standard [mʌdə] 'mother', [fɔ̝də] 'father'.) Now, these are only the developments that we have a reasonable basis for surmising; other details might have been involved that we have no inkling of.

Note that these six developments are of very diverse structural significance: the first three changes are components of a huge restructuring affecting all Germanic languages (Grimm's and Verner's Laws); item 4 is a specifically West Germanic development of relatively small structural significance; and both item 5 and the subsequent change of /ð/ > /d/ are details limited to some English dialects.

Similarly indirect was the development of Sp. /χ/ from Lat. /g/ as in Lat. *gentīlis* /gen'tīlis/ > Sp. *gentil* /χen'til/. This could have been a straight shot, or nearly so, analogous to the Dutch development [g] > [ɣ] > [χ], as in *gulden* 'guilders' [χöldə]. But the evidence is clear that in Spanish the evolution in fact included at least the following steps: [g] > [gʸ] > [ĵ] > [ž] > [š] > [χ].

a. The relationship between earlier and later structures often is not a change in the structure itself but an artifact of another change.

An example is the change in the rules for the location of the tonic accent the evolution of Proto-Romance into French. They are given here in simplified form:

LATIN (Proto-Romance): the accent of polysyllabic words lies on the third syllable from the end of the word, except when it lies on the second syllable from the end (the penultimate) because (a) the word has only two syllables or (b) the penultimate is heavy, i.e., contains a diphthong or long vowel or ends in two or more consonants. Examples: *ámō* 'I love', *ópera* 'works', *témerunt* 'they defile', *árborēs* 'trees', *temeruntur* 'they are defiled', *catēna* 'chain', *adhaérō* 'I stick to', *animadvértō* 'take notice of'.

FRENCH: the accent lies on the final syllable.

The rules that describe the location of the accent in Latin are significantly different from the rule for its descendent French. However, the CHANGE was not actually in the rule itself, but in the French loss of Proto-Romance posttonic syllables. As a result, wherever the tonic accent stood, anciently, it would be found on the final syllable in French. Put differently, the accent has not actually moved; what has changed is the relationship between the tonic syllable and the rest of the word.

EFFICIENT CAUSES OF PHONETIC CHANGE

35. Why do the sounds of a language change in one way rather than in another? Why do they change at all? These questions are as old as historical linguistics. The underlying assumption often seems to be that speech sounds would not change in the absence of some kind of dis-

ruptive influence or other impetus. In fact, it is useful to focus on the truth that language structures are pretty stable, overall: change may be incessant, but is not very drastic in the short term, and the surprising alterations paraded for the astonishment of non-linguists usually represent the acumulation of small changes operating over time. In other words, Lat. *Augustus* did not become Fr. *Août* /u/ 'August' overnight.

Not only is there in fact no generally-accepted cause of phonetic change, is it hardly likely that there is any single cause: languages are complex, phonologies are complex, the functions of language in society are complex, and phonological changes are complex; it is not reasonable to assume that only one or two mechanisms are sufficient to account for all that is observed. And when we get down to actual cases, our achievements so far are disappointing: one or another causal theory is or once was regarded by some scholars as important or dominant, but all have failed to withstand any kind of test—assuming they are framed in a way that makes them testable in the first place, which is very often not the case. (Logical traps and other flaws in reasoning, in fact, have been as much an obstacle to progress in this area as lack of knowledge.)

Supposed efficient causes of sound change may be subdivided into *external* and *internal* causes, depending on whether they are part and parcel of the structure of the language itself, or bear upon it from the outside.

EXTERNAL CAUSES

36. It has been suggested that geography and climate (warm vs cold, wet vs dry, flat vs hilly) might have favored certain changes. This notion has been discredited, not because it is silly, but because it doesn't work: the changes thus supposedly favored—the spirantization of stops, say— are regularly observed in very different geographical conditions, and fail to occur in closely similar ones.

It has also been suggested that national character can influence sound change; but the impossibility of measuring anything so ethereal (not to say mystical), and among long-dead populations at that, forestalls any possibility of evaluating such theories.

37. Substratum influences

More plausible is the substratum theory. Since it is well known that whole peoples will from time to time adopt a new language (as happened with Latin throughout most of the Imperial Roman world, 120), it is reasonable to think that speech habits proper to the original language of the population (the *substratum language*) will bring about changes in the structure of the new language (the *superstratum*). A claim to this effect, of long standing, attempts to explain the 'weakening' of postvocalic stops—voicing, spirantization, loss altogether—in the Romance languages spoken in what is now France and Spain. The indigenous languages of France and parts of the Iberian peninsula were Celtic, we know; and the theory holds that the weakening of postvocalic consonants characteristic of Celtic languages was carried over into the phonology of the local varieties of Latin.[1] However, as plausible as the theory is in the abstract, it is supported by scarcely any evidence. Worse, this kind of theorizing leads inevitably to two absurdities:

(1) All changes that strike the beholder as in any way unexpected are attributed to such influences—the implication being that languages would hardly change at all without substratum influence; but for this there is much counter-evidence.

(2) To ascribe specific changes to the influence of a language whose structural features are totally unknown should be obviously futile; but

---

[1] Thus to take French as the example: medial *p* and *b* weaken to /f/ or /v/: *lupa* 'she-wolf' > *louve* /luv/, *faba* 'bean' > *fève* /fɛv/; apical and dorsal stops drop: *status* 'stood' > *été* 'been' (*ét-* is from the *st-*), *gaudia* 'pleasures' > *joie* /žwa/ 'joy', *iocus* 'game' > *jeu* /žö/, *fragilis* 'weak' > *fraglis* > *frêle*. (Dorsals in palatalizing environments have a different outcome: PRom. *recipére* 'to receive' > *recevoir* /rəsəvwar/, *decalciare* 'to remove shoes' > *déchausser* /dešose/; *plaga* 'district, zone' > *plage* /plaž/ 'shore'.)

It is perhaps necessary to remark that in Old Irish and Middle Welsh—the two varieties of Celtic with known lenition—ALL consonantals are affected, not just stops, so e.g. PIE *kʷr̥m-* 'worm' > PCelt. *kʷrim-* > W *pryf* /prəv/; but there is no hint of this sort of thing in French.

doing so is not merely a temptation which has proved hard to resist, it is logically unavoidable.

For example, let us take it as a given (for the sake of the argument) that the changes in Romance postvocalic stops in Iberian and Gallic Romance are indeed to be explained as the influence of a Celtic, specifically Gaulish, substratum; however unprovable, this notion at least rests on an observed fact of Celtic languages—the Celtic phenomenon known as the *lenition* ('weakening') of postvocalic consonants. So far, so good, apart from the drawback that lenition is not actually evident in Gaulish itself. But: if such developments are too eccentric and unexpected to be spontaneous in Romance, then how could they be spontaneous in Celtic? It follows that lenition in Celtic must necessarily also have a substratum explanation; and indeed, substratum influence has been invoked to explain Celtic lenition—despite the fact that NOTHING AT ALL is known of the linguistic features of Pre-Celtic languages.

This should remind one of the logical fallacy that goes by the tag *difficile per ignotum explicare*—'to explain that which is difficult by appealing to that which is unknown'. However, while the languages of the precursors of Indo-European speakers in Celtic Europe are indeed 'ignotum', the systematic weakening of consonants in certain environments is hardly 'difficile': it is something that has happened in the history of many languages.

Substratum influence is a language contact phenomenon, discussed more generally in 122.

38. Children's speech

The pronunciation of small children is faulty, and it is tempting to suppose that some sound changes might originate in the mistakes that occur in the acquisition of language by children. However, though the occasional hypocoristic detail obviously does work its way into standard speech, such as the Gothic word for 'father', *atta* (used even when addressing God), there is no evidence that permanent changes of a highly systematic character originate with children. Besides, such a theory about language change succeeds altogether too well: if the mistakes of children really were the ruling variable in language change, or even moderately important, languages would surely change much more rapidly and dramatically than they do. Further, the status of small children in any community is typically minimal—they may not even qualify as 'persons' at all—and for purely sociolinguistic reasons it seems unlikely that much influence would flow into the adult community from such a low-status source. Children might of course carry their pronunciation into adulthood, but anyone endorsing such a theory must explain why it is that the mistakes that small children most commonly make (lisping and substituting stops for affricates and fricatives, for example) are unlike the commonest kinds of diachronic sound changes, while some of the commonest diachronic developments are radically unlike known hypocoristic substitutions, for example palatalization, intervocalic voicing, or a change like [s] > [h].

39. Social dislocation

It has been speculated that traumatic experiences (like the Norman invasion, in the case of English) cause people to lose interest in matters of low survival value like endings or gender concord or vowel length. Hence the many differences between the Old English of Alfred's time and the English that reemerges a mere couple of centuries later. A variety of the theory may be regarded as a special case of substratum effect (37 and 122): it holds that persons of quality have more conservative —'correct'—speech than the many, and that in the social dislocations of invasion and revolution, people who 'know how to talk' are pushed aside (if they survive at all) by the lower orders. Since ignorant people more or less make up language as they go along, supposedly, the linguistic upheavals that sometimes follow such political experiences as the Norman Conquest are thought to be only natural.

However, though the uncouth many may well speak a dialect that differs more or less greatly from the norms of the former elites, any such dialect necessarily evolved following the same diachronic principles; furthermore, features of non-standard dialects often differ from the standard by being MORE CONSERVATIVE. What we are actually seeing in such cases is very much the same sort of thing as the shift of standard dialect bases from one geographic region of a country to another, such as happened when the French standard dialect base shifted from Provence to Burgundy, or has happened repeatedly in the history of Imperial China. In the specific example of the evolution of Old

English to Middle English, there is nothing to explain in the first place: large as the changes are, it has been recently recognized that they are not in fact out of line with the duration of time involved.

INTERNAL CAUSES

40. Much more attractive are theories that trace sound changes directly to the properties of phonetic givens, or to phonological structures themselves. But plausible as such theories are, they too have failed remarkably to withstand testing, or even less formal kinds of scrutiny.

41. **The ease theory**

Several internal-cause theories suffer from a fundamental logical flaw, namely, they propose an effect as a cause. This is particularly close to the surface in the *ease theory*. As is well known, many changes—particularly conditioned changes, such as assimilation or the loss of consonants—RESULT IN a less intricate articulatory shift in getting from one segment to the next, or even reduce the total number of segments. Thus, the *imp-* of Lat. *impotēns* 'powerless' might be thought to be somehow more economical, or maybe just a bit less tricky, than the preexisting sequence **inp-*, ditto Lat. *multus* 'fined' vs earlier *mulctus*.

First, note that the crucial 'diminution of effort' is asserted, not demonstrated; and even if the validity of the assertion is granted for the sake of the argument, converting the effect ('greater ease') into the cause means ascribing the change to some sort of purposeful behavior on the part of speakers—the articulators themselves can hardly 'know' what benefits await them if they switch from apical to bilabial closure in a certain segment. Besides, oddly, even banal phenomena like nasal assimilation manifest themselves very unevenly. In the Germanic group, PGmc **un-* has remained unchanged right up to the present in German and (to a large degree) in English, and it is debatable whether a native speaker of English would agree that *unpardonable* is 'more effortful' or 'less efficient' to pronounce than *impossible*, by reason of the cluster *np* vs *mp*.

A different problem with the ease theory is seen in the example of Lat. *octō* 'eight'. If its Italian reflex *otto* is merely what the ease theory would predict (*-tt-* being held to be more economical to pronounce than -*kt*-), this leaves us with the puzzle that this -*kt*- was pronounced by the Romans for hundreds of years, and by their ancestors for thousands; and it did not assimilate in such a fashion, even in the other Romance languages (though it underwent various other changes, as in Fr. *huit,* Sp. *ocho,* Rom. *opt*). In Gk *oktő* (now *okhtő*), the dorsal has remained unassimilated to this day. Inexplicably, that is, whole populations seem to be almost totally deaf to the advantages of a more economical pronunciation, with only fitful and erratic exceptions.[1]

But in some ways the gross logical flaw is only incidental. The real problem is that without some objective measure of ease, all such speculations are simply futile. Articulatory ease, relative or absolute, has remained unassessable to date. Indeed, the few crude approaches to the question that are possible yield unreassuring results: [či] is not found as a substitute for [ki] in the speech of drunks or of small children, whereas the norms of sound change indicate that [či] is somehow easier to pronounce than [ki]—very much easier in fact—since the latter so often turns into the former. Yet it is hard to imagine by what measure [či] might be shown to be 'easier' than [ki].

42. Functionalism

Another family of theories suffering from the same logical flaw of conflated effects and causes comes under the general heading of *functionalism*. Functionalism argues that the structure of the phonological system itself accounts for (or, at a minimum, influences) what sound laws do or do not take place.

---

[1] The mystery of whole communities of speakers remaining stubbornly heedless of the advantages of assimilation can sometimes be gotten around by invoking other, equally untestable, principles. It has been seriously asserted, for example, that the Germanic preservation of uniform *un-*, mentioned here, and the Italic assimilations of **in-* (see 107), is only natural, given coarse-natured Teutons on the one hand and, on the other, Italic peoples sensitive to 'euphony' or some other linguistic grace. (Two can play at that game, of course. Others have asserted, with equal seriousness, that the stability of the Germanic nasals testifies to the integrity and steadiness of the Teutonic character, in favorable contrast to Mediterranean *Schlamperei*.)

Note, in the case of Modern Gk *okhtő* 'eight' that speakers have actually added to the complexity of the articulation by INTRODUCING a transition from a fricative manner to a stop manner.

One manifestation of this is *gap-filling*. Many phonological systems have gaps—combinations of phonetic features that would be normal in such a system, considered as a whole, but which fail to occur. An example would be the absence of [p] in the stop system of Proto-Celtic:

	labial	apical	velar	labiovelar
Voiceless	–	t	k	k^w
Voiced	b	d	g	g^w

It is indeed true that sound laws often have the effect of filling gaps. In the example of Celtic languages, PCelt. $*k^w$ > Welsh *p*: PIE $*k^w etwor$- 'four' > W *pedwar*.

There are however three problems with this theory. First, such gaps are usually CREATED by sound laws in the first place, suggesting that sound laws are just as often heedless of functional imperatives as mindful of them.[1] Second, like so much speculation in diachronic linguistics, the theories' claims are teleolgical: that is, they redefine an effect as a cause. Third, there is no time limit: the theory's predictions are equally 'valid' whether it takes a generation or a thousand years for a gap to be filled. This means, inter alia, that the theory is unfalsifiable: no matter how long a gap survives, the theory can hold that the predicted effects have not been seen YET.

Besides, in a puzzle reminiscent of many other theories of causation, one and the same situation may have different outcomes. The *p*-less Proto-Celtic is the ancestor of both Old Irish and Welsh, and in Welsh as we have just seen this gap was filled when $*k^w$ > *p*. But in Old Irish, where k^w likewise disappeared, it did so by merging with *k*—leaving the inherited gap unfilled. (It was eventually filled even in Old Irish, not by phonological changes but through the agency of loan

---

[1] Although loss is very much the most usual explanation for phonological gaps, there are other causes. In the history of English, for example, the development of $*sk$ to *š* and the much later split of /f θ s/ into voiced and voiceless pairs of phonemes, /f v θ ð s z/, left /š/ as the only obstruent in the phonology with no voiced counterpart. (This 'defect' was repaired when—beginning ca 1600—/z/ split into /z/ and /ž/.)

words, e.g. *peccad* 'sin', but only after a struggle. In early borrowings, Prim.Ir. *k*ʷ was substituted for Latin and Welsh *p*, as in OIr. *Cothrige* /koθρʸəγʸe/ 'Patrick' < *k*ʷ*atrikios*, borrowed from Lat. *Patricius*.)

Another functional theory is that merger (27) is least likely to take place between elements bearing a *high functional load*, and most likely to take place between elements with lighter load. (Functional load has to do with the general idea that some structural contrasts do more work than others.) Phonetic similarity has to be taken into account, of course: even if there were zero functional load between [š] and [ŋ], say, no one would expect them to merge, owing to the huge phonetic difference between them.

However, functional load is considerably easier to name than to define in a way that both makes linguistic sense and can be measured. To date, there has been only one serious attempt at definition and measurement, and it failed to discover any correlation at all between functional load and merger. In any case, language is so extravagantly redundant that even the largest of functional loads of individual pairs of phonemes must necessarily be so minute that it is hardly to be expected that differences between loads would have detectable diachronic consequences.

    a. A striking reproof to the whole notion that functional load plays any significant role in merger is afforded by languages with small phoneme inventories such as Hawaiian, a language with a mere 14 phonemes in its phonology: /i e a o u p k ʔ m n l w y h/. This parsimony is the end result of an extended history of mergers operating on a phonology whose contrast system to begin with was on the rich side of average. Further, merger was not the only phonological change: other developments were acting to simplify syllable structure in the language as well, such as the loss of all consonants in word-final position.

    With each merger and simplification, the functional load of the remaining elements necessarily increased geometrically. If functional load were a ruling variable in mergers, one would have predicted on the basis of 'typical' phonologies of 30-odd phonemes that the Hawaiian merger binge must have come to a halt long before it actually did.

43. Spelling pronunciation

In *phonographic writing systems* the written signs represent elements in the phonology, either individual phonemes (in an alphabet) or sequences of phonemes which always include a syllabic (in a syllabary). Early in the histories of most written languages, the fit between sign and referent is fairly close to one-to-one. But often the written form will become more or less fixed, such that the fit between writing and language will deteriorate as the language changes while the orthography remains faithful to the practices of an earlier age. This means that with the passage of time the normal way of writing words will relate to the phonological facts of the living language in more and more inconsistent and complicated ways. Given such inconsistencies, if the written form of a language is felt as authoritative, the spelling may actually bring about a change in pronunciation. Such an innovation is called a *spelling pronunciation*. A confusingly-written language like English is inherently more prone to the influence of spelling pronunciation than languages like Greek, Latin, or Russian, whose written forms represent the facts of the language more straightforwardly. Yet even in such languages, spelling pronunciation is thinkable.

For example, there is strong evidence (including the Romance reflexes of the sequence; and see 128.1) that Lat. *-gn-* < PItal. **kn* and **gn* was originally pronounced /ŋn/: *ignis* [iŋnis] 'fire', *magnus* [maŋnus] 'great'. But at the same time there is reason to think that educated Romans said [ignis], [magnus] and the like. Influence of the spelling on pronunciation would reconcile this contradiction. Perhaps less hypothetical, the dropping of final *-s* in Latin, which is attested very generally in early inscriptions, is discussed by grammarians and rhetoricians, who describe it as an old-fashioned or ignorant pronunciation. This assessment fits with the idea that pedantry or exaggerated respect for spelling accounts for the uniform pronunciation of final *-s* in the classical period.

In English the phenomenon is abundant and very securely attested. ME *langage* came to be spelled *language,* with the etymological *u* restored, and it is now pronounced accordingly. The same cause accounts for present-day *perfect* for Chaucer's *perfit*, and *medicine* pronounced in three syllables.[1]

---

[1] British English still generally has /medsən/, and likewise /figə/ *figure* next to the spelling pronunciation /figyər/ of standard American English.

Spelling pronunciations based on etymological spellings, as most of them are, have in a sense turned the clock back, and this raises at least the possibility (remote in most cases) that the pronunciation itself is conservative rather than an innovation inspired by the spelling. But in the case of NE *equip* and its derivatives, the *qu* is not etymological at all: it is a purely graphic convention of French for writing the sound /k/ before /i/. (The word is ultimately from Low German *skip* 'ship'.) Likewise general in English is the /b/ in words like *obscure* and *obtuse,* for which we have ample evidence that the actual sound was voiceless in Latin and Romance, despite the usual spelling.

As in the case of Latin /gn/ mentioned above, spelling pronunciation can be fairly systematic: in Early Modern English earlier /sy/ everywhere became /š/, thereby falling together with the /š/ which had been in the language since Old English times: thus *portioun* /porsi'ūn/ (Chaucer) > /'porsiŭn/ > /'porsiŭn/ > /'porsyun/ > /poršun/ > /poršən/. Similarly *sure* /syur/ > /šur/. Where the results of this development are spelled *ti* or *ssi* or *ssu* (*portion, passion, tissue*) they usually survive unaltered in pronunciation; but for some reason, almost all cases of the letter sequence *su* representing /šu/ or /šə/ < /syu/ reverted to /syu(w)/ (*consume, sue, suitable*—then in most dialects of American English there was a subsequent loss of /y/). The surviving exceptions are *sugar* and *sure* and, dialectally, *sumac.*

Given the inconsistencies of English spelling, proper nouns are particularly vulnerable to spelling pronunciation. A striking but not extreme example is *Rothschild* /roθčayld/ (Ger. /rōtšilt/ lit. 'red shield'). The Scottish use of the 'insular' form of the letter *g* ⟨ʒ⟩ led to *Mackenzie* and *Menzies* changing from /məkiŋiy/ and /miŋiyz/ to the familiar /məkenziy/, /menziyz/. Similarly, the silent *th* of *McGrath*—properly just an etymological spelling of the name also written *McGraw* and *McCray*—has been so to say lifted off the page when the name is pronounced /mə'græθ/.

Not all spelling-pronunciations become standard, however generally they may be heard. Widespread without being standard is /oftən/ *often* for standard /ofən/, and /forhed/ *forehead* for /farəd/ or /forəd/.

Finally, there is the possibility of what might be called MIS-spelling pronunciations: a change in pronunciation based on a mistaken perception of the spelling in the first place. Certain examples of this are

/eriyeyt/ *aerate* and /ǰadfərz/ *jodhpurs*. This is probably also the explanation of the very general American English forms /riylətər/ *realtor* and /riylətiy/ *realty* (often from the lips of realtors themselves). The substitution of *lamblast* for *lambaste* 'berate soundly' might be a folk-etymology (53) or have a folk-etymological component, but may in part be due to a misreading of the word; and the same may be the basis for the widely-heard *enroach (on)* for *encroach (on)*, and *larnyx* for *larynx*.

P A T T E R N L E S S   C H A N G E S

44. Dialect Borrowing

Forms in a language will sometimes be seen to deviate in a detail or two from what is expected on the basis of sound laws, likely analogies, and ascertainable morphological innovations. Now, what makes one dialect different from another (113-6) is that they have undergone different innovations; and one of the commonest explanations for unexpected details in a form is that the form is proper to a (neighboring) variety of speech, and accordingly reflects the sound laws and morphology of that dialect and not of the matrix dialect.

In Latin, words with labial reflexes of Proto-Indo-European labiovelars, like *lupus* 'wolf' < *$luk^w os$ (< PIE *$w\underset{\circ}{l}k^w os$) and *bōs* 'cow' < *$g^w ōws$, can be confidently ascribed to borrowing from some non-Latin form of Italic in which such developments resulted from their own (regular) sound laws. In this case, our confidence comes from our certain knowledge that sound laws of the type *k^w > *p* are proper to the development of Italic forms of Indo-European speech which, furthermore, early Latin speakers had intimate contact with. The same confidence, based on the same kind of definite knowledge, applies to the interpretation of NE *vixen* for expected *fixen* < OE *fyxen* 'female fox'. That is, it is known that in a sizable area west and south of London, and not far from it, initial spirants regularly become voiced, unlike the English of the matrix dialect, and this form of speech is the source of the voiced initial consonant of *vixen* and several other words.

Many times dialect loans will coexist with forms proper to the matrix dialect, as in the Latin dialect borrowing *popīna* 'fast-food restaurant, snack bar' next to matrix *coquīna* 'kitchen' (PItal. *$k^w ok^w īnā$ or the like). Similarly NE *hale* is from a northern source next to the matrix dialect cognate *whole* (with bogus *w-*); and doublets like *strap, plat* next to *strop, plot* (of land) come from closely-related dialects.

It must be stated, however—indeed, insisted upon—that 'dialect borrowing' is too often a guess rather than an explanation. For example, PIE **snusos* 'daughter-in-law' is reflected as Lat. *nurus*, whereas the sound laws of the matrix dialect would give **norus*. Nor are we disappointed in that expectation: Sp. *nuera*, It. *nuora* and so on vouchsafe a PRom. **nǫra* 'nurus' < **nor-*, which proves that we are correct in our formulation of the Latin sound law decreeing the lowering of high vowels before -*r*- coming from -*s*-. But whence the offending *nurus*? It is almost reflexive for historical linguists to ascribe any such surprising detail to dialect borrowing. Indeed, that may be the simple truth; and the very existence of PRom. **nǫra* beside standard Latin *nurus* perhaps adds to the likelihood. But in this case we know nothing of any nearby dialect in which **us* > *ur*, and as a result such a suggestion is necessarily a hunch rather than a genuine explanation.

See also **119** regarding the complex ancestry of *compromise dialects*.

45. Truly sporadic (random) changes

It sometimes appears that a word has changed pronunciation for no reason at all, such as the replacement of /g/ by /ǰ/ in NE *margarine*. It remains an open question, however, whether there really is any such thing as a totally unmotivated innovation. It is more likely that we are dealing with limitations in our knowledge rather than with anything truly random. That is, it is probable that there is in fact a reason why *margarine* changed pronunciation, a reason of a familiar and recognizeable type (contamination probably); it is only that we have no hint as to what it was. In perfectly clear cases, at least—like that of *margarine*—inexplicable innovations present no real problems of interpretation. We know that *margarine* with a /g/ and *margarine* with a /ǰ/ are one and the same word, and we know which one is earlier. The same goes for reflexes which are merely puzzling in their details, like the *hi-* of Gk *híppos*, Myc. *i-qo* 'horse' for expected **éppos* (PIE **eќwos*). In more complicated cases, particularly when dealing with vexed etymologies, if a sporadic change in pronunciation is part of the mix, it can make the puzzle virtually insoluble.

SUGGESTIONS FOR FURTHER READING

The basic idea of analyzing sound change as structural change is exhaustively (if often obscurely and confusingly) discussed in **Hoenigswald** 1960, but for an important earlier treatment see **Twaddell** 1938. See also **Bynon** 1977 chapter 1 §4, **Hock** 1991 chapter 8, **Hock & Joseph** 1996 chapter 4 §§1–4 and §6.

Regarding causes of sound change, see particularly **Thomason & Kaufman** 1988 passim but especially chapters 2–4 for language contact as a source of phonological innovation, and **Bynon** 1977 chapter 5 for other social motivations. See **Hock** 1991 chapter 20 on lexical diffusion. Functionalism is discussed in **Martinet** 1958 and (much more elaborately) 1964; **King** 1967 manages to frame one central Functionalist claim in a testable form. (It fails). See **Hock & Joseph** 1996 chapter 4 §5.5 for sporadic changes.

ANALOGY

The following technical terms will be discussed in this chapter:

Analogy (short for analogical change) – the influence of one
    form or class of forms on the pronunciation of another
Leveling – the elimination (or reduction) of functionless
    alternation
Analogical proportion – a display which makes explicit the
    similarities between differences, in the explanation of
    leveling
Contamination – the patternless influence of the pronun-
    ciation of one word on another
Portmanteau words (synonyms: *blending, telescoping*) – the
    combination of elements of two words of similar
    meaning into a new word
Folk etymology – a change in pronunciation which alters an
    inherited form toward some nonhistorical connection[1]
Back formation – the creation of an etymologically false
    morpheme boundary
Metanalysis – the relocation of a morpheme boundary
Hypercorrection – the creation of a new form in place of an
    inherited one which is perceived as erroneous; a near
    synonym is *hyperurbanism*

46. Analogical changes

As previewed above (25), analogical changes (informally, *analogies*) alter the forms of a language in a fundamentally different way from phonological changes (sound laws). Sound laws deal in phonological
givens alone; that is, the inputs and conditions are all exclusively in
phonological terms. Formulations of analogical change, however, always identify specific words or affixes, or whole classes of forms. That

---

[1] When a similar alteration clarifies a genuine derivation, the process may be either
leveling, above, or else (depending on the authority) *recombination* or *refreshment.*

is because analogical changes are the influence of one form (or class of forms) upon the pronunciation of another form or class. The differences between sound laws and analogies all follow logically from this. Phonological changes are prevailingly regular; analogical changes are prevailingly sporadic. Phonological changes usually apply to forms present in a language at a given time, and then quit (but see 32); analogical changes may affect one or another suitable form, ever and anon, over a very long period of time, perhaps eventually dealing with all suitable forms, perhaps stopping when there are a few forms left unaffected, or perhaps affecting only a sprinkling of forms in the first place.

Thus, in English, comparatives of the vowel-mutation type (*old, elder, eldest*) are now extinct except for that one example, which is marginal. The plurals *teeth, geese, mice, oxen, sheep* and a handful of others are the only remnants of the once diverse varieties of English noun inflection. But now the analogical processes which 'regularized' virtually the entire lexicon of nouns seem to have ceased: in even the most peculiar of nonstandard dialects, no such forms as *ˣtooths* and *ˣfoots* seem to be encroaching on the inherited forms.

A somewhat different picture is presented by the verbs of English. The once-vigorous analogical transfer of verb paradigms of the type *help, holp, holpen* to the type *help, helped, helped* has ceased in all dialects. In the verbs, unlike the nouns, a considerable number of the earlier 'irregular' types were still left in the lexicon when this trend lost steam. There the matter has rested, in the standard dialects; in some dialects, however, a fresh round of analogical remodeling has arisen, but one which is quite unlike the previous type: the 'irregular' types remain irregular, but are remade so that the preterite tense and the past participle have the same form, just as they do in the dominant type (the 'regular' verbs—*look, looked, looked*—and also some inherited irregular classes like *buy, bought, bought*, or *meet, met, met*). Thus we find nonstandard *see, seen, have seen* (or *see, saw, have saw*, rarer and possibly from hypercorrection, 55); *drink, drank, have drank; go, went, have went;* but NOT *drink, drinked, have drinked; go, goed,* and the like.

Analogical innovation is based on function, that is, lexical or grammatical meaning. Forms which influence the pronunciation of other forms must be appropriate in meaning as well as in form. This formulation is vague on purpose: 'semantic appropriateness' includes all manner of things, including very commonly in fact the relationship of antonymy (opposite meaning).

   a. 'Analogical change' is a conceptual terrain with overlapping provinces and few landmarks. There is no standard terminology or analysis beyond a few general notions, and the taxonomy in this discussion has the chief aim of organizing inherently indistinct categories. You will find with experience that these terms will be used in published works in somewhat different (usually vaguer) senses than those set forth here; for some authorities, for example, a term like *leveling* (47) is virtually a synonym of *analogical change*. Notions like *folk etymology* (53) and *hypercorrection* (55) obviously overlap, as do *back formation* (54) and *leveling* (47). Even if it were possible to run up an unambiguous and exhaustive taxonomy of analogical changes, there would be little actual gain in understanding and equally little resemblance to the terminology and actual usage of any other historical linguist.

   b. Scholars of earlier generations spoke of analogical changes in terms of 'mental associations of ideas', but psychologizing brings nothing to the table. Mental states are elusive even when they can be directly studied, and can hardly be held to explain the facts of languages attested only in ancient history. In any case, these appeals to mental states are circular: the only evidence for the presumed mental state is the analogy which the presumed mental state is adduced to explain.

LEVELING ANALOGY

47. Leveling is the most important analogy which acts on morphologically complex languages. It is an interplay between PATTERNS, as a rule, not between individual forms. It serves to remodel form classes, and to remove alternations resulting from sound laws. Functionless alternation (as in *old, elder* vs *bold, bolder*) is so pervasively attacked by leveling analogies that one must infer that the simplest relationships between form and meaning must have some kind of special survival value in language. Sound laws of course are unconcerned about such matters, figuratively speaking, and the operation of REGULAR conditioned changes routinely results in the very complexities that are so typically leveled by the action of analogy. Regular sound laws acting on the Proto-Greek root *leyk^w- 'leave (over)' would have resulted in a Greek paradigm on p. 76 built to *leip-*, *leit-*, and *leik-*, depending on the vowel following the root (the details of the endings are not relevant here).

	Pre-Greek	'regular' form	form actually occurring
1 sg	*leykʷoH	leipō	leipō
2 sg	*leykʷesi	leitei	leipeis
3 sg	*leykʷei	leitei	leipei
1 pl	*leykʷomos	leikume(-)	leipomen, -mes
2 pl	*leykʷete	leitete	leipete
3 pl	*leykʷonti	leikunti, -ūsi	leiponti, -ousi

Such an alternation of stems would have been found in all thematic verbs whose roots chanced to end with a PIE labiovelar stop. However, and despite the fact that the changes merging PGk *k^w with the other three stops (p. 46) occurred quite late in the history of Greek, no such alternation is attested: the elimination of the alternants *leit-* and *leik-* (and some other changes as well, such as the restoration of the theme-vowel *-u-* to *-o-*) are the work of leveling analogy. The model, or inspiration, for eliminating the alternation is the prevailing pattern of thematic verbs, namely: the same form of the root is seen in all persons and numbers. (The triumph of the shape *leip-* rather than *leit-* or *leik-* is harder to rationalize; see note **a**, below.)

In a like manner, sound laws by themselves would have produced such English singular/plural noun paradigms as *day, dawes; gloof, gloves; shade, shadow; glass, glazes; mother, mether.* However, a series of developments led the prevailing pattern for English to be (in so many words) 'The plural of a noun is formed by adding the plural suffix to the singular without change'. According to such a scheme the plurals of *day* and the rest should be *days, glasses,* and *mothers;* and so it came to pass.

Glove (where the singular has been modeled on the plural rather than vice versa) and the differentiation of two nouns, *shade* and *shadow,* also exemplify leveling phenomena, with interesting differences in detail only.

Leveling applies to affixes as well as stems and roots. Both Latin and Greek should have inherited two forms of the ending of the neuter plural: -ā (Att.-Ion. -ē) in the o-stems, but -ă in consonant stems. In both languages this diversity was replaced by a single ending; but despite the generally similar patterns overall in the two languages, the leveling proceeded in opposite directions. Greek leveled the difference in favor of the short vowel and Latin leveled in favor of the long vowel (which subsequently shortened). Here at least a half of a rationale is possible: when alternations in vowel length are leveled in Latin, it is almost always in favor of the long alternant. (That doesn't really qualify as an explanation, obviously; and of course it leaves out the Greek facts altogether.)

a. The Greek example is typical: there is no (obvious) explanation for why *l(e)ip-* won out. In fact, given the pivotal status of the third person singular in the remodeling of verb paradigms, it might be expected that *l(e)it-* would have been generalized. When explanations for the precise details of an analogical leveling are discoverable, they are very welcome; but the lack of a clear rationale in this or that case is no defect in the theory. (In this case, the form *leip-* would have been constant in the future and aorist stems, which could have favored that form in the present.)

A lesson in the difficulties of discovering rationales for the details of leveling is afforded by the separate evolution of English and German strong (ablauting) verbs. Both started with the same inherited patterns; both leveled in generally similar ways; but the details are often radically inconsistent. Consider the verb 'to freeze' ('pret.sg.' in the table below means first and third persons):

	infin.	pret.sg.	pret.pl.	pple
OE	*fréosan*	*fréas*	*fruron*	*(ge)froren*
OHG	*friusan*	*frōs*	*frurun (-umēs)* 1pl.	*(gi)froran*

The modern forms are *freeze, froze, frozen* and, for German, *frieren, fror, gefroren,* respectively. That is, the consonant alternations of the English paradigm were leveled on the basis of the present tense/singular preterite, whereas the German ones were leveled on the basis of the plural preterite/past participle.

b. Some authorities use the term *generalization* for leveling, others reserve it for the spread of sentential (or phrasal) alternants beyond the original distribution:

In standard French there are two phrasal forms for 'you', /vu/ before a consonantal in e.g. *vous même* /vumɛm/ 'yourself', or in final position, e.g. *pour vous* /purvu/ 'for you'; and /vuz/ before a vocalic, in e.g. *vous aussi* /vuzosi/ 'you too'. This pattern is echoed in a number of basic French forms, such as the plural article (/le/ and /lez/). In some varieties of French this has been the model for *mois aussi* /mwazosi/, *tois aussi* /twazosi/, even though *moi* 'me' /mwa/ and *toi* 'you' /twa/ originally had no such forms as /mwaz/, /twaz/.

In Proto-Romance, the vowel of **dę* 'from' truncated before a word beginning with a vowel, such that there were two forms of the preposition: /d/ before a vowel and /de/ before a consonant. This is still the rule in French (*de vins* 'of wines', *d'hôtel* 'of the inn'). In Spanish, the preconsonantal form /de/ has spread, thus *de eso* 'of that'. (But the previous existence of /d/ in the history of Spanish is evidenced by fossilized forms like *donde* 'where' < *d'unde*.)

Forms like English *idear* for *idea* in Standard British English and parts of New England are the prevocalic allomorph of *idea* and other forms (*I sawr it* and *the idear of it* but *I saw them* and *the very idea*). This generalization started with the loss of postvocalic /r/ before consonants but not before vowels, thus /fɪə/ in *fear not* but /fɪər/ in *fear of flying* and spread to words like *idea, vista,* and *Gloria.*

The LOSS of alternant forms like English *my/mine* or Italian *e/ed* 'and' is not usually described as generalization, though it fits the definition.

48. Leveling as simplification

Although analogical leveling nearly always simplifies the structure of the language somehow, it must not be assumed that the process is necessarily one of replacing more complex patterns with simpler ones. Further, 'simplification'—and non-trivial simplification at that—includes the reduction of the total NUMBER of patterns serving the same functional purpose, and an important facet of analogical remodeling is the transfer of elements from one form class to another. On occasion a more complex pattern may be favored over a simpler one. An example of this is seen in the interplay between *a*-stem and *i*-stem nouns in High German. (These stem-vowel classifications are etymological; in Old High German, as in all historical Germanic languages, the stem-forms themselves are no longer transparent.) In Old High German, the *a*-stem inflection is one of endings only, as *tag/tac* nom. sg. 'day', *taga* nom.pl. The *i*-stems however, in addition to having somewhat different endings, have vowel alternations (umlaut; pp. 21-2, anticipatory assimilation) in the root. These are the result of regular sound laws conditioned by the high front vocalics of certain *i*-stem endings acting on any preceding back vocalic: *gast* nom.sg. 'guest', *gesti* nom.pl. In Old High German, the vowel mutations in the *i*-stem paradigm still correlated with the presence of an -*i*- in the case endings. By the Middle High German period, however, other regular sound laws had reduced the vowel contrasts in final syllables, and the two types now looked like this: *tac, tage* and *gast, geste*. Where the root contained a front vowel, of course, the old *a*- and *i*-stems simply fell together; but analogical leveling has transferred most *a*-stem back-vowel nouns to the historical *i*-stem type. Put differently, a sizable percentage of German nouns of the *Gast/Gäste* type, for example *Wolf* 'wolf', *Wölfe* pl. and *Baum* 'tree', *Bäume* pl., are old *a*-stems. In fact, only slightly more than a dozen nouns in modern German go like *Tag, Tage,* and forms like *Täge* are found in dialects as well as in beginning German classes.

   a. Some have speculated that an inflected form like *Gäste* (next to *Gast*) is inherently more potent than the *Tage* type, because it has two markers of plurality against the single marker of *Tage.* It is natural therefore that it would be favored in the leveling process. This notion is reasonable, but reasonableness is not the same as evidence, and in fact there are many countercases. The ouster of the *old, elder* type in English has already been mentioned, and that process seems to have started in prehistoric times. Similarly, the 'doubly-marked' morphology of the English *wolf, wolves* or *keep, kept* types have shown no signs of spreading; indeed, they are retreating if anything (e.g. *cloths* for *clothes, dreamed* for *dreamt*).[1]

49. Proportional Analogy
A useful tool for explicitly framing the givens of leveling analogies is the *analogical proportion.* Such a proportion as it applies to the evolution of English plural nouns might take some such form as:

$$\text{hand : hands :: crow : crows :: day : } X$$

Englished as: '*hand* is to *hands* as *crow* is to *crows* as *day* is to what?'. That is, a form ('X') would be said to 'solve' the proportion if it bears the same relationship to *day* that *crows* and *hands* bear to *crow* and *hand*—and also bears the same relationship to *crows* and *hands* that *day* bears to *crow* and *hand.* In this case only one shape fits: *days.*

   It is vital to note that most such proportions are nothing but a

---

[1] The *-f* of *dwarf* continues OE /χ/ (cf. NHG *Zwerg*); such a reflex is sometimes spelled *gh* (as in *enough* and *laugh*) and sometimes *f* (as in *draft*), but no matter how spelled, the sound would not be expected to alternate with /v/. The OED (2nd ed.) does not even acknowledge a plural *dwarves*, but it is common in American English. And the author has encountered a native of Wisconsin for whom the plural of *shaft* is /šævdz/.

compendious way of identifying a PATTERN. It is a form of shorthand and nothing else. There are no reasons for supposing that the words *crows* and *hands* themselves, or any other word or words in particular, played any special role in the coining of *days*. Rather, the role of the nouns in the *hand : hands :: crow : crows* proportion is to REPRESENT A PATTERN, in this case a particular relationship between singular and plural formations (crudely, 'plural = singular + *s*').

In some cases, a formal proportion hardly seems necessary. For example, according to English sound laws, the second and third principal parts of *swear* should be *sore* and *sor(e)n*, and in the 16th century they are in fact attested as such. (The same sound law is seen in NE *sword*, whose conservative spelling, incidentally, hints that some attestations of *swore* and *swor(e)n*—so spelled—were written by people who actually pronounced the words without a /w/.) If one wished, one could easily run up a batch of proportions of the type *wear : wore :: swear : X*, or *strive : strove :: swear : X* to account for the reappearance of /w/ in *swore/sworn*. Such a proportion would define a pattern paraphrasable as: 'preterites and participles involve assorted vowel changes but the consonants of the root are the same in all forms'. But it is no loss of genuine rigor to state that the *-w-* of *swear* was reintroduced (or 'imported') into the other forms.

Nevertheless, as the following example shows, it can be rewarding to pay attention to details. As we've seen above (**28**), sound laws pure and simple yield such Latin paradigms as *mōs, mōris* 'custom' and *genus, generis* 'race'. In both paradigms, in accord with the sound laws the stem-final *s* of *s*-stem nouns is unchanged in the nominative singular but becomes *r* between vowels in all forms with an ending. The same should be the case for nouns like *honōs, honōris* 'worth, honor; public office', but instead of *honōs* and the like we find *honor*. (The *ōs*-stem type is enormously common in Latin; other minor *s*-stem types are seen in *arbor, arbŏris* 'tree', and *mulier, mulieris* 'woman'). We know that we are dealing with *s*-stems here, because of etymology, remarks by Roman grammarians, archaic inscriptions, and such derivatives as *honestus* 'worthy', *arbustus* 'wooded', and *muliebris* 'womanly' (*-br-* < *-sr-* is regular). As with NE *swore*, above, we might simply say: '*r* was introduced into the nom.sg. after *honōris* etc.' But, while this is a fair statement of the facts, it provides no hint as to (a) why such leveling in favor of *r* is found throughout Latin only in *s*-stems; (b) why it is so very uniform in the case of *honor, arbor,* etc.; and (c) why it is NOT found in two namable categories of *s*-stem: monosyllables like *mōs,* and neuter nouns like *genus.* (The exemption of the neuters from this analogy is seen even in the comparative degree of adjectives, where we find e.g. *maiior* 'greater' m.f. < **-yōs,* but *maiius* n. < **-yos.*)

The answer to all these questions is not to be found in the *s*-stems themselves, but only by looking at OTHER Latin noun patterns, specifically the Latin *r*-stems. Latin inherited several types of *r*-stems, including the prominent (if isolated) item *soror, sorōris* 'sister', and the productive agent noun type *āctor, āctōris.* By the combined action of sound laws and analogies, the *honōs* type came to differ from the *āctor* type in a single detail:

		s-Stems	*r*-Stems
Sg.	nom.	honōs	āctōr[1]
	acc.	honōre(m)	āctōre(m)
	dat.	honōrei, -ī	āctōrei, -ī
	abl.	honōre	āctōre
	gen.	honōris	āctōris
Pl.	nom.	honōrēs	āctōrēs
	acc.	honōrēs	āctōrēs
	dat., abl.	honōribus	āctōribus
	gen.	honōru(m)	āctōru(m)

The proportion *āctōris : honōris :: āctōr : X,* such that *X = honōr* in this case is more than a convenient summary: monosyllabic and neuter *s*-stems do not undergo a parallel remodeling because of a lack of suitable patterns—there are no inherited monosyllabic *r*-stems to influence *mōs, mōris* and the like, which accordingly show no replacement of word-final *-s* by *-r.*

RECOMPOSITION

50. Leveling is often seen among derivatives with a common basis ('word families'). Sound laws are always distorting the similarities between

---

[1] The shortening of long vowels before all final consonants except *-s* took place much later.

cardinal and ordinal numbers, for example, and the similarities are often then reconstituted by analogical leveling: to OE *tíen* 'ten' was built *téoþa* 'tenth' (> NE *tithe*), which has been replaced by *tenth*—but only as a counting term; the noun in the sense of a levy (whether actually ten percent or not) has been left untampered with. This kind of inconsistency is wholly typical of leveling analogies. Further examples: leveling has replaced the phonologically regular vowel and consonant of the plural *glasses* and derived *glassy* but not of the derived *glaze* and *glazier;* the phonologically regular tonic vowel of *regency* has been replaced but not the (etymologically) corresponding vowels of the semantically remote *regimen* and *regular.*

Given how difficult it is to rationalize the direction of an analogical influence after the fact, it follows that trying to predict such things is futile. For instance, although it is common for cardinal numbers to influence the 'derived' ordinals (as has happened repeatedly in English: cf. OE *seofeþa, nioþa, téoþa* with NE *seventh, ninth, tenth*), it is by no means the inevitable direction of influence. Latin has *quīnque* 'five' for expected **quĭnque,* with -*ī*- imported from the ordinal *quīn(c)tus* (where it is phonologically regular); and in Slavic languages, the direction of influence in the numerals is prevailingly FROM the ordinals TO the cardinals.

In Latin verbs formed with a preverb, both the normal vowel weakening of the root syllable and regular consonant assimilations are frequently counteracted in the image of the simple verb or more distinct forms of the prefix, respectively, as in both *conlocō* and *collocō* 'set' in place of the phonologically regular **collicō.* (The analogical process that results in forms like *conlocō* is sometimes called *recomposition.*)

a. The actual PROCESS of leveling—that is, what cognitive route a speaker travels to come up with a leveled form—is (like all psychological events) uncertain. The main choices are between a sort of tinkering with the details of a segment or two, like what happens in spelling pronunciation (43), or starting over with an entirely new derivation fitted to some perceived pattern of relationships between parts and wholes. Certainly, tinkering must be the case in some other types of analogy such as contamination: the pronunciation /kow'vərt/ *covert* in place of /'kəvərt/, discussed below (51), must be of this sort—there being no derivational relationship either before or after the change. On the other hand, forms like /tenθ/ *tenth,* or *latest* in place of *last,* must be cases of starting over (so to say) with the raw ingredients.

Cases like *regency*, where we have the replacement of expected /rejənsiy/ (like *regiment* /rejəmənt/) by /riyjənsiy/, or /hawsəz/ for /hawzəz/ *houses*, or *fifth* for *fift*, are undecidable, and different speakers may well use different strategies. The same goes for the most common sorts of leveling, as in *older* for *elder*.

CONTAMINATION

51. The association between words of the same semantic group, such as numerals, kinship terms, colors, antonyms, and so on, may result in the influence of one form on another.

Greek dialectal *hoktō* and *optō* 'eight' for PGk **oktō* show the influence of the adjacent *hepta* 'seven', manifested in two different ways. LLat. *Octember* shows the influence of *September* and *November*. Both of these cases are a very common type of contamination, namely *contamination in compact series*—stereotyped sequences such as numbers, the letters of the alphabet, days of the week, and the months. In such compact series, elements contaminate immediate neighbors in the sequence; thus Lat. *novem* 'nine' for expected **noven* is to be traced specifically to the influence of *decem* 'ten' rather than *septem* 'seven'.

Antonymic or otherwise contrastive words very often contaminate one another—much more commonly than synonyms do, in fact. Thus LLat. *sinexter* (for *sinister*) 'left', after *dexter* 'right'; PRom. **grevi-* (whence OFr. *gref*, NE *grief*), for *gravis* 'heavy', is traceable to *levis* 'light' (and possibly also *brevis* 'short'); NE *female* for earlier *femell* (which would— and in fact did—ultimately give NE *fimble*), owes its shape to contamination by *male*.[1] NE *covert* was until recently pronounced /'kəvərt/ (in fact, *cover* and *covert* are doublets). But under the influence of *overt* /ow'vərt/, the pronunciation has become /kow'vərt/.

The words *riches* and *richness* are an interesting case. They are historically the same word, traceable to Fr. *richesse*. It appears that original /'ričes/, a singular noun, was variously tampered with, once by contamination (the English suffix *-ness*; such a remodeling affected many forms, e.g. *gentleness* for Chaucer's *gentilesse*); and once by reinterpreting the form as a plural, so present-day /ričəz/.

A curious kind of analogical creation is seen in Gk *andrápoda* 'cap-

---

[1] *Fimble* occurs in English as the term for the male (that's right) hemp plant.

tives, slaves', based on *tetrápoda* lit. 'quadrupeds'. It looks as though *-poda*, properly 'footed', was reinterpreted as 'booty' or the like in contexts where *tetrápoda* referred to spoils of war. This is reminiscent of coinages like *petrodollars* based on a clipping (87) of *petroleum*, etymologically 'rock-oil'. Modern English is rich in such creations: the suffix *-(o)mat(ic)* from *automatic* (whence *laundromat, vedg-o-matic*, the *Instamatic* camera, and other forms) rests on a prior metanalysis (p. 89) which created an element whose morphological status in English seems to have properties of derivation and compounding simultaneously. A similar metanalysis split off *-rama* from *panorama* (and perhaps *motorama*, though the latter is probably simply the earliest of the newly-minted forms like *cinerama* and *kitchenorama* 'a kitchen show'—a type of formation now becoming rare); *-burger* from *hamburger* (the catalyst presumably being the utterly irrelevant *ham*), whence *cheeseburger, steakburger,* and many others such things including the unobvious (*pizzaburger* and *kiwiburger* e.g.).

Stray formations are *skycap* from *redcap*; *shrimpkabob* and other forms in *-kabob,* from *shishkabob* (in which incidentally the *shish* comes from Turkish *şiş* /šiš/ 'skewer'); and so on. These things are somewhat outside normal morphological patterning. In fact, they are little more than a playing with syllables, which in extreme cases creates morphological partials out of thin air, as in *clamato* (a drink consisting of a mixture of clam juice and tomato juice); *prequel* 'a sequel (a movie or television drama) which takes up events preceding those of the original work'; or *workaholic.*

a. A problem with inherently sporadic, patternless, and sui generis innovations, as contaminations are, is that in ambiguous cases it is impossible to determine the course of a change. The pronunciation of NE *February* as /febyuweriy/ is plausibly taken as a case of anticipatory dissimilation (as presented above, 16); but contamination by *January* might be a contributing factor, and may even be the sole cause.

b. Morphological cross-pollination at least looks like contamination, whether it is properly so or not: Hom. *huiási* dat.pl. of *huiós* 'son' has the ending *-asi* rather than *-oisi* (the ending proper to *o*-stems) under the influence of such consonant-stem kinship terms as *patrási* dat.pl. of *patḗr* 'father' (where Gk *ra* is the regular reflex of PIE *$*r̥$, the zero grade of the stem). Similarly in Indic, the *r*-stem gen.sg. *-ur* (as Ved. *pitúr* 'father's') shows up in the non-*r*-stem paradigms of words of appropriate meaning: for *pati-* 'master, husband' the gen.sg. is *patur* for 'husband's' (next to *patyas* for 'master's'), and the stem *sakhāy-* 'friend' has the irregularly-formed genitive singular *sakhyur*. Note than in all these examples there is nothing remotely resembling a 'proportional analogy' available.

PORTMANTEAU WORDS

52. *Telescoping* or *blending* results in what are commonly known as *portmanteau words:* two words of similar or merely associated meaning are merged into a new word. Many portmanteaus are slips of the tongue, such as *remaindants* (*remainder + remnants*) or *cheat* (*chair + seat*) and, like spoonerisms, vanish as soon as they are uttered; but some are deliberately created for picturesque effect, as *insin(n)uendo* (*insinuate + innuendo*) or *disastrophe,* and maintain a foothold of sorts because their jocular tone appeals to some users. Occasionally, however, such blends become standard, as in NE *brunch, happenstance,* and *smog.*[1]

Blending also occurs in inflection, as Lat. *iter, itineris* 'way', instead of expected *iter,* **itinis* (the blended form attests a period when the inherited **itenes* gen.sg. was in competition with the straightforward but unattested coinage **iteres,* but the resulting paradigm is formally more chaotic than what preceded, and resembles nothing else in the language except one or two blended forms forms with similar histories like *iecur, iocineris* 'liver'). Arguably *unloosen* and the stigmatized *irregardless* in English are cases of derivational blending.

> **a.** Coinages like *sexpert* (*sex + expert*), *cremains* 'ashes from a crematorium', *motel,* and *Destroylet,* a patent name for a sort of electric privy, are reminiscent of blends, but differ importantly: they entail the combining of elements of a phrase or com-

---

[1] The term *portmanteau* is Lewis Carroll's, and occurs in Humpty Dumpty's explanation of the word *slithy* in 'The Jabberwocky' to Alice. The image—a portmanteau is a sort of carrying case for a cloak—is not self-explanatory (it may refer to the way the contraption, which was hinged along one side like a book, was briskly clapped shut over its contents), but there is no reason to think that *slithy* is a genuine portmanteau anyway. Rather, it is just a nonsense word, like *mome, outgrabe,* and *wabe,* made up for the sound of it with no meaning in mind. The opening (and closing) quatrain of 'The Jabberwocky', in which it occurs, predates the Alice books, in fact, so in any case Carroll's portmanteau analysis came long after the fact.

pound rather than a mingling of components of lexical items of similar meaning. There seems to be no specific term for innovations like *sexpert;* the term telescoping would be more appropriate for these forms than for forms like *smog,* but it is probably too late to make any such terminological change stick.

b. Morphological markers are commonly portmanteaus in a slightly different sense, viz., they mark more functions than they have formal parts. In Lat. *bona* 'good (nominative singular feminine)' there is no way to disaggregate the three specific functions of the *-a.* NE *am* is specifically 'present tense' and 'first person' and 'singular' as well as the verb 'be'. Fr. *au* /o/ is specifically 'to', 'definite article', 'masculine', and 'singular'.

FOLK ETYMOLOGY

53. Since *etymology* means 'the history of a form', the term *folk etymology* (and its synonym, *popular etymology*) look as though they should mean simply an uninformed (and probably incorrect—otherwise, why bring the matter up?) notion as to the derivation of a word, such as casually supposing that there is a connection somehow between NE *ear* and *hear,* or that *real estate* has something to do with 'reality'. There is to be sure guessing in folk etymology as the term is correctly defined, which is to say: folk etymology is a CHANGE IN THE PRONUNCIATION of a word, based (evidently) on some sort of rationalization which results in a pseudo-morphology.

So far from being freakish or unusual, such innovations are commonplace. A book published in 1882, under the (revealing) title *Folk-Etymology; a dictionary of verbal corruptions or words perverted in form or meaning by false derivation or mistaken analogy,* runs to 664 pages of text treating forms in English alone.

PIE **nomn* 'name' should give Lat. **nŏmen;* the form we find instead, **(g)nōmen* 'name'—the **g* still evident in *cognōmen* 'family name' and *agnōmen* 'surname'—gains both its initial **g-* and its *-ō-* from fancied association with **gnō-* 'know' (represented by a large number of forms: *(cog)nōscō* 'become acquainted with', *ignōtus* 'unknown', *nōbilis* 'well-known', for example). OE *útemest* and *fyremest* give NE *utmost* and *foremost,* as if formed from *most;* in fact, originally the morpheme boundary came after the *-m-* (cf. *former*) and, untampered with, the regular reflex of OE *fyremest* would have been homophonous with

NE *firmest*. OE *brýd-guma* lit. 'bride(s)man' (*guma* 'man' cognate with Lat. *homō;* cf. also NHG *Bräutigam*) gives NE *bridegroom* as if formed from *groom*. (Incidentally, *bridegroom* simultaneously shows the effects of recomposition, 50, as it has replaced phonologically regular **bridg(r)om* with *bride-*.) NHG *Hängematte* 'hammock' comes ultimately from the same Carib source as the English word, but it has been touched up to make it look like a regular German compound, 'hang-mat' or the like. (Dutch *hangmak* has been so to say half-folk-etymologized. A similar half-a-loaf achievement is NE *belfry* 'bell tower' < ME *berfray* 'movable tower', a kind of siege engine. The clarified forms *hang-* and *bel(l)-* have the side-effect of creating the pseudomorphemes *-mak* and *-fry*.) As a term for 'butterfly', Hausa has the expression /mālam būɗe littāfi/ lit. 'the scholar opens a book'; this delectable image is apparently an elaboration of a folk-etymology starting with the English word *butterfly*.

Folk etymological disturbances can alter meaning as well as form. NE *outrage* from Fr. *outrage* 'gross insult' < **ultragium* has had its meaning as well as its pronunciation affected by a fancied connection with *out* and *rage*.[1] Another example is seen in *noisome* /noysəm/ 'annoying, especially by cause of an obnoxious smell'. This relative of *annoy* is very commonly pronounced /noyzsəm/, and at least sometimes is clearly used as a synonym of 'noisy'. In the case of *touchy* 'easily angered', the original form *te(t)chy* survives but has been reinterpreted as a rusticism.

A curious point about folk etymologies is that the premises they are based on, and the results achieved, are not notable for their appropriateness—or even their sanity. The only advantage that *bridegroom* has over the original form is that the two halves of it are recognizable English elements. A folk etymology like *sparrow-grass* for *asparagus* (widely found in US dialects) borders on the lunatic, as does Persian *jālī-kāftar* lit. 'screen-pigeon', a folk-etymological distortion of English *helicopter*. (Borrowed forms, being opaque by definition, are much subject to

---

[1] In both Shakespeare and Spenser *outrage* is accented on the second syllable, /uˈtrɛ̄j/ or the like. Accent retraction in the absence of folk etymology should have given ˣ/ˈuwtrəj/ if not ˣ/ˈətrəj/.

folk-etymology in the course of borrowing. Further examples from English: *carry-all* for Fr. *cariole,* a kind of covered cart; *mohair* < Arabic *muχayyar*.) Lunacy is not of course a requirement: some of the examples cited above are rational enough; and a different folk distortion of *asparagus,* namely *spear-grass,* has much to recommend it.

   a. Folk etymology may affect spelling only, as when evanescent mistakes like *hairbrained* or *tow the line* or *straight-laced* indicate, if the spelling can be trusted, that the writer has misunderstood the expression. But some such wrong ideas have actually become established spellings. NE *sovereign,* from OFr. *souverain* < LLat. *superānus,* has been influenced by the completely unrelated *reign* < Lat. *rēgnum.* The spellings *abhominable* (once common for *abominable*) and *posthumous* (still standard) have been influenced by fanciful ideas about their derivations—the former as if from Lat. *homō* 'man', rather than *ōmen,* and the latter as if connected with Lat. *humus* 'earth' rather than from *postumus* 'last' (see also **67**).

   b. In some cases it appears that folk etymology has been at work, but it is not clear what has happened. It is thus with the English pairs *gat-toothed/gap-toothed* and *cat-nip/cat-mint.* The usual reasoning employs the utrum in alterum principle ('which one into the other'—which here functions as a variation of the lectio difficilior principle; see note c, next): a structurally obscure form is more likely to be turned into a transparent one than vice-versa. By such reasoning the first item in each pair would be the original one, and indeed the dates support that inference in the case of *gat-toothed* (Chaucer) vs *gap-toothed* (first seen several hundred years later). But the dates do not cooperate in the case of *cat-mint,* which is well attested some 500 years earlier than *cat-nip.* The latter appears to contain a form of Lat. *nepeta* 'mint'—so it would appear to be a case of a LEARNÈD folk etymology (as it were) rather than a lay one.

   c. *Lectio difficilior* 'the more difficult reading' is a shorthand way of referring to a principle of text criticism. In the simplest case: you have two copies of the same text which differ in a certain passage such that one copy reads more or less straightforwardly and the other contains an unknown word or something otherwise somehow unexpected, difficult, or obscure of interpretation. The correct method is to assume that the more difficult reading is the original one, and that the clear reading is the result of an editorial decision (or perhaps scribal inattention). It might not be so, in fact; many garbles ARE introduced into texts in the copying. However, a real possibility is that a scribe, confronted with something obscure, will decide that it is a corruption in the source text and will correct it to something that makes sense.
   This phenomenon is not of course limited to scribal practice: an every-day (or

rather, seasonal) example occurs in the song 'The Twelve Days of Christmas', in which the unfamiliar *coll(e)y-birds* has been corrupted into *calling birds*—not a miracle of clarity, but at least more intelligible on some level than *coll(e)y-birds*.

The real point, however, has little to do with the absolute probability of one kind of textual change or another. Rather, it has to do with the consequences of different assumptions. If one assumes that the clear reading is the correct one, then a possibly corrrect (but difficult) reading will simply be discarded without proper consideration. If one assumes that the more difficult reading is the correct one, then it demands explanation, and in the process of digging around and trying to figure out what the text really means, and so on, true understanding might be reached. Only after every possibility of explaining the lectio difficilior has been exhausted is one justified in (provisionally) endorsing the easier reading as genuine.

MORPHOLOGICAL ANALOGY

54. There are two ways in which something like folk etymology affects the formal properties (morphology) of certain words, while altering the actual pronunciation either not at all or only incidentally. These are *back formation* and *metanalysis.*

BACK FORMATION

Back formation (or *morphological reinterpretation*) is used here to mean the INVENTION of a morpheme division where none historically existed.[1] For example, *peddlar (-ler)* 'itinerant merchant of small wares' was a morphemic simplex, originally, but appears to contain the agent suffix *-er* as in *singer;* on such a basis was created the previously non-existent verb *to peddle* 'to hawk small wares' (these days more often figuratively than literally). A similar example is *lenten,* originally a noun ('spring[time]') whose reinterpretation as an adjective was nudged along perhaps by forms like *golden* and *wooden,* with the result that a new noun, *Lent* (now exclusively ecclesiastical), was created by back formation.

---

[1] Some authorities also use back formation to mean the REASSIGNMENT of a genuine division, either as to place or function. The term endorsed here for that is *metanalysis*, next. Others use the term back formation for the kind of leveling (47) where a 'derived' stem is generalized, as when the present-tense *live* /liv/ was manufactured on the basis of the Old English pret. *lifde* [livdɛ]. See note **b**, below.

This process can have significant influence on a lexicon; indeed, it accounts for the very numerous NE verbs which are apparently (but only apparently) based on Latin past participles, such as *act, inspect, defect* 'desert', *profess, imitate,* and the rest. These are actually back formed from *action, inspection, defection, profession, imitation,* and so on, perhaps with some help from borrowed nomina agentis like *actor, inspector,* and other models, like the noun *act* < Lat. *āctus, -ūs.*[1] These back formations, like the more recent *diagnose* and *donate,* have been fully accepted into the lexicon. Others, like *burgle,* are still jocular (except that *burgle* is standard in British English). Still others, like *a kudo* (based on misapprehending *kudos* 'fame, reputation' as a plural noun), *to orientate,* and *to enthuse* are used seriously but are disparaged by usage authorities. A few authorities are still tilting at such windmills as *diagnose, donate,* and other standard forms.

    a. Back formation is sometimes hard to distinguish from leveling (47-50), as in the case of Lat. *iūnxī* perf., *iūnctus* pple. based on *iungō* 'join', whose *-n-* is properly a component of the present stem and not of the root as such; but a new root *iung-* was manifestly abstracted from *iungō* and made the basis for a new paradigm. Such a process, which is common in morphologically complex languages, could with equal justice be treated as either back formation or leveling. Similarly, many authorities would surely describe the singular *(bee)hive,* based on pl. *hives* and replacing expected [x]*hife* < OE *hýf,* as a back formation rather than (as here) as leveling. Perhaps a case could be made for classifying *hive* e.g. as both.

    b. Some authorities identify innovations like *to baby-sit* as back formations, on the grounds that the term *baby-sitter* had been in use for a long time before the previously non-existent verb *to baby-sit* was coined. Coinage it definitely is, but in terms of language history the question is this: is there is a difference between creating a morpheme division and exploiting one?

METANALYSIS

Metanalysis is the repartitioning of a morphological complex into

---

[1] The nomina agentis are usually attested later than the verb, when they are attested at all—for example, there never was an English [x]*detestator* to help account for *detest* (which, in a typical alignment, is attested 100 years after the first occurrence of *detestation*).

novel components. The usual catalysts are (a) morphological ambiguity and (b) semantic confusion.

In English, the indefinite article is *a* before consonants, *an* before vowels (and formerly *my/mine* and *thy/thine* paralleled *a/an*); the phrases containing forms with *-n* are therefore indistinguishable from phrases where the article is followed by a word beginning with an *n-*, as *a neighbor* or *my name*. Native speakers of a language usually keep such ambiguous sequences straight, of course, as they know perfectly well what the components are; but ambiguity at least opens the way to confusion—and in fact confusion occasionally arises. Thus in the history of English, *auger, orange,* and *apron* have lost their word-initial consonant through metanalysis of *a nauger, a norange,* and *a napron;* and *nickname* has acquired its initial consonant from the reverse process. In the same way, the Attic conditional particle *án*, which corresponds functionally to dialectal *ke(n)* and *ka*, seems to spring from misprision of neg. *ou-kán* as *ouk-án* on the basis of the regular alternation between *ou* 'not' (before consonants) and *ouk* (before vowels).

In these cases, semantic confusion seems to play no role. There are some cases, however, where function does seem to be a player. When *fyrem-est* 'first' was reinterpreted as *fyr-* and *-most* (53), with the creation thereby of a whole new class of adjectives, the reanalysis was inspired by the chance similarity of the form with the semantically suitable *most*. The Latin creation of *ubī* 'where' and *ut* conj. from **ne-kubei* (cf. *alicubī*) and **ne-kutei* (cf. Osc. **puz** 'ut')—all from a pronominal stem **kʷu-* —presumes a stage of development where *ne-que* 'and not' had already apocopated to *nec*, and in the case of *ubī* (for **kubī*) the restructuring was undoubtedly abetted by the form *ibī* 'there'.

c. It appears that ambiguity is not indispensible, if a form by chance resembles a morphological element in the language. We have already seen a case of this in the remodeling of *fyremest*. It also seems to be the explanation for the reinterpretation of a number of nouns as plurals in the history of English, as *cherries* (of complicated history, but ultimately from LLat. **cerasia* or **cerasea*), pl. *cherrieses*: this paradigm should always have been no more ambiguous than NE *fox, foxes* or *rose, roses*. But the Siren's song of plural morphology resulted in *cherries* being reinterpreted as a plural, with the back formation of a new singular *cherry*.

NE *peas* < Lat. *pisum* is similar but interestingly different: from earliest times *pease*, as it was usually spelled, construed as either singular (i.e., a mass noun) or plural, and therefore was a wide target for reinterpretation leading to the back formation of a singular *pea*. But even mass nouns were subject to the same process, as when *sherry* was back formed from *Sherries*, itself a place-name in origin (Sp. *Jeres de la Frontera*) like many other wine terms (*port, canary, Bordeaux, Mosel*).

The metamorphosis of other mass nouns into pluralia tantum is something of a mystery: the etymon of Fr. *richesse* 'opulence' shows up in English as *riches;* Lat. *eleemosyna* 'charity, mercy' > OE *ælmysse* > NE *alms;* OE *efes* 'brim, brink; edge of a roof' > NE *eaves*.

HYPERCORRECTION

55. Hypercorrection is a mistake in morphology or, more commonly, in pronunciation, made in the course of trying to avoid a mistake (or what is perceived as a mistake). The near synonym *hyperurbanism* is particularly applied to hypercorrections that aim at some form of speech thought to be somehow 'higher' than the speaker's own, such as the 'careful pronunciations' *kitching, chicking* for *kitchen, chicken,* on the pattern of careful *going, coming* in place of colloquial (if ancient) *goin', comin'*.

Lat. *saeculum* 'age' for *sēculum* is probably to be explained as a hyperurbanism (though perhaps in spelling only); and there is an anecdote from Suetonius about the emperor Vespasian teasing a puristic client, one Flōrus, by addressing him with the deliberately hypercorrect pronunciation *Flaurus*.

Morphological hyperurbanism in English is seen in bungled classical phrases like *magnus opus* or *e pluribus unus,* and plurals like *apparati* and *ignorami*. Most such mistakes are of course transient—however common they may be, they rarely become accepted as standard.

Chronology is important. The phrase *between you and I* looks like a hypercorrection (and is confidently described as such by some) starting with latter-day harping by school teachers on such supposed errors as *It is me*. But *between you and I* is far too ancient and persistent to be any such thing.

   a. The term *mistake* is used here not normatively but descriptively. The speaker who utters a form like *kitching* or /nyuwn/ for *noon* may be presumed (without pernicious psychologizing) to have a purpose in mind—and to have failed to achieve it.

It is probably fairly rare for a hypercorrection all by itself, that is without the assistance of spelling pronunciation (43) or folk etymology (53) or some other prop, to become standard. *Terlet* for *toilet* and other forms with /ər/ for /oy/ probably enjoy a certain status regionally. *Coupon* /kyuwpan/ for /kuwpan/ (very general) may or may not be a hypercorrection. It is not clear whether /perkyəleyt/ *percolate* (common) and /simyələr/ *similar* (somewhat less so) are hypercorrections pure and simple, or result in part from contamination by common if irrelevant shapes (and in the case of possible influence from *simulate,* not so irrelevant).

SUGGESTIONS FOR FURTHER READING

Bynon 1977 chapter 1 §§5, **Anttila** 1988 chapter 5, **Hock** 1991 chapters 9–11, **Hock & Joseph** 1996 chapter 5, **Campbell** 1999 chapter 4. See particularly **Hock** 1991 chapter 10 for a clear presentation and analysis of the analogical theories put forward by Jerzy Kuryłowicz and by Witold Mańczak (whose fame exceeds their merits). For one of the few twentieth-century attempts to identify psychological processes in analogical innovations, see **Esper** 1973, which is interesting as well for his searching discussion of a tangential matter: the oft-repeated claim that Greek and Roman linguistic theory was dominated by a dispute between 'analogists' and 'anomalists' regarding the basic nature of human language. (Esper shows that there was no such dispute.)

No reasoning can hold Lat. *iter, itineris* (52) to be 'simpler' in any way than the inherited paradigm; see **Thomason** 1974 for a discussion of even more elaborately complexifying analogies.

See also **Anttila & Brewer** 1977 for further titles.

SEMANTIC CHANGE

A discussion of semantic change, even one which is on a relatively modest scale, can be fatiguing to read through. You may find that coming and going on this chapter is more rewarding than tackling it in a single go.

56. Linguistic meaning below the level of the sentence is called *semantics.* Like all components of linguistic structure, the semantics of any language are constantly in flux. Of course, the meaning of a given word or affix may remain stable for very long periods, and the Proto-Indo-European etyma of NE *sit, fill, udder, foot, wheel, red, name, egg,* and *mouse* had pretty much the same meanings seven thousand years ago as their present-day English reflexes (if one disregards a host of added meanings, like *red* 'Communist'). But these semantic Methuselahs are in fact the exception: words usually do not retain meanings unaltered for any length of time, so in historical and comparative linguistics some understanding of the nature of semantic change is vital for dealing with the routinely divergent semantics of cognate forms.

It must be emphasized that the examples in the following discussion are culled from countless possibilities. Anyone who spends a few minutes glancing at entries in a large dictionary must be impressed by both the quantity and extent of the semantic change chronicled there. As is true of so much of language study, the sheer luxuriance of the subject is an obstacle to clear understanding. The following discussion has only the limited object of highlighting the things that go on in semantic change.

Any attempt at a systematic study of semantic change, in fact, will yield only limited rewards, for two reasons: with rare (and not very helpful, however interesting) exceptions, semantic change is completely patternless; and, second, insight is forestalled by our nearly perfect ignorance of the real nature of the semantic component of language.

Both these points merit discussion.

57. Lack of pattern in semantic change

Each semantic change in a language is likely to be independent of other changes, apart from often conforming generally with tendencies widely found in semantic change. The result is that within a lexicon, the meanings of different forms in the same 'word family' will very commonly diverge, sometimes so widely that a common source is hard to prove without detailed philological study. The following examples are typical: NE *tempest, temper, tempera,* and *temperate* are now semantically remote from one another, as are NE *seethe, sod,* and *sodden; secret* and *secretary; consider, considerate,* and *considerable; thrive* and *thrifty; cosmic* and *cosmetic; emerge* and *emergency; candidate, candor,* and *candle; album, auburn,* and *albino; veteran* and *veterinarian; discreet* and *discrete; road* and *raid; make* and *match; blood* and *bless; read* and *ready; salad* and *sausage; vindicate* and *vindictive.*

Actual patterns of change (such as semantic shifts) occasionally occur in tightly-knit semantic systems. A striking example is the coherent semantic shift in Latin legal terminology: the interconnected terms in a judicial sequence all shifted meaning one notch from cause to consequence (80). The same shift is attested, albeit less systematically, in English: for example, *damage(s)* originally 'harm done' now has the legal meaning 'compensation paid for harm done'.

Occasionally one finds semantic changes linked in a looser sort of system. In Winnebago (a Siouan language spoken in Wisconsin), for example, there has been a general transfer of terms for various native fruits and vegetables to more or less European cultivars. For example *nąąpák* 'choke cherry' now means 'cherry' (Bing, pie, and so on). As a result, newly-coined compounds are used for the original referents of these words, so in this example 'choke cherry' is now *nąąpáksep* verbatim 'black cherry'.

58. Semantic accidents

Some abrupt semantic changes result from chance similarities in the FORMS of unrelated words.

NHG *leiden* 'suffer, endure, put up with' originally meant 'fare; experience' (cognate with OE *līþan*, Old Saxon *līthan*, among many others). In Middle High German it developed, quite naturally, the new meaning 'get through, escape'. Its current meaning seems not to continue either of these, but to have resulted from confusion with the totally unconnected *Leid* 'pain, distress, injury' < OHG *leit* 'injury, offense, disgrace'. Cf. the same range of meanings in the Old English cognate of this form, *láþ*, which is the etymon of NE *loath(e)*.

The verb *to sap* is (or was) synonymous with *to undermine* (cf. *sapper*); it is likely, however, that all or nearly all English speakers, native and otherwise, take an expression like *it sapped their strength* as equivalent to *it drained their strength* (as one takes sap out of a maple tree, say).

The expression *friendly fire* has a long history in legal terminology; it is defined thus in Black's law dictionary: 'Fire burning in [a] place where it was intended to burn, although damages may result.' (The implied contrast is with arson, fire handled irresponsibly, general conflagrations, and so on.) Some time in the 1960's, presumably owing to the ambiguity of the term *fire*, the phrase was misinterpreted and imported into a military context as the discharge of weapons by one's own side, especially when inflicting injury or damage on one's own troops or facilities.

Some such abrupt changes are in effect just slips, and may continue to be widely judged as such, as when *fortuitous* as used as a substitute for *fortunate; interpolate* 'insert' is used for *interpret;* or *hypothecate* 'take a mortgage' is used for *hypothesize.* But some such mistakes take root: *fortuitous* is encountered with the sense 'by fortunate chance' often enough for that meaning to qualify as established (however much it may grate on some ears); and NE *meld* has indisputably shed its original meaning. That meaning, 'show, display', is still current in the German cognate *melden,* but in English the verb had become obsolete except as a technical term in certain card games. The current use of *meld* to mean 'mix together, blend' presumably results from associations with *melt* (?—and *blend*).[1]

59. Unique and extreme

Some semantic changes are so extreme as to be startling: the etymon of NE *cardinal* 'red bird native to eastern North America' is Lat. *cardō* 'hinge'; Lat. *minium* 'cinnabar' (HgS, a red pigment) underlies NE *mini-*

---

[1] Some important authorities hold that *meld* 'mingle' is a coinage, a portmanteau form (52) of *melt + weld* and only coincidentally homophonous with *meld* 'show'. However, the first attestation of the word, in 1936, is for the mingled aromas of different cooked fruits, regarding which neither 'melt' nor 'weld' seems especially appropriate, semantically—certainly not in the same degree as *smog < smoke + fog.*

ature; and Lat. *fīcus* 'fig' underlies *fīcātum, fīcatum, fecatum* literally '(be)figged' > Fr. *foie,* Sp. *hígado,* and other Romance forms meaning 'liver'. In all these cases, the immense semantic distance was traveled incrementally; and all furthermore owe one or more important factor in their semantic evolution to specific circumstances in culture (the use of red in the decoration of capital letters in manuscripts, for example, and the further evolution of such decorated capitals into little vignettes) rather than to any general properties of semantic change. Explanations of extreme semantic changes, however, depend upon KNOWN facts: the meaning of a word simply cannot be accounted for by making up the crucial links, though exactly that is very often done.

a. One consequence of the overall lack of system in most semantic change is that earlier meanings may survive in fossilized expressions. Earlier USES, at least; it remains a question whether the meaning as such comes through. Thus, NE *tell* originally meant 'count', and this acounts for the expression *all told* and—less obviously—(bank) *teller.* But it is unclear whether native speakers of English actually think of *all told* as specifically meaning *summed-up* or *in total.* Similarly, NE *with* reflects OE *wiþ* 'against' (= NHG *wider*), and this accounts for *withstand, withhold,* and expressions like *fight with* and *disagree with.* NE *other* has always had its current meaning, but in addition used to mean 'second', hence *every other* 'every second' and (less obviously) in *the other day,* which once meant specifically 'the day before yesterday'; *throw* used to mean 'rotate', which accounts for the technical senses of *throwing* a pot on a wheel and the *throw* of a crank in mechanics; *pretend* (65) is used in an earlier sense when speaking of the *pretender* to a throne, e.g. to the Stuarts in exile. It is however unclear whether these are fossilized MEANINGS or fossilized USAGES. That is, do speakers truly understand *with* as MEANING 'against', in any context? Or take *other* as meaning 'second', or keep at bay the latter-day connotations of falsity that inhere in the meaning of *pretend?*

b. Most diachronic semantic changes run in well-worn grooves, but sharp changes in direction are possible because any given stage in semantic evolution can provide the basis for fresh departures. The semantic progress of PGmc **wōpijana^n* 'to scream, shriek, cry out' to NE *weep* 'ooze liquid, as from an abscess' is not a straight line. First came the change—a commonplace one, in fact—from 'cry out' to 'sob, weep and wail, keen'; but loud vocal noises are not the only thing characteristic of weeping, hence the application of the word to the (silent) exudation of moisture from sources other than tear-ducts.

And in the same vein, there is no predicting what the basis for a semantic development will be. The verb *to telescope,* for example, does not mean 'to look at distant objects with optical assistance', as would be expected, but rather refers to figurative intussusceptions (such as 'telescoping cause and effect'), from the way in which familiar kinds of hand-held telescopes are collapsible to reduce their length.

60. Limited understanding of linguistic semantics overall

The second obstacle to studying semantic change is even greater, namely the extreme obscurity of the semantic component of lexicon— what it is and how it works.

One line of inquiry has attempted to represent linguistically significant meaning in terms of a system of irreducible semantic *features* which are said to be *binary*, i.e., either present in or absent from the meaning of a lexical element. Such features would include for example 'human/non-human', 'animate/inanimate', 'count/mass', and 'edible/ inedible'. Constellations of such features would add up to the total meaning of a word.

Superficially—very superficially—such a system is attractive: it seems obvious that one of the ways in which the two words *chair* 'president of a meeting' and *chair* 'a kind of furniture designed for sitting' differ semantically is that the first has the semantic component [+human] in contrast to the latter's [−human]. But in fact any serious attempt to work out 'the semantic features' of a natural language's lexicon comes to grief very quickly.[1]

Nevertheless, as long as we avoid specifics, the concept of semantic features has its uses. We might say, FOR CONVENIENCE, that the more of these (imaginary) features a word or expression has, the smaller its semantic range: *puppy* has the same features as *dog* (whatever they are) plus some in addition, and therefore refers to fewer real-world objects

---

[1] For instance, in one standard example, the oddity of the utterance *The table sneezed* has been explained by the fact that *table* is semantically [−animate] while the verb *sneeze* occurs only with subjects coded [+animate]. But *The lobster sneezed* and *The firefly sneezed* meet this requirement, and are nevertheless odd. You have to have lungs and vocal cords as well as animacy to sneeze. A shrewd suggestion is that a feature like [+mammal] will do the trick, and such a feature would have some claim to linguistic salience (though including [−mammal] among the semantic properties of *table,* even by implication, would open another Pandora's box).

than the more general *dog;* similarly *dog* vs *carnivore,* and *carnivore* vs *mammal.* In verbs, the same relationship may be observed in *walk* vs *saunter, kill* vs *murder* vs *assassinate,* or *leave* vs *flee.*

Much semantic change can be thought of, FOR CONVENIENCE, as adding and subtracting such features, even though the 'features' thus 'added and subtracted' resist any approach to rigorous definition. Semantic changes that can be thought of in this way make up two large categories, *semantic widening* (losing features) and *semantic narrowing* (adding them)(61-6).

The second major category of semantic change comes under the label of *figurative usage,* which falls into two subgroups, metaphor (69-74) and metonymy (75-84).

Finally, there are several other kinds of influence on the meaning-bearing system of languages, such as cultural changes, which will be taken up separately (85-90).

CHANGES IN THE

NUMBER OF SEMANTIC FEATURES

61. Semantic widening and narrowing

When features are dropped, we speak of *widening* (or *generalization* or *extension*) of meaning; when features are added, of *narrowing* (or *specialization* or *restriction*) of meaning. *Melioration* and *pejoration*—the improvement or decline in the connotations of a word—are in these categories, but are often discussed separately and will be handled thus here (64-6).

Not uncommonly, the original and semantically altered meanings survive side by side. Thus *grow* 'change by getting bigger' loses features to come to mean 'increase in any quality' (including, without any sense of incongruity, *grow smaller* and the like), but the original meaning 'get bigger' is fully alive. On the other hand, it is common for the earlier meaning to be lost, as in the case of NE *speed.* This reflects OE *spéd* 'success; prosperity' (cf. the now opaque blessing *God speed!*)

a. Note that when what appear to be related words differ in the wideness or narrowness of their meaning, it is impossible to decide without additional information which meaning is the earlier. For example, given NE *hound* 'hunting dog' and NHG *Hund* '(generic) dog' there is in principle no way to reason out which meaning is closer to the common point of departure. That matter can be settled only by other evidence, such as earlier records (which in this case reveal that OE *hund* was a generic) or by the geographic distribution of meanings (as when the original sense is found in discontinuous areas around the periphery of an area with a different, new sense). There are of course general trends: words for 'young human male' much more readily acquire negative connotations than lose them; words for the young of animals raised for table routinely displace the generic (as in NE *pig* 'young swine' and *chicken* 'young fowl' displacing *swine* and *fowl/cock/hen*).

WIDENING (LOSS OF SEMANTIC FEATURES)

62. NE *control* (Fr. *contrôle*) continues a noun which is a contraction of *contre-rôle* or its Late Latin antecedent, meaning a file-copy of a record. The derived verb meant straightforwardly 'to compare originals and file copies for verification'. From this have evolved various equally specific senses (such as *controls* in statistics or experiment design) but also the very general senses of 'to rule, guide, regulate, restrain'.

NE *batch* (derivationally related to *bake* the same way that *speech* is related to *speak*) originally meant 'quantity of bread baked at once'. Cookies still come in batches, but otherwise the word now refers to anything connected with a single operation, even figuratively (such as *a batch of job applications* or a *batch file* in computerese).

For some reason, words properly meaning 'very new' and 'rather young, quite young' commonly lose the explicitly emphatic or contrastive force and come to mean simply 'young; new': PIE **new-yos-* 'very new' > Ved. *návyas-*, still 'very new' in the Rigveda but already in that text it is also attested with the meaning 'new'.

Forms morphologically marked as 'diminutive' may lose the specifically diminutive sense and become generic. Thus NHG *Mädchen* '(little) girl', diminutive of *Magd*, has replaced the latter as the generic word. (This seems to be a case of cooperative effort in the lexicon, as the meaning of the simplex was evolving from generic 'young woman' to the meaning 'servant-girl'.) The Romance languages are full of leached diminutives: It. *sorella* and *fratello* 'sister, brother', for example. As in the case of *Mädchen,* the process here was probably facilitated by the concurrent semantic specialization of the simplexes as synonyms of 'nun' and 'monk'. Fr. *abeille* 'bee' reflects *apicula; oreille* 'ear', *auricula; soleil* 'sun', *sōliculus*—the etyma being the diminutives of *apis, auris,* and *sōl,* respectively.[1]

a. The limiting case of semantic widening is seen in words with practically no meaning at all, like 'go', 'thing', 'do'. These generally come from words of more robust semantics: It. *cosa,* Fr. *chose* 'thing' < Lat. *causa* 'cause, reason; lawsuit'; Modern Greek *kánō* 'do' < Gk *kámnō* 'toil, labor'.

NARROWING (ADDITION OF SEMANTIC FEATURES)

63. ME *stove* was borrowed from a middle Low German source which meant—as Du. *stoof* and NHG *Stube* still do—'heated room'. Its change in meaning to 'appliance to contain burning fuel' is a metonymy (78), but the development of that sense to 'cookstove' is a narrowing. (Likewise a narrowing is the meaning of *stove* in the now technical sense of 'heated greenhouse'.)

OE *corn* 'grain' is now in American English specifically '*Zea mays,* maize, "Indian corn"'. (The original meaning is still seen in *peppercorn* and, more removed from ordinary experience, the term *corn laws.*)

LLat. *capitāle* 'wealth, in the form of money or movable property' > NE *cattle* formerly 'livestock', now 'bovine livestock' only.

OE *sellan* 'give (up)' > *sell.* (Words in many languages meaning 'buy'

---

[1] Occasionally one hears that the displacement of the original generic forms by diminutives is at least partly functional in cause: the French reflexes of the simplex forms, here, had they survived, would have been 'too short'—thus **ap* [a] 'bee', **sou* [su] 'sun'. But the opinion that words that are too short are somehow liable to replacement can hardly be based on observation, considering the large number of very short words in many languages (note Fr. [o] 'high' (*haut*), 'water' (*eau*), 'to the (pl.)' (*aux*), 'bones' (*os*), 'the letter *o*', and so on). A second opinion suspects that avoidance of homophony might have favored the Darwinian success of the diminutives; but French, for one example of many, is bursting with homophonous forms, like those in the example; so this surmise too raises more questions than it tries to answer, particularly if the claim is not framed in a testable (i.e., falsifiable) form. A good case for 'homophonic collision' might of course be made when e.g. OE *blác* 'white' and *blæc* 'black' dangerously converged in the oblique forms of the latter (as seen in the family name *Blake*) and northern forms of the former (as seen in *blake* 'pale; become, make pale').

and 'sell' are specializations of forms which originally meant generally 'take' and 'give (over), give up'.)

OE *tilian* 'strive for; labor; earn' (cf. NHG *Ziel* 'goal') > NE *till* 'work the soil for planting; tend crops', whence *tillage* 'farmland'.

Specialization routinely takes place in specific utilitarian or technical contexts:

Type 'kind, sort, genre' > specifically 'pieces of metal with raised designs of letters, used in printing' and also 'style or design of letters; typeface, font'.

Pattern means different specific things depending on whether one is speaking of dressmaking, oriental rugs, flatware, baldness, or shotgun chokes.

Draw means different things depending on whether one is talking of a picture, a bow, a sword, or a wagon.

Such specialized meanings often emerge as the only meaning of a word:

Gk *presbúteros* 'older', as a noun 'elder(s)' > Fr. *prêtre*, NE *priest*. The same word, by a different route, gives the equally narrow NE *presbyter* 'member of a decision-making body in a church organization'.

PGmc **fehu* 'money, valuables' > NHG *Vieh* 'cow' (cf. Go. *faihu* 'money', NE *fee*).

Lat. *prīnceps* 'leader' (in general) > NE *prince*.

In Old High German, *gift* meant what it looks like; in present-day German *Gift* means 'poison'—a specialized notion of something to give someone. (The English word *dose* has a similar semantic history—Gk *dósis* 'gift', specialized in a specifically medical context—and the English word *poison*, which is a doublet with *potion*, originally meant 'a drink'.)

OE *rǽdan* meant 'advise, discuss, deliberate, decide, decree, rule, possess, plot, scheme, try to benefit, help, provide for, guess, solve (of riddles—the word *riddle* is cognate with *read*—or problems), interpret (of dreams), tell a fortune, read (any written matter, but particularly a book)'. Of these meanings, only 'process written language' (and metaphors based on that meaning) have survived in NE *read*, whose functional link with the cognate *ready* (57) is no longer evident.

a. One must be careful about the details of such families of words of specialized use. Consider the word *key* which, like the forms just mentioned, means different specific things depending on whether the context is musical tonality, pianos, machinery, botany (= *samara*), design (*Greek key*), concepts, or encryption. However, these meanings, or most of them, are not cases of specialization—adding semantic features—but of figurative language, specifically metaphor (**69**).

PEJORATION AND MELIORATION

64. Words will gain or lose negative or positive connotations with or without changes in other semantic features. These are sometimes treated as special phenomena—*pejoration* ('getting worse') and *melioration* ('getting better')—but in fact they are merely subcategories of the addition and subtraction of semantic features. Presumably a movement from a decidedly negative meaning to a neutral (or less negative) one, as in *envy*, below, counts as melioration, and conversely the loss of specifically positive connotations, as in OE *hros/hors* 'steed' > NE *horse,* might be held to be a kind of pejoration.

Note that specific contexts will force pregnantly meliorative or pejorative readings of words, as *You'll pay for that* (*pay* = 'suffer a penalty') or *Very clever!* (*clever* here = 'dishonestly or meretriciously ingenious'). As an example of melioration: *I can give you a price on that,* that is, 'a reduced or otherwise especially attractive price'. It is uncertain just how lexicalized many such pregnant senses are. This question of lexical status vs diction is returned to in **75** and **77**, **79** below.

65. Pejoration

NE *facetious* used to mean 'witty, droll'; its meaning has shifted to something like 'characterized by out-of-place efforts at jocularity; waggish', that is, the value of the word has gone from approbation to disapproval.

NE *pretend* used to mean simply 'maintain, represent, claim' (as is still the meaning of Fr. *prétendre*); but now, the negative nuance of falsity has been added. (See **59a**.)

Lat. *cōnspīrātiō* (componentially 'a breathing together') 'unison, harmony, agreement'; already in Roman times also 'plot, conspiracy'.

OE *dóm* 'judgment, verdict' > NE *doom* (cf. the neutral—if obsolescent—cognate *deem,* and the semantically negligible contribution of the element to the meanings of compounds like *wisdom, martyrdom, kingdom* and even, with a semantic shift, the recent—1867—coinage *boredom*).

LLat. *christiānus* 'Christian' > Fr. *crétin*, NE *cretin*.

NE *fiddle* (a loan word from Late Latin) once was simply the word for 'violin', and is still used pretty freely by professional musicians. It has become informal by comparison to *violin*, however, and a radio announcer or preacher would be unlikely to use it.

Some few generalizations are possible:

Words meaning 'inexpensive' have an inherent likelihood to become negative in connotation, often highly negative. Lat. *vīlis* 'at a good price' (i.e., inevitably, 'low price') > 'commonplace' > 'trashy, contemptible, low' (the current meaning of It., Fr. *vile*, NE *vile*).

Words for 'clever, intelligent, capable' commonly develop connotations (and eventually denotations) of sharp practice, dishonesty, and so on:

LLat. *latīnus* 'Latin, cultivated' > Sp. *ladino* 'dishonest' (see also **66**).

NE *crafty* 'dishonestly clever' is from OE *cræftig* 'strong(ly); skillful(ly)' (= NHG *kräftig* 'strong'; the ancient sense 'strong, strength' of this family of words fades very early in the history of English, where the usual senses pertain to skill).

NE *cunning* has very negative connotations in present-day English, but in Middle English it meant 'learned, skillful, expert' (the word is not attested before the early 14th century, but on various grounds is assumed to be much older). The related *canny* is closer to neutral, but still implies some degree of unexpected or unwonted cleverness.

NE *sly*, a borrowing from Scandinavian, at its first appearance in Middle English meant 'skillful, dexterous' (note the derived noun in *sleight of hand*). Now it is a synonym, connotations and all, of *crafty*.

Very occasionally, words in this semantic field do meliorate, at least to some degree: *shrewd* originally meant 'spiteful, malicious' (it is related to *shrew*); *wily*, though hardly a postive descriptor, originally meant 'pertaining to sorcery and witchcraft' (grave matters in those days).

66. Melioration

Early NE *emulate* 'be jealous, envy' > 'desire to surpass' > 'desire to resemble/equal in some positive quality'. *Envy* itself has undergone considerable melioration, having lost its earlier semantic ingredients of malice and viciousness. As a result, the inclusion of Envy among the Seven Deadly Sins necessarily strikes most present-day speakers of English as odd.

NE *tempt* 'test, try (usually by torment)' > 'entice with promises of pleasure, payment, or other alluring things'.

NE *look forward to* was originally neutral, 'anticipate' or the like, now it means only 'contemplate a future event with relish or eagerness'.

Success 'what comes next' (as in the related *succession*) > 'wished-for or admired results'. The same evolution is seen in NHG *Erfolg* which, however, unlike *success,* still has both the generic and the pregnant meanings: 'outcome, effect' and 'success'.

OE *prættig* 'tricksy, sly' > NE *pretty.*

OE *cwén* 'woman; wife' > NE *queen.*

PRom. **bravu* 'savage, ferocious' underlies NE *brave* 'courageous, noble'. A similar evolution has taken place in the Romance languages, but with differences: for example, It. *bravo* 'able, clever, skillful, capable, honest', only incidentally also means 'plucky'.

Derivative affixes may acquire specifically positive or negative connotations: the English affix *-ish* (building adjectives from nouns) often has a negative flavor compared to other derivatives, as *childish* vs *childlike.* There are invariably exceptions to such generalizations: ethnonyms like *English* and *Netherlandish* are neutral, and *boyish* is downright positive. The Latin adjective suffix *-ōsus* underlies both English *-ous* and *-ose.* In Latin already such formations had connotations of excess, as in *cūriōsus* both 'careful' and 'excessively careful'.[1] In English, any good or bad flavor for adjectives in *-ous* inheres in the lexical item itself, so: *devious* (negative), *virtuous* (positive), *various* (neutral). There are some 300 adjectives in *-ose* in English, all but a few being

---

[1] There may be a lesson here. The common adjectives, like Lat. *cūriōsus,* are descriptors which place the thing described against a background of behavioral norms, and the mere fact that such qualities would be mentioned at all implies that something is cause for comment. A descriptor like *well-meaning,* that is, inevitably communicates the sense of missing the mark: if the good intentions of an action can't be taken for granted, something is wrong already. (I owe this insight to Jeffrey Wills.)

technical like *pilose* 'having fine hairs', *rugose* 'ridged', *tomentose* 'woolly'. These are all neutral, whereas all the similarly-formed adjectives in ordinary use have implications of excess or some other undesirable quality: *verbose, lachrymose, morose, grandiose, bellicose.*

The same word may undergo divergent semantic evolution in different reflexes:

Lat. *vitiōsus* 'weak' > 'faulty, blemished' > Fr. *vicieux*, NE *vicious* but It. *vezzoso* 'charming'.

OE *cniht* 'boy, servant' (the former is the original meaning, as indicated by Old English compounds like *cnihthád* 'youth; virginity—of a man', *cnihtlíc* 'boyish') > NE *knight*. The cognate OHG *cneht* became NHG *Knecht* 'farmhand; menial'.

LLat. *latīnus* 'Latin (adj.), Roman' > Sp. *ladino* 'crafty, dishonest' (pejoration, 65) but Port. *ladino* 'learnèd, cultured'.

Curiously, words may in effect change places connotatively: as recently as the 19th century, the connotations of *zeal* and *enthusiasm* (originally 'inspiration or possession by a spirit or divinity'), and their derivatives, were essentially the reverse of what they are now: *enthusiasm* implied wretched excess while *zeal* was praiseworthy. (*Zeal* had itself already traveled a long semantic road, starting out with the exceedingly negative sense '(impassioned) jealousy'—*jealous* and *zealous* are doublets, incidentally—then moving to the more or less objective-to-approbative sense 'ardent devotion to any cause'.)

a. It might be predicted that if a term is profoundly taboo, it would be impossible for it to shake its connotations. But there are good examples of just that: *screwed up* is as harmless as *balled up* (earlier *ballsed up*), and *nuts!* is an almost laughably mild expletive; but all three items, like *shafted* and *hosed,* were to begin with crudely obscene. These all belong to a highly informal register, to be sure, and far more startling is Sorbian *jebać* 'to deceive' which continues the root that elsewhere in Slavic (and in Proto-Indo-European) means 'fuck'.

FOREGROUNDING OF CONNOTATIONS

67. Sometimes the change in the relative importance of denotations and connotations can completely alter the meaning of a word. The routine changes in the meaning of words for 'inexpensive' and 'clever/skillful' as described above (65) are cases of such foregrounding. Attempting to

keep such negative connotations in the background can be an unequal struggle, as is evident in the following advertising copy encountered on television: *This is not inexpensive furniture; it is quality furniture at a low price.*

Lat. *precārius* 'begged for, obtained by prayer' (Lat. *prex* 'prayer') > 'uncertain, insecure' (NE *precarious*).

Words meaning 'well-born, well-connected' routinely develop some positive metaphoric sense which often becomes the only sense: NE *generous* is borrowed from Lat. *generōsus* 'of good family'; NE *noble* and its Romance cognates are from Lat. *nōbilis* 'well-known'; specifically, 'of well-known or aristocratic family'.

OE *spinnan* 'draw out, specifically draw out staple fiber into thread' (cf. NE *span* and NHG *spannen* 'draw, pull') > 'rotate rapidly' (from the characteristic action of the spinning wheel—a machine which first appeared in Europe in the 15th century). In present-day English the historical meanings have changed place: 'rotate rapidly' is the basic meaning, and 'make thread' is a secondary, derived sense.

In England, Lat. *tandem* 'at length' (of time) was used with donnish jocularity to denote a two-horse rig in which one animal is harnessed behind the other, and a little later the same term was used for a 'bicycle built for two'. These uses all involve things joined together, and now the meaning of *in tandem* refers exclusively to the LINKING of (usually two) things, and not to their spatial arrangement; indeed, the commonest use of the word nowadays is probably metaphorical.

In Latin, a *postumus* child was simply a man's last; the term to be literally valid was understood as denoting a child born after its father's death, and therefore by definition his last-born legitimate offspring. The 'after death' concomitant in the meaning early moved from incidental to central, so that now the term refers to anything at all coming to light after its begetter's death—possibly a child, but much more commonly a work of art or something similar, as in a sentence like *The final volume of his memoirs was published posthumously.* (Amusingly, the change in spelling is the orthographic equivalent of folk etymology, **53**, and results from the shift in denotation: it is based on a fanciful association with Lat. *humus* 'ground'. The word is in fact just the superlative degree of *posterior* 'later'.)

Venerable means, or meant, 'worthy of respect' (cf. *venerate*); persons in this state are not uncommonly advanced in years, and *venerable* is now only a flattering synonym of *old*.

FIGURATIVE MEANINGS

68. The second major division of semantic change can be gathered together under the heading of FIGURATIVE MEANINGS. Of these there are two large subsets, *metaphor* and *metonymy*.

A caveat: a semantic link (of whatever necessary complexity) can almost always be invented between any two meanings, and not every polysemy discloses a valid historical semantic development. Chance similarities, mentioned in **95a** & **b**, occur frequently WITHIN lexicons; and these include homophonies as well as mere resemblances like *see* and *seem*. NE *ear* of grain (in American usage practically limited to corn) is unrelated to *ear* 'hearing organ'; the former continues OE *éar/œhher* (= Go. *ahs*, NHG *Ähre*; PGmc **aχaz-*, an *s*-stem); the latter continues OE *éare* (= Go. *auso*, NHG *Ohr*, PGmc **awson-*, an *n*-stem). NE *light* (opposite of *heavy*) and *light* (opposite of *dark*) are unrelated words, reflecting PIE **le(n)ǵh-u-* and **lewk-o-*, respectively. Unrelated are NE *calf* 'gastrocnemius (the muscle mass on the lower leg); young cow'; and *corn* 'grain; hard growth on a toe'.

METAPHOR

69. Metaphors are figurative uses based on some similarity of form, function, relationship, appearance, and so on, between the normal (literal) referent of the word and some new referent. That is, metaphors always imply some sort of COMPARISON: the mouth of a river or a jar is in some sense LIKE the anatomical mouth.[1]

---

[1] The operative word *new* describes the creative aspect of metaphorical language. But of course many metaphors, such as the ones catalogued here, are not continually reinvented. Rather, the use of *mouth* to mean 'the aperture of a jar' is simply a term in the lexicon. These are sometimes called *faded* metaphors, but for our purposes the distinction between creative and faded metaphors is immaterial, because behind every faded metaphor is a semantic innovation.

The basis for the 'implied comparison' of a metaphor may range from the obvious (*teeth* of a gear wheel) to the obscure (as in Gk *kúklos* 'circle; wheel' and also 'place of assembly', virtually a synonym of *agorā́*). The similarity invoked is not necessarily very salient, or very realistic, and may be downright inappropriate: *sweat* 'moisture condensing on a COLD surface' (of a glass, e.g.). Even many of the *mouth* metaphors (70) are not, upon reflection, easy to explain.

Of course, many very strange-seeming metaphors turn out to be transparent in the proper historical context. OE *spinnan* 'make thread', mentioned above in a different context (67), had also the metaphorical senses 'twitch, jump; struggle'. In the present day, it is impossible to see how twitching and struggling could have anything to do with spinning, but when thread-making involved the use of a distaff and spindle the story was different:

> The primitive thread-making implement consisted of a wooden spindle, from 9 to 15 in. long, which was rounded and tapered at both extremities.... Near the top there was usually a notch in which the yarn was caught while undergoing the operation of twisting, and lower down a whorl, or wharve, composed of a perforated disk [i.e., doughnut-shaped] of clay, stone, wood, or other material was secured to give momentum and steadiness to a rotating spindle. Long fibres were commonly attached to a distaff of wood, which was held under the left arm of the operator [who was standing up].... After attaching some twisted fibres to the spindle, a rotatory motion was given to the latter either by rolling it by hand against one thigh, or by twirling it between the fingers and thumb of the right hand, after which the fibres were drawn out in a uniform strand by both hands and converted into yarn. When the thread was of sufficient strength, the spindle was suspended by it until a full stretch [NB the term] had been drawn and twisted, after which that portion was wound upon the body of the spindle, and the operation continued until the spindle was filled....
>
> *Encyclopaedia Britannica*, eleventh edition 25:685 (1911)

The dominant visual impression of thread-making by this technique would be the motion of the spindle, which, having been twirled and dropped, would twitch and jerk as it rotated at the end of the newly-drawn and lengthening yarn. Given this information, the metaphorical transfer from 'draw thread' to 'twitch, struggle' is straightforward.

Note that figurative meanings, however obvious they may seem, are never inevitable. In English, machinery *runs* (except in England, where clockwork and any analogous device *goes*), but French machinery 'walks' (*marche*). English-speaking needles have an *eye*, in German they have an 'ear' (*Nadelöhr*).

Conversely, in different languages the same term is used for unlike metaphors: NE *wing*, when applied to a building, denotes a subsidiary structure relative to the main body or axis of the building, or a branching out from one such subsidiary structure to another. But Lat. *āla* 'wing' (from which NE *aisle*—the -*s*- is an unetymological whimsy) in Late Latin referred rather to a feature of large church buildings, namely, side passages or galleries running parallel to the axis of the main space. NHG *Flügel* 'wing' has metaphorical senses which are not paralleled in the English or Latin lexica, e.g. 'sail' (of a windmill; but *wing* is formerly attested in this sense, too), 'blade' (of a propeller), and 'grand piano'. Lat. *āla* itself is used metaphorically in several senses that have no close parallel in the later languages: '(human) armpit' and analogous structures in quadrupeds; 'the point where a branch joins the trunk of a tree'; and (in the plural) 'apartments on opposite sides of a courtyard'—the starting point of the 'gallery' sense, above.

70. Human body parts

One generalization that can be made about metaphors is that mankind is indeed the measure of all things: the human body is probably the single most prolific source of metaphors in all languages. The relationship is usually body-part → other.

> *foot* of a mountain, tree, sewing-machine, bed, or page.
> *head* of the class; of a page, bed, or table; of lettuce, or of a boil. (As is typical, these examples embody diverse metaphors: 'shaped like a head', 'on top, like a head', and so on.)
> *mouth* of a river, a jar, a cave, the opening between the *jaws* of a vice; Scottish Gaelic *beul na h-oidhche* 'dusk' (verbatim 'mouth of the night').
> *eye* of a needle, of a potato, of a storm, of Swiss cheese. Similarly, Spanish *ojo* 'eye' in *ojo de agua* 'spring', *ojo de la cerradura* 'keyhole' (verbatim 'eye of water' and 'eye of the lock').
> *leg* of a table or of a pair of compasses, or of a journey, or of a sur-

veyor's layout; *hand* of a clock; *snout* of a glacier; *nosing* and *knees* of a stair-tread; *heel* of bread, of a mast, of a scythe.

This kind of metaphor is abundant also in morphological complexes: the *cheek-piece* of a harpsichord; *wrist-pin* of the piston of an internal combustion engine; *elbow macaroni; breastworks* of a fortification.

There are two chief categories where metaphors in the reverse direction are common: the body-parts involved in taboos (sex and excretion, mainly), for which the reasons are obvious; and the head, for which they are not. Examples of the former are NE *cock* and *muff*.[1] Examples of the latter are Lat. *testa* 'pottery' > Fr. *tête,* It. *testa* 'head'; OHG *copf* 'cup, mug' > NHG *Kopf* 'head'. Many such terms are slangy or jocular, like NE *noodle, bean,* and *gourd,* and probably now-standard terms like *Kopf* and *tête* started out in that register.

In the case of sex taboos, metaphors BASED ON the body-parts are rare (except of course abundantly as insults). An exception is the use of *male* and *female* for plugs, jacks, and other connectors, where the sexual metaphor is at a remove or two, at least (for all its anatomical explicitness). In the case of 'head', metaphors of the usual body-part type are copious—as sampled above, to which add Fr. *chef* and NHG *Haupt,* both formerly the every-day words for 'head' but in current usage all but restricted to metaphorical uses, as *chef de cuisine* 'person in charge of the kitchen', *chef d'œuvre* 'masterpiece' (verbatim 'head of work(s)'), *Hauptbahnhof* 'main train station', *Häuptling* 'chief', *Hauptbetrag* 'sum total', *überhaupt* 'on the whole'.

71. Quantity and number

Words denoting number ('many, few') and size ('large, small') not uncommonly interchange. Transfers in both directions occur; if one is favored over the other, it is not apparent. Thus Lat. *paucī* 'few' is the source of It. *poco,* both 'few' and 'little'. Contrariwise, for younger

---

[1] *Cock* in this sense is probably a double metaphor: first, from *cock* 'male chicken' > 'spigot', and then from 'spigot' to 'penis'. Parenthetically, this example embodies another diachronic truth: homophones of taboo words become taboo themselves, so *cock* 'rooster' and (in America) the utterly innocent *ass* 'donkey' are avoided and fall into disuse.

speakers of English, *less*, originally 'littler', also means 'fewer' (*There are less ants over here*).[1] Synchronically, a language can be inconsistent in such matters: in Latin the same stem signifies 'much' (*multus*) and 'many' (*multī*) in contrast to 'large' (*magnus*); but the antonyms are parcelled out differently: one stem (*parvus*) signifies both 'small size' and 'small amount' in contrast to 'few' (*paucī*):

	quantity	*number*	*size*
large	multus	multī	magnus
small	parvus	paucī	parvus

Note that in English, *little* is used of either quantity or size, *small* now only of size, but this has not always been the case: note Jonson's famous (if often misquoted) remark about Shakespeare's *small Latin and less Greek*.

72. Sense transfer

There is growing evidence that sense-conflation, or *synaesthesia*—seeing sounds, feeling flavors, and so on—has a physiological basis, at least for a very few people. For most of us, however, the transfer of terms from one sense to another is metaphorical, and commonplace. (Interestingly, the metaphors commonly met with bear little resemblance to the recorded experiences of synaesthetes.) We speak of *dull* or *loud* colors—a tactile and an auditory term, respectively, used of visual stimuli. A study of these transfers has concluded that there are constraints on such metaphors; for example, although auditory terms are used for appearances (as above), visual terms rarely applied to sounds, even though one of the commoner forms of neurological synaesthesia is 'seeing' sounds.

Sensory words are of course used as metaphors per se, as *sweet* or *sour* of disposition, or *bright, sharp, dim*, and *dull* of intelligence.

NE *smart* at present has the meaning 'painful' only in the derived

---

[1] *Less* used of countables taken as amounts, for example *less than ten dollars*, has been standard for 800 years. The phrase *or less* is standard with ALL countables: *25 words or less, vehicles with three occupants or less*. These are different matters from the use discussed here, but probably have contributed to its rise.

verb *to smart* (and compounds like *smartweed*); the adjective now means 'quick-witted, intelligent' or in some contexts 'impudent'.

73. Concrete to abstract

A very strong generalization about metaphors is that when a concrete and an abstract meaning are associated with the same word—for example, Gk *horáō* both 'see' and 'take care of, look out for'—the concrete meaning is almost invariably the basis for the figurative metaphor.

NE *sad* orig. 'full, sated', then 'heavy' in any sense (including, say, thick cloth), finally 'doleful, dejected'.

Skt *guru-* 'heavy' was also used metaphorically in early (Vedic) literature to mean little more than 'very'. Later, by a different metaphor, it came to mean 'venerable, respectable; a venerable person, e.g. a parent; a spiritual teacher'; and finally '(any) teacher'. (As borrowed into English the meaning has shifted slightly to something like 'an expert, an adept'.)

The Latin source of NE *involve* meant 'roll up in' or the like; of NE *confuse* 'baffle' meant 'pour together'.

Lat. *integer* is etymologically 'untouched', but in Latin already only 'entire, whole; untainted'. A new formation, *intāctus*, had the literal sense 'untouched', but already in Latin the meaning of that word underwent the same extension, as still seen in NE *intact*.

Examples of the concrete-to-abstract motion are literally innumerable; by contrast, metaphors in the reverse direction, that is, a word of non-concrete significance being figuratively used concretely, are very rare. There must be others, but in English the following is the only example known to me:

OE *céne* (NE *keen*) meant 'bold, brave, eager, enthusiastic', just like the Modern German cognate *kühn* 'brave, audacious'. It still has that meaning—especially in British English—but how this evolved into 'sharp, well-honed' of blades is a standing puzzle. (It has been pointed out that already in Old English weapons are described in poetry as 'eager for battle'. Some regard this as the key; but the presumed semantic progression remains very doubtful.)

a. These examples all involve the more or less complete loss of the original (concrete) sense; but in the initial stages, the literal and figurative senses are naturally found side by side. That was certainly once the case with all the above examples, and such a state of affairs may last a long time, as in NE *inflate* 'blow up (like a balloon); exaggerate', and *way* 'road, route; method, procedure'. Contrariwise, it is very common for once-current figurative senses to vanish, as in the example of *spin* 'twitch, struggle', above (p. 109), and *versatile* 'fickle, opportunistic; devious'.

     b. The use of NOUNS of abstract meaning to refer to objects or persons is commonplace: *a beauty* 'a beautiful thing or person', *counsel* 'attorney', *dominion* both of the exercise of power and the territory in which it is exercised; and some, like *magistrate,* are exclusively concrete now. These are metonymies, however (75 ff), not metaphors.

74. Transfer from physical to mental

This phenomenon is similar to the preceding, and similar as well to the metonymic transfers between subject and object (82) but is nevertheless distinct from both.

     Very commonly one finds a transfer from the physical notions of 'grasp, take in the hand' to 'comprehend, understand'. Thus Lat. *comprehendō* 'grasp, take hold of' and also 'understand, perceive'. This figurative meaning is the earliest, and the most commonly-attested, for the English borrowing *comprehend*. Note also the very common mental uses of NE *grasp, gather,* and *get* (this type of metaphor is enormously commonplace; possibly it is a semantic universal).

     Similarly, notions of the type 'weigh, heft' routinely come to mean 'ponder, think seriously about'. The polysemy is still on the surface in NE *weigh;* but NE *ponder* no longer has any remnant of the meaning of its etymon, Lat. *ponderō* 'weigh' (which had the sense of 'consider, think about' already in Latin), though clear traces of the original semantics are to be found in other derivatives such as *ponderous*.

     Very commonly verbs meaning 'perceive visually' come to mean 'notice; know', as in *I see that Fred and Alice are getting divorced.*

     The etymon of NE *patient* meant 'suffering, experiencing' and the like; nowadays the word applies to a frame of mind. (The 'Patient Griselda' of fable was notable not for her composure but for her suffering.)

     NE *regard* (noun and verb) originally had to do with literally keeping in sight, looking at, inspecting; now in addition the noun means 'high opinion, esteem', the verb more generically 'hold an opinion', good or bad. In a similar way, *view* (noun) is etymologically a visual impression or scrutiny of something; now also a synonym of *opinion*.

METONYMY

75. Metonymy is the figurative use of a word which is suggested by some physical or temporal proximity, cause-and-effect, material, relationship, or similarity of use. In a broad and vague way, the thread running through most metonymies is *adjacency*. This may not always be obvious, and probably a more reliable test is negative: given a semantic development that appears to be figurative but which involves no implied COMPARISON (which would make it a metaphor), we are probably dealing with a metonymy.

It is important to note that many metonymies are a matter of DICTION rather than lexicon. This distinction is important: it is not wise to regard all of the ways a word is UNDERSTOOD in discourse to be inherent, i.e., among its 'meanings'. This is easy to demonstrate in the case of irony. Just about every word in the language can be made to mean its opposite through irony; for example a sentence like *We should certainly pay attention to what Fred says because Fred is an expert,* if signaled by whatever means to be heavily ironical, would require us to understand *expert* to mean 'by no means an expert' and *pay attention to* to mean 'disregard'. This is pretty straightforward, pragmatically, but it is certainly a matter of discourse only: it would obviously not be a good idea to list, among the meanings of all words, also the opposites of those meanings.

Probably the great majority of metonymies belong to diction (discourse), in fact. We routinely say that someone *doesn't like Wagner* when the topic of discussion would properly be the operas (or perhaps more generally, the music) composed by Wagner; but we would not like to put *Wagner* in a dictionary glossed as 'opera; music'. Similarly *the whole village was in bed* really means 'every person in the village … '. We speak of turning on a light when the literal event is turning on the electricity (if not arguably turning on a switch).

Some examples are hard to call. In English, the expression *seeing things* means 'imagining (in error or delusion) that one is seeing something', that is, it specifically means NOT seeing anything. This does seem to be a case of lexicalization, but even so it is not usually included in dictionary definitions of *see*.

Even lexicalized metonymies are endlessly various, but many can be catalogued under headings: part for the whole; whole for the part; cause for effect and vice versa; material for object; and others. The following selection is only a sampling.

76. Part for the whole

NE *train* (clipped (87) from *train of cars*) now usually refers to the whole lash-up, including the locomotive.

NE *wheels* is a (slangy) synonym for 'automobile'; Skt *rátha-* 'chariot' is etymologically 'wheel' (cf. Lat. *rota*), and the same metaphor is seen in Toch. *kukäl* 'wagon' or 'chariot' < *k^wek^wlo- 'wheel'.

NE *head* of cattle; in various trades, customers are known as *heads*.

NE *hand* 'assistant; member of a crew'.

NE *press* 'a company in the business of setting in type, printing, and distributing printed matter'. A different metonymy on the same word means 'the industry, part and parcel, which gathers news and writes, prints, and disseminates periodicals or newspapers'.

Lots of poetic (if not indeed euphuistic) expressions are part-for-whole metonymies: *sail* 'ship', *blade* 'sword', *cloth* 'clergy', *crown* 'king', *boards* 'the stage', *hearth* 'home'.

In everyday terminology, NE *strings* = 'violins, violas, cellos' (but not instruments with keys); similarly *reeds* = 'oboes, clarinets' and the rest.

77. Whole for the part

This kind of metonymy is rare, maybe non-existent, in the lexicon—despite the fact that it is enormously abundant as a matter of diction: the *village* example, above (75); we *start a car* when what we are starting is its motor; we *vacuum the living-room* when what is actually being vacuumed is the floor and rugs of the living-room.

78. Container for the thing contained

Like whole-for-part (above), this relationship is exceedingly common in discourse: when you offer further liquid refreshment you will likely ask if someone would like *another glass* or *another cup* or *another bottle*. However, such relationships do occasionally become lexicalized:

NE *dish* (a borrowing from Latin) literally 'platter' > 'prepared food'; the same transfer is seen in *casserole* 'covered baking dish' > 'a preparation cooked and (usually) served in such a dish'.

Sp. *paella* originally denoted a sort of frying pan (from Lat. *patella*); it now means 'a preparation of rice with chicken, meat, or seafood' prepared in such a vessel.

79. Contained for the container

This metonymy is commonplace in diction, as in *Pass the beer* 'pass the pitcher with the beer in it'; but it seems to be only rarely lexicalized.

Bushel originally 'a certain quantity of grain' (the exact quantity originally depended on what crop), then 'a container of bushel capacity'; ditto *peck*. (Both are now rare; the one is probably most commonly encountered in the Biblical quotation about putting a lamp 'under a bushel'.)

Salt 'NaCl', also 'salt cellar; vessel for holding/dispensing salt'.

Lat. *aqua* 'water' also 'aqueduct'.

Lat. *arēna* 'sand', also 'the area of an amphitheater with sand in it'.

80. Effect for cause, result for purpose

—and (rather less commonly) vice versa. These closely-related types of meaning shift are observed very commonly in diction, as in the turning-on-the-light example above (75, end), but also may become lexicalized.

Lat. *probō* 'test, examine' was borrowed as NE *prove* (noun *proof*) with the same meaning, from which evolved 'find satisfactory (by testing)', whence the *proof-marks* on sterling silver, suits of armor, and the like; and it further evolved to the usual present-day meaning of 'demonstrate an impregnable conclusion'. The original sense of trying out and testing is still current in technical applications, such as *(a printer's) proof* 'a trial impression for the purpose of finding and eliminating imperfections', and also encapsulated in the saw *the exception proves* (i.e., tests the validity of) *the rule*—which is cheerfully incoherent if understood with the usual present-day meaning of *prove*.

Vintage originally 'year's output of wine' (cf. *vintner* 'wine producer') but now also an attributive with the meaning 'old and fine' (as in *vintage automobiles*) or just plain 'old' (as in *vintage humor*).

NE *drink* (noun) 'something [to be] drunk'.

Notions meaning 'lack, be missing' commonly acquire the additional or even exclusive meaning of 'be (urgently) desirable' or 'be necessary':[1]

NE *want* 'lack' > 'need (*It wants to cook a little longer*); desire'.

Gk *khrēízei* 'lacks' > 'needs'.

Lat. *fallit* 'tricks, deceives' > 'escapes notice' > 'fails, lacks' > Fr. *il faut* 'it is necessary'.

The reverse semantic development is evident in OE *níed* 'inevitableness; requirement, what is required; duty; compulsion; hardship, distress'. Of these meanings, all still more or less evident in NE *need,* the original seems to have been something like 'distress'.

'Tasting' and 'testing' are routinely connected metonymically. One may take a taste of something for various reasons, including investigation (so 'taste' > 'test'); or one may try out something by tasting it (so 'test' > 'taste'). As it happens, a semantic widening (62) is at the root of the NE *taste* words, which ultimately go back to LLat. *taxitō* 'touch, feel of' (> OFr. *taster,* Fr. *tâter*) whence by metonymy 'find out something about a thing by touching or feeling it' whence (by widening) 'find out something via any means', then renarrowed to the gustatory sense specifically, and then, by metonymy, 'the sense of taste (no matter what its function)'. (*Taste* n. in the sense of 'sensitivity, delicatesse, aesthetic or moral judgment' is of course a metaphor.)

a. It is wise to recognize that in all varieties of semantic change, mere common sense is an inadequate analytic tool. The 'obvious' relationship between the words *taste* and *test* in English—obvious to anyone with some experience in semantic change—turns out to be wrong: in fact, these words resemble each other by chance (95a). Similarly, at first sight the meanings of NE *hurt*—both 'cause pain' and 'injure'—look like a typical cause/effect metonymy, though it cannot be determined prima facie which is the metonymy on the other. This is indeed a case of metonymy, but one whose history cannot be guessed from the meanings themselves: the original Middle English verb, from a French word of unknown history, meant 'strike a blow'. The meanings 'cause pain' and 'injure' both seem to have been pres-

---

[1] It is in fact often difficult to tell, especially in periods of transition, which of these several meanings is intended: *She is old and wants someone to take care of her* makes equally good sense whether *wants* is taken as 'lacks', 'needs', or 'desires'.

ent from an early time; but both are metonymies on 'strike a blow', neither one is a metonymy directly on the other.

81. Material for object

is a very common type of metonym, and highly lexicalized; some, like the words for 'money', are paralleled in many languages. The converse metonymy—object for material—occurs, but is rare.

Silver 'the metallic element Ag', then 'flatware eating utensils' (not necessarily actually made of silver). But Lat. *argentum* 'silver' > Fr. *argent* 'money'—though not usually coins (which are *monnaie*). Incidentally, Lat. *argentum* itself meant, metonymically, 'tableware', that is, dishes, platters, and such.

In contrast to the part-for-whole metonymy of *strings* and *reeds*, mentioned above (76), *brass* in the sense of 'trumpets, trombones, flügelhorns' and so on is a material-for-object metonymy.

Lat. *penna* 'feather; pen' > NE *pen* (now never made of a literal feather). The metonymic polysemy is still alive in Fr. *plume*, NHG *Feder*, and many other languages.

OE *línen* 'flaxen' (the adjective from *lín* 'flax', formed like *golden* and *oaken*) > NE *linen* 'bedsheets' and 'tablecloths and napkins'; formerly also 'burial shroud'.

Cane 'stout plant of the grass family' > 'walking stick' (now rather rarely made of literal cane).

Glass 'fused silica' > 'a vessel for drinking', 'a barometer' (on the obsolete side), and in British English also 'mirror'. In the plural, and (if rarely) more fully *eyeglasses*, 'spectacles'.

The *glass* example demonstrates that metonymies may be commonplace among languages without being anything like universal:

Fr. *verre* 'glass' means 'vessel for drinking' and also 'lens', but NOT 'mirror' or 'barometer';

It. *vetro* 'glass' means 'barometer' and 'window', but NOT 'drinking vessel' or 'mirror';

NHG *Glas* means only 'drinking vessel' in addition to the substance;

Swedish *glas* 'drinking vessel' and 'window'; but also 'chimney' (of a lamp), as well as the substance;

Hu. *üveg* 'glass' means only 'bottle' in addition to the substance.

One might predict that material-for-product metonymies would continually lead to a bothersome sense of incongruity when, say, speaking of an *aluminum cane* or *silk linens*. But for whatever reason, these metonymies seem to 'fade' (if not indeed 'die')—as the metaphors have it—very quickly.

Very much less common is a transfer from **object to material**, as in the evolution of Sp. *plata* 'silver'. This reflects LLat. *plat(e)a* (probably a borrowing from Greek) 'any flat thing' > 'a flat piece of metal' and often specifically 'bowls, cups, dishes and the like fashioned of silver'.[1]

82. Transfer from objective to subjective

and vice versa. That is, terms originally characterizing objects come to characterize a mental or emotional state, and vice versa.

NE *pitiful* originally meant, as its morphology would seemingly require, 'full of pity' (subjective); but now it is used exclusively of objects, 'exciting pity' or the like.

Lat. *ēlegāns* originally meant, of persons, 'discriminating, choosy' but then of objects 'choice, outstanding'. Cf. NE *choice* (noun) 'a selection' or 'the act of selecting' (subjective) but as an adjective 'particularly desirable, outstanding' (objective).

The original meaning of NE *difficult* was 'hard to do'; now it also means, of people, 'hard to please'.

The process can be zigzag. NE *curious* once applied to a quality of objects; that is still so, but now the word applies also to a mental disposition. But the reverse metonymy happened earlier in the history of the word: Lat. *cūriōsus* 'diligent, attentive'—the word is related to *cūra* 'care, responsibility'—was originally purely subjective, but by Augustan

---

[1] This is one of the senses of *plate* in British English, and by yet another metonymy, with the rise of the manufacture of such items out of a sort of metal sandwich consisting of a copper or brass core surrounded by silver—often specifically *Sheffield plate,* from the place of its early development—the term *silver plate* comes to mean such items specifically, that is in contrast to solid (sterling) silver; and then, by metaphor this time, to any thin layer of any metal on metal, even one which is deposited electrically or chemically and is only a few atoms thick.

prose also of objects 'requiring care' (and later, 'receiving care' as in *curiously fashioned*).

Sometimes the meanings of different words evolve in tandem. Until the early 19th century the terms *contemptible* and *contemptuous* were synonyms: both of them referred either to the object of contempt or to the contemner. The problems with this state of affairs were resolved when *contemptible* lost its subjective meaning and *contemptuous* lost its objective one. (Like most semantic change, this process was both gradual and spontaneous, and not in response to the dictates of usage authorities, dictionaries, and the like.)

83. Adjacency, similarity of condition, or functional connection

NE *hand* of cards (cf. the previously cited *hand* 'assistant, worker' (76), a metonymy too but of a fundamentally different kind).

OE *dǽl* 'part, portion' > NE *deal* 'business transaction' (the original meaning still in *a good deal* 'a lot' and even in *deal* (of cards)).

NE *board* and *panel* both are metonyms for a committee; *board* (in a metonymy based on an earlier, now obsolete, figurative sense, 'table' —it is not clear whether it is a metaphor or a metonymy) > 'meal', as in *room and board* and *boarding house* 'a rooming house with meals provided' (though it is probable that most Americans think that *boarding* has something to do with being put up for the night).

NE *meal* < OE *mǽl* '(appointed/regular) time'.

NE *coffee* 'an informal daytime get-together with light refreshments' (and of course the similar metonym of *tea*).

84. Temporal creep

Words meaning 'immediately' regularly come to mean 'soon' and then 'by and by'. In fact, NE *soon* and *by and by* are themselves examples of this very thing, as is the obsolescent *anon* (formerly 'at once'). In light of this, consider the discrepancy between American (and Scottish) *presently* 'at present, right now' and British 'after a short while'. This might represent conservatism on the part of American and Scots English (the usual view); or else it might be the fresh creation of a new derivative from *present*. The one thing it cannot plausibly be is a retrograde change of meaning from 'soon' to 'right now'.

A species of converse is seen in the English phrase *the other day*, originally 'the day before yesterday' (59a), but now referring to an indefinite, very often rather remote, past.

We now know, thanks to evidence from Hittite, that there was an Indo-European root *nek^W- 'grow dim', which was the basis for the noun *nok^Wt- 'dusk'. But the reflexes of the latter in the familiar Indo-European languages—Lat. *nox,* Gk *núx,* Skt *nakt-,* and many others—all mean 'night', not 'dusk'.

A *matinée* was originally something that happened in the morning, now it means an afternoon (as contrasted with an evening) theatrical performance.

This process is oft-repeated in the names of specific meals:

LLat. *disjējūniārium* 'breakfast' (lit. 'disfasting') is reflected in two different French words, *déjeuner* 'lunch' and *dîner* 'evening meal, dinner'. *Dîner* formerly, and still dialectally, meant 'lunch', and must have been borrowed into English at such a stage: the sense 'midday meal' for *dinner* is still very general in certain regions of the USA, and that meaning cannot be imagined to have evolved from the sense 'evening meal'.

A long semantic journey is traveled by LLat. *collātiō* 'study group', typically of monks, and typically an evening gathering. By metonymy, it came to mean 'a snack, a light repast', such as often accompanied such sessions. This is the source of NE *collation* 'light, informal meal', rarely used of breakfast, perhaps because breakfast is by nature light and informal, though otherwise *collation* is time-neutral. In Italian we find *colazione,* formerly (and still dialectally) 'breakfast', but now more commonly 'lunch', while *prima colazione,* like Fr. *petit déjeuner* verbatim 'little lunch', is still 'breakfast'. In a sense, *collātiō* has traveled through the night to arrive at daybreak, since that is the only way a term for an evening meal could show up in the morning.

The only case of retrograde motion of a time-expression known to me is NE *noon.* Since it is etymologically *nōna (hōra)* 'ninth (hour)', that is ca. 3 PM, it has retreated some hours to become the term for 'midday'.

CHANGES RESULTING FROM CHANGES IN THE
STRUCTURE OF THE LANGUAGE,
REINTERPRETATION OF AMBIGUITIES,
AND CHANGES IN THE PHYSICAL OR SOCIAL
ENVIRONMENT

85. Changes in the structure of a language

Morphological categories can be *reindexed,* that is, marked by new or additional formal features, as a result of changes (elsewhere) in the language structure itself. The changes may be phonological, and more or less intrinsically unrelated to the affected features, but may be morphological or syntactic.

In NE *ox, oxen* (one of the few survivors of an important Old English noun-class) the element *-en* was originally the stem-marker, and essentially functionless; the actual endings that marked different cases fell off prehistorically by the action of regular sound laws. As a result, in Old English the formal difference between the singular and the plural was the absence vs presence of the old STEM, which by default assumed the function of number-marker. The same history accounts for the German noun type *Kalb* 'calf' *Kälber* pl., *Buch* 'book' *Bücher* pl.

In the most extreme case, the affixal material is gone altogether and all that is left is some change originally conditioned by the affix. In Old English many nouns had word-final (voiceless) fricatives, whereas derived verbs had endings and therefore the root final fricatives were intervocalic and voiced; and in addition, the syllable shapes of the verbs triggered vowel lengthenings in Middle English. Taken together, these factors result in NE *breath* vs *breathe, house* /haws/ n. vs *house* /hawz/ vb., *half* vs *halve, glass* vs *glaze.* But of course the actual affixes of the derived verbs are nowhere to be seen, now, only the phonological effects triggered by them when they existed.

A similar (earlier) phenomenon explains plurals like *mouse, mice.*

The French negatives are examples of this process, but the arena is morphosyntactic rather than morphological: in the sort of Late Latin underlying French there occurred emphatic expressions like *nōn ... passum* 'not a step', *nōn ... persōna* 'not a person' *nōn ... rem* 'not a thing' > Fr. *ne ... pas, ne ... personne, ne ... rien.* In early French, *ne* (the

negative marker per se) dropped in some contexts for purely phonological reasons; the pendant words, originally reinforcing, became—
and remain—negative themselves: *pas du tout* 'not at all', *personne ici*
'there's no one here', *rien de plus beau* 'nothing finer', *rien au monde*
'nothing in the world', and so on. There is a second souvenir of the
period when *ne* was lost: in sentential negation, even though *ne* was
subsequently restored, the once-optional pendants are now obligatory
in the syntax of French negative sentences.

Phonetic changes at word-boundaries made for far-reaching changes in Old Irish morphosyntax. The Proto-Celtic forms **osyo* 'of him',
*osyās 'of her', and **oysom* 'of them' all give Old Irish *a*; but thanks to
the word-boundary changes, many actual phrases were not homophonous: to *teng(a)e* 'tongue' would be found *a theng(a)e* /aθ'eŋge/ 'his
tongue', *a teng(a)e* 'her tongue', and *a deng(a)e* /ad'eŋge/ 'their tongue'.

English forms of the type *thou art* and *I ask thee* and *thine enemy*
were from an early time explicitly INTIMATE, in contrast to the formal/
deferential ('polite' is the usual misnomer) *ye/you/your*, historically the
plural of *thou*. In Christian usage, in Early Modern English just as in
all modern European languages, the deity and Satan are addressed intimately. The disappearance of the inherited second person singular
forms from modern English, together with their mummification in
religious texts (preeminently old translations of the Bible), has resulted
in a total semantic reversal: *thee/thou/thine* are now explicitly marked,
not as archaic (which is the case), but as high register RELIGIOUS/SOL-
EMN. To some modern ears, prayers addressing God or Jesus or Mary
as *you* are shocking. In the sixteenth century, by contrast, testimony
like 'And then he did *thou* me most vilely...' occur in court records as
an extenuating circumstance for starting a brawl. Note that this sancti-
fication of *thou* etc. did not affect all archaic forms in holy texts: *durst,*
spake, wroth and so on are simply quaint. (Other forms, such as *meat*
'food' and *nations* 'non-Jews', are simply misunderstood.)

86. Reinterpretation in specific contexts

Abrupt semantic changes are possible in specific phrases. These are not
necessarily pivots about an ambiguity: abrupt resemanticizing often
results from a paucity of contexts, such that there is little to shepherd
the hearer's interpretation of a word's function.

In Early Modern English the Italian word *firma* 'signature' was borrowed into commercial vocabulary as *firm* n. in the same sense. By a trifling metonymy it came also to be used to mean 'title, style'. In this sense it was applied to the official or public style of joint enterprises, as referring to a legal establishment as *the firm [of] Honeycutt & Finch*. From such uses the meaning of the term *firm* changed from denoting the name of the enterprise to denoting the enterprise itself, and this is its only present-day sense. This use seems to have started with law firms, and is still conspicuous in that connection; but it has spread to every branch of organized business activity and is now virtually a synonym of *company*.

The English verb *like* originally meant 'suit, conform, seem suitable to', and functioned the way German *gefällt* and French *plaît* do now, i.e. *Das gefällt mir, cela me plaît* 'I like that', verbatim 'that pleases me'. The switch in thematic roles in English seems to have started in subjunctive phrases of the type *Do as like you best,* where *like you* meant 'may agree with you'. The mediating factors were the ambiguity of the second person plural pronoun coupled with an ending system in verbs reduced to the absolute minimum (one single form—third person singular present indicative).

Stereotyped phrases are the limiting case of contextual poverty, and naturally they are liable to reinterpretation. The phrase *carrot and stick* originally was nothing more than a compendious description of (or allusion to) an apparatus consisting of a carrot tied to the end of a stick, which a wagoner dangles in front of a stubborn draft animal to entice it, Tantalus-wise, to move forward. It was therefore a kind of metonymy for getting your way non-violently by means of enticement (with perhaps a whiff of sharp practice). The phrase has been generally reinterpreted, however, as a pair of metonymies: *carrot* = 'inducement' and *stick* = 'threat (of beating or the like)'. That is, the collocation is now understood to mean something like 'getting your way by a judicious combination of inducement and coercion'.

a. A good many saws, literary allusions, and the like, have undergone an abrupt change in meaning as a result of contextual poverty.

The Dutch phrase *verloren hoop* 'storming party; suicide squad' (lit. 'lost troop') was perhaps inevitably remodeled in English as *forlorn hope,* and the sense of the expression has changed accordingly.

The expression *(give someone) free rein* is a term connected with the management of horses, a matter that was once familiar to everyone. The disappearance of horses for transport has allowed the expression to be relexicalized as *give free reign*.

The devil to pay, which is now normally construed to be an allusion to some Faustian bargain (or lesser imprudence of a similar nature), was originally a nautical expression involving the verb *pay* (from Lat. *picāre*) 'to caulk or otherwise make waterproof with pitch' and *devil* 'seam in a ship's hull at or below the waterline' (the thrust of the saying originally pertained to helplessness in the face of emergency: the full expression was, *There will be the devil to pay, and no pitch hot*).

Compounds can undergo a process similar to phrases, as when *harebrained* is reappraised as *hairbrained*.

Under cause/effect metonymies, above (80), the original meaning of the expression *The exception proves the rule* was discussed.

87. Clipping

Semantic change can result from *clipping*, that is, shortening a phrase or compound such that the remaining portion has the meaning of the whole expression. This is presumably a conscious process, unlike the more or less accidental consequences of phonological changes as discussed in 85.

Lat. *via strāta* 'paved road' was the usual term for what we call Roman Roads; by clipping, *strāta* ('paved') was used to mean 'paved road', whence It. *strada* and (by borrowing) NE *street*, NHG *Straße*.

Lat. *sōl oriēns* 'rising sun', also (by metonymy) 'east' > *oriēns, -entis* (verbatim 'rising') > *orient(al)*. This is also the source, via semantic widening, of the verb *to orient* 'to site, situate, point in the right direction' (not necessarily east).

Skt *ekonaviṃśati* 'nineteen' comes apart morphologically as *eka-ūna-viṃśati*, verbatim 'one-lacking twenty'. But this commonly was clipped to *ūnaviṃśati*, verbatim 'lacking-twenty', which on its face makes no sense.

NE *China-ware* 'porcelain' > *china*.

NE *piano* for *pianoforte* lit. 'soft [and] loud' (Italian).

NE *remote* for *remote-controle(r)*; *air* for *air conditioning*.

Note that much clipping entails a functional shift at the grammatical level, namely an attribute (*oriēns, China*) becomes a noun head; but this is not invariable, as was seeen in the *piano* example, and Fr. *chef de cuisine* 'head of the kitchen' > *chef* 'cook' verbatim 'head'.

Some clipping is limited to compounded forms: *petrochemical* is in effect a clipping of expected *petroleum chemical,* likewise *petrodollar.* As in the case of *shrimp-kabob* (p. 84), the wrong part of the underlying form is preserved (*petrochemical* looks as though it should mean 'chemical(s) from stone').

a. Clipping of a phrase is sometimes called *elision,* literally 'a leaving-out' (a term also applied to syntactic features like *Alice will sing but Bill won't* and *Alice was drinking coffee and Bill, tea.*) Fundamentally different but sometimes treated as clipping is *truncation,* as in *lab* for *laboratory, trank* for *tranquilizer, bod* for *body.* This is creating new lexical items out of fragments which contributed nothing to the meaning of the whole in the first place. Most such truncations are jargony, but some, like *lab, auto,* and *plane* 'aircraft' are all but standard, and *zoo* and *(cotton) gin* (< *engine*) are thoroughly so.

88. Changes in physical or cultural environment

Lat. *volūmen* 'roll' also meant by metonymy 'a book'—the leaves of long written works were glued together horizontally and rolled up. The figurative meaning lives on in NE *volume* even though now the word is never applied to a scroll.

Lat. *libra* 'pound' (clipped, 87, from 'pound of silver'—a very large denomination of money indeed)—is the etymon of It. *lira,* the standard unit of account, now worth a small fraction of a cent in exchange. The word *libra* was not borrowed into English as such, but like the standard appreviation for 'penny', *d.* < *denarius,* it was indexed (and stylized) in British English usage as the symbol £ 'pound (sterling)'.

PItal. **lowkos* 'clearing' (PIE **lewk-* 'be bright') > Lat. *lūcus* 'grove'. Now, Lat. *lūcus* figures in a stock example of an explanation that utterly fails to explain: *lūcus ā nōn lūcendō* '[it is called] *lūcus* ('the shiner' or so) from the fact that it doesn't shine'. But, remarkably, the connection between *lūcus* and *lūcēre* 'shine' is etymologically correct—not of course for the (non-)reason given. In heavily forested areas, such as once were common in Italy, there are natural clearings, which still mystify scientists and in ancient times were regarded with awe; and more specifically they were commonly thought to be the abode of forest spirits. With deforestation, woodsmen would steer clear of these spots (and the shrines that were in them), with the consequence that what started out as a clearing in a forest turned into an isolated stand of trees. The term remained unchanged through the process, but what made a *lūcus* a *lūcus*—in other words, its meaning—necessarily changed radically with the change in physical circumstances.

    a. *Lūcus ā nōn lūcendō* is the type-specimen of a Greek and Roman etymological strategy of last resort. Classical etymologists assumed that words of similar form were etymologically related; since they often were (a fact hinted at by their similar semantics), mere guessing usually accords tolerably well with what we now know to be historical fact. But there were stumpers, like the similarity between *lūcus* and *lūcēre*, or the similarity between *bellum* 'war' and *bellus* 'handsome'. In the absence of any better rationale, then, the argument was made that the functional connection was negative—either simply lacking (as in the case of *lūcus*, where surely a failure to glow can hardly have been seen as one of the defining criteria of a grove) or based on (ironical?) opposite meanings: war is designated *bellum* because it's the opposite of 'lovely', *pāvō* 'peacock' from *pavēre* 'to be timid' because peacocks are anything but.

CALQUES

89. A *calque* (French 'a copy, a tracing') is an abrupt semantic change due to borrowing: a word acquires a new meaning by importing it from another language. This process is also called *loan-translation*. Calquing is usually more or less incidental, but in the history of some languages there have been occasional episodes of *systematic calquing*, whereby a large 'native' lexicon is created in the image of a source lexicon. This has happened in the history of German, Czech, and Hungarian, among others. This kind of conscious program often has the overt aim of preserving linguistic purity (a purely mythological concept in any case), or at a minimum nurturing a sense of cultural independence. The irony, of course, is that the lexicons of such languages are parasitic on Latin and Greek (or English) lexicons after all: translation rather than direct borrowing does not cancel the cultural subservience.[1]

---

[1] For new terms in commerce and science, the government of Indonesia generally supports the idea of creating 'native' forms (often by calquing) in preference to borrowing the terms themselves. The body entrusted with guarding the purity of Indonesian is called *Dewan Bahasa dan Pustaka* 'Council on Language and Literature'. The only native (Austronesian) word in this title is *dan;* the other three are borrowings from Indo-European languages, viz. Indic and Iranian.

A program of systematic calquing may be limited only to certain semantic fields, as in the extensive calquing of Greek in the Latin grammatical terminology, and Cicero congratulates himself for creating Lat. *quālitās* and *quantitās* on Greek models. But otherwise for the most part Romans had few qualms about simply borrowing Greek words.

90. Monomorphemic calques

Gk *ptôsis* meant literally 'a fall(ing)' (cf. the verb *é-pet-on* 'I fell'). It was also used—apparently metaphorically, though the metaphor is an unobvious one—to mean '(grammatical) case'. When Roman grammarians applied Greek models of description to the structure of Latin, they did not borrow any of the Greek terms, only the Greek polysemy. That is, they used the Latin word for 'a falling'—*cāsus*—to mean 'grammatical case' as well. Note that this is not a parallel and independent metaphor in Latin: the meaning 'grammatical case' was grafted on to the existing meaning(s) of *cāsus* in conscious imitation of the Greek lexicon. (The same semantic borrowing took place hundreds of years later in German, whereby *Fall* orig. 'a fall(ing)' also was used to mean 'grammatical case'.)

Another Greco-Roman example: Gk *kósmos* has the general sense of 'order, arrangement' (hence the denominative verb *kosmeîn* 'to arrange'), but among the special meanings which evolved from this basic sense were both 'world, physical universe' and 'ornament(ation), facial makeup' (whence the curiously divergent semantics of the English loans *cosmic* and *cosmetic* mentioned in 57). In imitation of this polysemy, and with the help of the adjective *mundus* 'clean, elegant', the Romans took to using the Latin word *mundus* 'world, universe' to mean also 'facial makeup, ladies' toilette'. Here even the possibility of a parallel or independent metaphor is out of the question, as the polysemy in Greek is the result of two separate metonymies on a third (original) meaning, and cannot be connected with one another directly; there are no such figurative underpinnings for the Latin polysemy, as *mundus* meant ab origine simply 'world'.

Since Lat. *nāvis* 'ship' also meant 'nave (of a church)' (and thereby hangs a tale; see 92 below) the meaning 'nave' was grafted onto the German word *Schiff* 'ship'. The same calque shows up in Hungarian *(templom) hajója* '(church) ship', that is, 'nave'. (Formerly, a model ship more or less ornately fashioned, often from precious materials, was a standard decoration of churches in some European countries, presumably the result of some species of word magic.)

91. Calquing compounds

Many treatments of calquing imply or even state explicitly that calquing entails translating a morphologically complex foreign word 'component by component'. This is obviously not true, given the phenomena just discussed, but probably the majority of loan-translations do indeed translate a morphological complex piece by piece; and the bulk of the 'systematic' calquing of Latin and Greek models in the lexicons of several European languages are of this sort:

Lat. *ac-cidēns* lit. 'at-falling' is the pattern for NHG *Zu-fall* 'accident'.

Lat. *ex-pressiō* lit. 'out-squeezing' begets NHG *Aus-druck* 'expression' (*aus* 'out', *drücken* 'press, squeeze').

Lat. *ex-positiō* lit. 'out-putting', NHG *Aus-stellung* 'exposition'.

Lat. *in-dē-pendēns* 'not hanging from', NHG *un-ab-hängig* 'independent' (*hängen* 'to hang').

Fr. *weekend* is common despite efforts of French purists to promote the calque *fin-de-semaine*.

Even portmanteau forms (52) can be calqued: Indonesian *asbut* 'smog' is composed of *asap* 'smoke' and *kabut* 'fog', apparently on the model of NE *smog*.

a. Note that a morpheme-by-morpheme calque, unlike a one-word calque, usually does not entail any change in meaning; rather, what is involved is coining a new word on a foreign model. It actually has more in common with calquing phrases or sentences of the sort seen in NE *it goes without saying*, a calque of Fr. *il va sans dire*, which has been in English for only about a hundred years, or NE *with a grain of salt* from Lat. *cum grānō salis*. Note that such examples as German calques on the French *en tout cas* 'in any case' and *en ce cas* 'in that case' (*auf alle Fälle* and *in diesem Fall*) presuppose the prior translation of Lat. *cāsus* as NHG *Fall*.

b. There are also what might be called calques at one remove: the German word for 'letter' (of the alphabet) is *Buchstabe*. But 'literal(ly)' in German is *buchstäblich*, even though *Buchstabe* itself is neither a calque on nor a borrowing of Lat. *lītera/littera*.

92. Loan-mistranslations

A loan-translation is not always slavishly literal: NE *sky-scraper,* closely traced in Fr. *gratte-ciel,* is calqued in German as *Wolkenkratzer* literally 'cloud-scratcher'. Gk *hippopótamos* literally 'river horse' (itself probably a calque, since the order of the elements is backwards for Greek) is the source of Hungarian *víziló* verbatim 'water-horse', German *Nilpferd* verbatim 'Nile horse'.

The limiting case of a non-slavish translation, of course, is missing the target altogether—a loan-mistranslation as it were.

The polysemy of Lat. *nāvis* 'ship; nave' mentioned above (90), is the result of a botched calque from Greek: in Pre-Greek times the ingredients for the confusion were not particularly similar at all: **naw-s* nom. sg. (stem **nāw-*) 'boat' and **naswo-* 'temple, sanctum sanctorum, cella'. In the variety of Greek earliest familiar to Latin speakers, these still would have been generally different: *naus* nom. 'boat', *nā(w)es* nom. pl.; and *nā(w)os* nom. 'temple', *nā(w)oi* nom.pl. But the two Greek words were associated by the Romans (and by the Greeks themselves, it might be added), whence the mistaken use of Lat. *nāvis* 'ship' to mean 'temple' as well.

Gk *psilós* means 'smooth; free of underbrush or hair; plain; simple; lacking in substance'. Applied to the Greek phonemes /p t k/—the plain stops of Greek—the metaphor is exactly the same as the English phonetic term *plain,* the opposite of *aspirated.* Roman grammarians called the voiceless stops of Latin *tenuēs* 'the thin ones'—literally thin, that is: 'attenuated; very small in one or two dimensions; watery, insubstantial'. Plainly, an inappropriate alternative from among the various senses of *psilón* was hit upon. This is very odd, as grammarians, of all people, ought to have been able to keep such things straight. But there are a number of striking loan-mistranslations from the Greek in the Latin grammatical terminology.

THE ETYMOLOGICAL FALLACY

93. 'Living etymology'

In conclusion, it cannot be overemphasized that a word's etymology is not its meaning. And emphasis is truly called for, here: the *etymological fallacy* is immemorial, and shows no signs of exhaustion. We know the Greeks suffered from it, and it is enshrined in the very word *etymology,* from a Greek term that means 'the study of true [meaning]'. Greek thinkers believed that there could be a difference between the 'true meaning' of a word and its workaday use. The Brāhmaṇas and Upaniṣads provide copious evidence for a similar belief on the part of ancient Vedic scholars. In our own day the etymological fallacy is widely honored, as revealed in countless statements by columnists, in letters to editors, and other public fora, which declare for example that the real meaning of *doctor* is 'teacher'; or that the verb *orient* properly means 'to arrange something to face east'; or that *gyp* 'cheat' is derived from *Gypsy* (probably), and therefore its use in any context is de facto an ethnic slur; or that *decimate* correctly means only 'to punish a mutiny or other serious breach of military discipline by killing one soldier in ten'.[1]

The etymological fallacy appears from time to time in puristic prescriptions, too, as when we are warned by usage authorities that because the real meaning of the verb *grow* is 'get bigger', expressions like *grow weaker* or *grow smaller* are incoherent; or that it is impossible to *climb down;* or that only stone structures can be *dilapidated.*

Of course, if there were anything at all to the notion that some previous meaning of a word is its 'real meaning', it would be very hard to utter a single sentence that wasn't semantically peculiar, and most utterances, no matter how humdrum and straightforward they seemed, would have to be judged incoherent from top to bottom.

It doesn't stop there: a rigorous adherence to the etymological fallacy would necessarily mean that any given word could have one and only one meaning—and, given the incessant change of meaning in a lexicon, in a very large number of cases that 'one meaning' would turn out not to be the meaning proclaimed by the purist in the toils of the etymological fallacy. For example, the real meaning of *dilapidated* would have to be 'squandered', NOT 'of a structure (stone or other-

---

[1] The sense 'to subject to severe loss, slaughter, or mortality', at present the usual meaning of the word, is attested from the 17th century and was well established in the 19th. The so-called correct sense is very rare, being necessarily limited to discussions of Roman antiquity. The word is MENTIONED many dozens of times (for the purpose of proclaiming its true meaning) for every time it is so used.

wise), run down, ruined', since its source is a Latin verb *dīlapidāre* 'dissipate, squander'. For another example, the ORIGINAL meaning of Lat. *decimātiō*—the word on which *decimate* is based—was actually something like 'a tithe, i.e. a tax in the amount of one tenth', and in fact *decimate* is early attested (1656) in English with the meaning 'to levy a tithe'. One doubts that those who take arms against using *decimate* to mean 'to subject to severe loss, slaughter, or mortality' would welcome the news that even the meaning 'execute one soldier in ten' is also wrong, on the grounds that the real meaning of the word—according to their own reasoning—is 'to levy a tithe'.

On the basis of observation, however, we see that even the most outspoken purists along such lines have no coherent ideology or program. They are, rather, preoccupied with pet peeves and a handful of stock examples which have somehow become a sort of canon. Few who pontificate about *decimate* and *orient* will also tell you that only popes can pontificate, or that *revise* can only be used to mean 'look at again', or that *inflate* means 'blow into' and only that, or that *class* means 'fleet (of ships)', or *plant* must mean 'a cutting, a graft', or that *anthology* can mean only 'a bouquet of flowers', or that *December* actually means 'October', and so on ad infinitum.

Not only will they not tell you these things, they will probably be indignantly unreceptive to such assertions. And that, ironically, is the right attitude: the real error lies in fallacious assertions about a handful of forms like *decimate*.

SUGGESTIONS FOR FURTHER READING

Semantic change is not treated very extensively in most general discussions of diachronic linguistics, or is the subject of many monographs. **Anttila 1988** chapter 7 and **Hock 1991** chapter 12 are excellent general discussions. **Hock and Joseph 1996** chapter 7 treats the question under the wider heading of changes in lexicon, which for that reason is of special interest. A similar approach, different in detail, is taken in **Campbell 1999's** chapter 10. **Stern 1931** is a book-length treatment.

Also at the interface of lexicon and semantics is **Haugen 1950**, a foundational work which effectively defined for the ages the types and kinds of lexical borrowing (including calquing). The only work known to me that attempts to apply Haugen's analysis rigorously, indeed monumentally, is **Teschner 1972**.

The discussion of semantic change in **Williams 1976** is unusually fruitful in large part because the problem can be clearly stated (and is an interesting one besides).

Countless passages in the Merriam-Webster *Usage Dictionary* are concerned with semantic history and the proper significance of it, and contain much else of interest to students of language change. (For other reasons as well the book is one of the more interesting dictionaries to read.)

RECONSTRUCTION

94. Similarities between languages

When looking at the features of any two languages, similarities between them will be apparent. Some of these mean only that all languages are similar by virtue of being human languages—all known languages have phonologies made up of a mixture of resonant and obstruent sounds, for example, and all have more than one 'part of speech'. Some similarities, e.g. NE *fire* and Fr. *feu* 'fire', have no significance whatever (see **95a** & **b**, below).

Two other kinds of similarities result from languages having a historical relationship to one another. First, there are the results of *borrowing*, that is, when one language takes over (or 'copies') a feature of another language. As a consequence of such a taking-over, the two languages will resemble one another more than they did before the borrowing took place; and when borrowing is extensive, one may think of the progressive increase in similarity between the two languages as *convergence*. (Such convergence may also result when two languages borrow from a third, as for example the extensive borrowing of Arabic words into Swahili and Indonesian, or of English words into many different languages.)

The second kind of historically-significant similarity between two languages is a PATTERN of similarities and differences which is so detailed and interpenetrating that the only thinkable explanation is that both languages are changed forms of what was once a single language. The traditional way of putting this is that the two languages are 're-lated' and belong to the same 'language family'.

These are biological metaphors, and not very apt ones. When we say that languages belong to a 'language family', what we really mean is simply this: they used to be the same language.

95. Proof of relatedness

More specifically, we say that two languages are related—used to be the same language—if they exhibit *recurring correspondences* in *basic vocabulary*.

These three concepts merit separate discussions:

RECURRENCE

The requirement that correspondences RECUR eliminates (or anyhow greatly reduces) the possibility that the similarities are nothing but ahistorical accidents, as discussed in notes **a** & **b**, below.

CORRESPONDENCES

Correspondences include not only identities and similarities—though naturally that sort of correspondence is the easiest to spot—but also any regular alignment.

The following is an example of a correspondence with a high degree of similarity. Specifically, all three languages have correspondences between voiceless bilabial stops, i.e. /p/, but in addition, the general level of formal (and functional) similarity is high throughout the list of words:

Latin	Greek	Vedic		PIE
pro	pró	prá	'forth'	*pro(H)
pater	patḗr	pitár-	'father'	*pH̥tér-
septem	heptá	saptá	'seven'	*septm̥

In the following example the alignments show less similarity, but (to the practiced eye, at least) quite a lot of similarity nevertheless:

Gothic /h/	Greek /k/	Vedic /ś/		PIE
taihun	déka	dáśa	'ten'	*déḱm̥t
weihs	oîkos	viś-	'village; clan'	*weᵒyḱ-/*wiḱ-
ga-teihan	deíknūmi	diś-	'point out'	*deyḱ-/*diḱ-

The limiting case—an example of a correspondence in which similarity plays no role whatever—would be a case where a language has systematically lost a sound, as is seen in the following table showing reflexes of PIE *p. Here we see the effects of the loss of PIE *p in Celtic, and the phonetic similarity between [p] and no sound is necessarily zero. Some correspondences involving very little actual phonetic similarity are commonplace in diachronic linguistics, however, so much so that

Old Irish	Other IE Languages		PIE
ath(a)ir /aθəрʸ/	Lat. pater	'father'	*pḤter-
ro	Lat. pro	'forth'	*pro(H)
il	Ved. purú-	'many'	*pḷHu-
	Go. filu-		
nieth *gen.sg.*	Skt. napātas	'nephew'	*nepotos
(= Prim.Ir. NIATTA)			

to experienced linguists they seem obvious, even banal. For example, [r] = [s], [č] = [k], [s] = [h], [d] = [y], and [w] = [g]. Others are more unusual, even peculiar, such as *y > t /p__ in Greek (that is: *y becomes t immediately after p, as for example *klepyō 'steal' > Gk kléptō) or the celebrated if recently contested Armenian development of PIE *dw > erk as in *dwō 'two' > Armenian erku.

BASIC VOCABULARY

Basic vocabulary is a notion easier to name than to define. What is at stake is that certain lexical items in language, experience shows, are likely to be replaced only at wide intervals, whether by forms borrowed from other languages or by a different word from within the same lexicon. Put differently, these are the words which show the highest level of LEXICAL CONTINUITY through time. Thus it is among these words that we are likeliest to find forms retained from earlier historical periods.

But obviously this definition is circular, and in fact it is practically necessary to define by example. Tenacious lexical continuity is likeliest in terms for (public) body parts, low numbers, certain colors (red, yellow, black), some basic physical notions like 'light' and 'heavy', 'long' and 'short'. Even the safest-seeming generalizations are risky, however. Numerals have been highly tenacious in the Indo-European languages, but in other language groups numbers have been borrowed readily, and for some reason the number 'one' is lexically unstable compared to other units (whereas 'two', by contrast, is preternaturally tenacious). For body parts, due allowance has to be made for tabuistic replacements and a certain functional plasticity overall (historically, NE *chin* aligns with Lat. *gena* 'cheek' for example, and NE *bone* aligns with NHG *Bein* 'leg'. This kind of semantic near miss is found throughout the lexicon, of course, but is characteristic of body parts). And finally, many unquestionably basic verbs are highly mutable lexically, so that notions like 'take', 'move', and 'turn' are less useful for historical linguistics than one might suppose.

Basic kinship terms like 'father' may be useful in the case of bulky, derived forms, such as the Indo-European words (Lat. *pater*, Gk *patḗr*, Ved. *pitár-*, Go. *fadar*, OIr. *ath(a)ir*), but the more customary shapes of a hypocoristic sort (*pa(pa)*, *tata*, *aba*, *atta*, and so on) are useless for proving relatedness.

a. CHANCE RESEMBLANCE. As alluded to in 94, there is another kind of similarity, one which has no historical significance: pure chance. Given that most meaning-bearing units of language are rather short, and that phonologies are generally made up of three dozen or so elements arranged in commonplace systems (one or more series of stops with three or four points of articulation, for example), it is inevitable that the inspection of the lexicons of any two languages will turn up items with both similar form and similar meaning which totally lack historical significance. Such *chance resemblances* are not freaks: they abound. Latin *maria* 'seas' and Kikuyu *maria* 'lakes', strikingly similar in form and meaning, are unrelated (in the sense defined above). Gk *hólos* and its English gloss *whole* have no historical connection, nor do Hindi *kaṭ-* [kəṭ] and the English word of the same meaning, *cut*, nor OIr. *glas(s)* 'green' and NE *glass*, nor Gk *theós* and Lat. *deus* both 'god'. A three-way accident of similarity is seen in Lat. *hodie*, NHG *heute*, and W *heddiw* all 'today' (though to be sure the 'day' elements in the Latin and Welsh are cognate). A remarkable coincidence in the morphology of verb person-markers is evident in a comparison of Miwok, a language of the Penutian family (California and Oregon), and Indo-European, here represented by Latin:

	Miwok	Latin
1 sg.	-m	-m
2 sg.	-š	-s
3 sg.	-ø	-t [1]
1 pl.	-maš	-mus
2 pl.	-toš	-tis
3 pl.	-p(u-)	-nt

b. Chance resemblances are frequent within lexicons, too. Words of similar

---

[1] Proto-Indo-European also had zero 3rd person singular forms, like Miwok.

form and meaning in a single lexicon usually do have some historical (or derivational) connection, of course; but that can't be taken for granted. A sampling from
English of the numberless cases of this sort of thing include *island* and *isle*, which
are unrelated historically (the *s* of native *island* is a bogus spelling—the first syllable
is actually cognate to Lat. *aqua*—whereas *isle* is a loan word from French, ultimately
Lat. *insula*); *miniature* has no connection with *minute, diminish, diminutive* and the
rest (see 59); *king* and *queen; hear* and *ear; ear* (of corn) and *ear* 'pinna' (68); *savory*
(the herb—a loan word from Lat. *satureia*) and *savory* 'tasty'; *cow* 'overawe, render
helpless from fear' and *coward; sorrow* and *sorry* (the former is cognate with NHG
Sorge 'care, anxiety', the latter with NHG *sehr* 'very' = NE *sore*, OE *sár*). NE *soil* in
the sense of 'earth' is unrelated to *soil* 'to dirty, to contaminate' (though the apparent polysemy may be responsible for the parallel semantics of NE *dirt*). *Compound* 'enclosure, enclave, village' is a Malay loan (somewhat roughed up by folk
etymology, 53), unrelated to *compound* 'mixture' from Latin. The English past tense
marker *-(e)d* and the past participle marker *-(e)d* have no historical connection, or
are very unlikely to have.

Similar arrays can be found in any language whose history is well enough understood to permit accurate sorting out of the facts, which is what allows us to say
with perfect confidence that Gk *goné* 'offspring' and *guné* 'woman' are unrelated,
the former being from a root *$\acute{g}enH_1$-* and the latter from PIE *$g^{w}enH_2$-*.

96. Proto-languages

In the event that the lexicons of two languages exhibit recurring correspondences in basic vocabulary, the hypothesis of choice is that the
two languages used to be one language. The test of this hypothesis is
the systematic *reconstruction* of the features of that language, called the
proto-language.

In principle, reconstruction is a down-to-earth matter: it amounts
to nothing more than imagining a language whose elements might
have turned into the attested languages by means of economical, plausible, and (above all) regular changes. Further, the normal properties
of human languages are a necessary guide: one is not reconstructing
isolated items but a system.

THE COMPARATIVE METHOD

97. More can be learned from doing reconstruction than from talking
about it.

Consider the list of words from two artificial languages, A and B,
on the following page. (Artificial data avoid the distractions and com-

	A			B	
1.	wapo	'hand'	lap		'hand'
2.	waka	'salt'	lak		'salt'
3.	lipu	'mouth'	lip		'face'
4.	woli	'beam'	lol		'roof'
5.	puku	'gravel'	puk		'spoke'
6.	like	'heavy'	lič		'morose'
7.	kewo	'red'	čel		'red'
8.	tika	'amulet'	tik		'magic'
9.	peli	'fish'	pel		'eel'
10.	kiwu	'early'	čil		'tomorrow'
11.	kuti	'tree'	kut		'wood'
12.	waki	'sister'	wač		'sister'
13.	weli	'sit'	wel		'rest'
14.	wapu	'push'	wap		'beat against'

plexities of natural languages, which get in the way of the basic principles without contributing anything.)

Even a cursory inspection of the forms will note many cases of similarities of meaning coupled with regular formal correspondences which, given the particular vocabulary, can reasonably be explained only by the theory that these two languages were once the same language (and not so very long ago, at that).

The semantics all either match outright or, with one important exception, are easily connectable: (3) 'mouth' is a commonplace metonymy (76) for 'face'; the metaphorical relationships between (6) 'heavy' and 'morose', and between (13) 'sit' and 'rest', are transparent; the 'wood/tree' polysemy (11) is commonplace (in many languages, both meanings are found in one word, as in Finnish *puu*); (9) 'fish' and 'eel' are easy to relate semantically, as are (14) 'push' and 'beat against', (8) 'amulet' and 'magic', and 'morning, early, tomorrow' (10). The semantics of the pair (4) 'beam' and 'roof' seem to be nothing remarkable, but with more thought (or more experience) they may turn out to be a little difficult to connect, as discussed below (102a & b).

In the last five items mentioned, it is not obvious what the meaning of the reconstructed form should be; but the general semantic field is evident at least. This is emphatically NOT the case with (5) 'gravel' and 'spoke': as we will see, the forms permit unambiguous reconstruction of a proto-FORM, but there is no thinkable meaning (or field of meanings) which might evolve naturally into both 'gravel' and 'spoke' —it makes no difference whether the latter is the past tense of 'speak' or a component of a wheel.

a. GLOSSES. The ambiguity of the gloss 'spoke' is significant. The problems of reconstructing meanings—or even identifying possible cognates in the first place— are aggravated by the limited information provided by *glosses,* i.e. short (commonly one-word) translations. Glosses caricature the semantics (properly speaking) of natural languages. For example, in the present case, it would be typical enough for real knowledge of the languages to reveal that A *kuti* and B *kut* BOTH mean both 'tree' and 'wood'; and that B *lič* means 'morose' only in poetry, and otherwise means simply 'heavy'.

Glosses in certain languages, English and French for example, are especially liable to misinterpretation owing to the very large number of homographs in those languages (French *vers* 'verse; toward', *râpe* 'grater; stalk'), but the danger is present in most European languages: German *Reis* 'rice; brushwood', *Ton* 'clay; tone, music'; It. *populo* 'poplar; people', and so on.

The treachery of glosses is actually only one aspect of a truism: A RECONSTRUCTION CANNOT BE BETTER THAN THE DESCRIPTIONS ON WHICH IT IS BASED. If the available 'description' of a lexicon is limited to glossed word-lists, the reconstruction will have serious flaws directly traceable to that circumstance.

98. First step: start with the obvious

When reconstructing a proto-phonology (and the forms expressing it), the best procedure is to start with the obvious things. Put differently, we would not begin our reconstruction by puzzling over the pair (10) A *kiwu* / B *čil.* The reason for starting with the most straightforward facts is, partly, that their historical reconstruction is the most straightforward, of course; but more importantly, every reconstruction you make will guide your choices in how best to make sense out of the less obvious matters.

The most obvious gross difference in the two lists of words is that the forms in A all end with a vowel, those in B never do. The question then is whether the words of A have added a vowel, or those of B have lost one. If (and only if) it proves possible to write a RULE which stipulates which vowel 'grows' in A at the end of an originally vowelless form, can we reconstruct Proto-AB in the image of the forms reflected in B. Such a history is not impossible, though it is a priori very much more likely that B has lost proto-vowels which are still preserved in A, because languages very much more commonly lose elements by sound change than add them, and furthermore this phenomenon is especially likely to delete elements from the ends of words.

In any case, a careful study of the forms will reveal no pattern for the vowels occurring at the end of the A forms (and in fact we will find several kinds of evidence that support the hypothesis that word-final vowels were present in the proto-language). This means that we reconstruct Proto-AB words with final vowels as attested in A, and write a sound law to the effect that all such vowels are lost in B. Evidence for which particular vowel occurred in Proto-AB is somewhat slender as long as A provides the only information on that point; but as we shall see, B actually does confirm some of the information in A. And besides, there is always the possibility that additional languages belonging to the same family will be discovered which might shed more light on the matter, whether confirming our reconstruction or—equally likely, in fact—requiring its modification. (There is no point in worrying about the latter possibility: you can't analyze data you don't have.)

Turning to other correspondences, the most straightforward are the vowels of the first syllables: they match, and should simply be reconstructed as such; and wherever A has p or t, B has the same, so they too would be reconstructed as Proto-AB $*p$ and $*t$.

99. Reconstructing phonemic split

Things turn more interesting in the case of sets involving the sound k: here, there are two *partially similar* correspondences:

A	B	
k	k	e.g. tika : tik (8)
k	č	e.g. like : lič (6)

The simplest reconstruction strategy would be to posit two kinds of dorsal stop in the proto-language, one for each correspondence; say $*k$ and $*k_2$ (or, with greater phonetic specificity, $*k$ and $*\acute{k}$). The sound laws would state that $*k$ and $*k_2$ fall together (merge, 27) in A, but that $*k > B\ k$ while $*k_2 > B\ č$.

However, when one strings one's reconstructed phonemes together in reconstructed lexical items, one will notice that $*k_2$ always and only occurs before the vowels $*i$ and $*e$–the natural class of front vocalics (A15)–and $*k$ never occurs there: (11) $*kuti$ 'wood, tree', (8) $*tika$ 'magic' but (12) $*wak_2i$ 'sister', (6) $*lik_2e$ 'heavy'. As it it sometimes put, the CORRESPONDENCE SETS $k = k$ and $k = č$ are in complementary (mutually-exclusive) distribution, and the most economical reconstruction is not the merger of two phonemes $*k$ and $*k_2$ in A, but a SPLIT (28-9) of a single proto-phoneme in the history of B: Proto-AB $*k$ remains unchanged in A, and also in B before back vowels; but it becomes $č$ in B before original (Proto-AB) front vowels.

This reconstruction has two virtues. First, it's natural: the change of $*k$ to B $č$ in palatalizing environment is a diachronic commonplace; in fact, it's at the opposite pole of probability from the merger alternative, which would envision a change of $*[\underset{\circ}{k}]$ or $*[č]$ to k in Language A. Second (and more obviously), the fewer proto-phonemes the better. Of course, splits can be hypothesized if and ONLY if, as here, it is possible to state unambiguously the environments for each outcome, with reasonable excuses for what look like exceptions.

In addition to being both economical and natural, a split hypothesis has two interesting consequences in this situation.

First, we see here a case of *relative chronology* (31): the two sound laws $*k > č$ and the loss of final vowels in B will give different outcomes depending on what order they apply in. Proto-AB $*like$ would give B *lič* if the loss of final vowels in B happened after the patatalization of $*k$, and would give *lik* if the loss of final vowels predated the palatalization. Since *lič* is the form in B, it follows that the two sound laws in B must have occurred in the order: (first) palatalization (then) loss of final vowels.

Second, we have here a case of *secondary split* (29). When the palatalization effect seen in B first took place, the result was a small increase in the complexity of B's phonology, as now the element /k/ would have had two automatic variants, or allophones: [k] before any back vowel, [č] before any front vowel. With the loss of the word-final vowels there was no longer any exhaustively statable relationship between [k]/[č] and their environments, as shown by say *lak* 'salt' vs. *wač* 'sister'. In this way, what had been non-contrastive allophones became *phonologized*, that is, became two contrastive phonemes.

Note, too, that this hypothesis of secondary split means that Language B, as hinted above (98), actually provides evidence for our reconstructed word-final vowels hitherto based solely on evidence from A, thanks to the difference between *lak* and *wač*.

100. A case of primary split

The three remaining correspondence sets make up a partially-similar threesome:

A	B	
l	l	e.g. lipu : lip (3)
w	l	e.g. kiwu : čil (10)
w	w	e.g. waki : wač (12)

Here again the most elementary hypothesis would be one proto-phoneme for each correspondence set: starting with the straightforward cases, for *l* = *l* we reconstruct *$*l$, for *w* = *w* we reconstruct *$*w$. For *w* = *l* we might either add a second proto-lateral, *$*l_2$, or surmise some third phone type altogether, say *$*\gamma$. Whatever we reconstruct for the last, it merges with *$*l$ in B, and merges with *$*w$ in A.[1]

But here, as before, we note that two of the three correspondence sets, *w* = *l* and *l* = *l*, are in complementary distribution: the former occurs only when the following sound in Proto-AB is a back vowel (*$*u$, *$*o$, *$*a$), and so both correspondence sets can be reconstructed as *$*l$, which splits in A depending on the cavity features of the following vowel. But, unlike the case of the split of *$*k$ in B, above (99), this time one of the two split products merges with a phoneme already present in the phonology of A, namely /w/. That is, we end up with the same number of contrasts in the phonology that were present in Proto-AB. This is therefore a case of *primary split* in A (28). At all times in the history of A, then, /w/ and /l/ remained in contrastive distribution. While

---

[1] Two kinds of lateral are more likely than two kinds of *w*, since the development of a glide from a lateral is commonplace whereas labial glides rarely turn into laterals. A totally different phone in the present case would be just guessing, even if plausible phonetically, since one has so little evidence as to what its phonetic features might have been.

Proto-AB   A

it is true that /l/ is only found before front vowels in A, /w/ occurs before both front and back vowels, and there is no way of telling from A alone whether a given *wa*, say, reflects Proto-AB *la* or **wa*. (Of course, any example of *we*, say, must necessarily reflect **we*.)

101. Recovering lost contrasts

The possibility considered (and rejected) in 99-100—that the proto-language had more contrasts than are apparent in EITHER daughter—is sometimes the correct hypothesis in fact. One of the most interesting achievements of the comparative method is the possibility of recovering a contrast in the proto-language which is not independently attested in any daughter. For example, consider the following additional data from our two languages:

	A			B	
15.	kiwo	'hut'	čel	'house'
16.	piwa	'pearl'	pew	'pearl'
17.	lite	'cut'	let	'cut'
18.	tika	'kindling'	tek	'twig'

Here we see that in addition to the five previously-analyzed matching vowel correspondences, we have a sixth: *i* = *e*.

The first step is to see if we can combine this correspondence set with one of our five reconstructed vowels through a conditioned split in either A or B (or both). The most likely candidates are *i* = *i* and *e* = *e;* but all five should be examined. If the correspondence set cannot be shown to be a conditioned split—and in this example it cannot be—then it MUST be accounted for by reconstructing a sixth proto-vowel, which merges with reflexes of other vowels in both A and B.

In the interest of phonetic plausibility, this new vowel would be phonetically similar to both [i] and [e], and furthermore front enough to palatalize **k* in B (item 15). The two choices for the newly-emended proto-vowel system are shown in the following table; the 'new vowel' in each system is indicated with an arrow.

Reconstruction I		Reconstruction II	
i	u	i	u
→ ɪ		→ e	
	o		o
e		ε	
			a
	a		

These two alternatives differ in phonological plausibility: a system with two high front vowels and one mid front vowel—the chart on the left—is less likely, by far, than the system on the right with one high front vowel and two mid front vowels (a common so-called 'square' configuration in fact).

But if our new vowel in (15-8) is *e (that is, a vowel that might easily fall together with *i in one language and with a lower mid front vowel, *ε, in the other), that means rewriting the previously reconstructed *e as Proto-AB *ε.

a. A consequence of our now-refined reconstruction of the proto-phonology is that some of our reconstructed ETYMA, straightforward before, are now in doubt. The problem is this: A has the same five vowels in medial and final position, but we now know that the medial five reflect an original SIX-VOWEL system. Information regarding a six-vowel proto-system necessarily comes from a comparison of A and B; but for the FINAL vowel of *peli, *kuti, and *waki, B provides no information.

The best reconstruction of the final vowels can be decided only by evidence from some third source (another related language, or earlier stages of either A or B that shed light on this question), but pending fresh discoveries the alternatives— all plausible—are as follows.

(1) Proto-AB may have had a six-vowel contrast only in initial syllables in the first place. (Though if so, this would hint there was an earlier stage of the language, PRE-AB, in which all six vowels were found in all positions.)

(2) Proto-AB may have had six vowels in all syllables, and *i and *e merge in all syllables as /i/ in A;

(3) Six vowels as in (2), but the three front vowels fall together in A differently in different syllables, for which at least two scenarios can be imagined: in final syllables *ε and *e fall together as e; or *ε and *a fall together as a.

In the absence of additional information, option (2) is the most ECONOMICAL reconstruction. It is necessarily provisional: the most economical reconstruction is in fact very often the historically correct one, but it is by no means always so.

102. The proto-language

We are now ready to reconstruct our proto-lexicon:

1.	*lapo	'hand'		10.	*kilu	'early'
2.	*laka	'salt'		11.	*kuti, -e	'tree/wood'
3.	*lipu	'mouth'		12.	*waki, -e	'sister'
4.	*loli, -e	'beam? timber'? (see notes **a** and **b**)		13.	*wɛli, -e	'sit'
				14.	*wapu	'push?'
5.	(not cognate)			15.	*kelo	'dwelling' (see note **a**)
6.	*likɛ	'heavy'		16.	*pewa	'pearl'
7.	*kɛlo	'red'		17.	*letɛ	'cut'
8.	*tika	'magic'? (see note **a**)		18.	*teka	'twig? kindling?' (see note **a**)
9.	*pɛli, -e	'fish? eel?' see note **a**)				

a. A NOTE ON SEMANTIC RECONSTRUCTION. Semantic matches, like formal matches, are easy to reconstruct. So are the commonplace metaphors and metonymies ('heavy' > 'glum' is a commonplace development, but not the reverse; likewise 'mouth' > 'face' but not the reverse).

In principle, however, the correct prehistory of *semantic widening* and *narrowing* (61-3, especially 61a) cannot be reconstructed on the basis of only two glossed forms. That is, the etymon of 'fish/eel' might with equal plausibility have meant either thing. A trickier question is posed by alignments like (4) 'beam/roof', (14) 'push/ pound on', (15) 'hut/house', and (18) 'twig/kindling'. A time-honored but obviously jejune strategy is to distill the semantic common ground of the attested words, and reconstruct meanings like 'timber for the upper reaches of a structure', 'apply force to', 'dwelling', and 'small pieces of wood' to the reconstructed etyma.

'Dwelling' is thinkable, at least; but in most cases the common-ground strategy leads to a highly improbable lexicon. The chances are that (for example) Proto-AB (18) *teka meant something quite specific and concrete—whether 'kindling' or 'twig' or some third thing is impossible to say—and that (4) *loli, -e meant something either much less or much more specific than 'wood used in the construction of the upper reaches of a structure' (assuming the pair is cognate at all—a question visited in **b**, below). Presumably the urge to put a gloss on all etyma is what accounts for the plethora of reconstructed forms in our etymological dictionaries with distilled meanings like 'set in motion', 'make a dull sound', 'shine', and 'move rapidly'. No natural language needs, or has, a dozen words meaning 'move rapidly'.

b. To return to the problem in item (4), it is worth remembering that the A form could reflect four different proto-shapes (*loli, -e, and *woli, -e) and B could reflect six different proto-shapes (*lolV$_{1-6}$).

Now that we know what the sound laws are, given the slightly troublesome nature of the semantic alignment in this pair, this is a case where it might be fruitful to troll through the lexicons of both languages looking for better alignments. And the item *wowa* 'eaves' from the lexicon of A would be just such a better bet for cognate status with B *lol* 'roof'. It almost certainly would have been missed in our first pass through the two languages, owing to the lack of similarity between the forms; but now, combined with B *lol*, it would point to Proto-AB **lola* 'roof' (or the like). The original A form in the pair (4), *woli* 'beam', is for now left without a cognate in B.

103. Standards of acceptability

In principle, unless the form of a word or affix can be accounted for by its strict conformity to sound laws, or can be reasonably explained as a more or less defensible 'apparent exception' as discussed in 44-55, then the words cannot be held to reflect a common ancestor. It is this principle that allows us to declare with confidence that words like Lat. *deus* and Gk *theós*, or NE *whole* and Gk *hólos*, mentioned in 95a, are unconnected historically despite the high degree of similarity of both form and meaning.

In practice, however, this principle is more or less relaxed. How far one is justified in disregarding it is necessarily a subjective matter. Gk *híppos* 'horse' and Lat. *canis* 'dog' are widely, perhaps universally, believed to reflect the firmly-established PIE etyma **ékwos* and **ḱwon-/ *ḱun-*, respectively, even though in each case the exact developments are neither in accord with the sound laws nor easily rationalized as 'apparent exceptions'.

A more localized example is seen in the pan-Germanic words for 'head' (OE *héafod* and Go. *haubiþ* for example), which point to a PIE **kawpVt-* (*V* denotes a short vowel of uncertain phonetics). The similarity to Lat. *caput* 'head' is obvious, and many scholars hold that the words are connected, the discrepancy in the first syllable—**kawp-* vs. **kap-*—being explained as dissimilation (in Latin) or epenthesis (in Germanic). But the most scrupulous stance, methodologically, would be that the discrepancy in the first syllable is irreconcilable. Ad-hoc guesses do not change that fact, and so a theory of etymological connection is untenable.

Part of the problem here is lack of data: cognates in other Indo-European languages would increase the likelihood of figuring out what is going on here (either unrelated forms for sure, or else, if related, what the likely story is). But in the absence of such data, insisting that these words cannot be shown to be cognate is not mere pickiness. The too-casual assumption of exceptions to sound laws is a major threat to knowledge. Great progress has been made, and continues to be made, in the principled explanation of apparent irregularities; but no such progress is likely if oddities are incuriously taken for granted.

Another problem is that there are many cases where the exact history of a form is ambiguous. This is more often true of affixes than of words (owing to the shortness and functional ambiguity of affixes), but there are tolerably many of the latter: is Lat. *septimontēs* (a sort of nickname for Rome and its environs) the 'seven hills'—the traditional but numerically puzzling interpretation—or the 'fortified (*saeptia*) hills', with an unexpected development of -ae-? (Part of the problem is we do not know whether the first vowel of *septi-* is long or short here). Is Lat. *nox* adv. 'by night' a nominative or a genitive? Is Gk *mnáomai* 'woo' from *men-* 'think' or $*g^w neH_2$- 'woman'? (The latter would regularly give Gk *mnā-*). For Lat. *ēbrius* 'drunk', nine different reasonably plausible histories have long been on the books, and recently a tenth (and an especially plausible one) was suggested by a Hittite verb (*e-ku-i-e-ir* 'they drink' for example), root apparently /eg^{w-}/. This does mean taking *ēbrius* to be a borrowing from a P-dialect (115a), a bit of a complication but not by any means a fatal one.

RECONSTRUCTION OF FEATURES
OF MORPHOLOGY, SEMANTICS, AND SYNTAX

104. This book will not explore the reconstruction of the morphology (if the proto-language has any), semantics, and syntax of proto-languages. The the reconstruction of morphology, e.g. the markers of case, number, tense, person, and so on, is special only in being more difficult because of the nature of the data. The two chief problems are the shortness of the elements involved (often a single phoneme—if that) and the plasticity of their functions. As a result, a generally-accepted reconstruction of affixes—apart from the most obvious facts, of course—tends to take shape much more slowly and tentatively than the reconstruction of phonology and lexicon.

Reconstruction of a proto-semantics is by definition no more feasible than an account of the semantics of an attested language, and that, as we have seen (60), is still not realistic. And reconstructing any-thing like an explicit proto-syntax is very questionable, despite the fact that an overall similarity of syntax (or rather, morphosyntax) is usually apparent among cognate languages. For example, notwith-standing the relatively recent evolution of the Romance languages and the detailed and pervasive similarities between them, it is sobering to ponder how little of Latin morphosyntax can be accurately deduced from a study of the morphosyntax of the modern Romance languages.

INTERNAL RECONSTRUCTION

105. Internal reconstruction employs exactly the same kinds of reasoning as the comparative method. The only difference between the two is the source of the evidence: the comparative method infers facts of history from the features of several languages, whereas internal reconstruction draws its evidence from the features of a single language.

In phonology, evidence for a phonological structure predating that of the attested language comes from two principal sources: alterna-tions, and peculiarities of distribution (see 109).

Latin rhotacism (28) affords a clear example of this procedure as it applies to alternations. In Latin morphology there is alternation be-tween the two phonemes /s/ and /r/: *gerere* 'to comport, carry (on)', *gerō* m. (stem. *gerōn-*) 'a carrier', *gerundum* '(something) to be done', next to perf. *gessī* (with the tense-marker -*s*- between the root and the person-marker), pple. *gestus* (with the affix *-to-*), *gestāmen* 'something carried', *gestiō* (stem *ges-tiōn-*) 'management, performance', *gestāre* 'to carry (about), wear' (based on the participle), and so on. There are many similar sets of words with intervocalic *r* alternating with an *s* that occurs in other environments.

On the other hand there are word families with non-alternating *r*, like *morior* 'die', *moritūrus* 'about to die', *moribundus* 'dying', *mors* (stem *morti-*) 'death', *mortuus* 'dead', *mortālis* 'a human'.

Between Vowels	*Elsewhere*
gerō, gerōn-, gerundum	gessī, gestus, gestāmen, gestiōn-, gestō
morior, moritūrus, moribundus	mortuus, morti-, mortālis

That exhausts the patterns—there are no cases of *s* everywhere (except where there is some obvious explanation), nor is there any other system of *s/r* alternation. A concomitant rarity of intervocalic *s* points to a fairly recent (because still largely intact) primary split of Pre-Latin **s* into *r* between vowels and *s* elsewhere. In other words, we infer that the historical shape of the root of the first example was **ges-*, in contrast to that of the second example, **mor-*. (The thought that **r* might have split into *s* and *r* is ruled out by the impossibility of PREDICTING whether a verb like *ferō* 'carry' will or will not alternate with *s*, whereas given a form like *portō* 'carry' one knows already that no forms in *s* will occur anywhere in the word family, and likewise given a form like *ustus* 'burnt', one can be confident that *-r-* instead of *-s-* will appear in intervocalic position—as indeed it does in e.g. *ūrō* 'kindle' and *ūrēdō* 'an inflamatory itch'.)

To repeat: ALTERNATION is the key to this analytic technique: an *r* which is always intervocalic, as in the gen.pl. ending *-ārum* or *mora* 'delay, interval' (and all its derivatives), is uninterpretable: there is no way of telling whether it used to be an **s* or always was an **r*. (In these particular examples, we know from comparative evidence that the former was in fact **s*, the latter was always **r*.)

106. The uses of internal reconstruction

Internal reconstruction is useful in historical linguistics in several ways. Let us consider two.

First, it simplifies the comparative method. In the present example, once one determines that intervocalic *r* in Latin aligns with both *r* and *s* in Latin itself, then one is ready from the outset to look for correspondences in cognate languages (or possibly-cognate languages) between sibilants and Latin *r*. For example, the similarity between Lat. *nurus* 'daughter-in-law' and Ved. *snuṣā́-* increases strikingly if the pair is looked at with the foreknowledge that an alignment of a Latin medial *r* with a sibilant in other languages is a possibility.

To pursue the example of rhotacism, in the Sanskrit stem-class corresponding to the Latin first declension (*fēmina* 'woman'), the genitive plural ending is *-ānām*, as in *senānām* 'of armies'. A different feminine genitive plural marker, *-āsām*, occurs in a few pronoun paradigms: thus *tāsāṃ senānām* 'of those armies'. (The nouns and pronouns share many endings, of course: *tāṃ senām* acc.sg., *tās senās* nom.pl.) Now, the Latin genitive plural ending in this form class, for both nouns and pronouns, is seen in *hārum fēminārum* 'of these women'.

Either of the two Indic genitive plural endings might be the cognate of Lat. *-ārum*, though naturally Skt. *-ānām* would get first consideration, since it is the form in noun paradigms. But internal reconstruction in Latin reveals that an intervocalic *r* may reflect a historical **s*, which means that the connection between Lat. *-ārum* and Skt *-āsām* is the more likely by far—unless, of course, evidence aligning Skt. *n* and Lat. *r* can be found. (This would not be implausible phonetically; but there is no such evidence.)

107. **Internal reconstruction of morphemes**
The second role of internal reconstruction, probably the more important one, is the recovery of the historical shapes of morphemes in situations where comparative evidence is ambiguous or lacking. In a sense we have already seen this: internal reconstruction establishes that of the pair *ger-* and *ges-* in Latin, the latter is in a very true historical sense the 'real' form of the root, overruling any competing consideration (such as reasoning that because *ger-* occurs in the present stem and infinitive, it might be taken as basic on the grounds that such forms are FUNCTIONALLY basic). More dramatically, the paradigm of the Greek verb *blṓskō* 'come, go' includes the stems *blōsk-*, *(e)mol-* and *memblō-*, and despite the perhaps startling variety—or, more exactly, BECAUSE of it—it is possible to state with confidence that the root was **melH-* (and further that the laryngeal was specifically **H₃*) even though the root happens not to be attested in any cognate language. (Of course, it may not in fact be inherited even though its shape is faultlessly Indo-European.)

Another example would be a comparison of the patterns of alternation of the verbal prefixes *in-* and *com-* in Latin.[1]

---

[1] The meanings of the verbs derived by these prefixes are, as is often the case with verb-deriving elements, quite various. It is sufficient for our purposes to say that it is clear that we are dealing with just two elements here.

Both prefixes have exactly the same alternants before consonants:

Before labials	im-plorō 'call upon'	com-plicō 'fold together'
	im-bibō 'drink in'	com-būrō 'burn up'
	im-mergō 'dip into'	com-mūtō 'change entirely'
Before apicals	in-tendō 'stretch out'	con-trahō 'draw together'
	in-dō 'put in'	con-dūcō 'collect'
	in-nō 'swim, float on'	con-nectō 'fasten together'
Before dorsals[1]	in-crepō 'rattle' (trans.)	con-crescō 'become stiff'
	in-gredior 'enter'	con-gerō 'bring together'
Before glides	in-vīsō 'go see'	con-vellō 'pluck off'
	in-jungō 'fasten to'	con-jūrō 'take an oath'
Before fricatives	īn-sideō 'sit upon'	cōn-sonō 'sound together'
	īn-fundō 'pour in '	cōn-flō 'flow together'
Before l and *r*	il-lūdō 'play with'	col-luō 'wash thoroughly
	ir-rumpō 'break in'	cor-rigō 'make straight'

But before vowels there is an interesting discrepancy:

in-eō 'begin'	com-itor 'go with'
in-ungō 'anoint'	com-edō 'eat up'

Now, it is obvious that both of these prefixes must originally have ended with a nasal, and equally obvious that the various forms that occur before consonants have undergone assimilation to the following consonant—routine enough, though with interesting details such as the complete assimilation to the liquids, and the lengthening of the vowel before fricatives (plus the curiosum that the articulatory difference between *s* and *f* is not mirrored in the spelling of the prefix). But in all these regards both prefixes have identical properties. What then can be the explanation for the difference between *in-* and *com-* before a vowel?

As a matter of experience we do not normally expect vowels to influence the point of articulation of consonants, though they sometimes do; here it is evident that there is no rationale connecting the

---

[1] Here the letter -*n*- stands for the dorsal nasal [ŋ].

difference between *m* and *n* with the following vowel. The only alternative is to assume that before a vowel the etymological point of articulation of the nasal is unaltered; and that in this environment, and here alone, we find the key to the original consonant. This inference tells us relatively little new about the prefix *in-*, which is well-attested in cognate languages (which unanimously confirm the **n*), but the evidence that we are dealing with an Italic **kom-* rather than **kon-* is helpful in sorting out the history of that element which, as it happens, presents a number of etymological problems.

108. English plural suffix

A more challenging test for internal reconstruction would be applying the method to finding the original form of the regular English plural suffixes. In contemporary English these take three forms: /əz/ after sibilants and (what amounts to the same thing) affricates: *bushes, roses, foxes, pouches*; /s/ after all remaining voiceless obstruents: *cats, rocks, cliffs*; /z/ after everything else (resonants—all of which are phonetically voiced—and voiced obstruents): *beds, plugs, buns, oils, boys, sofas*. In the latter category are included the nouns with voice alternation in the final consonant, as *wolves* /wulvz/ and *paths* /pæðz/.

Here, unlike the Latin example just discussed, we have no environments at all which do not fit the phonetics of the affix snugly: voicing always matches, and /əz/ is found in cases where the noun ends with a sound matching several basic phonetic features of the consonant in the affix.

The first question is whether /əz/, the form with the vowel as in *bushes*, is the conservative form or the innovation.

Two arguments suggest the syllabic form is conservative. First, when two closely cognate forms differ in the number of segments, the odds greatly favor the loss of a segment in the shorter form over the addition of a segment in the longer one. Additions do occur, of course (17), but loss is by a wide margin the better bet. Second, the enclitic forms of the verb *is* have exactly the same distribution as the plural marker, as in *Ted's* /z/ *here* but *Pat's* /s/ *going to be late and Janice's* /əz/ *still at the office; I think Fred is* /iz/, *too*. In the case of the enclitic forms /z/ and /s/ of *is*, there can be no question that a vowel has been lost—it is right there in NON-ENCLITIC /iz/, as in the concluding clause—while it survives (after a fashion) in /əz/. To be sure this PROVES nothing regarding the plural suffix, but especially taken with the purely statistical likelihood that the vowel is old, it is a suggestive parallel.

Of course, in the case of the plural suffix we have no way of knowing what our reconstructed vowel originally was: a study of synchronic English vowel alternations (another example of internal reconstruction, even though the conditions cannot in fact be recovered; see 110) indicates that ALL atonic short vowels in English can become /ə/.

Finally there is the question of whether the reconstructed form should be */Vs/ or */Vz/ (where *V = any vowel). This might seem to be hopeless, but here we get crucial evidence from a couple of plural forms, *dice* and *pence*. The form of the plural marker here, /s/, is unexpected ('irregular'). We have two ways of explaining it: either it once was the expected /z/, and somehow became devoiced in these two words; or else it ALWAYS WAS voiceless. There is no thinkable rationale for the first alternative, whereas the notion that the sound always was voiceless in these words is a straightforward hypothesis.

The concomitant inference is that the voiced pronunciation of the allomorphs /z/ and /əz/ is the innovation. Since we started out with the certainty that one or the other of the voicing states was an innovation, this conclusion is unproblematic.

Putting all our inferences together we conclude that the oldest shape that we can recover is /Vs/, which—note—is different from ALL present-day reflexes of it.

Parenthetically, dictionaries tell us that *truce* and *bodice* are also historically plural forms, though that information is not evident in the lexicon itself; that is, there is no way a normal native speaker of English could know such a thing. It is nevertheless further evidence (for the historian) that we are correct in taking the sibilant as originally voiceless. Further confirmation comes from the histories of *riches* and *sherry*, which originally ended in /s/; neither was a plural to begin with, and their reinterpretation as plurals (p. 83, 54c) would be difficult to fathom, to put it mildly, if the original form of the plural affix in English had always ended with a /z/. Finally, there are no crypto-plurals (like *truce*) that end in /z/.

a. The reasoning called for in the interpretation of 'irregular' forms like *dice* seems to be counter-intuitive, since without training in historical linguistics, instinct seems to point straight to the wrong conclusion—namely, that 'regular' patterns are real language (so to say) and 'irregular' forms have somehow gone off the rails. In reality, however, an 'irregular' form often reflects some earlier linguistic structure which, for whatever reason, has not been roped into the regular patterns.

b. The reasoning used in (descriptive) morphological analysis is often identical to the reasoning of historical linguistics, but this last example highlights the differences. The currently-fashionable morphological analysis of the English plural suffix takes |z| to be the morphological 'base form': the shape /əz/ is then arrived at by *insertion*, presumably for reasons of economy (insertion acts on relatively few forms; many more forms would have to have the vowel deleted if you start with |əz|); and for the same reasons of economy the voiced alternant is posited as the starting point. The net effect is that in this case internal reconstruction and morphological analysis arrive at exactly opposite inferences.

c. A third use for internal reconstruction is the recovery of features of *pre*-proto-languages. By definition, proto-languages are postulated on the basis of their daughters, but proto-languages have histories too, and the only access to these matters is internal reconstruction. Sometimes, however, hints offered by internal reconstruction can lead to a rethinking of COMPARATIVE reconstruction. The famous Indo-European laryngeal consonants, for instance, were in the beginning largely internally-reconstructed curiosities until it was noticed (after a long delay) that these constructs actually correlated with features in the daughter languages. Nowadays, therefore, most scholars take for granted that one or more such consonants were in fact actually present in PROTO-Indo-European.

THE RELATIONSHIP BETWEEN
PHONOLOGICAL RESTRUCTURING (26-9)
AND INTERNAL RECONSTRUCTION

109. Merger

Merger (27) is not usually recoverable by internal reconstruction. Occasionally a merger will result in statistical or structural oddities such as the superabundance of the vowel /a/ in Indo-Iranian (below) or a *gap* in a phonological system, but gaps (such as the absence of dorsal fricatives in standard English, or the absence of /ŋ/ from initial position) can have various commonplace causes, and explaining a phonological gap as the result of a merger is usually just a guess.

Sometimes there are changes in the ENVIRONMENT of a former contrast which disclose a merger—or might do so. A supposed case of this is the Indo-Iranian merger of Proto-Indo-European non-high vowels into *a*, alluded to just above. One of the merger ingredients, *e*, palatalized preceding dorsal stops, with such results as are seen in reduplicated forms like Skt *jagama* [jəgəmə] 'I went', root *gam*.[1] Now, according to some authorities, we can detect here two different kinds of *a*, historically speaking: one that palatalized a preceding consonant (*ja-* < *ga-*) and one that didn't (*-gam-*). This inference is supported by the disproportionate frequency—extraordinarily disproportionate—of *a* in Indo-Iranian languages relative to the other vowels.

No such inference is really justifiable, however, on the basis of an honest scrutiny of Indo-Iranian evidence alone—honest, that is, as opposed to marshalling evidence for a historical event previously discovered by means of other kinds of evidence. The crucial data for Indo-Iranian palatalization were so extensively disturbed by analogy that even with the richer and much more powerful tool of the comparative method, brilliant scholars stared at the evidence for something like fifty years before concluding that palatalization phenomena SUPPORTED the theory that InIr. *a* was a merger product. To be sure, a number of factors got in the way of a correct perception, mainly the fledgling state of diachronic theory and the potent distraction of the a priori conviction that Sanskrit was virtually a dialect of Proto-Indo-European. But even if the reasoning about *jagama* and the like is somehow seen

---

[1] *Reduplication* is a type of affixal morphology where the affix consists not of a form or list of forms, but of a pattern or 'blueprint', whose actual phonological content is provided by the root. Examples of this in Sanskrit are given in the text. From Tagalog note the following verb-paradigms:

past	*future*	
naʔalis	ʔaʔalis	'leave'
nahalik	hahalik	'kiss'
naʔulan	ʔuʔulan	'rain'
nasulat	susulat	'read'
nagawaʔ	gagawaʔ	'do'

The prefix marking the past tense is of the usual type, a uniform /na-/. The future prefix, however, is rather /CV-/ 'consonant + vowel', that is, a sort of phonological recipe whose actual phonemic matter is copied from the particular verb root.

as cogent, the selfsame reasoning as applied to verb-forms like *cikitur* 'they notice' (root *cit*) and *cukūja* 'groaned' (root *kūj*-; *c* is the voiceless counterpart of *j*) would oblige us to infer that Indic *i* and *u* likewise continue two different vowels, one palatalizing and the other not. This time, however, the inference does NOT conform to any historical fact. Inferences of a merger by internal reconstruction, in fine, are unlikely to be any better than guesses until confirmed by comparative (or some other) evidence.[1]

110. Primary Split

Primary split or conditioned merger (28) often results in alternations which allow the recovery of the split by internal reconstruction, if the facts are not obscured by other changes, either phonological or ana-logical. The passage of time of course makes it more likely that such overlays will occur, as accumulating sound changes and leveling anal-ogies make the vital facts harder and harder to see. The split of PItal. **s* into Lat. *r* and *s* is easily recoverable from Latin; it is highly doubt-ful whether it could be retrieved from an inspection of, say, Middle French.

Furthermore, note that not all primary splits result in alternations in the first place. In the history of English, a number of short vowels merged with /u/ before /r/: as the (not always reliable) differences in spelling hint, forms like *word, birth, fur, verse,* and others originally had the usual array of short vowels despite their uniform pronunciation now as /ər/ (or /ə/). Since ME *ŭ* regularly becomes /ə/ in standard English, this is a conditioned merger (primary split) of ME *i, e,* and *o* with *u* when followed by tautosyllabic /r/:

---

[1] 'Some other evidence' could be earlier states of the same language. For example, even though it might be possible to infer an earlier merger in the history of NE /i/ on the basis of pairs of words like *chin* and *kin*, in which one ancestor of /i/ pal-atalized and the other didn't, given the poverty of the evidence it is unlikely that reasoning along such lines would ever occur to anyone, let alone be judged strong enough to sustain a hypothesis. Earlier-attested forms of English, however, reveal it directly, as in the etyma of the above forms *ćinn* /činn/ and *cynn* /künn/.

druncen	>	/drəŋk/
fur /u/	>	/fər/
birth /i/	>	/bərθ/
verse /e/	>	/vərs/
word /o/	>	/wərd/

However, there is no resulting alternation. The reason for this is that the segments affected are never to be found sometimes followed by *r* and sometimes not, in the same morpheme. Contrast this with Lat. *ger-ō, ges-tus* (105) in which the same segment—the root-final consonant—is now between vowels, and now not, depending on the affix.

And finally, even when primary split does produce typical alternations, the resulting patterns can be rendered uninterpretable by a very few subsequent innovations. A case in point would be the extremely abundant alternations in English between reflexes of pairs of long and short vowels in words of Latin derivation, such as *divine/divinity, proceed/procession,* and *opaque/opacity.* This is largely the product of the shortening of originally long vowels in unstressed syllables, which appears to have have taken place a little before the Great Vowel Shift.[1]

This was a straightforward set of primary splits: original /ī/, for example, split into /ī/ and /i/, the latter being identical with the vowel /i/ already present, and so on for all the other pairs of vowels. As already stated, the alternations resulting from this split are abundant, comprising literally thousands of forms. Thanks to two subsequent phonological developments of no great complexity, however, the split itself is completely unrecoverable by internal reconstruction. (Honest internal reconstruction, that is. If you know in advance what your goal is you can always marshall evidence, however elusive or inadequate it is in fact, to support the analysis; but that is not what we are talking about here.)

The first obstacle to recovering this innovation by internal reconstruction is that English teems with length alternations which reflect

---

[1] The Great English Vowel Shift has complicated the PHONETIC statement of these alternations: what was originally a banal matter of [e·] vs. [ɛ], [i·] vs. [ɪ], and the rest, has become /iy/ vs. /e/ as in *meet, met* and /ay/ vs. /i/ as in *wise, wisdom,* and so on. Fortunately, this descriptive complication is irrelevant for our purposes.

some seven or more unrelated events in the history of the language. Some alternations reflect features already present in Proto-Indo-European, such as the alternations seen in the Class I strong verbs (*ride : ridden*). Some of them are traceable to the lengthening of short vowels in certain environments but not in others, so for example the short vowel seen in *weft* and *web* lengthened in the (formerly) open stressed syllable of the present stem, *weave* < OE *wĕfan*. Differently, the alternations seen in *wild : wilderness* and *wind* (the verb, i.e. /waynd/) : *windlass* come from the Middle English lengthening of short vowels before certain consonant clusters in monosyllables. Contrariwise, the length alternations seen in *sheep : shepherd, wise : wisdom* and *sleep : slept* are the result of the shortening of originally long vowels, but under conditions unrelated to (and much earlier than) the shortening seen in *divine : divinity*. Some alternations, even some pretty systematic ones, are mysterious: the long tonic vowels in *basis, vapor, sequence, female* and many others result from a Middle English development whereby the first vowel of Latinate words of two syllables with a single intervocalic consonant is usually long, regardless of its quantity in Latin or French. The short vowel seen in a trisyllable like *feminine* is regular; but that in *manic, vapid, Spanish, second* etc., is just as mysterious as the long vowel of *mania*.

On top of this, there has been a great deal of recomposition (50) and leveling (47) in all classes of the data: hence *housewife* next to *husband* (both reflecting OE *hús* 'house' and cf. the regular outcome of OE *húswíf*, namely NE *hussy* /həziy/ or commonly, by spelling pronunciation (43), /həsiy/); *wildness* next to *wilderness; leaped* next to *lept; nation* should have a short vowel in the first syllable (like *vision*), ditto *regency* and *basic* and the penultimate syllable of nouns in the huge class built with *-ation*, such as *damnation*.

However, even assuming for the sake of argument that one could by some clairvoyance identify the coherent core of regular Latinate vowel alternations in English, there is no way the historical facts could be recovered by internal reconstruction. As stated above, the key to these alternations is an unremarkable, even banal sound law: the shortening of originally long vowels when atonic. But note that in *divine* and *divinity* the tonic accent is on the SAME syllable in present-day English. And the same is true of *sane, sanity; profound, profundity; regent, regicide,* and countless others. The explanation (we know) is that at the time of the shortening, the tonic accent was sometimes on the same syllable that it is on in present-day English, and sometimes not. Specifically, at the crucial time the tonic accent of *sanity, profundity,* and *regicide* was on the last syllable of the word. Then, subsequent to the shortening of the atonic vowels, there was an innovation known as the *three-syllable retraction rule,* whereby a tonic accent in English that stood three or more syllables from the beginning of the word moved two syllables to the left.[1] In this way the tonic accent very often came to rest on a short vowel that was previously long, as in the examples.

The real problem for internal reconstruction, here, is that present-day English provides no reason at all for thinking that its word-accents were ever different from the ones attested, nor (if such a suspicion should occur to the analyst) would there be any basis for assigning the earlier accent to any particular syllable.

It doesn't stop there. Subsequent to the time of the events outlined above, words like *vision, division* and *nation* lost a syllable: the *-ion* suffix of English had two syllables at the time of the vowel-shortening and accent-retraction developments: *di-vī-si-ón > di-vĭ-si-ón > di-ví-si-on,* after which *-i-o- > -yo-* and /zy/ > /ž/, whence modern /dǝ'vižǝn/. There is no reason for 'reconstructing' an extra syllable in these suffixes (and also in some other formations, e.g. *vicious* next to *vice*): indeed, it is hard to imagine on what basis one might even suspect that such a reconstruction is called for.

The upshot: a couple of simple and straightforward changes (accent retraction and syllable loss) of no great age have thoroughly covered the tracks of the 'atonic vowel shortening rule'. The true historical events can in fact be confidently recovered, thanks to the rich variety of evidence available to historians, but the evidence in question does not include (and is inaccessible to) internal reconstruction.

---

[1] The tonic accent probably did not of course actually move anywhere. The likelier innovation was the rise of a secondary accent two syllables before the tonic, and a subsequent shift in the relative prominence of the two.

III. Secondary Split

Secondary split, or phonologization (29), often but not always creates alternations. In the artificial example of reconstruction discussed in 99, the secondary split of Proto-AB *k into /k/ and /č/ in Language B was not accompanied by any alternation. Given any kind of morphological complexity in a language, however, one would expect to see at least some alternation. But: a major difference between primary and secondary splitting is that secondary split is rarely, perhaps in principle never, recoverable by internal reconstruction. Apparent examples to the contrary turn out to be, on inspection, either a guess or a marshalling of evidence a posteriori to support a conclusion arrived at by other means, rather than a deduction FROM evidence. This is the case with the Indo-Iranian example, above, where a merger of *e with *o and *a creates a secondary split of *k, *g, and *gh into k g gh before original *o, *a and č j h before original *e; this was discussed in 109 in connection with the vowel merger.

Another example is the voicing alternations of English fricatives: *breath/breathe, glass/glaze, wolf/wolves, life/live*. The immediate and obvious inference is that splitting has created these alternations, and in fact that inference is historically correct. But precisely because the alternations were created by secondary splits, Modern English provides no intelligible evidence for what conditioned the split. On top of that obstacle, alternation of voicing in fricatives in English is utterly chaotic even on its face. (See the table on the facing page.) The obvious inference is that leveling has been extensive here, which would make the task of digging out the history of these things especially difficult in any case. But it cannot be over-emphasized that no matter what one thinks might be the best guess for the prehistory of these alternations, a guess is all it ever can be. This is no fault of the data (battered as they are); it is simply a property of secondary split, which after all comes about precisely because the defining pattern has been lost (29).

noun sg.		noun pl.		verb		adjective (etc.)	
rose	+	roses	+			rosy	+
glass	–	glasses	–	glaze	+	glassy	–
wolf	–	wolves	+	wolf	–	wolfish	–
breath	–	breaths	–	breathe	+	breathy	–
brass	–	brasses	–			brazen	+
						brassy	–
tooth	–	teeth	–	teethe	+	toothy	–
elf	–	elves	+			elfin	–
						elvin	+
						elvish	+
use	–	uses	–	use	+	usual	+
goose	–	geese	–	goose	–	gosling	+
earth	–	earths	–	(un)earth	–	earthling	–
						earthy	–
worth	–					worthy	+
cloth	–	cloths[1]	±	clothe	+	clothy	–

A plus means 'voiced fricative', a minus means 'voiceless fricative'

SUGGESTIONS FOR FURTHER READING

Anttila 1988 chapters 10 and 11, **Hock 1991** chapter 18, **Hock & Joseph 1996** chapter 16, **Crowley 1997** chapter 5, **Campbell 1999** chapter 5 are all ample discussions of the comparative method both as such and (with varying emphasis) as it touches on other topics such as subgrouping, linguistic relationship, and so on. All but **Hock 1991** provide data for analysis, based on the diverse areas of expertise of the several authorities. **Fox 1995** provides the most searching account of both the method and some of its theoretical implications (with a large bibliography). **Hoenigswald 1960** is searching as well, but it is not an easy work to read; **Hoenigswald 1950** adumbrates some of the material in the later work very much more transparently. **Hall 1950** provides a

---

[1] For the author, the usual plural *cloths* has /θ/, but *washcloths* has /ð/. And of course *clothes* is nothing but the original plural of *cloth*.

lucid demonstration of the reasoning and methods in a practical arena, the reconstruction of Proto-Romance phonology.

See **Hock 1985** and **Anttila 1988** for comments on reconstructing syntax, a topic not mentioned here and rarely touched on in handbooks of historical linguistics. **Matasović 1996** is a good introduction to the complex and delicate question of reconstructing 'texts'.

Internal reconstruction is discussed in **Anttila 1988** chapter 12, and much more elaborately in **Hock 1991** chapter 17, **Campbell 1999** chapter 8, and **Fox 1995** chapters 7–8.

On language families: an invaluable work on Indo-European is **Mallory 1989** (large bibliography); a good summary of the Indo-European family is presented in **Hock & Joseph 1996** chapter 2; and **Bynon 1977** pp. 68–9 arranges the basic facts of Indo-European attestation on a time-line. Further on language families: **Hock & Joseph 1996** chapter 16 §8 and **Campbell 1999** chapter 6 (somewhat sketchy). **Meillet & Cohen 1964** is a recent edition of a much earlier work; it contains mountains of information on language families, albeit conservatively.

Long-range (great time-depth) reconstruction of super-families or even 'Proto-World' is touched on in Mallory 1989 but discussed more thoroughly in **Hock & Joseph 1996** chapter 17 and in **Campbell 1999** chapter 13. See also **Matisoff 1990** for a pointed (and often droll) commentary, and **Salmons 1992**.

On the question that similarities between forms of similar meaning might be pure chance (a matter of concern in long-range comparison: as the time-depth of the putative reconstruction increases, recurring correspondences dwindle in both number and cogency) see **Ringe 1992** and **1995** and **Hock & Joseph 1996** chapter 16 §§1–2.

EXTERNAL ASPECTS
OF LANGUAGE CHANGE

LANGUAGE AND DIALECT

112. One of the questions most frequently asked of linguists is 'what is the difference between a language and a dialect?' The questioners assume that their own uncertainties are the result of ignorance, and that the matter will prove straightforward with proper explanation. In reality, however, what linguists know about the matter is probably of no great use to laymen.

In the first place, part of the problem is that the term *dialect* is freely used in at least three distinct senses. First, it is used in regard to the degree of difference between two forms of speech (113). Second, it is viewed as a matter of the relationship between a *standard language* and other forms of speech used at the same time in the same polity (114). Third, there are conventional uses of the term that do not come under either heading, such as calling the different languages of China 'dialects' (115).

These three categories will be discussed separately.

113. **Degrees of difference between languages**
This is the heart of the problem: systems of speech may differ from one another in a few trivial traits, or by so many traits that communication is impeded or completely impossible. There are infinitely many gradations between *same language* and *mutually unintelligible languages*, and there is no conceivable principle for deciding where, along this continuum, the dividing line between 'different dialects' and 'different languages' is to be found.

This impossibility leads to futile disputes over whether two different forms of speech are dialects or different languages. Such disputes most often take the form, curiously, of insisting that very similar forms of speech are really 'different languages' (thus Ukrainian and Russian; Serbian and Croatian; Hindi and Urdu; and even American and British English).

You might suppose that mutual intelligibility, or rather the lack of it, would be the simplest test for 'languagehood', but in fact it is anything but simple. First, intelligibility is not objectively definable. Two very different forms of speech may 'work' for mutual communication as long as rough understanding is sufficient and philosophizing is avoided. Besides, the nature of the differences between two somewhat similar forms of speech may be such that it is easier for a speaker of language A to understand language B than vice-versa. It is well known that monolingual speakers of Portuguese can understand Spanish better than monolingual hispanophones can understand Portuguese (though the degree of the directionality has probably been overstated). Finally, even small differences in structure can be highly disruptive: there are reported to be varieties of tone languages here and there which have undergone a tone shift, which in effect scrambles the assignment of lexical tones. As a result, to an interlocutor speaking another form of the language, most common words would have a meaning—but the wrong one. The differences in structure, even though descriptively trifling, would be an immense barrier to communication: if a perfectly normal remark as uttered in one dialect comes across, clear as a bell, to a speaker of the other as 'pour elder-sister thunder rope if-not', communication on even the most elementary level is going to be difficult.

These factors are all linguistic, at least; but it turns out that intelligibility is not a purely linguistic property in the first place: the WILLINGNESS of the participants is a prime variable.

For cultural reasons people will claim to understand speech where genuine understanding is unlikely or impossible. For example, many Lithuanians seem to be convinced that speakers of Lithuanian can understand Sanskrit—or could, if they ever heard any spoken. And the author knows of an incident in Sitka in 1937 when an unkind joke was played on a fellow of Russian descent who was proud to claim that he knew Russian. He seems to have claimed this once too often. Some friends rigged a phonograph turntable to rotate backwards and a record, actually of someone speaking in English, was played thus for the unfortunate. He listened intently; at the end, while he conceded he had not understood all of it, he claimed to have gotten the gist of it—when, in fact, there was no gist to get.

On the other side of the coin, people will insist they cannot make head or tail of some culturally stigmatized form of speech when a linguist would be hard pressed to find much actual difference in structure at all.

Finally, intelligibility varies with experience: one's ability to understand a different but similar form of speech will improve with practice, in extreme cases moving from nearly complete lack of communication to reliable intelligibility.

114. Standard Language vs dialect

The term *language* is commonly used in the narrow sense of a literary and national standard of speech and writing, as defined by academies or other authorities on usage, and disseminated by public schools, news media, and governmental organs. *Dialects,* by contrast, are forms of speech coexisting in time and place with the (standard) language, but lacking the status, and the symbols of status, of the standard speech. The actual historical and linguistic relationship between a *language* and *dialects* in this definition is of no importance. Thus, Low German (*Plattdeutsch*) of northern Germany is called a dialect, or rather a collection of dialects, of (High) German, the standard language of the country.[1] In fact, though, the closest relative to Plattdeutsch in terms of historical development is actually Dutch—itself (thanks to the sovereign status of the state where it is the vernacular) by this definition a *language,* not a *dialect.* Further, wholly within the genuine High German dialect continuum (116), as diachronically defined, one finds far greater structural differences than are to be found between the Danish and Swedish *languages* (so-called). Since the distinction between language and dialect as defined this way is based on cultural and political considerations rather than on linguistic ones, it has been aptly quipped that a 'language' is a dialect with an army and a navy.

a. In earlier periods—15th century England, ancient Greece and Rome, Imperial China, for example—some of the present-day tokens of standard language status as listed above did not of course exist. But in many such societies 'correct usage' was the object of some degree of conscious cultivation, as when for example the opinions of noted Attic or Roman rhetoricians and grammarians were studied and fol-

---

[1] *Low* and *High* (German) refer to the terrain, not the status of the speakers or their speech, though that misinterpretation is probably inevitable.

lowed. Depending on time and place, the civil and judicial bureaucracies of such polities as Imperial Rome or Medieval England and France, owing to their sheer size as well as the importance of their functions, were an especially potent standardizing influence—in the opinion of some, outweighing the literary influences conventionally credited in this connection. See 119.

115. Conventional uses

A further source of confusion in the lay perception of the language/ dialect question is that the terms themselves have arbitrary and contradictory conventional uses. We speak of the Greek dialects, which would seem to imply that there was some sort of difference in the status of say Spartan and Phocian, but in reality there was no Standard Greek in early classical times: paradoxically, ALL varieties of Greek speech were 'dialects' (and all, within their polities, equally 'standard'). A similar but more extreme case is the so-called Chinese language, made up of dialects (also so called) which are in fact no more dialects in any of the usual senses of the term than Spanish, French, Italian, Romanian, and so on, are dialects of something called 'the Romance language'. (At different times in China's history, one or another among the local varieties has served as the official and literary language, all other local varieties being for the time subordinate. But all of them, official or subordinate, are commonly known as *dialects*.)

   a. In some technical contexts *dialect* means something like 'form of speech distinguished by a specific trait', without regard to any overall degree of similarity. In this sense of the word Indo-Europeanists speak of Celtic languages as divided into 'P-dialects' and 'Q-dialects', according to a single datum: their treatment of PIE *k^w. Now, by this usage Welsh and Gaulish are 'P-dialects' and Gaelic is a 'Q-dialect', but there is no question that by the time of their earliest attestations, all three were in fact different LANGUAGES by any normal measure.

116. Dialect continua

There is another kind of indeterminacy in dialectology: the geographic boundaries between dialects—or rather, the lack thereof. Important discoveries at the end of the 19th century revealed that different individual dialect *traits* (or *features*) rarely cover precisely the same territory. In fact, in areas of long-term settled populations we encounter not *dialect boundaries* as the usual terminology plainly envisions, but a *dialect continuum.* Any given community will be found to share certain traits with the folks to the west and other traits with the folks to the east, and each of these other communities will also be dialectally ambivalent.

Consider the following two experiments. As one figuratively travels the linguistic map from Paris to Munich, pausing frequently to chat with the locals, there is a sharp discontinuity where French ends and German begins, fuzzed up only to the extent that there are communities where both languages are in use concurrently. Of course, there has never been any question that German and French might be anything other than 'different languages', so this experiment results in no discoveries.

But if one similarly travels from Paris to Rome, say, staying wholly within Romance territory, there is no such abrupt discontinuity where French ends and Provençal begins, or even where French ends and Italian begins. Rather, as one goes along one finds detail-by-detail changes in pronunciation, vocabulary, syntax, and so on. As more ground is covered, the details accumulate commensurately; and eventually, the accumulated differences will be sufficient to hamper free communication, and finally will make communication impossible altogether.

A consequence is that a list of traits thought to define two dialects will be found together consistently only in so-called *dialect focal areas* at a certain distance from the dialect boundary. The term 'boundary' itself is a misnomer for what is, in reality, a more or less extensive area, sometimes called a *transition zone* or *transition dialect,* where the boundary lines between SPECIFIC TRAITS will be found to be congruent only sometimes, while more often diverging or converging and even crossing and recrossing one another. As a result, the only chance of finding a sharp and unequivocal geographical division between two dialects is to define them in terms of a single trait, which however linguists and everyone else would judge trivializes the whole enterprise.

The languages 'French' and 'Italian' differ as much as they do because the regions which provide the *dialect base* for the National Standards are geographically remote from one another in their *dialect continuum.* In a dialect continuum, two forms of speech will differ in proportion to the distance between the communities in question, with few if any local discontinuities ('dialect boundaries') of any importance. The prehistoric map of Indo-European Europe was certainly similar to what we see by direct observation in the Romance dialect continuum; the subgroups of Celtic, Germanic, Greek, and the rest, as we know them, are so sharply distinct mainly because the intermediate gradations are unattested. As soon as even a moderate amount of detail is known, problems of classification arise. For example, the conventional grouping of the Germanic languages into North, West, and East Germanic achieves its purposes by selecting a few differentiating traits and ignoring others which cut across the standard divisions; and the dialect structure within the West Germanic subgroup is still disputed (as is the very existence of such a subgroup).

a. The technical name for the line DEMARCATING the distribution of a linguistic trait is *isogloss*. This is an unfortunate coinage for what was intended (it is patterned after terms like *isobar* 'locus of points [a line] of equal atmospheric pressure'), and occasionally nowadays one sees the term *heterogloss* instead. This is a better term, but only time will tell whether it can dislodge its long-standard predecessor.

117. Speech styles and social dialects

A final complication: the discussion so far, like the bulk of all written material about dialects, treats GEOGRAPHICAL phenomena, that is, the distribution of features over terrain. There are two other types of linguistic variation: *stylistic levels* (or *registers*) and *social dialects*.[1] *Style* (or *register*) refers to the observed fact that people's speech will differ according to whom they are talking to, the subject being talked about, and other circumstances. The adjustments involved affect all components of linguistic structure, and the styles are not ragbags of stray details but coherent structural wholes. Each speaker commands several such styles—one authority has gone so far as to state categorically that all speakers of all languages have five, and exactly five, such registers—and shift between them efficiently; and since each individual is fully in command of the styles, they are generally kept straight, that is, features of one tend not to be introduced into another, which would strike speaker and hearer alike as incongruous and jarring. According-

---

[1] The terms *horizontal* and *vertical* dialects are sometimes used for the geographical and social distribution of language variation, respectively.

ly, exceptions like NE *fancy* (presumably from a casual speech register) side-by-side with *fantasy* (from more careful styles), or *varsity* vs *university*, are unusual.

Possibly the most common mingling of styles is also the most drastic, namely, when a slang term may become standard. Once such a transition is made, of course, the previous status of the word becomes irrelevant, and in fact only historians will be aware of it: nothing about the current acceptability of *won't* hints that in the middle of the 19th century it was condemned in the same breath as *ain't* as 'utterly vulgar'; and *pants* 'trousers' and *mints* 'mint-flavored sweetmeats' were witheringly disparaged as recently as World War II. *Its,* which occurs in the King James Bible (in editions from 1660 onward) exactly once, seems to have had similar status problems in the beginning. Many such adoptions remain informal in tone, *kid* 'child' and *mob*, e.g.; but a word's status in present-day language is no guide to its historical status.

Contrariwise, some items of ordinary vocabulary can become, if not slang, at least slangy; and rare or technical terms can unexpectedly become current in less rarified styles.[1]

SOCIAL DIALECTS

Social dialects are a very important type of language variation. These are distinctively different forms of language spoken more or less in the same community but peculiar to specific social or occupational groups. As little as is known about geographical dialects in ancient times, it is a wealth of information compared to what is known (or even guessed) of social dialects, which are difficult to study even in vivo. Unlike register features, features of social dialects appear to be readily borrowed, at least under some circumstances, and such borrowings probably are

---

[1] It is risky to venture examples of these things in a printed book, as by nature fashions in slang change rapidly. But in the 1970's *gross* and *excellent* became for all practical purposes slang terms, as had *neat* and *cool* before them. (Well before them, in fact; *cool* in particular may hold some kind of record for slang longevity.)

As an example of the domestication of a highfallutin' term, *oxymoron* abruptly emerged from the dim light of the pedant's cave into shopworn currency in the 1980's.

the explanation for many peculiarities in the histories of all languages. But owing to our ignorance of the necessary details, any appeal to such borrowing as the explanation for particular forms is usually mere speculation. For example, it has been suggested that the unexpected vowel of NE *great, steak,* and *break* (the words should rime with *cheat* and *freak,* and actually do in some dialects) is because the pronunciation is a borrowing from a social dialect. This is a shot in the dark.

    a. PRESTIGE. Normally, a standard language (118) is the form of speech which enjoys the highest status in the community, but there are exceptions. In Catalunia, Castilian Spanish is the low status (or anyhow, stigmatized) language. In large areas of the Philippines, the official language of administration, Pilipino (Tagalog), does not enjoy high esteem. In Switzerland, the local forms of High German have a somewhat schizophrenic standing: high status is claimed for them, and emphatically; but they nevertheless usually yield to standard German for such purposes as belles-lettres and formal communication. At the same time they are the favored form of speech for intimate conversation and 'saying what you really mean'. And beer ads are in Swiss, not standard, German.

    In some communities, the highest status language may even be a form of speech not native to the community at all, such as Greek among the Roman upper classes, or French in Czarist Russia. On occasion such a state of affairs arises naturally, as when, in early 15th century England, native-speaker knowledge of the supposedly prestige speech, French, had all but died out, but French was maintained as an official language of administration and admired as a vehicle for literary expression. In the practical sphere this burden was eventually felt to be intolerable and French was dropped for all administrative purposes. Such an outcome cannot be taken for granted: cultures will cherish and cultivate far more inconvenient exercises of status than a knowledge of French. All things considered, in fact, the privileged position of French in England was surprisingly brief. (See p. 177.)

DIFFERENTIATION OF LANGUAGES

118. The evolution of separate languages is mostly a continuation of ordinary dialect differentiation as noted above and in 2. As pointed out in 116, the national languages known as French and Italian are not distinct developments radiating out independently from a common source: they are points in a dialect continuum that happen to be geographically distant from one another and hence structurally distant. But a former dialect continuum may naturally develop real discontinu-

ities as the speech of one particular locality spreads at the expense of local varieties (as discussed below). Abrupt and complete partitioning of a speech community may come about by migration, either by the speakers themselves or when their speech community is split by an intruding population.

Migration from what is now southern England to Brittany resulted in the differentiation of Breton from Cornish, and migration to Iceland was the first step in the division of early Norse into Icelandic and Norwegian. Migration in Indo-European prehistory has often been assumed to explain the differentiation of the Indo-European branches, but has probably been overestimated as a cause. For one thing, the separation of ancient language groups may well be only apparent, a consequence of our ignorance of the geographically and linguistically intermediate forms of speech (as noted in 116 above). There is no reason to think that little bands of speakers of Proto-Germanic, Proto-Celtic, Proto-Baltic, and so on, had scattered from the original homeland far and wide and for millennia lived completely out of touch with one another.

Migration is not itself the CAUSE of linguistic change; in fact, the language of a small isolated speech community, whether a relic area or a result of in-migration, will usually be more conservative than that of larger populations, as in the case of Icelandic compared with Norwegian. There is nothing mystical about this: innovations in the isolated group will be limited to those that arise locally. By contrast, a group in contact with other similar forms of speech will both make its own innovations and be influenced by changes originating elsewhere.

Migration as a plausible explanation for prehistoric developments is realistically limited to two cases: where we find a form of speech that is totally surrounded by unrelated languages (a *speech island*), and languages spoken on literal islands. Even the latter is less cut and dried than it might appear at first, since open water can be an avenue of contact rather than a barrier. For example, the rise of 'r-less' forms of English, now standard in England but retreating and regional in the United States, postdates the establishment of permanent English colonies in North America by a century or more. (It is also an example of the truism that even if an innovation becomes established, it sometimes happens that the speech of the community reverts to an earlier structure.) In other examples, it is significant that, following the settlement of Iceland, coastal Norwegian shared more innovations with Icelandic than with the Norwegian of the hinterlands; and Polynesians seem to have gotten about from island to island very ably.

The isolated émigré community has a converse, namely a speech community that is a RELIC of a once more extensive area, such as Welsh in Britain or Basque in the Pyrinees. Naturally, in the absence of reliable historical documentation, it is often hard to tell whether a speech island is a remnant or an intrusion.

> **a.** One keeps hearing that in some hollow in West Virginia, or on an island in Chesapeake Bay, the populace 'speaks pure Elizabethan English'. It would be 'pure Jacobean English' if anything, but in fact it is pure moonshine. There are no genuinely isolated settlements in this country, and the traits by which one form of regional speech differs from another will always be seen to be a MIXTURE of innovative and conservative details, with the latter being no more numerous or conspicuous than the conservative linguistic details of out-of-the-way communities in, say, Maine or villages in Yorkshire.

119. The evolution of a standard language

Standard languages (114) have various origins. Rather rarely, the emergence of a standard can involve a straightforward codification of the speech of a smallish community, as seems to have been roughly the story of the early history of Latin. Standard languages more usually emerge from a dialect continuum (116) by a sort of centralizing process: the speech of important centers becomes the norm for certain districts; and of these larger units the speech of one becomes the basis of a standard literary and administrative language. Note that BASIS is the operative word at every stage of this process: by their nature, 'important centers' are places where people of diverse backgrounds mingle. Thus, it is not the case that some regional dialect simply becomes preeminent, part and parcel; rather, it forms a starting point for an often elaborate (as well as continuous) process of compromise and accommodation of dialect features. Some such process lies behind the rise of standard English based on the speech of the upper classes in London of Chaucer's time; of Italian based (more approximately) on that of Florence in Dante's time; and so on. This process greatly complicates the accurate charting of the linguistic histories of standard languages, and scholars have long been aware that with regard to the regularity hypothesis (30), out-of-the-way dialects are usually better-behaved than standard languages.

Conventional wisdom holds that influential texts play a significant role in the rise of standard languages from a local vernacular; but the current view is that while individual authors such as Chaucer, Dante, and Luther have been influential, their importance has been overestimated, and other influences (such as civil administration) have been underrated.

However a form of speech evolves into a standard, its preeminence is due neither to any intrinsic merit from the linguistic point of view (at least, linguists have never been able to measure degrees of merit), nor to the quality of the works of art composed in it, but to external circumstances—usually the political or economic importance of its center. These are changeable fortunes, and it follows from this that linguistic preeminence is changeable, too. Among the many dialects of France, the speech of Paris by the 13th century was firmly established as the literary language, but it was in competition with an earlier literary standard based on southern (Provençal, or Occitan) dialects, which it supplanted only after a struggle. It is evident that the dialect base of Alfredian (West Saxon) Old English is different from the dialect base of London (South Midlands) English; and a shift in dialect base accounts for the many structural details of Proto-Romance—which is based on colloquial rather than literary or normative speech—which do not jibe with Ciceronian Latin.

At the opposite extreme from the comparatively simple evolution of standard Latin (and even standard French) was the tardy and complex development of standard Greek and German. The reasons for that are, as always, mostly political and economic, with long-lasting linguistic decentralization being merely a reflection of political decentralization. In Greece the dialect of Athens by the 5th century BC had became the standard for literary prose, supplanting an earlier preference for Ionic. Prior to the rise in Attic prestige, Athenian prose writers avoided certain Attic peculiarities which must have been felt as provincial, such as the native -tt- (*thálatta* 'sea') and -rr- (*árrēn* 'male') for which they substituted the -ss- and -rs- (*thálassa, ársēn*) of Ionic and the majority of dialects. In the German states, during the heyday of the Hanseatic League, Low German, while never exactly standardized, enjoyed high prestige in letters as well as affairs. The considerable body of German loans in Scandinavian languages, for example, are early enough to be prevailingly from Low rather than High German. Only later, with the rising power and influence of High German areas to the south, did a sort of synthetic High German speech (or rather, *Schriftdeutsch* 'written German') emerge. A milestone in this process was the vernacular translation of the Bible by Martin Luther, who was concerned to produce a text that would not strike any potential reader as too alien, and so avoided forms he understood to be narrowly regional. However, while conceding that more Germans must have read the *Lutherbibel* than the documents of the imperial and ducal chanceries, the fact is that the latter laid much of the groundwork for Luther's compromise dialect, and reinforced it.

It has been suggested that the development (and recognition) of a linguistic standard, or the failure of one to develop, can be important variables in determining how successful a minority language is in maintaining itself against 'mainstream' cultural pressures. Arguably Plattdeutsch, Scottish Gaelic, and Irish would have fared better under the aegis of some sort of standard, whereas the sturdiness of Catalan may be indebted to successful standardization efforts.

LANGUAGES IN CONTACT

120. One of the commonest explanations for the occurrence of more than one language in a polity is invasion or conquest. The languages of the invader and the indigenous population may exist side by side indefinitely; but often there emerges a single language. This is sometimes the language of the intruder and sometimes the language of the native population. The two opposite outcomes are largely unpredictable, as they are determined by complex factors in which numbers play only a part. In exceptional cases (122b, below), the emergent language is a genuine amalgam, but most commonly the surviving language is a continuation of one of the competing languages. Thus, English is unquestionably a Germanic language, however obvious the Romance admixture, which was in any case due to several different, and widely-separated, episodes of borrowing.

THE INDIGENOUS LANGUAGE PREVAILS

The Franks, a High German-speaking people, conquered the Romanized Gauls in Burgundy (whose very name comes from an earlier brush with East Germanic groups). They lost their Germanic speech and adopted the Romance speech of their subjects, which however came to be called French (literally 'Frankish'; cases of languages and peoples with the wrong names, as it were, are very common). The Manchu conquerors of China, who founded the Qing (Ch'ing) dynasty in 1644, adopted the language of the native population. Scandinavian 'Northmen' established major colonies in England (the Danelaw, ca. 875–925), France (Normandy), Sicily, and elsewhere, and in all of them the language of the native population prevailed within a few generations (with, however, in the case of England, lasting effects on English). The Normans of Normandy conveyed their adoptive Romance speech to England in the aftermath of the Conquest (1066), where the same thing happened in the course of about 200 years: by the end of the 13th century there is increasing indirect evidence that French was a foreign language for many of the ruling elite, and 1362 was a watershed year: by order, English was henceforth to be used in the proceedings of the sheriff's court of London and Middlesex. There is evidence that English had played some role in the legal arena all along, but this decree was a benchmark. The decline of French as a vernacular was obviously well along, and in a very short time it would disappear from literature, law, and administration. A sort of terminus post quem is the year 1417, when the language of the official correspondence of King Henry V abruptly changed from French to English.

THE INTRUDING LANGUAGE PREVAILS

An example is Latin in the Roman Empire, in which virtually all local languages disappeared. (Remember that subsequent events, such as the spread of Semitic, Germanic, and Slavic languages, reshuffled the deck.) This extinction, especially over such a large area, is not easy to account for. Subjectively, Latin has been called a 'killer language' (as has English, vis-à-vis North America), but this is only a colorful phrase, not an explanation.

Factors involved in Roman Europe included the following. First, whole populations in the Roman world were avid to learn Latin (competence in which was essential for success in social, political, and economic affairs); and second, examples of native-speaker-quality Latin were readily available—that is, although ethnic Romans were a pretty small minority, they made no attempt to withhold their language by, say, addressing locals in baby-talk or dealing with them through intermediaries. Similar circumstances prevailed in Byzantium—*Rhôma*, no less—but the failure of the same thing to happen in Greece can be accounted for, at least in part, by the inherent prestige of Greek language and culture. (Byzantium was sociolinguistically complex. Success in civil administration depended upon an excellent command of Latin, by ethnic Greeks as well as everyone else. But Greek was nevertheless the prestige language of art, letters, and polite society, among ethnic Romans as well as Greeks. Nevertheless, along the way, Greek borrowed a fair number of words from Latin.)

A more complex puzzle is Britain, where the social, political, and economic circumstances were virtually identical to the mainland; but Welsh and related forms of Celtic manifestly survived next to Latin as the vernacular, at least in certain social strata.

On the face of it, the position of the Anglo-Saxons in England resembles the situation of the various Northmen colonies much more closely than Roman Europe. Speakers of the ancestor of Old English once occupied the coast region from about the mouth of the Scheldt to Schleswig-Holstein, inclusive, and in England were definitely intruders into a going concern with a higher culture. Nevertheless, Old English early became the only speech on the island apart from pockets of surviving Celtic speech in the west (Welsh) and south (Cornish); and West Saxon can boast of being the first non-Latin language of administration in Europe.[I]

a. To whatever degree Celtic Britain had been Romanized during the nearly 400 years of Roman occupation, events in the country after the withdrawal of the Ro-

---

[I] What was going on in what is now Scotland is unclear, beyond the fact that eventually the use of English penetrated where Latin, and perhaps even Celtic, failed to (the latter question depending on just what language the 'Picts and Scots' spoke).

man imperium are obscure, and just as doubtful is the explanation for the incursion into Britain of 'Angles, Saxons, and Jutes'. There are two contradictory traditions; neither is reliable.

According to the 6th century Welsh chronicler Gildas, in the 5th century AD the Britons induced some continental Teutons to help in dealing with raids by Picts and Scots. The strategy was a success, but then the Teutonic warriors, claiming they had not been sufficiently paid, seized land.

A different and somewhat later story has it that two noble Saxon refugees, Hengest and Horsa, sought the protection of the British king Vortigern. They proved to be a great help, somehow, in dealing with the Picts and Scots, though what exactly two 'refugees' could do to turn around a situation like that is not obvious and is not described in the chronicle. What happened next is obscure, but may have involved a gift of land, and in one version of this account Vortigern married Hengest's daughter. Eventually, the Saxons 'by treachery' (why, and by what means, is not related) induced their patron to send for large numbers of their countrymen, and these freebooters were the spearhead of the invasion of Britain by continental Germanic tribes.

For purely linguistic reasons, neither of these traditions is plausible: given the success of the English language in Britain, we surmise that we are dealing with more than troops here—family groups, probably, and in non-trivial numbers too.

For historiographic reasons, both of these accounts are strange. The later tradition would better fit a view of history by an aggrieved and oppressed populace, while the specifically Welsh account has all the earmarks of a self-justifying myth concocted by a successful invader.

121. The prehistory of Indo-European

The spread of the Indo-European languages is apparently a case of the imposition of the language of intruders upon the earlier populations of India, Anatolia, and Europe. Archeological evidence suggests that there were actually three separate and distinct incursions of Indo-European peoples into Europe, which raises the possibility that the languages of some of the populations overrun by speakers of the direct ancestors of known Indo-European languages were themselves Indo-European, who had arrived in earlier movements. The likely numbers and status of Indo-European newcomers vis-à-vis their precursors, whether pre-Indo-European or Indo-European, have been hotly discussed. The extreme positions are (1) that 'waves' of Indo-European-speaking invaders more or less exterminated their predecessors, and (2) that they were very few in number, hardly more than raiding parties. Neither extreme seems likely, and the latter is particularly implausible:

according to all analogies in history, mere raiding-parties would have been absorbed linguistically—if not in every single case, then at least in the majority of cases. The actual outcome, therefore, argues for considerable numbers of people, and stable social groups including women and children.[1]

In the case of the Hittites in Anatolia, thanks to written records, the cultural complexities are more overt than in the case of Romans, Germans, and so on. It is clear that the Hittites took over a going concern; but the indigenous Hurrians retained prestige personally and their language continued to be spoken and used in important rituals. Many Hittite kings with Hittite throne-names are known to have had Hurrian names prior to ascending the throne, and they had wives, viziers, seneschals, and so on, with Hurrian names. For all that, Hittite was the language of administration, of official records, and so on. In general and in detail the situation is reminiscent of the early phases of the Norman conquest of England.

   a. The reliance upon onomastics for our understanding of history is a little risky. A culture can take over the naming practices of another culture wholesale, as for example the enduring popularity of male Germanic names in France (they include most of the commonest male given names—*Roger, Roland, Robert, Louis, Albert, Alain, Charles, Frédéric, Gilbert, Guillaume,* and so on), or the vogue for Hebrew names in Puritan New England. The Hurrian names in our Hittite records, therefore, are not guarantees of Hurrian ethnicity.

122. The results of language contact
Different from the question of what language emerges as the only language of an area in the aftermath of conquest, and an issue more interesting to the historian, is the question of the linguistic consequences of periods of coexistence (*language contact*). Recently there have been some major advances in our understanding of this question. At the same time, at the center of all such matters is a major intangible: the single most important factor seems to be social and cultural *attitude*—tricky to analyze, under the most favorable circumstances, and

---

[1] A third view—that there were no non-Indo-European paleo-Europeans, i.e., that ALL prehistoric peoples in Europe were speaking Indo-European languages—is associated chiefly with the opinions of Colin Renfrew.

difficult or impossible to recover in the case of cultures long gone.

The nature and extent of the influence of one language on another —if any influence is shown at all—will differ somewhat depending on whether a populace clings to its traditional language (a situation called *language maintenance*) or, such as happened in Roman Europe, takes over a different speech (*language shift*).

LANGUAGE MAINTENANCE

In the event of relatively shallow contact—that is, little bilingualism and not much access among the population to native speakers of the other language—the results will be borrowing of lexicon only. This may be extensive, if the cultural pressures are strong or long-term, but the words borrowed will include little basic vocabulary (p. 137).

On the other hand, in the event of intimate contact and much bilingualism, one expects extensive lexical borrowing and appreciable structural borrowing. The structural borrowing will be most apparent in the syntax and the phonology, though some of the derivational morphology of English has been imported from Latin and even Greek.[1] The lexical borrowing, 'intimate borrowing' in Bloomfield's term, will include function words (conjunctions, adverbial elements) and even some basic vocabulary, particularly personal pronouns and low numbers. The deep penetration of specifically Scandinavian features into the recesses of English vocabulary (including pronouns—such as *they*— and a preposition or two—*(un)til*) resulted from this kind of contact.

    a. These consequences are typical, but other outcomes are found. Given vast differences between two phonologies, for example, coupled with incompatible morphosyntax, even lexical borrowing can be at a minimum, and cultural attitudes (harder to chart) probably play a role too. For example, Zoque (northern Mexico)

---

[1] Examples are *-able* as in *breakable, -ation* as in *vexation,* and *-ize* in *Balkanize* or *brutalize.* Of course, these suffixes were not borrowed per se; they have been abstracted from borrowed words built with them (which still account for the bulk of the formations in question). But certain Uralic languages in northern Russia seem to have borrowed a substantial number of Altaic derivational affixes directly, that is, without borrowing much Altaic lexicon in the process.

is virtually free of Spanish loan words. Flathead (Montana) is on the point of extinction due to cultural pressure, but even as it is being displaced by English it shows no structural influence and has notably few loan words or even calques.

LANGUAGE SHIFT

When the target language is readily available and bilingualism is widespread, or where the shifting population is relatively small, there will be little influence of the indigenous language on the (prevailing) new one. The larger the shifting population, and the less accessible the target language is—it makes no difference whether this unavailability is purposeful or incidental—the more influence there will be of the indigenous language on the structure of the surviving target language, particularly in the areas of phonology and syntax. Significantly, there will be little effect on the vocabulary, with the obvious exception of terms for local plants, animals, social customs, food—i.e., items for which the target language provides no equivalents.

The explanation for this is simple enough, however counter-intuitive the fact itself may seem: despite what a despairing first-year language student might think, the lexicon of a language is in fact its most accessible component, and the easiest to get right. Gauls struggling to be accepted by Latin-speakers, for example, who can't remember (or don't know) a Latin word will presumably paraphrase around it, not plug in the Gaulish equivalent; still less would they purposely salt their speech with Gaulish words for which Latin equivalents are available. (They would be more likely to salt their Gaulish with Latinisms.) It is this which probably explains the meager Gaulish influence on Romance lexicon, which has struck many authorities as odd. This may also be the explanation for the lack of Britannic influence on English, though we really know too little about the early days of Saxon Britain to tell. (Note, by contrast, that in Ireland there HAS been significant influence of Gaelic on English, and along the predicted lines: the extensive Irish-English lexicon is largely limited to matters without English equivalents, but there has been a good deal of influence on syntax and phonetics. One striking form of syntactic influence is the frequency of the characteristically Gaelic use of a presentational verb *to be* with a relative clause, in place of one independent clause: *It's working at the shop all day I am, while it's sitting home you are, and....*)

b. The most extreme outcome of a language contact situation is the emergence of a true amalgam, that is, a language whose lexicon and grammar are conflated from two or more different sources. It has been argued, ably, that such a language represents a basic discontinuity: it does not belong to the language family of either source, i.e., it is *nongenetic*. Such nongenetic languages have either of two histories. In the case of *abrupt creolization,* a population for some reason tries to shift to a target language but, owing to the fundamental unavailability of models of the target, only the most superficial component of the target—the lexicon—is acquired (and that incompletely).

On the other hand, if for some reason a language is MAINTAINED by a populace despite heavy cultural pressure from another language over a long period of time, and given a favorable social atmosphere, the result may be a form of speech in which some of the original vocabulary is maintained (including, significantly, the basic vocabulary, p. 137) but the morphology and syntax are largely imported from the other language. An example of this is the East African language Ma'a (or Mbugu), whose vocabulary remains about fifty percent Cushitic—including the basic items—but whose morphosyntax, as well as the balance of the lexicon, is Bantu. (Indeed, some authorities have actually been led to classify Ma'a as a Bantu language, albeit a very odd one.)

Both of these extreme outcomes are rare.

123. Language and race

Any discussion of language and race is hampered at the outset by the problems of defining the term *race* in a way useful for this or any other purpose. Much human misery has resulted from more or less crassly superstitious views of races as not only physical but mental or moral types, and nowadays scholarship tends to avoid what is seen as a tainted subject. However, even the most dispassionate and abstrusely scientific attempts to pin down what race is and what 'the races' are have met with little acceptance.[1]

---

[1] The anthropologist W.W. Howells wrote as follows in 1959: 'UNESCO in 1950 assembled in Paris a panel of anthropologists and others, to draw up a general statement on the nature of race, as it is understood today. This was to be a long and full definition and explanation, a scientific reference for laymen of any sort. The panel did its work and made public its statement with hopeful satisfaction. But the other anthropologists fell upon this document with such vigor that the English journal, *Man,* was for some months running what amounted to a department of criticism, correction, and amplification, in the form of letters from Great Britain, France, and the United States. So UNESCO quickly got together another panel in

Even if we grant for the sake of argument (and against much objective evidence) that there are such things as distinct physical and genetic types which are fairly constant over populations and through time, between race so defined and language there is no connection. Linguistic and racial classifications, however defined, commonly cut across each other. A people (? race) often adopts the language of another people; a few of the many cases of this were mentioned above (120). In an example of the opposite relationship, Hungarians have kept their Finno-Ugric language, but are now indistinguishable from their Indo-European neighbors, and physically resemble their cognate Finns much less. There is no way to predict on the basis of physical or genetic type whether a citizen of India will be a native speaker of an Indic or Dravidian language.

In fact, most nameable languages or language families are spoken by peoples of assorted ethnicity. The French, who latterly portray themselves as a homogeneous society, are in fact descendants of Gauls, Romans, various flavors of Germans, and who knows what else—and none of these ingredients were homogeneous to start with, nationalist fantasies to the contrary notwithstanding. The Greeks and Celts were of mixed race at the dawn of history (and knew it), and some have theorized that the Roman historical myth of the 'rape of the Sabine women' was in part an attempt to account for racial diversity in Rome. (Less colorful modern theories suggest that the settlements in the region that became the Roman City State were partly Latin and partly Sabellian to begin with, and likely some Etruscans as well, such that the evolving city was an ethnic amalgam from the start.)

All told, Indo-European languages are spoken by peoples of such diverse physical types that it is futile on its face to think in terms of a 'Proto-Indo-European race', still less to hope to identify what 'it' was.

1951 to do the statement over again. This time the draft was circulated widely, so that the rest of the profession could get its comments and abuse in early. By compressing the results UNESCO was able to publish the statement and the gist of the exceptions to it—a sort of minimum anthropological description of race—in a relatively small volume.'

a. Until much too recently, it was usual for discussions of the spread of the Indo-European languages to include paeans to the cultural, moral, and probably physical superiority of 'the Indo-Europeans' over the indigenes they overran. This never was anything more than self-congratulatory nonsense, and advancing archeological knowledge has revealed that the cultures overrun by 'the Indo-Europeans' were largely peaceable, technologically and socially advanced, and in no obvious way inferior to what came after. Indeed, Greece—the one locale where the Paleo-European culture survived in an amalgamation with invading elements—was the scene of the only genuinely advanced culture in the ancient Indo-European world, unless (as seems likely) something similar happened in the Hittite Empire and in northwestern India. Incidentally, even in Greece, the importance of Semitic cultural influence has probably been underrated as part of the mix; such cultural influence was obviously very strong on the Hittite Empire.

The attempt to reconcile the notion of Indo-Europeans as culturally and morally superior with their destruction of advanced cultures—perhaps such cultures were merely effete, for example, rather than advanced—was an unequal struggle from the outset and has largely been given up (apart from crannies here and there on the Internet).

SUGGESTIONS FOR FURTHER READING

The subjects treated in this chapter are well-served in standard texts: see **Bynon 1977** chapters 4–6, **Hock 1991** chapters 14–16, **Hock & Joseph 1996** chapters 10–11, **Lass 1997** chapter 4, **Campbell 1999** chapter 12. **Mallory 1989** contains a number of interesting passages on Indo-European prehistory. A classic already is **Nichols 1992.**

On the consequences of language contact, one of the most important books on historical linguistics of the 20th century is **Thomason & Kaufman 1988. Weinreich 1968** is another indispensable reference.

A diverting but solid discussion of speech registers will be found in **Joos 1967.**

Koineization is an important and under-studied aspect of language formation. For a discussion of koineization, both in theory and in the history of Spanish specifically, see **Tuten 1998.**

WRITTEN RECORDS

THE INTERPRETATION OF WRITTEN RECORDS

124. For both historical and comparative work, linguists work with the earliest possible attestation of a language. The more time that passes between the proto-language and the daughters, the more changes have taken place; and the more changes, the more complex the task of recovering the history of the language family. The written records of earlier periods of a language's development are for historical linguistics something like what a telescope is for astronomy; weak or strong (that is, depending on whether the records are 300 or 3000 years old), it shows us things we wouldn't know if we didn't have it. On the other hand, projecting forward, in a sense, when we study the more recent history and development of a language, it is also the case that the more detailed our knowledge is of what the structure of the language was a hundred or five hundred or a thousand years ago, the better our understanding of its current features will be. But if linguists are going to work with a state of the language earlier than the childhood of the oldest living speaker, that means dealing with written records.

Pinning down the details of historical phonology inevitably leads to questions of what the written symbols of ancient languages actually represent. Theoretically, one can get along well enough dealing with the symbols qua symbols, since locating recurring correspondences in basic vocabulary (p. 137) is all that is required. Thus, at least in theory, finding that @9 in Language A several times corresponds to &% in Language B will do. But observation of behavior suggests that most linguists prefer to have at least a general idea of the phonetic or phonemic values of the words they work with. In fact, phonetic reality is more than merely reassuring: if you were to find somehow that @9 in the example stood for [š] while &% stood for [æn], you would probably be inclined to discount the significance of the correspondence.

The following is a survey of the principal lines of reasoning for recovering at least some of the phonetic features of written languages. It treats only phonographic signaries—writing systems that represent (however erratically) the phonology of the language. Morphographic writing systems such as Sumerian cuneiform or Egyptian hieroglyphics have been decoded too, of course, but the crucial facts and the reasoning based on them are hair-raisingly complex, and do not lend themselves to a brief rehearsal.

Finally, the quality of evidence available for different languages no longer spoken differs greatly from one case to the next. For Latin, say, we have a large literature in both poetry and prose, discussions of pronunciation by contemporary authorities, and epigraphic attestations covering a good stretch of time; on top of that, there was extensive contact with speakers of other languages, leading to much borrowing of lexicon in both directions, a potentially valuable source of information (127); and in the Romance Languages we have a large and diverse Latin progeny. Collectively, these afford a broad spectrum of evidence for almost every detail of Latin phonology. But even here, under almost ideal circumstances, problems remain.

At the other end of the cline would be a language like Cornish. Despite its very recent demise (conventionally put toward the end of the 18th century), there is a paucity of written records, indited moreover in an anarchic orthography influenced by both Welsh and English scribal practices. As a result, there are many mysteries about the pronunciation of Cornish.

The lines of reasoning discussed below are weak: it is rare that any single datum is decisive in recovering a feature of an ancient phonology. The usual situation is that motes of evidence point this way and that; if enough of these grains of sand wind up on the same side of the question they may tip the scales in favor of a particular interpretation. Of course, how much is enough is subjective at bottom, and what convinces one scholar may be seen by another scholar as a mare's nest of fugitive evidence and flawed arguments.

TRANSLITERATION

125. There are two subvarieties of reasoning from transliteration: (1) a form is found represented in a FOREIGN alphabet or syllabary; (2) a given language routinely uses more than one SYSTEM for written representation.

1. Greek had three series of symbols for obstruent consonants, as seen in the following table:

$$
\begin{array}{lllll}
A & - & \Pi & T & K & /p\ t\ k/ \\
B & - & B & \Delta & \Gamma & /b\ d\ g/ \\
C & - & \Phi & \Theta & X & ?
\end{array}
$$

First, there is no reasonable doubt that the series here called A stood for /p t k/, respectively; and that series B stood for /b d g/.[1] Second, there is no question that in a later period, as still in present-day Greek, the sounds represented by the C-series are voiceless fricatives on the order of [f θ χ] (see pp. 56-7). But: what sounds did they represent in, say, Periclean Athens?

An important source of evidence is the rendition of Greek NAMES in the Roman alphabet. When these contain consonants from the C-series, the earliest Roman practice was to use the Latin letters P, T, C respectively (which normally stand for /p t k/, like Greek Series A). Thus:

Greek	Roman
ΦΙΛΙΠΠΟΣ	PILIPVS
ΑΧΙΛΛΕΥΣ	ACILES
ΑΓΑΘΟΣ	AGATO

Note that these facts tell us little in the case of C for X and T for Θ. If these were fricatives of some sort in Greek, there would have been no way to represent them directly in Latin letters anyhow. The crucial datum is the Roman choice of P, rather than F, for Φ: it indicates that Φ is some kind of voiceless stop, not a fricative like its later value.

In the absence of evidence to the contrary, we assume that Θ and X also represented voiceless stops.

2. 'The Greek alphabet' was actually a number of closely-related scripts, not all of which had the special symbols of the C-series here. In C-less versions of the alphabet, the sounds written with the C-series of the fuller signaries are variously represented, the two main alternatives being: the use of the A-series to write the sounds represented

---

[1] These are taken as givens here; but of course, the values of A and B have had to be determined by the same kinds of reasoning that are set forth in this chapter.

by the C-series in the fuller alphabets (e.g. ΑΚΙΛΛΕΥΣ 'Achilles'); and writing a sequence consisting of the A-series letters plus H (for example, ΑΚΗΙΛΛΕΥΣ). Both of these conventions accord with the inference drawn from the first analysis, above, namely that the C-series sounds were stops, not fricatives.

Conclusion: the best sense that can be made of these two kinds of evidence taken together is that the Greek C-series letters represented VOICELESS ASPIRATED STOPS, /p^h t^h k^h/ or so (A7).

a. The Greek transliteration of Latin names, *Sulpicius* and *Appius,* for example, as ΣΟΛΦΙΚΙΟΣ and ΑΠΦΙΟΣ, with Φ rather than Π—the reverse of subvariety (1), above —points in the same direction. It makes sense only if Greek Φ stood for a stop of some sort, and further suggests the interesting phonetic detail that Latin /p t k/ were aspirated enough to leave the Greek ear in doubt as to whether the best Greek equivalent for Latin stops was the C-series /p^h t^h k^h/ or the plain stops /p t k/.

126. The importance of names

Names, of both people and places, are crucial in these arguments. In rendering names, the writer/transcriber is presumably aiming to represent a particular pronunciation as closely as possible; so if something about the pronunciation of the name in the original language is already known, this sheds light on the value of the symbols used in the transcription. In the decipherment of wholly unknown scripts, such as Egyptian hieroglyphics, Babylonian cuneiform, and Linear B, names were vital keys to the values of the characters. It was the discovery of the groups of hieroglyphs on Egyptian inscriptions such as the Rosetta Stone which corresponded to the known name *Ptolemaios* 'Ptolemy' that provided the first clue for what the signs represented. Similarly the first reading values for signs in the cuneiform scripts came from names, though with a difference from the Egyptian situation. The Rosetta Stone provided a readable key (albeit fragmentary) in the Greek bilingual, whereas all three of the *languages* in the trilingual cuneiform inscriptions of Persepolis and Susa, as well as the *writing systems* themselves, were unknown. (The key to cracking the code was the hunch that certain stereotyped phrases at the beginnings of the inscriptions, in combination, named three generations of kings, and the only trick was to pick the right dynasty. The one that worked turned out to be Achaemenid; but see note a.)

a. In both the Egyptian and cuneiform decipherments there were many difficulties, however. It was a while before anyone realized that the phonographic signs in the hieroglyphic script represented only consonants. In the cuneiform case, in addition to the hit-or-miss business of guessing which royal dynasty was involved, there were sizable discrepancies between the known (Greek and Hebrew) versions of the Persian names and the actual names themselves: for example the Achaemenid king known to us in Greek sources as *Xérxēs* /kserksēs/ and in Old Testament Hebrew as *Akhashverosh* emerged from cuneiform Old Persian as χšayā̆ršā̆. And finally, in both cuneiform and hieroglyphic systems of writing, the relationship between writing and the language represented is bewilderingly complex.

BORROWING

127. Loanwords offer evidence for pronuciation, interpreted using principles very similar to the reasoning connected with transliteration (125), but with one large difference: in the case of borrowing the pronunciation of the 'target' form is not merely REPRESENTED (as accurately as the sophistication of the adapter and the makeup of the writing system will allow)—its pronunciation will probably have been ADAPTED to the phonology of the borrowing language. This introduces complexities of interpretation which are not always taken into account in discussions of these phenomena.

A standard, and good, example of this kind of evidence—and also exemplifying the aforementioned complexities of interpretation—bears on the question of the value of the Latin consonant written V.

In later forms of Latin, as still seen in the modern-day Romance languages, the sound continuing Latin V depends on the position in the word. Initially, it is a voiced fricative in French, Italian, Portuguese, and the rest; medially it generally falls together with Latin B:

Latin	French	Spanish	Italian
lavāre 'wash'	laver /lave/	lavar [laβar]	lavare
ōvum 'egg'	œuf /øf/	huevo [weβo]	uovo
caballus 'horse'	cheval /šəval/	caballo [kaβaʎo]	cavallo
faba 'bean'	fève /fev/	haba [aβa]	fava

That this is an innovation is evident on its face, as the distribution of V and B in classical Latin is contrastive in all environments.

And there are a number of good reasons for believing that in early times the consonant sound represented by V was [w]. One datum is the English word *wine*. It is a Germanic borrowing of very early date from Lat. *vīnum*, and can be taken as indicating that [w] was the value of the Latin consonant letter V.

It does not, however, PROVE that V was [w]. The problem is that Old English, like all early Germanic languages, did not have [v] in word-initial position. What then if the actual pronunciation of the Latin target word were [vi·nũ] or the like, rather than [wi·nũ]? To be borrowed into any early Germanic language, such a form would have to be adapted in some way. This raises the non-trivial possibility that the [w] of the English pronunciation is not in fact a sort of snapshot of the pronunciation of contemporaneous Latin, but a SUBSTITUTION of a native sound for an impossible Latin one.

However, there is reasoning that points away from such an idea:

The phonetically thinkable substitutes for Latin word-initial [v] in Old English would have been /b/, /w/, /hw/, and /f/. On phonetic grounds alone, it is a toss-up whether OE /w/ or /hw/ would be the very least likely of these; but /w/ is nevertheless possible.

Second, Lat. V occurs medially as well as initially. Medially it shows up in Romance reflexes as sounds of the type [v ~ β], as in Sp. *huevo* [weβo] 'egg' or [f], as in Fr. *œuf* [œf] 'egg' (both from Lat. *ōvum*). Now, what is important about medial Lat. V is that Old English DID have an intervocalic [v], so that if its pronunciation in Latin were in fact [v], in a loan word it could be pronounced without trouble in English and could be unambiguously indicated in its orthography as well. Accordinging to Old English evidence, Latin source-words with medial V contained [w], not [v]: Lat. *pāvō* 'peacock' gives OE *péa* (*éa* is the regular OE development of PGmc **aw*. Cf. NHG *Pfau* = OE *péa*). Likewise, Lat. *pervinca* 'Vinca minor' (a kind of plant) gives NE *periwinkle*.

Third, as mentioned above, the word-initial sound written V in Latin is known to turn into [v] in the LATER development of the language en route to Romance; and there are loan words in English which on various grounds are known to be later than borrowings like *wine*. Such words disclose a struggle to accommodate an alien sound. Lat. *verbēna* '*Verbena officinalis*' (a kind of herb) shows up in Old English as *berbene* (accent on the first syllable); Lat. *versus* 'row, line; verse' shows up as

OE *fers* 'sentence; verse'. Thus did speakers of OE accommodate the impossible Late Latin word-initial [v]. And, significantly, it appears that OE *w-* is NEVER used for Romance *v-* in borrowings of this date.

English borrowings provide evidence for the phonetic details of Medieval French sibilants. French reflexes of Latin *c* before front vowels come into English uniformly as /s/, thus *face, embrace, entice, cent*. However, French reflexes of Latin *s*, and also of Latin *t* in assibilating environment (earlier than the palatalization of Lat. *c*), are inconsistently represented in English: now as /š/, in *push, leash, varnish, punish*, and the like; now as /s/ in *miss, press, gross, abbess*.[1] A pertinent datum here is that we have evidence from a variety of sources that many languages of Europe in the Middle Ages had two kinds of sibilants: an alveopalatal [s] generally similar to NE /s/, and a lamino-alveolar [ṣ] like present-day Spanish (Castilian) /s/ and Finnish /s/. Modern French has no evidence of any such contrast—the French versions of the words in question all contain /s/ (or no sibilant at all); but the collective evidence of English borrowings from Medieval French suggests that something about the sibilant in the French sources of *push, press, varnish, abase* and the rest left the English ear in doubt as to whether to assign the sound to English /s/ or /š/. Thus, even though there is no evidence from French itself that the general European contrast between [s] and [ṣ] obtained in Medieval French, the treatment of English borrowings from French would plainly indicate that it did.

a. Two interesting details: borrowing into English provides no evidence for such a French distinction in INITIAL POSITION; nor for a pronunciation of French /z/ (from Latin *s*) as [ẓ] parallel to [ṣ].

But the significance of these two facts is different, and points up the necessity of paying attention to the phonological details of both the lending and the borrowing language. Since English had both /s/ and /š/ in initial position at the time of the borrowings, the consistent representation of the French reflexes of both Latin *c* (*cent*) and *s* (*sense*) as English /s/ indicates that the distinction between Fr. /s/ and /ṣ/ had already collapsed in word-initial position (as it was to collapse in all positions eventually).

---

[1] The /š/ in *pressure, issue,* and *sure* (and also in words like *facial* and *nation*) is unconnected with this phenomenon, and reflects earlier /sy/.

The lack of any evidence in loans for Fr. [ʐ] is a different matter, since at that point English itself did not have the sound [ž] anywhere in its inventory.[1] Therefore, the uniform occurrence of English /z/ (as in *rose*) in borrowings from French can provide no evidence for the phonetics of contemporaneous French.

MULTIPLE VALUES OF SYMBOLS

128. This has two complementary forms: (1) hesitation between different spellings within an orthographic system; (2) the use of a symbol for more than one function within a system.

1. In early Latin inscriptions, the sequence properly spelled *gn* is sometimes written NGN, for example INGNEM (*ignem*) 'fire' acc.sg. On still other occasions the sequence is spelled NN, as in SINNV (*signum*) 'sign, insigne'. There are a number of reasons for thinking that proper *gn* stood for [ŋn], not [gn]; the epigraphic substitutions of NGN and NN for proper *gn* are further evidence for this view.

Note the importance of INSCRIPTIONS in this kind of argument: once written, they aren't recopied, changed, brought up to date, normalized, or otherwise edited. It is the case that Latin manuscripts rarely (if ever) show things like epigraphic INGNEM.

2. Touching on the matter treated under 127 (borrowing) is the following additional evidence that Latin 'consonantal V' stood for [w] originally, not [v]: the letter V actually had three functions. It was used not only for the consonant that later became [v] etc., it was also used for the vowels /u/ and /ū/, as in CO(N)SVL (*cōnsul*) 'consul', AVGVSTVS (*Augustus*), and FORTVNA (*Fortūna*, a goddess). It is easier to accept the idea that the selfsame letter might be used to write [w], [u(·)], and the offglide of the diphthong [aw], than the idea that it was used, from the beginning, to write sounds as unalike as [v] and [u(·)].

---

[1] Like /š/ < /sy/ in the previous footnote, English /ž/ in loanwords like *vision* and *pleasure* is a later development of /zy/ within English, and unrelated to French sibilant phonetics.

CHRONOLOGY

129. Regarding the Latin letter V, at some later date it certainly stood for a fricative (or [b]) rather than [w], and that is still the value of the letter in all the standard Romance languages. The facts cited in 128 are good evidence that the value of Latin consonantal V was [w] around the time that the orthography was crystallizing; but note that they cannot shed any light on whether it was still [w] in (say) Nero's day. This is an important principle which even authorities sometimes lose sight of: a change in pronunciation will be reflected by a change in spelling only if the spelling is being invented on the spot, and then only if certain kinds of changes in pronunciation are involved.

Spelling out words anew mainly involves two kinds of situation: amateur writers, that is, people who more or less 'know the letters' but do not write or read often; and outsiders, who are possibly unfamiliar with local orthographic customs.

Amateurs are commonly foxed by changes in pronunciation which result in syncretism of two different sounds. In the history of Latin, the diphthong *ey* and the vowel *ī* fall together as *ī*. In early Latin inscriptions, the spellings EI and I are used consistently and correctly; later, one starts to find cases of EI used to spell words containing *ī* < *ī*. (And in any such inscription we may be sure that e.g. DEIXIT for *dīxit* 'he said', even though the spelling is etymologically correct, is an ARCHAISING spelling of a word actually pronounced /dīksit/.)

As for outsiders, Frederick the Great's *asteure* for standard French spelling *à cette heure* 'at this time' contains information about the actual pronunciation of French that the approved orthography lacks. Similarly, Greeks who at one point in history would have substituted Gk *ou* for Latin consonantal *v* might well decide at a later period—after a change in pronunciation in Latin itself—that it would be better to render the sound in Greek letters with *b*.

But—and this is important—it would never occur to a NATIVE SPEAKER of a Romance language, at any time in its evolution, that a change from [w] to [v] in the pronunciation of a word like *vīnum* called for rethinking the orthography.

Here is an example of the pitfalls sometimes encountered in this kind of reasoning. The value of the Greek letter theta, Θ, as shown in

125. I was originally [tʰ], a voiceless aspirated stop. Evidence shows (pp. 56-7) that by the third century AD, [tʰ] had become a fricative, [θ], its value in present-day Greek. However, as early as seven hundred years before that, we have inscriptions in certain Greek dialects in which the letter sigma, Σ, normally [s], is substituted for Θ; for example, Laconian (Spartan) *anesēke* '(he) dedicated' for standard Greek *anéthēke*.

Some scholars have taken this as evidence for the change to a fricative, as attested later in standard Greek, already in 4th cent. BC Laconian. Now, SOMETHING had definitely happened in Laconian, but a mere change from aspirated stop [tʰ] to fricative [θ] absolutely cannot be the explanation for the respelling: so long as the sounds written with Θ and Σ were different, no matter what their phonetics, it could never have occurred to native speakers to change the spelling. So, either the inscriptions in question were written by non-Laconians, or else a spelling like *anesēke* means exactly what it looks like—the likelier interpretation, in fact—namely, that Pan-Gk [tʰ] had simply become /s/ in Laconian.

BORROWING THE SYMBOLS

130. There are two situations: (1) borrowing BY a language whose written representations are otherwise well understood; (2) borrowing FROM a language whose written representations are well understood.

1. If, say, the Romans felt pressed to import special symbols from Greek to write Greek names and loan-words, it is safe to assume that the value of no Latin letter will do even approximately. Thus we note that Latin routinely uses *u* to render the Greek digraph *ou,* as in *Ūrania* from Gk *Ouranía* (one of the nine muses—Lat. *mūsa,* from Gk *Moûsa*), and in very early loans *u* also represents the Greek sound spelled Υ, such as *scutula* 'a roller for moving very heavy objects' < Gr. *skutalā.*[1] In the great majority of loans, which are from a later period and fur-

---

[1] The change of *a* to *u* before 'fat *l*' (133.1) and the non-Attic-Ionic ending of the *ā*-stem nouns both point to an early borrowing. Cf. the much closer approach to the (Attic) form in *scytala, -ē,* below.

thermore are from Attic specifically (the prestige dialect), the Attic vowel written Υ is represented by *y*, a letter based on Gk Υ: so ΝΥΜΦΑ 'young wife'·> Lat. *nympha*, ΜΥΡΤΟΣ 'myrtle' > Lat. *myrtus*, ΚΥΑΘΟΣ 'ladle (for serving wine)' > Lat. *cyathus* (3 syllables), and so also even in the later borrowings of the same Greek word that formerly resulted in *scutula*: Lat. *scytala, scytalē* 'roller' (Att. ΣΚΥΤΑΛΗ).

Now, whatever sound Gk Υ stood for in Attic, no Latin sound evidently was very close to it, so our knowledge of the Latin inventory of vowels limits the possibilities of what the value of Attic Υ might have been. (Evidence, parenthetically, points to the high front rounded vocalic, [ü(·)]; and there is also a variety of evidence suggesting that no such vowel was found in native Latin vocabulary.) In later Latin, of course, it is clear that *y* and *i* are merely allographs, a state of affairs continued indirectly in the French and Spanish name for the letter *y*, namely 'Greek *i*'.

a. On p. 56-7 the creation of a special symbol in the Gothic alphabet to render Greek words containing Χ /kʰ/ was discussed in a different connection—whether Greek /kʰ/ had become a fricative at the time of the creation of written Gothic. But that is tantamount to saying that a Greek-alphabet-inspired letter was necessary in *Saixaineia* because no Gothic sound was close enough to the sound in Σεχενία(ς) 'Shechaniah'. But nearly all instances of the special Gothic letter transliterated *x* are found in the epithet *Xristus* 'messiah' (lit. 'annointed'). In North Germanic languages, the sound represented by *h*- before liquids remained a fricative until hardening into a stop in modern Scandinavian languages, and Go. *Xristus* certainly supports the idea that the sound written with Greek Χ was not a fricative yet; but this must NOT be thought of as proof. The problem is that given the particularly sacred character of the word itself, Greek orthography might well have been carried over for it even if Go. *h* was an apt way to write it. Certain Greek orthographic habits (themselves presumably influenced by e.g. Hebrew taboos regarding the ineffable name of God) did in fact carry over: like the word for 'God', *Xristus* is not actually written out in Wulfilian Gothic, but is instead always abbreviated: $\overline{Xus}$ = *Xristus (nom.), $\overline{Xau}$ = *Xristau (dat.), and so on. The form is actually written full in only a single word, the compound *galiuga-xristus* 'false messiah'.

2. The value of the Latin letter O was for a virtual certainty a mid, back, rounded vowel. If therefore this letter is used to render a vowel in a previously unwritten (ancient) language, such as Old Irish or Old High German, it is to be inferred that the phoneme in question was prob-

ably some kind of middish, backish, rounded vowel, or more accurately, included such phones prominently in its allophonic range.

a. As self-evident as this principle may seem, there are of course exceptions to it. For example, we are confident that Lat. *h* stood for a sound very much like English [h]. But the letter *h* is used by Old Irish scribes in two ways, seemingly, neither of which makes sense from the point of view of the (Classical) Latin phonetics. First, it is used as a diacritic, such that *th* = [θ] and *ch* = [χ]; second, it appears haphazardly at the beginnings of words which, on good evidence, actually began with no consonant at all. Furthermore, there is strong evidence that Old Irish itself actually had an [h], the lenited form of *s*. For example [aherk] 'his love' is written either *a serc* or (less commonly) *a erc*—but never ˣ*a herc*. These facts can all be explained by the hypothesis that by the time of the earliest efforts to write Old Irish in Latin letters (and even long before, probably), the Latin sound represented by the letter *h* had ceased to be pronounced at all, leaving the scribes at liberty to use the letter any way they wished. (Evidence from other quarters also points to the early disappearance of Lat. [h]. For one thing, there is no trace of it in Romance languages.)

COMPARATIVE EVIDENCE

131. There are two dimensions to the evidence provided by cognate languages: (1) what sorts of sounds in cognate languages CORRESPOND to the sound in question; (2) what sorts of sounds in daughter languages REFLECT the sound in question.

1. Gothic (an early-attested Germanic language, now extinct) was written in a special alphabet invented expressly for the language; it distinguishes graphically between long and short vowels thus:

	Written (*transliterated*)	*Phonemic* *Value*
short:	i	i
	ai	e
	au	o
long:	ei	ī
	e	ē
	o	ō

However, there is no graphic distinction between /u/ and /ū/, or between /a/ and /ā/. The question then is: do the letters corresponding

Gothic	OE	OHG	ON	
wulfs	wulf	uuolf	ulfr	'wolf'
lustus	lust	lust	lyst	'pleasure'
ufar	ofer	uber	yfir	'over'
-hus	hús	hūs	hús	'house'
brukjan	brúcan	brūhhan	—	'use' (verb)
rum	rúm	rūm	rúm	'room'

Table showing regular reflexes of PGmc *u* and *ū;* all other details are regular as well. Go. *-hus* is attested only in a compound, *gudhus* 'temple'. The modern English reflex of OE *brúcan* is *brook* 'allow, tolerate'.

to *a* and *u* in Gothic script stand sometimes for long and sometimes for short phonemes? Or was there just no length contrast in the case of high and low back vowels?

One piece of evidence bearing on this point is the observation that all other Germanic languages have a contrast between long and short vowels in forms corresponding to the Gothic words in question, such that all the Germanic language apart from Gothic agree as to which *u* is short and which is long; and there is similar (if less copious) evidence regarding *a* vs *ā*. So it is to be inferred that Gothic *u, a* probably stood for both *u, a* and *ū, ā*.

Since this signary was invented for Gothic by a Goth, however, one might worry about an inventor who conceived of ways of distinguishing length for only six out of ten vowel phonemes. Happily, there is a good reason why the written representation of the four vowels—and just these four in particular—would be *underdifferentiated*. The key is the state of Greek phonology at the time of Wulfila's invention of the Gothic alphabet (third century AD). By way of background: there are a number of saliently Greek traits from this period carried over into Gothic spelling conventions, such as the use of *ai* for /e/ and *ei* for /ī/. The Greek syncretism of *ei* and *ī* as /ī/ provided Greeks for the first, time with a ready means of distinguishing in writing between /i/ and /ī/. But at no point in the history of Greek was there ever a means of distinguishing length for the low back and high back vocalics. It is unlikely to be a coincidence that it was exactly these length contrasts, and only these, which were unrepresented in Gothic script as well.

2. Old English scribes use a Latin signary except for two special letters, þ and φ, called *thorn* and *wynn* (the symbol φ is a crude approximation of the Old English letter). These are seen in e.g. *þorn, þynn, forþ,* and *φín, φolf,* and *hφít.* These words yield modern English *thorn, thin, forth, wine, wolf,* and *white,* respectively. The inference is that—in absence of evidence to the contrary—þ stood for OE /θ/, and φ stood for /w/. (In some scribal practice, *u* and *uu* are used in place of φ which, per the reasoning set forth in 128.1, is consistent with this conclusion.)

Another example: as mentioned above (128.1), there are reasons for thinking that in Latin the letters -*gn*- (as in *signum* 'sign' and *dignus* 'seemly') stood for [ŋn], not [gn]. In West Romance languages, this sequence is reflected by [ñ], as in Fr. *signe, digne,* It. *segno, degno.* It is easier to get to [ñ] from [ŋn] than from [gn]. This is not to say that [gn] > [ñ] is impossible, however, and in fact even better diachronic evidence comes from Romanian. Its reflex of -*gn*- is [mn], as in Rom. *lemn* 'wood' < Lat. *lignum.* The sequence [mn] is the EXPECTED Romanian development from [ŋn], but it is nearly impossible from [gn].

TYPOLOGY, PARALLELISM

132. Appeals to both typology and parallelism come down to interpreting ambiguities in writing systems on the basis of what is known about the typical properties of the structures of phonologies.

Typological reasoning bears on the question of vowel length in Gothic, just discussed under 131.1. Gothic inherited (and wrote) a distinction between various long and short vowels, but it writes reflexes of **u* and **ū* with the same letter. It is however unlikely that a language that faithfully preserves the Proto-Germanic contrast between /i/ and /ī/ would efface the contrast between /u/ and /ū/, so we infer that a length contrast going unwritten.

a. This kind of reasoning must be used with caution. Many phonologies are in fact atypical or asymmetrical in detail. For example, modern standard French has only low nasal vowels, whereas in most languages with a contrast between oral and nasal vowels, there is either a complete two-way contrast or there are trifling gaps in the opposition between them. In Classical Arabic, the final consonant of the definite article, ʔal, assimilates to all following coronal consonants with the single exception of ǰ. In Hindi, the contrast between (true) dental and retroflex articulation is found in nasals only when the nasal is adjacent to stops: [n̪t̪] vs [ṇṭ], for example. Intervocalically, the phonetics of the sounds written with the letters that lie in the dental and retroflex series are apico-ALVEOLAR for /n/, and a nasal flap for /ṇ/

STATEMENTS BY

CONTEMPORANEOUS AUTHORITIES

133. 1. The Roman grammarian Consentius tells us that there were two kinds of *l* in Latin: *exilis* (lit. 'thin') and *pinguis* (lit. 'fat'). 'Thin' *l* occurred before high front vowels and another *l*, so in *velim* 'I would like', *olīva* 'olive', *villa* 'estate'. 'Fat' *l* occurred everywhere else. On its face, we are dealing here with a more or less velarized lateral ('fat'), like the English lateral in *silt*. It is less clear whether the 'thin' lateral was specifically palatal, or palatalized, or only neutral.

2. The groupings of words in the old Chinese 'rime tables' provide information about what words sounded alike, however much they have diverged subsequently. (But the interpretation of the tables is an exceedingly complex matter—a study in itself.)

3. Tennyson's statement in a letter that he'd 'sooner lose a pretty thought' than indite it in a rime between *sister* and *vista* is tantamount to saying that the words DO rime (and, on the basis of other evidence, had rimed for a hundred years and more).

4. The English orthoepic manuals of the 17th and 18th centuries are full of evidence regarding the pronunciation of the period. For example, the *Orthoepia Anglicana* (1640) of Simon Daines puts *beauty, Beaumont, Beaufort, dew, few, fewer,* and *ewe* in a list of words with 'Latin *eu*' as distinct from '*u* single', which he says occurs in *new, lieu, adieu, view*. It is fairly easy to figure out what Daines is driving at: something like [iw] for *beauty* and the rest, and by '*u* single' for *new, view* he means something like the value [yu] for -*u*- in *music*.[1] Note that this distinction has collapsed in present-day English, and further that there is

---

[1] The value [yu] rather than [yuw] is presumed, as no orthoepists mention anything that can be interpreted as referring to offglides in the so-called 'tense' vowels like those in present-day *say, me,* and *go*.

nothing in the standard spellings of either our day or Daines's own to point to that earlier contrast. (It is an incidental detail that *Beaumont* has since been Frenchified into /bowmant/.)

POETRY

134. A literary form with rigid structural constraints—that is, poetry—can provide evidence about pronunciation. What kind of evidence, naturally, is determined by the specific rules of the form. In modern English, *greet* and *meat* rime, and as a rule the digraphs *ee* and *ea* are simply different ways of spelling the same sound. But the rimes of Chaucer, Shakespeare, and even more recent poets, make it clear that in their day the words thus distinguished in present-day orthography had different vowels; that is, the list of words that rime with *greet* is different from the list that rimes with *meat*. (On the other hand, a different kind of evidence is provided when Gay rimes *great* and *cheat,* and Pope rimes *obey* and *tea*.)

In Old English, outcomes of Proto-Germanic *$*y$ are invariably written the same as the outcomes of PGmc *$*g$ in initial position followed by a front vowel; and both come into Modern English as /y/: PGmc *$*yuka^n$ > OE *geoc* > NE *yoke;* PGmc *$*gelwaz$ > OE *geolu* > *yellow* (cf. NHG *Joch* and *gelb,* respectively). But at what stage did the actual syncretism take place? Now, Old English poetry employed alliteration rather than rime as one of its organizing and constraining principles, and in all Old English poetry, reflexes of PGmc *$*g$ before front vowels and *$*y$ freely alliterate. This indicates that they had become the same phoneme before the 8th century (the date of the oldest texts).

It is even possible for poetry to reveal elements altogether unattested otherwise. The consonant /w/ can be reconstructed as a phoneme in the Greek poetry of Homer's time, even though it is never written in our manuscripts of Homer. Middle English poetry reveals accentuation and syllabification quite different from ours, for example words like *visio(u)n* 'vision' and *nacio(u)n* 'nation' had three syllables with the tonic accent on the ultima (p. 161); without poetry, in the absence of contemporaneous comment, we would know nothing of these matters. In a similar vein, where the present-day accentuation of words differs in American and British forms of English, Shakespeare confirms that

in his day the pronunciation was like the American one, for example
Ulysses [yuw'lisiyz] next to the British pronunciation ['yuwləsiyz].

135. Having outlined the various strategies for pinning down—or at least,
trying to corner—the phonetic features of languages no longer spoken,
let us now bring all these principles to bear on a specific question:
what was the pronunciation of the sounds represented by the Latin
letters G and C when they stood before a front vocalic? As it happens
there is relatively little evidence bearing on the value of G in Latin;
whatever we can figure out about the value of C will presumably be
valid for the voiced counterpart, in the absence of evidence to the
contrary.

What is at stake is whether these letters represented dorsal stops in
all positions, or else when before front vowels represented some kind
of affricate—[č ǰ] or [tˢ dᶻ] or something similar.

i. In the familiar Romance languages, without question, the sounds
at stake are reflected differently depending on the following vowel.
Thus, when a front vowel follows: Lat. *centum* '100' > Fr. *cent* /sã/, Sp.
ciento /θyento/ or /syento/, It. *cento* /čento/; Lat. *princeps* 'chief, leader'
> Fr. *prince* /prēs/, It. *prence* /prenče/; but when a back vowel follows:
Lat. *comitem* 'companion; courtier' > Fr. *conte* /kõt/, It. *conte* /konte/;
Lat. *cuneus* 'wedge' > Fr. *coin* /kwẽ/, Sp. *cuña*, It. *cuneo*.

This distribution might well reflect some phonetic difference dating
back to Roman times.

ii. Latin words borrowed into Old English have /č/ before front
vowels, as Lat. *acētum* 'vinegar' = OE *eċed* /ečed/, *picem* 'pitch' = OE *piċ*
/pič/. This too might point to [č] in the source language.

But further scrutiny of the Old English lexicon discloses that not
only in loan words but also in native vocabulary, *k* becomes OE *ċ* before a front unrounded vowel, as PGmc *kinwiz* > OE *ċinn* 'chin'. In
fact, the conditioning 'front vowels' include not only Proto-West-Germanic and Latin front vowels but certain front vowels which arose
within the early history of Old English by various routes. It is espe-

cially significant that these include words borrowed from Latin with *ca* sequences, in which the palatalizing vowel is a development within the history of English itself: for example Lat. *castra* '(en)camp(ment)' = **kastra* > PreOE **kæɹstr* > OE *ċeaster* /čæəster/ 'city' (whence the place-names in -*chester*) and Lat. *causa* 'lawsuit, quarrel' (the etymon of It. *cosa* and Fr *chose* both 'thing', **62a**) = **kawsa* > **kæɹs* > OE *ċéas* 'strife'. This indicates that the words in question were borrowed before the Old English fronting, which necessarily predated the Old English palatalization; so the presence of /č/ in words like *ċed* and *piċ* actually tells us nothing of the details of Latin pronunciation of C at the time of the original borrowing.

iii. It is clear that Latin's ancestor, Proto-Indo-European, had no distinction of velar stops as they occurred before front vs. back vowels; thus Proto-West-Indo-European **g* is uniformly attested as Celtic /g/, Germanic /k/, Greek /g/, and so on, regardless of the following vowel. Had there been some kind of palatal or palatalized pronunciation of **k* and **g* before front vowels, it is implausible (in the extreme) that there would be next to no evidence for such a pronunciation in early-attested Indo-European languages in the so-called Centum group.

iv. As mentioned in item 1, above, it is clear that in Romance languages the reflexes of C and G are determined by the phonetics of the following vowel (front vs. back); but there is an important exception to this. In the variety of Romance spoken on the island of Sardinia, all Latin C and G are reflected as stops, regardless of the following vowel: next to Italian /čento/, French /sã/, and the rest reflecting Lat. *centum* '100', as given above (**i**), there is Sardo *kentu*. Now, the development of /k/ to /č/ in palatalizing environment is a very straightforward matter; a development of /č/ to /k/ is close to inconceivable—anywhere, never mind in a palatalizing environment. That is, the facts of Romance can be explained with greater phonological plausibility if we start from a phonology similar to Sardo's rather than with one similar to any other Romance language.

v. Roman grammarians themselves nowhere mention anything different about the 'powers' of these letters in different environments, whereas they do talk about 'fat *l*' and 'thin *l*', the assimilation of *n* to a following velar, the assibilation of *t* before *i* + vowel (as in *nātiō*), and other allophonic details. This however is an example of the weakest of all reasoning, the *argument from silence*.[1]

vi. In Umbrian (an Italic language spoken in a number of important cities near Rome), inherited *k WAS seemingly assibilated or strongly altered in some way before front vowels, and the altered sound is written with a special letter in the native (Sabellian) alphabet: it looks something like **d** and is probably in origin a digraph of **C** and **I**. It is variously transliterated ś, ç, and ṣ, and its likeliest value was [č]: thus **śerfe** [červe] < *kerese 'O Ceres'. Now, when Umbrian is written using the LATIN alphabet, letter C is used only before back vowels, and Lat. Ś (with or without the diacritic) is used where Umb. ś would occur. That is, C, however it was pronounced before front vowels in Latin, was not a possible representation of whatever the sound was that was represented by Umbrian ś.

vii. In Greek names and loan-words, Greek aspirated stops in cultivated Roman speech were pronounced with aspiration and written so (as in *philosōphia* and *Achillēs*). But unetymological aspirated stops also intruded into native vocabulary as hyperurbanisms (55), and as such are criticized by rhetoricians such as Cicero. There is a lesson in these blunders, however: attested spellings (and presumably the concomitant Greekified pronunciation), and forms mentioned by rhetoricians and grammarians, include such words as *pulcher* 'handsome' (so general that even Cicero grudgingly accepted it) and *chenturiō* 'squadron leader'. The point is that the bogus *ch* in these words stands before a FRONT vowel, whereas there is no shadow of a possibility that Greek *k* and *kh* (letter X) were assibilated or palatalized in any environment. That being the case, it is hard to understand how an aspirated *ch* in e.g. *chenturiō* can have arisen, if the initial consonant of *centuriō* was

---

[1] What makes it so weak is that, by its very nature, there is always more than one reasonable explanation for silence. Some aver that the argument from authority is weaker still—which it would be, if it were clear that appeal to authority even rises to the level of an argument.

pronounced anything like the intial consonant of present-day Italian *cento* 'roo'. Of course there is admittedly the possibility that the pronunciation implied by *chenturiō* employed not only an un-Latin aspiration but also an un-Latin stop pronunciation of a normally affricated initial consonant. But this is far-fetched compared to the straightforward inference.

viii. The grammarian Varro, in a discussion of what is manifestly the allophone [ŋ] of the phoneme /n/, lists among instances of the sound the word *anceps* 'two-edged'. This example would be out of place if the letter *c* here stood for something like [č]. (Still, if in fact the sound WAS [č], it would not have been the first time, nor certainly the last, that a grammarian's example failed to exemplify.)

ix. In Latin loan-words in Greek, and in Latin names rendered in the Greek alphabet(s), the equivalent of Roman C is usually κ, occasionally χ /kʰ/, as Gk Κικερων /kikerōn/ = Lat. *Cicerō*. Admittedly, if the Latin target did in fact begin with a [č], Greeks would have had a hard time rendering the sound directly, but (a) they could easily have come a lot closer to it than the letters κ and χ /kʰ/, and (b) they would likely have shown some hesitation between various makeshift renditions. (It is unlikely that the occasional representation of C by χ /kʰ/ is an attempt to render something distinctive about the Latin phonetics of C, since letters for voiceless aspirated stops—φ /pʰ/, θ /tʰ/—show up in the Greek renditions of Latin *p* and *t* as well, and χ for C is not limited to position before front vowels. See **125a**.)

x. The other side of the same coin: Latin orthography makes no special effort to render Greek /k/ before front vowels in names or borrowings. Names, for the reasons mentioned above (**126**), are the more probative. Thus the Phocian city which was the main port of Delphi, *Kírra* in Greek, is rendered *Cirr(h)a* in the Latin character. If Roman CI normally stood for something like [či] or [tˢi], one might expect at least hesitation if not outright avoidance of the spelling CI for /ki/. (Latin had the letter *k*, after all; it was only used before -*a*- in an early period, to write either /g/ or /k/, and in the classical period this letter was confined to a word or two. But it was available and unambiguous, and its similarity in shape to the Greek kappa would have helped, if there had been a problem. The Romans did after all borrow Greek Y to represent Greek forms accurately, 130.)

xi. As mentioned in item **i**, above, Latin C > Romance *č before front vowels. But note that the Latin source of It. *cielo* /čelo/, Fr. *ciel*, Sp. *cielo* /θyelo/, and so on, all from PRom. *kẹlu*, was actually *caelum;* similarly Lat. *Caesarem* > Fr. *césar,* It. *cesare,* and so on. That is, IN LATIN the C- in these words was followed by a low back diphthong, which only later fell together with Lat. *e* to become PRom. *ẹ;* it is this product, and not the original Latin vowel, which is the environment for [č] and the like. Of course, it is possible that in Latin itself the real rule was that /k/ was pronounced differently both before the diphthong *ae* as well as before front vowels—a phonetically implausible idea, or at any rate far-fetched—or (more plausibly) that in the dialect that actually underlies Romance, the monophthongization of *ae* had taken place preternaturally early. The most straightforward interpretation of the facts, however, is the one endorsed here. (The early-monophthonization theory, for example, hinges upon an extra assumption which is unsupported by independent evidence.)

xii. In a similar detail, the change *k > č takes place in post-Latin forms in which the *k itself is a post-Latin development: Lat. *coquīna* 'kitchen' > PRom. *kokina* (the intervocalic *k* not via a regular change) whence—this time by regular change—Fr. *cuisine,* It. *cucina* /kučina/; similarly Lat. *quīnque* 'five' dissimilated to PRom. *kinkwe* > Fr. *cinq* /sẽk/, It. *cinque* /činkwe/, Sp. *cinco* /θinko/. (When Lat. *qu* is continued as PRom. *kw,* as it usually is, there is no palatalization: Lat. *quid* 'what' > PRom. *kwẹ* > *kẹ* > Fr. *quoi* /kwa/—French /wa/ being the regular development of PRom. /ẹ/ in tonic open syllables—It. *che* /ke/, etc.)

CONCLUSION: the preponderance of evidence points to a VOICELESS DORSAL STOP (however front or back to some degree, in different environments) as the value of the letter C in Latin. The letter G can be cautiously taken to have had the same same point and manner of articulation features, but voiced.

SUGGESTIONS FOR FURTHER READING

Most handbooks of old languages have a section on 'Schrift und Aussprache' and the like, containing interpretations of the pronunciation of the written representations of the language. The reasoning which underlies these statements is rarely discussed, however. Nor are such discussions as in this chapter typical of books on historical linguistics generally. They are to be found in **Hock & Joseph 1996** chapter 3 §4, **Campbell 1999** chapter 14, and preeminently **Lass 1997** chapter 2.

Book-length applications of the reasoning presented here (often with running discussion of the reasoning itself) may be seen in **Sturtevant 1940** and **Allen 1967** and **1985** (for the classical languages), and **Jespersen 1909** (for English, particularly notable for its exploitation of orthoepic resources, but excellent in all ways).

Writing systems are a study in themselves; **Anttila 1988** chapter 2 considers the ways language and writing relate to one another; more elaborate treatments are **Sampson 1985** and (from a different perspective) **Coulmas 1996.**

Still highly worthwhile is the meaty (and sui generis) discussion of written records in **Bloomfield 1933,** chapter 17.

A topic critically dependent on the question of language/ writing interrelationships is DECIPHERMENT, whether of comparatively simple systems (Mycenaean linear B script; see **Chadwick 1963**) or of dauntingly intricate ones (Egyptian hieroglypics and the cuneiform scripts; **Cleator 1961, Friedrich 1966**). A discussion less focussed on these traditional problems is **Barber 1974.**

APPENDIX : PHONETICS

THE MECHANISMS OF SPEECH
AND THE CLASSIFICATION OF SPEECH SOUNDS

AI. The phonetic segment

An utterance is said to consist of phonetic *segments,* each consisting of a constellation of *articulatory features.* Segments are easy to demonstrate with well-chosen examples, such as the eight English words *cats, tacks, stack, cast, task, asked, sacked,* and *scat,* each of which contains the same four, evidently discrete, components—in very crude phonetics, [s], [k], [t], and [æ]. (See note **a.**) From the phonetic point of view, it is clear that there are four separate phonetic events (the segments) in a complex articulation like [stæk], with easy-to-hear boundaries between them.[1]

Even with examples of this kind, on close examination the question of discrete phonetic segmentation turns out to be complex; and segmentation is downright elusive in the case of words like *warrior* or *yellow.* It is convenient, however, and usually not too much of an idealization, to regard all utterances as segmentable into discrete elements articulated sequentially, called *speech sounds* or (more formally) *phones.*

When people talk, the organs of speech produce vibrations in the air, which are perceived by the organs of hearing. The three components of the speech act at the phonetic level accordingly are: *articulation, acoustics,* and *audition.*

Articulatory phonetics describes and classifies phones in terms of the positions and movements of the articulators (which will be described below) at the time that a given phone is produced. It is axiomatic that a given configuration of the vocal tract (A2) will result in one and only one phone; if two phones sound different, there MUST be an articulatory difference. (The converse is NOT valid: particularly in the case of vocalics, but not limited to them, a variety of articulatory strat-

---

[1] For charts of phonetic symbols see pp. 222, 230-1, and 233-4.

egies may result in identical acoustic outputs. The term *vocalic* is defined in A6.)

Articulatory phonetics makes no attempt to describe the sound of a phone directly or synaesthetically, that is, naming sounds *thin, hard, soft, dark,* and so on. Rather, it catalogues the positions and activities of the articulators during the production (articulation) of the phone. Obviously, an inventory of the organs of speech and their repertories of movement is indispensable, and follows directly.

   a. To review: phonetic symbols are enclosed in square brackets. Words or letters from languages are given in *italics*.

   Unlike the letter s, which in English has at least four values, [s], [z], [š], [ž] (or no value at all, as in *Illinois* or *island*), the symbol [s] stands for one and only one sound, which is the initial sound of *stack* and the final sound of *tacks*.

   What makes the eight words cited above (*cats, tacks,* etc.) different from one another is that the four phonetic segments occur in different orders. Note that the phonetic segments themselves are functionally void; that is, individually they contribute nothing to the meaning of the whole (with the trivial exception of the plural marker in *tacks* and *cats* and the tense-marker in *asked* and *sacked*). They are exactly like the dots and dashes that make up the Morse Code: the individual dots and dashes are without significance; they have significance only in certain combinations.[1]

   b. Phonetic science is plagued by a changing and unstandardized terminology. This accounts for the many synonyms for basic terms that are mentioned below and in the glossary; however, no attempt has been made here to be exhaustive in this matter, especially since many synonyms are obsolete, e.g. *inverted* for what is now usually *retroflex* (though for that very reason they are likely to be encountered in older reference works). Fashions in terminology continue to change, and sometimes obsolete terms (like *plosive* for *stop*) will experience a revival; *coronal* as a late 19th cent. synonym of *retroflex* was hardly used at all but appears in Leonard Bloomfield's *Language* (1933) redefined as any sound articulated with the apex, front, or

---

[1] Occasionally, of course, a single sound does have meaning, as in [kæts] *cats* next to [kæt] *cat*. But [s] means 'plural' only some of the time. At other times it means 'possessive', '3rd person singular subject', and 'the verb *be*' (in e.g. *Jack's not here.*) Most of its occurrences in English, however, are like those in *scat* and *task* and *tax* where it has no function (meaning) at all.

blade of the tongue; as such it was largely ignored for thirty-five years until it was taken up as a (pseudo-)binary feature by some generative phonologists, and is now a familiar and standard term; of the half-dozen synonyms for the voice-producing structure (*vocal cords, vocal bands, vocal folds, vocal ledges, vocal lips, vocal ligaments*) in ordinary use, *cords* had long been far and away the most general, but has recently been dislodged by *vocal folds*.

There is a similar variability in the shapes and functions of phonetic symbols, a book-length subject by itself.

c. Rapid advances have been made in *acoustic phonetics,* the study of the physics of speech sounds, using increasingly refined and useful instruments. Some long-held phonetic truths, based on subjective (articulatory) analyses of speech, are being modified as a result. Other kinds of instruments, measuring rate of air flow, for example, or air pressure at specific points in the vocal tract, have in still other ways added to our knowledge of the relationship between articulation (which are physiological acts) and speech sounds.

At present our knowledge of *auditory phonetics*—how the acoustic signal becomes intelligible to the hearer—is meager.

A2. The vocal tract

There are four more or less independent mechanisms that make up the *vocal tract,* such that any reasonably accurate description of a phone must specify the configuration and action of each of the four. The components are:

(1) airstream initiation (both the initiating mechanism and the direction of air flow), A3;

(2) phonation (the state of the *vocal folds*), A4;

(3) the oro-nasal adjustment (the position of the *velum*), A5; and

(4) the positions and movements of the tongue and lips (*articulation* in the narrow sense), A6.

A3. Airstream

All phones require moving air for their production. Such a movement of air can be set up using any one of three airstream initiators, each of which may move the air either out of the body or into the body (called *egressive* and *ingressive* airstream, respectively). Of these six possibilities, however, only one is of major importance, and most languages rely on it exclusively: *egressive lung air*. This being the default case, a speech sound without specified airstream features may be assumed to be egressive/pulmonic.

During breathing, chest and abdominal mechanisms (muscles, bones, and elastic tissues) rhythmically inflate and (partially) deflate the lungs. At the onset of speech, this rhythm vanishes: instead, the lungs are quickly filled, and then deflated slowly in a controlled way that provides a finely-adjusted egressive flow of air through the windpipe, to and through the larynx (at the top of the windpipe) in which the vocal folds are located, and thence to the mouth and nose. When the supply of air is low, the lungs are again quickly refilled and the process is repeated.[1]

    a. The second most important airstream initiator (but still of minor importance compared to the lungs) is the larynx itself, which, when the glottis is closed (or nearly so), may be moved up or down like a piston. An upward movement produces a class of obstruent phones (A7-8) called variously *(glottal) ejective* and *glottalized*. A downward movement produces a class of obstruent phones called *(glottal) ingressive*. The former, e.g. [pʔ tʔ kʔ], are always voiceless; the latter, e.g. [bˤ dˤ gˤ], are usually but not invariably voiced. Hausa [ƙ] (= [kˤ]), for example, is voiceless.

A4. Phonation

The *larynx*, located at the top of the windpipe (or trachea), is an armature of cartilage which supports and protects a complicated and delicate mechanism known as the *vocal folds* (or *vocal cords*). These are not literally folds or cords, but a pair of adjustable membranes. They may be pulled quite out of the air stream at one extreme or, at the other extreme, clamped tightly together, cutting off all air flow through the windpipe. This latter state, *glottal occlusion,* is useful for such non-linguistic purposes as coughing and sneezing, but it is widely found as an element in language. As a linguistic element, especially if it functions as a consonant, it is commonly known as a *glottal stop* (or, less commonly nowadays, *glottal catch*). Its phonetic symbol is [ʔ].

The edges of the vocal folds that come in contact in glottal occlu-

---

[1] The intake of air prior to speech is so unlike normal breathing that it is one of the more obvious cues—in a conversation group, for example, or on the telephone —that someone is preparing to speak.

sion are formed of bands of a special kind of cartilage, the vocal bands proper. When the space between the vocal folds, known as the *glottis,* closes and opens rapidly because of pulmonic air passing through it, as explained below, the result is a sound (with musical pitch) called *voice.* Phones whose phonetic makeup includes this sound are classified as *voiced.* When, during a segment, the folds are held somewhat apart, so that lung air passes between them more or less soundlessly, the phone is said to be *voiceless.* (Examples below.)

VOICE

The production of voice is complicated, but is easily explained in outline. The vocal folds do not produce sound in the manner of a violin string, set in motion by friction (in effect, a very rapid plucking); nor do they initiate sound like a buzzer; nor reverberate like a bell. The closest analogy is the reed assembly of a woodwind instrument, double reeds in particular.

Like a wind instrument, the vocal folds 'work' only if there is a flow of air. Given such a flow, in both reed instruments and the larynx the sequence of events that results in sound is as follows.

First, there has to be a small, elastic aperture (between the vocal folds or the reeds, depending), through which air flows. In the larynx this aperture is called the *glottis.*

As the airstream increases in velocity by reason of squeezing through the aperture, there is a pressure drop in accord with *Bernoulli's Principle.*

This causes the aperture to collapse, blocking the flow of air completely. When the air flow ceases, so does the Bernoulli effect, and the aperture reopens, elastically; thereupon the air flow resumes, and we are back at stage one.

This closing and opening takes place very rapidly. The specific rate determines the musical pitch of the resulting sound. If it happens 440 times a second, for instance, the resulting pitch is 'concert A' (A below middle C, rather higher than the ordinary speaking voice of most men). More rapid interruptions produce higher pitches; less rapid ones, lower pitches.

Now, nearly all phones may be produced in two versions, articulatorily identical except for PRESENCE or ABSENCE of voice. However, this pairwise phonetic distinction is unevenly distributed in the sound systems of actual languages. It is commonplace for *obstruents* (A7-8) but relatively rarely encountered in *vocalics* (A14-20), *liquids* (A10-11), and *nasals* (A9).

English is typical. All native speakers of English can unhesitatingly (and without paying particular attention) tell which word is which in the pairs of examples given here, so sensitivity to the voiced/voiceless distinction is acute on a practical plane; but without practice it may be difficult to focus on the phonetic difference objectively.

Voiceless	Example	Voiced	Example
[p]	maple	[b]	Mabel
[t]	welter	[d]	welder
[k]	bicker	[g]	bigger
[f]	wafer	[v]	waver
[θ]	ether	[ð]	either
[s]	fussy	[z]	fuzzy
[š]	Confucian	[ž]	confusion

Here are two techniques for enhancing the effect while pronouncing the words in the table.

(1) Hold your hands over your ears; this will block out most of the normal airborne acoustic feedback, leaving as the dominant aural impression the sound—which is very loud—of the vibrating vocal folds as transmitted to the ears through the bone. This makes it easier to concentrate on the switching on and off of the voice while you pronounce the pairs of words. This switching back and forth between voiced and voiceless segments will be very rapid, however, and may not be easy to identify on the first few tries. It would be best to start out with pairs like *fuzzy* and *fussy*, in which the [z] and [s] can be somewhat prolonged at will, to make their phonetics more evident.

(2) Rest your fingertips lightly on your neck over the larynx to FEEL the vibrations of the vocal folds while hearing them. (You will find that the ring-finger is particularly sensitive to this sensation.)

a. By these definitions, the glottal stop [ʔ] is neither voiced nor voiceless but a third phonational state. If *voiceless* is defined disjunctively, however (as the term itself implies), then [ʔ] is voiceless, as it does indeed lack voice.

Other phonational states include *breathy voice* (also known as *murmur*), *creaky voice* (also known as *glottal fry*), *whisper*, and *falsetto*. Breathy and creaky voice play a role in the phonologies of some languages. Whisper and falsetto are both *voice surrogates*, that is, they never function as components of phonologies as such, and when they occur in an utterance they take the place of ordinary voiced phonation. That is, in normal English speech the adjustment of the vocal folds alternates between voiced and voiceless phonation; in whispering, it alternates between whispered and voiceless phonation, though the acoustic difference between the two states is minimal.

b. In earlier sources the term *sonant*—not to be confused with *sonorant*, which is a synonym of *resonant*—will often be found for *voiced*; the terms *breathed* (from *breathe*) and *surd* are equivalent to our *voiceless*.

A5. Oro-nasal adjustment

The distinction between *oral* and *nasal* phones results from the position of the *velum*. This is an adjustable flap of tissue, informally the soft palate, at the back of the roof of the mouth. It acts as a valve between the nasal passages and the back of the throat. When it is down, the valve is open; this is necessarily its position during normal breathing with the mouth shut. When the velum is up, the valve is closed. This position is necessary for swallowing or blowing up a balloon.

In acoustic phonetic terms, the nasal passages are nothing but an optional *resonator*. During speech, when the velum is up the nasal passages are not part of the vocal tract (acoustically speaking) and do not resonate. Sounds pronounced under these conditions are called *oral*. When the velum is down and the valve is open, however, the nasal passages are a part of the vocal tract, and resonate at a particular frequency determined by the size and shape of the individual's anatomy. Phones pronounced thus are acoustically very different from otherwise identical oral phones; they are called *nasal*.

Both consonantals and vocalics (A6) come in oral and nasal classes; the following pairs of sounds are articulatorily identical except for the velum adjustment.

French is a handy example of a language with oral and nasal vowels, but English too has both oral and nasal vocalics. The details differ from dialect to dialect

Velum up (oral)	Velum down (nasal)	Examples
[b]	[m]	chubby, chummy
[d]	[n]	tidy, tiny
[g]	[ŋ]	rigging, ringing [rɪŋɪŋ]
[a]	[ã]	French gras [gʀa] 'fat', grand [gʀã] 'big'
[o]	[õ]	Fr. beau [bo] 'handsome', bon [bõ] 'good'

in English, but the following is a common distribution: words like *spine, seen,* and *sewn*—that is, where a nasal consonant follows the syllabic—contain nasal vocalics, whereas *spy, spied, see, seed, so,* and *sewed* have exactly the same vowels except for being pronounced with the velum up. But—by way of an instant demonstration of the differences between phonologies—syllabics that are followed by a nasal consonant in French are in fact ORAL, so *Seine* is [sɛn], not [sɛ̃n].

A6. Articulation

Different positions of the tongue and lips (the active articulators) relative to the teeth and the roof of the mouth (the passive articulators) result in a very large array of acoustically distinct sounds. These fall into two general categories, different in character and different in overall schemes of classification: *vocalics* and *consonantals*.

VOCALICS are defined as: *all sounds produced with a pulmonic airstream passing through the mouth over the center of the tongue and with no audible local friction in the mouth.* CONSONANTALS—which cannot be characterized except disjunctively—are all other sounds.

The class of vocalics includes all vowels and glides. The glides—that is, non-syllabic vocalics—include not only the familiar [y] and [w] of English *yet* and *wet* but also [h] and the English *r* (whose phonetic symbol is [ɹ] or [ɚ]—the latter being the IPA symbol for the vowel of *bird* [bɚd] with a diacritic that marks it as non-syllabic): *red* [ɹɛd] or [ɚɛd].

This, then, is the explanation for the difficulty of partitioning a word like *warrior* into articulatory segments, as mentioned in A1. Segmentation is most apparent as articulators move from one consonantal to another, or from consonantal to vocalic and back again. Thus the example words *cats, sacked* and so on (A1), are easy to segment. In sequences of vocalics, however—and in articulatory terms *warrior* is vocalic from beginning to end—it is more difficult to pin down segment boundaries.

Consonantal articulation is various and complicated; the class includes most of what are commonly thought of as 'consonants'. We will take up consonantals first.

a. The terms *consonant* and *vowel* are phonological, not phonetic items. Structurally speaking, the English words *head, wed, red, said, Ted,* and *fed* all begin with CONSONANTS; but those of the first three examples are in fact phonetically vocalic and the last three are consonantal. Conversely, *button* [bʌtn̩] contains two syllabics, but only the first is a vocalic, the second is a consonantal. Syllabic consonantals are not unusal in the world's languages—Proto-Indo-European had four of them—and of course nonsyllabic vocalics (*glides,* A18) are commonplace.

CONSONANTALS

Consonantal segments are classified by the nature *of the narrowing in the oral cavity—for example, whether the flow of air is completely cut off or not—and by the* location *of narrowing. The nature of the narrowing is called* manner of arcticulation *and the location is called the* point (*or* place) *of articulation. The manners of articulation are presented here in order of decreasing degrees of interference with the airstream.*

MANNER OF ARTICULATION

A7. **Stops**

Stops are consonantals that are produced by an occlusion of the vocal tract, such that the flow of air is blocked and then released. For complete blocking there must be two simultaneous events: the velum (A5) must be up, and there must be a complete closure somewhere in the mouth. (Alternative, generally obsolete, synonyms for *stop* are *plosive, explosive,* and *mute.*[1])

Stops may be voiced or voiceless, as we have seen (A4); if the occlusion is released without particular commotion, a stop is said to be *plain* or *unaspirated*; if the release includes an audible puff of air or whistle a stop is called *aspirated.* In English, *spill* contains a plain [p]

---

[1] The phonetician Peter Ladefoged has recently promoted *plosive* as a compendious term for 'oral occlusion with egressive pulmonic airstream', in contrast to glottal ejectives and so on. As such it is practically a synonym of *stop* as the word is normally used.

(which can also be written [p⁼] if it is wished to indicate plain release expressly); *pill* contains an aspirated [pʰ]. In French, by contrast, voiceless stops are all unaspirated except occasionally in emphatic utterances. In Hindi (as in many other languages of India, and also in very many other languages of the world), plain and aspirated stops are in *contrastive distribution,* as exemplified by the following forms:

Plain	*Aspirated*
pal 'moment'	pʰal 'fruit'
tāl 'a beat'	tʰāl 'platter'
kān 'ear'	kʰān 'mine' (metal)

This is also confidently assumed to have been the case in ancient Greek, as discussed on pp. 187-8.

A8. Fricatives (or spirants)

When two articulators are very close together but not quite blocking the airstream, and the velum is up, so that air is forced through the oral aperture (small as it is), the result is turbulence in the airstream at the point of greatest constriction. This creates *noise,* the technical term for sound with a random distribution of frequencies. In the speech sounds thus characterized, the frequencies are concentrated around rather high pitches, resulting in one or another kind of hiss, for example in the initial sounds of NE *ship* [šɪp], *fit* [fɪt], *thick* [θɪk]. A major subset of fricatives, the *sibilants* (whistling sounds, literally), are the *s*-sounds; these include familiar [s] and [z], as well as the voiceless [š] of *pressure* and the corresponding voiced [ž] of *pleasure.*

Complex articulations called *affricates* entail a complete occlusion (i.e., a stop) released in such a way as to form a distinctly fricative interval as a sort of satellite to the stop segment. Such sounds occur in NE *etch* and *edge,* [ɛč] and [ɛǰ] respectively. There are many varieties of affricates. For example, an apical stop [t], if not released plainly, [t⁼], can have aspiration, [tʰ]; have a satellite [š]—that is, [tš] (an alternative notation for [č]); have a different kind of sibilant, [tˢ]; be laterally released, [tˡ] (as in NE *bottle*); nasally, [tⁿ] (as in *button*); laterally with voiceless friction, [tɬ] as in Aztec *čokolatl* 'chocolate'; with a slit spirant, [tᶿ] (as in *eighth*); and so on.

A9. Nasals

Nasal consonantals (commonly known simply as *nasals*) are sounds made with complete oral blockage, as in stops, but with the velum down. Nasals are usually voiced, and therefore differ from voiced stops by a single feature—the position of the velum. See table in A5.

A10. Laterals

Sounds made with the tongue blocking the midline of the oral cavity are called *laterals* (informally, the *l*-sounds). A detailed account of lateral phonetics is very complex; we can leave it with saying that during the pronunciation of a lateral, different acoustics result not only from details of the closure (different points of articulation), but also from different positions of the tongue-body itself. Most prominent of the numerous varieties are *palatalized* laterals, made with relatively high and front tongue-body, and, at the opposite extreme, *velarized* laterals, with the back of the tongue raised toward the velum.[1] Most dialects of English have the former in *leap*, the latter in *silty*, and an intermediate variety in *silly* and *silky*. In Russian, as in many languages, different laterals have a different kind of distribution. For example Ru. *stol* [stolɯ] (velarized *l*) 'table', but *stol'* [stoʎ] (palatalized *l*) 'so'.

A11. Trills and taps

Strangely, there is no standard term for the compact natural class of trills and taps.[2] They might be thought of as *assisted articulations*. They differ from all the consonantals described up to now, which are produced by a muscular effort which places the articulators more or less exactly and holds them steady, however briefly. Trills and taps, by contrast, entail an adjustment of the articulators such that the moving stream of air in the vocal tract does the work of bringing about the

---

[1] In one or another phonetic tradition, prior to or ignoring articulatory theory, palatalized sounds are known as *bright* (*light, clear*), *moist, soft,* or *thin*; velarized as *dark, dry, hard,* or *fat*.

[2] Ladefoged's term *rhotics* covers these, but includes as well things like the retroflex glides of English and the approximants of French, whose articulation has nothing in common with the sounds discussed here.

contact between the articulators (Bernoulli's Principle again, A4 and glossary). Put differently, while holding your breath you can 'silently pronounce' a [p] or an [l] or an [n]; but you cannot thus pronounce a trill or a tap. Without a moving stream of air, nothing happens.

All sounds of this type involve relatively flexible organs, principally the tip of the tongue (*apex*) and the *uvula* (the point of loose tissue depending from the edge of the velum at the back of the oral cavity). The phonetics of these sounds, like that of the laterals, is exceedingly complex in detail, but the commonest varieties are the apical trill familiar from Spanish, e.g. *perro* [peřo] 'dog', and the apical tap also familiar from Spanish, e.g. *pero* [peřo] 'but'. French and German have uvular taps in e.g. Fr. *France* [fřã·s] 'France', NHG *fahren* [fa·řen] 'to travel, to drive'. (In these words, and particularly in syllable-final position, the sound is often not a consonantal at all, but a *uvular approximant:* voiceless in the case of Fr. *farce* [faʁs] 'stuffing', voiced in NHG *Stern* [šteʁn] 'star'. *Uvular trills* also occur; in a certain style of French popular singing, strongly articulated uvular trills replace the usual taps and approximants, as for example in the singing of Édith Piaf.)

Taps and trills, together with the laterals, make up the natural class (A21) of *liquids,* though you should be warned that this term sometimes is used to include the nasals as well.

POINT OF ARTICULATION

A12. Consonantals are classified according to where, in the mouth, the narrowing or complete closure as described above takes place. There are two active articulators (lips and tongue) and two passive ones (teeth and the roof of the mouth). However, because various parts of the tongue may be voluntarily brought into contact with various parts of the passive articulators, between lips and throat there is a considerable range of choices for points of contact or narrowing; and even the crudest phonetics must partition the tongue into the tip (or apex) and the back (or dorsum); and the passive articulators are at a minimum subdivided into the (front) teeth, the alveolar ridge (just behind the teeth), the palate (just behind that), and the velum (the soft palate, discussed above in A5). Combining these, from front to back, we get the follwing eight divisions:

1. BILABIAL: contact between the two lips, as in [p b m].
2. LABIO-DENTAL: contact between the lower lip and the upper front teeth: [f v].
3. (APICO-)INTERDENTAL: the tip of the tongue in front of the upper teeth, as in careful or emphatic production of [θ ð] in NE *think, then*. (See item 5, below.)
4. APICO-DENTAL: contact between the tip of the tongue and the back of the upper front teeth, as in French or Italian *t, d, n*. Commonly called simply *dental*. The proper phonetic symbols for these phones are [t̪ d̪ n̪].
5. APICO-ALVEOLAR: contact between the tip of the tongue and the alveolar ridge, as in English *t, d, n*. Commonly called simply *alveolar,* the phonetic symbols for these sounds are [t d n]. (In fact, the normal pronunciation of [θ ð] for most speakers of English is apico-alveolar, not interdental.)
6. APICO-DOMAL: contact between the tip of the tongue and a portion of the roof of the mouth behind the alveolar ridge, symbols [ṭ ḍ ṇ]. (The usual term for these articulations is *retroflex;* the synonyms *cerebral, inverted,* and *cacuminal* are rarely met with nowadays, and *coronal* has been redefined; see glossary.) Many English speakers have a retroflex nasal in say NE *burn* [bɚṇ]; cf. the apico-alveolar contact in, say, *bun* [bʌn]. In many languages of India there is a full contrasting series of apico-dental stops [t tʰ d dʰ], on the one hand, and retroflex stops [ṭ ṭʰ ḍ ḍʰ], on the other.
7. DORSO-PALATAL: contact between the dorsum of the tongue and the palate. This category includes the affricates [č ǰ]—sometimes written [tš] and [dž]—and the [k̟] of NE *keep* (cf. the VELAR pronunciation [k] of NE *cool*); and the German 'ich-Laut' [ś] is in this series. These sounds are commonly called simply *palatal*. (*Palatal* thus defined must be strictly differentiated from *palatalized,* which refers to a consonantal of any point of articulation but with a co-articulated high front tongue-body; see fn. on p. 36.)
8. DORSO-VELAR: contact between the dorsum and the velum, e.g. [k g ŋ χ] ([χ] is the sound of the last consonant in *Bach,* also known in German as the 'ach-Laut'; [ŋ] is seen in *sing* and before [g] and [k] as in *finger* and *banker*). This point of articulation is commonly called *velar* for short; it was once generally called *guttural*.

a. Fully-specified terms like *apico-alveolar* are rarely used in actual practice; truncated terms like *alveolar* or *dental,* or compendious terms like *retroflex,* are explicit enough, and are usually self-explanatory.

b. It is often desirable to name consonantals without specifying irrelevant or unknown details of articulation. A term like *apical* subsumes interdental, dental, and alveolar sounds, or sounds not known to be specifically one or the other, or sounds indifferently so. *Dorsal* subsumes palatal and velar. (The terms *dental* and *velar,* respectively, are commonly encountered in these senses, but nothing can be said in favor of the imprecision of, say, designating a post-alveolar point of articulation as 'dental'.)

THE BASIC FRAMEWORK

AI3. Refined phonetics are vital for full understanding of some things, but the basic framework for consonantal articulation is simpler than the one just outlined, and may be summarized thus:

	Bilabial	Labio-Dental	Apical	Alveo-Palatal	Palatal	Velar
Stops						
Voiceless	p		t		ḵ	k
Voiced	b		d		g̰	g
Fricatives						
Groove ('sibilants')						
Voiceless			s	š	ś	
Voiced			z	ž	ź	
Slit						
Voiceless		f	θ			χ
Voiced		v	ð			ɣ
Affricates						
Voiceless				č		
Voiced				ǰ		
Nasals	m		n		ñ	ŋ
Liquids			l, r			

NOTE: As explained above, [h y w] are not consonantal in the first place, and [ʔ] (glottal stop) despite its name is a phonational state not a consonantal.

VOCALICS

A14. Vowels and glides

Vocalic syllabics ('vowels') and glides are equally vocalic (as defined in A6)—that is, they are exactly the same in *cavity features* (A15)—but they differ in a property that is easier to name than to define: *syllabicity*. Vowels are syllabic vocalics, and glides are non-syllabic.

One vocalic segment differs from another because they have different configurations of the vocal tract, as described below, which result in different patterns of *resonance*. These defining configurations, however, are more elusive than is the case with the articulatory features of consonantals. The interference in the stream of air which is characteristic of all consonantals facilitates their classification. By contrast, in vocalic articulation the vocal tract remains open, as a whole; so open, in fact, that it is futile to search for 'points of articulation' in the consonantal vein. The chief variables influencing resonance are two: changes in position of the tongue body in the vocal tract, and the position of the lips. (There are in addition less-often-encountered variables like lowered larynx, compressed fauces, and so on.)

A15. Cavity features

The most widely-used system of classification today dates from the work of Alexander Melville Bell (1867 and later), which attempts to describe the configuration of the vocal tract in terms of what the profile of the tongue looks like when a given vocalic segment is pronounced. The benchmark categories are *high, mid,* and *low,* in the vertical scale; and *front* and *back* horizontally. If the tongue body nearly fills the oral cavity and is pushed forward—it is actually visible between the nearly closed teeth—the *high front* vowel of Fr. *vie* [vi] 'life' is produced. If the tongue is near the roof of the mouth, but back and out of sight, the *high back* vowel of Fr. *vous* [vu] 'you' is the result.

These two vocalics differ in another way as well: the position of the lips. *Vie* is pronounced with the lips *unrounded* (indeed, somewhat spread), in *vous* they are *rounded* (and also somewhat projected; but *rounded* is the term). Vowels like [æ] in NE *lather* and [a] in *father* are *low* vowels, front and back respectively (both are *unrounded*). Vowels like those in Fr. *été* [ete] 'summer' and *haut* [o] 'high' are produced with the tongue at an intermediate height, and are accordingly called *mid*.

	front	*back*
high	i	{ u }
mid	e	{ o }
low	æ	a

(The vowels enclosed in curvy brackets are rounded; the others are unrounded.)

A16. Even in coarse-textured phonetics, it is usually necessary to subdivide the tongue-height scale one more time. The syllabics of English have off-glides and other complications which make them unsuitable for demonstrating such differences accurately, but they can afford a crude idea. In each of the following pairs of words, the vowels differ in that the first is higher than the second: *bead, bid* (higher-high front [i], lower-high front [ɪ]); *bayed, bed* (higher-mid front [e], lower-mid front [ɛ]); and *cooed, could* (higher-high back [u], lower-high back [ʊ]):

	front	*back*
higher high	i	{ u }
lower high	ɪ	{ ʊ }
higher mid	e	{ o }
lower mid	ɛ	
higher low	æ	
lower low	α	a { ɔ }

A17. **Lip rounding**
Tongue height, tongue advancement, and lip rounding are more or less independent variables, though in most languages there is the following correlation: mid and high back vowels, [o u] and so on, are rounded; all others are unrounded. That is the case in the otherwise radically different vowel systems of English and Latin. In Attic Greek, German, French, and Old English (and in present day Scots) there are in addition *front rounded* vowels, as in Fr. *dur* [dür] 'hard', NHG *dürr* [dür] 'dry'. In producing [ü] the tongue is in the same position as for [i], but the lips are ROUNDED, just as they are for [o u]. Contrariwise, high and mid back UNROUNDED vocalics are also encountered in vari-

ous languages, though less commonly than front vocalics that are rounded. Turkish has high back unrounded vowels (*kadın* [kaduɯn] 'wo-man', *kızlarınız* [kuɯzlaruɯnuɯz] 'your girls'), which is also seen in Romanian *pîîne* [puɯɪne] 'bread'.

Closer to home, the accent favored by Country and Western sing-ers and their imitators (including the Beatles in their Early Period, and many continental balladeers) have high back unrounded vowels in *would* and *could*; and many speakers of American English have [uɯ] in *wool* and the first syllable of *children*.

a. Traditional phonetic theory classifies [ɔ] as in NE *talk* (most dialects) as a lower-mid back vowel, and therefore predictably rounded. Instrumental investiga-tion indicates rather that its cavity features are closest to the low back [a], and in fact in many languages, e.g. Hungarian and Farsi, low back vowels acquire features of rounding. Being being both low and rounded, [ɔ] is a marked-feature vocalic, like front rounded [ü] and high back unrounded [uɯ], which fits with its relative rarity in the world's languages.

AI8. Non-syllabic vocalics (glides)

Any vocalic articulation can be represented as non-syllabic by means of the subscript [ˏ], and voiceless by means of the subscript [˳], e.g. [i̯ i̥], but certain special vocalic glide symbols are in wide use:

[y] high front unrounded, IPA [j] (the IPA has the symbol [y], but it is equivalent to our [ü]): NE *pie* [pʰay], *yes* [yɛs].
[w] high back rounded: NE *how* [haw], *wet* [wɛt].
[ɥ] (or [ẅ]) high front rounded: Fr. *puis* [pɥi] or [pẅi] 'then'.

Additional vocalic glides, though commonly overlooked in this con-nection, are [h], [ɹ] (the American English *r*, also written [ɚ], see A6), and [ʁ] (the uvular approximant, as in NHG *Stern* [štɛʁn] 'star').

The most frequently-encountered glides are the high front un-rounded [y] as in *yet* and the high back rounded [w] as in *wet*. These are produced with more or less the same tongue and lip features as [i] and [u], respectively, but differ in that the articulators do not remain in a fixed position: rather, for the duration of the segment, the posi-tion of the articulators is constantly changing, resulting in a constan-tly changing acoustic smear of vowel 'color'.

The most variable of the glides, both diachronically and descriptively, is [h], the only vocalic—indeed, the only resonant altogether—which is normally voiceless. Its distinctive phonetic features are 'voiceless' and 'non-syllabic'; its remaining phonetic features approximate those of the syllabic vocalic it shares a syllable with. This is typically a following vowel in English, German, the Scandinavian languages, and, evidently, Latin and Attic Greek. For example, the tongue position for [h] in the following forms is or was presumably high and front: NE *heed*, NHG *hiesig* [hi·zɪś] 'local', Lat. *hīberna* 'winter', Gk *híppos* 'horse'. In fewer languages it assimilates to a preceding vowel, as in Finnish *vihreä* ['vɪhreæ] (three syllables) 'green'. In all these examples, the phone transcribed [h] would be more fastidiously described as a *high front voiceless non-syllabic vocalic*—say, [i̥i·zɪś], [vɪi̥reæ], and so on.

The sound [ɦ] is often called *voiced h,* a serious misnomer: the phone is in fact *murmured* (A4a). It is found in Ukrainian (where it corresponds to Russian [g]), Czech, and Hungarian: Ukr. *гріх* 'sin' [ɦɪrʹiχ] (cf. Ru. [grʹɛχ]), Czech *Praha* ['praɦa] 'Prague', Hu. *halni* ['ɦɔlni] 'to die'. And many speakers of American English have [ɦ] in *ahead*.

Glides, just like syllabics, may be nasal, oral, voiced, voiceless, and so on: NE *nine* [nãỹn], *quite* [kw̥ayt], *cute* [k̥yʊwt], *barn* [bãɪ̃n]. Even [h] is found nasalized, as in the English affirmative grunt *uh-huh* [ʔʌ̃h̃ʌ̃].

In careful transcription, symbols like [i̥], [ɪ̥], [e̥], [y̥], and so on have an advantage over [y] and [w], because they indicate with some exactness the actual phonetics of the glide. The very vagueness of [y] and [w] usually is no problem, however, and often is convenient.

A19. Diphthongs

In Greek terminology a *diphthong* was any complex sound, and, since the distinction between language and writing seems always to cause trouble, the Greeks also called LETTERS like ξ /ks/ diphthongs. Most commonly, the term nowadays refers to complex vocalics, that is, vocalics produced while one or more articulator is in motion. Any change in the configuration of the vocal tract during the segment will result in changing resonances, and be different from the sounds produced with immobile articulators. (In fact, there is no such thing as a phonetically 'pure' vocalic except possibly for an utterance like *ah!* produced in isolation; but demonstrating this point would get us into

a discussion of the transitions between vocalics and adjacent consonantals which is beyond the scope of this work.)

Some phonetic theories speak of a complex nucleus like that of English *tie* [tʰay] as consisting of a *steady state* vocalic [a] followed by an
off-glide, during which the tongue moves up and forward from the
position it was in during the steady state. The usual notation reflects
this theory. Instrumental analysis of diphthongs reveals, however, that
the usual situation is that the articulators are in constant motion. That
is, during the WHOLE of the articulatory event transcribed as [ay] the
tongue and jaw are in motion, starting from the position for [a] and
moving up and forward toward an articulatory TARGET, here symbolized (vaguely) by [y]. A genuine steady state followed by an offglide is
theoretically possible, but if such an articulation occurs at all it is uncommon compared to the continuous-motion type.

A20. Not all languages have diphthongs—Finnish, Hungarian, and Japanese,
for example, do not; they do have vowel sequences, however, which
must not be confused with diphthongs. For example, Fi. *lain* /lain/
gen.sg. 'law' (the nominative is *laki*); *lain* has the same prosodics as
läkin /lækin/ 'of a game' (nominative *läkki*), and is quite unlike the
phonetics of English *line* /layn/.

In languages having diphthongs, far and away the commonest are
[ay] and [aw]. In general, [y] (raising and fronting) and [w] (raising,
backing, and rounding) are the commonest glide targets, but in fact
any configuration of the vocal tract may be a target. In-glides, that is,
toward a central vocalic target (say, [ə] or [ʌ]),also occur; they abound
in certain dialects of English, in fact, preeminently the 'r-less' dialects,
but are by no means confined to them.

The usual way of representing a non-syllabic vocalic is with a subscript arc, e.g. *hair* [heə̯], *here* [hɪə̯] in an *r*-less form of English. This
kind of transcription, as mentioned in A18, is necessary if phonetic detail is needed: a transcription like [ay] indicates the starting-point with
some phonetic accuracy but all it says about the target is that it is high,
front, and unrounded. For English, while a transcription of *tie* as [tʰay]
will do for many speakers it is more accurately rendered [tʰaɪ̯]; for some
southern types of speech [tʰɑɡ̯] would be the actual phonetics. And in
some types of southern speech there is no off-glide at all in such

words, and for them the word would be accurately transcribed as [tʰɑ·].

    a. Some phonetic traditions class ALL complex nuclei as diphthongs, that is, the vocalic portions of *yes* and *yacht* as well as the vocalic nuclei of *say* and *tie*. In this tradition, diphthongs are classed as *falling* and *rising*. In falling diphthongs the sonority diminishes ([ay ew] and so on); in rising diphthongs it increases ([ya we] and so on). The trouble with this terminology is that it gets tangled up with the Bell categories of tongue height: the most common 'falling' diphthongs, [ay aw], involve a RAISING of the tongue-body during the syllable, in fact, while most 'rising' ones involve a LOWERING of the tongue. Sometimes context is the only clue as to how the terms *rising* and *falling* are being used in discussing complex nuclei.

NATURAL CLASSES

A21. Phones sharing a feature or features of articulation belong to a *natural class*. For example, all apico-alveolar sounds, [t tʰ d n l] etc., regardless of their other articulatory features, make up a natural class; and more broadly, so do all apical sounds. Likewise all nasals; all high vocalics; all front vocalics; and so on. As a rule, a given sound will belong to more than one natural class. Thus [d] is, simultaneously, a member of the natural classes of: (all) voiced stops; (all) stops in general; (all) apicals; (all) occlusives; (all) obstruents; and various combinations of the above—voiced occlusives, for example, or apical stops.

    Indication that such concepts are not artificial, that is, that they are not mere restatements of the phonetic classification, is the marked tendency for members of a natural class to PATTERN TOGETHER in the phonology of a language: when for example as a group their distribution is limited in the same ways; when they combine with other sounds in the same ways; when they share the same subsidiary phonetic features, and so on. Thus, all voiceless stops in Modern English, regardless of their numerous other phonetic features, are aspirated when they occur at onset of tonic stress (indicated by [']) before a vowel, thus ['kʰip] *keep,* ['kʰul] *cool,* ['tʰɪl] *till,* ['pʰɪl] *pill,* and so on. And all such stops are NOT aspirated when preceded by [s], thus ['sk̄i] *ski,* ['sk̄ul] *school,* ['st̄ɪl] *still,* ['sp̄ɪl] *spill.*

    Natural classes are prominent in diachronic linguistics because of their tendency to undergo parallel developments in language change. It is convenient, time and again—or, more than convenient, revealing —to refer to changes in terms of SETS of sounds rather than individual sounds, item by item. Thus, one of the characteristic traits of Germanic languages is that ALL Proto-Indo-European voiced stops became voiceless stops (part of the large phenomenon known as Grimm's Law): PIE *kub-yo- > OE *hype* 'hip'; PIE *duō > OE *twá* 'two'; PIE *ĝṇHtis > OE *cynd* 'kind, race'.

On the other hand, natural classes en masse may serve as ENVIRONMENTS for conditioned sound changes. Any Proto-Germanic nasal consonant was lost before any fricative in Low West Germanic (with compensatory lengthening (20) of the preceding vowel), so *gans- 'goose' > OE *gós*, *fimf 'five' > OE *fíf*, *munθ- 'mouth' > OE *múþ* (cf. High German *Gans, fünf, Mund*). In the evolution of French, a sibilant developed between any labial consonantal and a following PRom. *y: *kripya 'manger' > *krepša > *crèche* (cf. *crib*; the details of the High Germanic source of the Romance word are a little complicated, and immaterial here); *rabyam 'anger' > *rabža > *raǰa > *rage* /raž/; *dīlūvium 'flood' > *diluvyu > *deluvžo > *déluge* /delüž/, *simiam 'ape' > *sęmža > *singe* /sēž/.

Commonly, both the environment and the altered sounds are natural classes. In West Germanic, all BACK vowels are altered when the following syllable contains *i, *ī, or *y—that is, all (and only) the HIGH FRONT VOCALICS in the Proto-Germanic sound system: PGmc *mūsiz > OE *mýs* [mü·s] 'mice', PGmc *þurstīþ > OE *þyrsteþ* 'thirsts' (cf. NHG *dürstet*), PGmc *fuljiþ > OE *fylleþ* [fül·eθ] 'fills' (cf. NHG *füll(e)t*).

Important (and large) natural classes are defined by manners of arcticulation. The following table shows these intersecting classes.

consonantals	stops	occlusives	obstruents
	affricates		
	fricatives	continuants	resonants
	nasals		
	liquids		
vocalics	glides		
	syllabics		

A22. Here is a chart of the symbols and (types of symbols) described and used here. These are 'American' symbols.

CONSONANTALS

Articulator:	Labial (lip)		Apical (apex)			Frontal (front of tongue)		Dorsal (back of tongue)		
	bilabial	labiodental	dental	alveolar	postalveolar (retroflex)	alveopalatal		velar	uvular	glottal
Stop: Voiceless	p	p̣	t̪	t	ṭ	kʸ	k̯	k	ḳ	ʔ
Voiced	b	ḅ	d̪	d	ḍ	gʸ	g̯	g	g̣	
Aspirated	pʰ		t̪ʰ	tʰ	ṭʰ	kʸʰ	k̯ʰ	kʰ	ḳʰ	
Ingressive	bˤ			dˤ					gˤ	
Ejective	pʔ		t̪ʔ	tʔ	ṭʔ	kʸʔ	k̯ʔ	kʔ	ḳʔ	
Affricate: Voiceless	pᶠ, pᵠ			¢		č				
Voiced				j		ǰ				
Fricative:										
Groove Voiceless			ṣ̌	s	ṣ	š	ṣ̌			
Voiced			ẓ̌	z	ẓ	ž	ẓ̌			
Slit Voiceless	ɸ	f	θ	θ̣		χʸ (ś)	χ̯	χ	χ̣	ḥ
Voiced	β	v	ð	ð̣		ɣʸ (ź)	ɣ̯	ɣ	ɣ̣	ʕ
Nasal:	m	m̟	n̪̆	n	ṇ	nʸ		ñ	ŋ	
(Voiceless)	m̥		n̪̥	n̥	ṇ̥	nʸ̥		ñ̥	ŋ̥	
Trill:				r̃					R̃	
Tap & Flap:				r̆	r̨̆, ɭ̆				R̆	
Lateral:				l	ḷ			ʎ		

A23. Here is the consonant chart according to the IPA.

		bilabial	labiodental	dental	alveolar	postalveolar	retroflex	palatal	velar	uvular	pharyngeal	glottal
Stop:	Voiceless	p		t̪	t		ʈ	c	k	q		ʔ
	Voiced	b		d̪	d		ɖ	ɟ	g	ɢ		
	Aspirated	pʰ		t̪ʰ	tʰ		ʈʰ	cʰ	kʰ	qʰ		
	Ingressive	ɓ		ɗ̪	ɗ		ᶑ	ʄ	ɠ	ʛ		
	Ejective	p'		t̪'	t'		ʈ'	c'	k'	q'		
Affricate:	Voiceless	pᶲ,pf			ts	tʃ						
	Voiced				dz	dʒ						
Fricative:												
Groove	Voiceless			s̪	s	ʃ	ʂ	ç				
	Voiced			z̪	z	ʒ	ʐ	ʝ				
Slit	Voiceless	ɸ	f	θ					x	χ	ħ	h
	Voiced	β	v	ð					ɣ	ʁ	ʕ	ɦ
Lateral	Voiceless				ɬ							
	Voiced				ɮ							
Nasal:	(Voiced)	m	ɱ	n̪	n		ɳ	ɲ	ŋ	N		
	(Voiceless)	m̥	ɱ̥	n̪̥	n̥		ɳ̥	ɲ̥	ŋ̊	N̥		
Trill:					r					R		
Tap & Flap:					ɾ		ɽ					
Lateral:				l̪	l		ɭ	ʎ		L		

Many possible combinations of features are not shown which can be inferred from the basic plan. For example, the voiced ingressive stops make a series ([bˤ ɗˤ dˤ ɖˤ ...], in the American notation) exactly parallel to the pulmonic stops; [ŋ̊ ŋ ŋ̊] parallel to the other dorsals; ALL resonants have voiceless forms, [l̥ ʎ̥]; and so on. At the same time, some spots are vacant because they are physically impossible (a dorsal groove fricative, for example).

As elaborate as it probably looks, these charts represent gross simplifications of articulatory phonetics in a number of different ways.

Sibilant phonetics are very complicated and furthermore the subject of much professional dispute. The root of the problem is that a number of articulatory strategies can achieve the same acoustic results. In this chart the whole matter is reduced to little more than a distinction between *hissing* [s z] and *hushing* [š ž] sounds, with some straightforward point of articulation indicators, [ṣ s ṣ] and the like.

The greatest source of complexity in **liquid phonetics**, though not the only one, is that laterals (A10) occur with the coarticulated tongue and lip positions of many of the VOCALIC syllabics (A14 ff). This accounts for the notably different laterals in NE *leap, pillow,* and *filter.*

Fricatives: regarding such details as the IPA classification (following an ancient tradition) of [h] as a fricative, see A18. In some other cases the facts are arguably less clear cut, but there is neverthelss room for a difference of interpretation, e.g. as to whether 'lateral fricatives' are really any kind of fricative (IPA and many other authorities) or are simply laterals with a judiciously managed pressure-drop (whether by increased air-flow or narrowing the aperture) that creates local noise.

And finally, it may be doubted whether there is actually any such thing as a 'velar lateral' (IPA [ʟ]) at all.

A24.   V O C A L I C S

Unrounded:

	front	central	back
high	i	ɨ	ɯ
	ɪ	ɪ̵	ï
mid	e	ə	ë
	ε		ε̈
low	æ	ʌ	a
	α	ὰ	ɐ

Rounded:

	front	central	back
high	ü	ú (ʉ)	u
	ü̈	u̇ (ʉ)	ʊ
mid	ö	ȯ (ɵ)	o
	ɔ̈		
low		ɔ̇	ɔ

The standard 'vowel triangle' looks like this:

```
        i             u
          e       o
              a
```

The asymmetries of the vowel arrays have several explanations. For one, since tongue height is augmented by the action of the jaw, the range of possible aperture adjustments in the front of the mouth is greater than the range in the back. And owing to the same circumstances, the feature *rounded* is at best a theoretical possibility for the lowest front vocalics.

Those familiar with traditional vowel triangles, such as the one given at the bottom of the previous page, will notice several departures from them. First, [a] is a back vocalic, not a central one (a major error of Melville Bell's which survived unchallenged for several generations). Similarly, [ɔ̃] and [ɔ] are shown as low, rather than the traditional (lower) mid; in fact, for most ordinary purposes [ɔ] is little more than a rounded [a].

A25. The vocalics according to the IPA notation (and classification). When two symbols are separated by a comma, the right-hand one stands for a rounded phone, the left-hand one for unrounded.

	Front	Central	Back
higher-high[1]	i, y	ɨ, ʉ	ɯ, u
lower-high	ɪ, ʏ		ʊ
higher-mid	e, ø	ə, ɵ	ɤ, o
lower-mid	ɛ, œ	ɜ, ɞ	ʌ, ɔ
higher-low	æ	ɐ	
lower-low	a, ɶ		ɑ, ɒ

A26. Additional vocalic features

Syllabic vocalics occur (like most sounds) in degrees of duration; these may be crudely compressed into *long* and *short*. The usual symbols indicating length are [aː] (IPA; less elaborately, [a:]) or, favored in American practice, [a·]. Also, all vocalics may be pronounced with the velum up (*oral*) or the velum down (*nasal* or *nasalized*) as defined in A5. The normal procedure is to write nasal vowels with a characteristic diacritic—[ã ũ] and so on (or, in some systems [a̜ u̜] and so on), and use the plan vocoid symbol to stand for oral. This method has the drawback that the plain symbol is also used when velum adjustment is unknown or immaterial; context is usually the only clue as to

---

[1] The IPA tongue-height nomenclature ranges from CLOSE [i, u] to OPEN [a, ɑ], with various compound terms ('close-mid', etc.) in between.

whether a symbol like [a] stands for a specifically oral vocalic or a vocalic indifferent to nasality.

Though vocalics (like all resonants) are mostly found voiced, they may be voiceless, as in Japanese, where high vocalics are regularly voiceless between voiceless obstruents: *kiku* [ki̥kɯ] 'chrysanthemum' and *suku* [sɯ̥kɯ] 'become empty'; and often voiceless in final position as well, after a voiceless obstruent, as in these words and the very common *desu* [desɯ̥] 'be'. (These are often erroneously called whispered vowels.)

SYSTEMS OF PHONETIC TRANSCRIPTION

A27. An unfortunate fact (but fact it is): there is no standardized system of phonetic notation. The International Phonetic Alphabet (IPA), based on various antecedents, was launched late in the 19th century with the hope that it would be the universal standard, and supplant the welter of symbol systems then in use. This hope was disappointed.

One of the aims of the IPA character set was to eschew diacritics, and this aim too met with only partial success. For one thing, distinguishing the apico-alveolar sounds [t d n r s] from the retroflex sounds by writing the latter as 'non-diacritic' [ʈ ɖ ɳ ɻ ʂ], rather than with diacritics as [ṭ ḍ ṇ ṛ ṣ], as favored here, is a distinction without a difference. In any case, even the IPA throws in the towel when it comes to release features like aspiration (IPA [tʰ pʰ kʰ] and so on) or fine distinctions in point of articulation such as [k̟] (more or less equivalent to [ḵ]) for a voiceless dorsal stop only slightly fronter than [k].

One particularly confusing concomitant of the prevailing chaos is that the selfsame diacritic mark may have different significance in different phonetic or philological traditions. Thus in the scheme favored by American linguists, a subscript dot indicates a backer point of articulation: whereas [t d] stand for apico-alveolar stops, [ṭ ḍ] stand for apico-domal (retroflex) stops, as shown above. But in romanized Arabic, the subscript dot has long been used to mark phones with a coarticulated high back tongue body (*emphatic* is the traditional but misleading term for the sounds in question), so *ṭ ḍ* = [tɯ dɯ] (in IPA, [tˠ dˠ]) etc. In Romance linguistics, *ẹ, ọ* stand for [e o], that is, higher-mid vocalics, in contrast to *ẹ, ọ*, which stand for lower-mid phones (something like [ɛ ɔ]). But very widely in West African languages, Yoruba for example, the selfsame ẹ, ọ stand for LOWER-mid vocalics, i.e., they are equivalent to Romance ẹ, ọ ([ɛ ɔ]). Among American linguists, the symbols [ę ǫ], if they occurred at all, would stand for *retroflex* vocalics, that is, vocalics with coarticulated tongue-bunching or raised tongue tip (the acoustic results are indistinguishable; IPA [e˞ o˞]). The symbols [ę ǫ] are the representations of NASALIZED vowels once common in American phonetics, especially by the followers of Franz Boaz (Pike and Smalley, e.g.), for which the alternative notation [ẽ õ] is preferred here.

In the traditional notation of Indo-Europeanists, m̥, n̥, r̥, l̥, represent SYLLABIC resonants, like the second syllables of *bottle* [bat l̥] or *button* [bʌtn̥]. The usual phonetic transcription for such sounds in both IPA and American practice is a subscript tick (as shown), so a surmise about the pronunciation of PIE *wl̥kʷos 'wolf' would be written something like [wl̥kʷos] in phonetic transcription. However—unhappily—the transcription [l̥] etc. does have a standard meaning in phonetics: it stands for a VOICELESS resonant, as in an English word like *plan* [pl̥æn].

> **a.** Systems of phonetic notation favored in the United States have traditionally inclined toward diacritics rather than special letter-shapes, and this preference is traceable to a specific technology: the type-bar typewriter. It is easy and inexpensive to modify such a machine by adding a few diacritic symbols on dead (nonspacing) keys which can be used to produce a very large number of distinctive signs built up from ordinary letters of the alphabet and one or more diacritics. Thus a series of alveopalatal articulations can be rendered [š ž ñ ĺ], in contradistinction to the IPA's special shapes [ʃ ʒ ɲ ʎ]; ditto retroflexes (apico-domals) [ṭ ḍ ṇ ṛ ṣ] next to IPA [ʈ ɖ ɳ ɽ ʂ].
>
> For either a typeset or a hand-written document, however, there is no practical difference in the choice between these alternatives, or between writing the initial consonant of *ship* as [š] or [ʃ] (the latter being the IPA symbol). But even here there are differences after all: many conventions that are convenient or easy in handwriting have no utility for the printer, or indeed may present the typesetter with challenges. And conversely: in place of [ṭ ḍ ṇ ṛ ṣ] for retroflex consonantals, for example, [t d n r s], or [T D N R S], or even [t ð ƞ r ʂ] would be very much easier for a typesetter to print than either the 'American' or the IPA symbols—but such conventions could be followed in handwriting only with difficulty. Of course, where typesetting is in question, ⟨š⟩ is after all an actual letter in the alphabets of Latvian, Lithuanian, and Czech, e.g., and therefore might be found in large fonts, whereas ⟨ʃ⟩ will be found only in a special IPA font.
>
> The type-bar typewriter, in any case, is now an obsolete technology. From a linguist's pont of view, the IBM Selectric machines (the kind with a type ball) and its

imitators, and machines with a daisy wheel, are retrograde steps on account of their inflexibility. A third-party supplier or two did offer balls with phonetic and other linguistically relevant characters, but dealing with both the suppliers and the mechanism itself taxed patience. But lately something with a flexibility similar to, and in some ways surpassing, the old type-bar machines has become available again, in electronic word-processing technology. In good word-processing programs, characters like [ḍ] or [ē] or [ṭ] or [ḫ] or [š] (or [r̥] or [ó]) can be created on the spot almost as easily as on a type-bar typewriter, and very much more easily than with metal type—and with as much typographic finesse as the operator is capable of.

GLOSSARY

The cues to the text in **bold face** refer to the numbered sections

ablative: (a) a case whose basic meaning is 'away from'. Such a case is found in Proto-Indo-European and several daughters. (b) Ablative denominative verbs are exemplified by NE *to skin, to gut, to brain, to seed, to core*.

ablaut: (a) any system of vowel alternation (or gradation). (b) In Proto-Indo-European, specifically an alternation between **e*, **o*, and no vowel at all, as in the root usually cited as **pet(H)-*: **petH-neH* 'feather', **pot-eyeti* 'flies about', and **ptH-rom* 'wing'. (c) In Indo-European languages, reflexes of (b), as in Gk *pétomai* 'fly (along)', *potéomai* 'fly about, hover', *ptéron* 'wing'; or OE *rídan* 'to ride', *rád* 'rode', *riden* 'ridden'.

  The different states are called *grades*: **pet-/pot-* are *e*-grade and *o*-grade, respectively; together they are called the *full grades; *pt-* is called *zero grade*. Traditional scholarship, and some scholars today, add the *lengthened grades* **ē* and **ō*, which are however secondary phenomena and glottogonically unrelated to the full grades.

affix *see* **bound.**

affricate: a complex manner of articulation involving a complete occlusion and a release so timed that the turbulence that forms in the air stream at the point of articulation is prominently audible, e.g. [č ĵ]. (A21)

agent noun *see* **nomen agentis.**

agglutinative: in morphology, characterized by ready formal segmentation with a simple relationship between form and function. Thus NE *cats* divides into /kæt/ and /s/ 'plural'. (By contrast, in *feet* 'foot' + 'pl.' it is not possible to assign formal elements to functions.) Hungarian *gyermekeknek* 'for children' is made of /dʸermek/ 'child', /ek/ 'pl.' and /nek/ 'to/for'. By comparison, in Latin *līberīs* 'for children', -*īs* is 'dative plural' and not further analyzable into components. *See* **fusion.**

Albanian: an Indo-European branch belonging to the satem group, spoken in Albania (east of the Adriatic Sea) and in many émigré enclaves in Greece, Yugoslavia, Sicily, and elsewhere.

allomorph: a term (and a concept) modeled on allophone—*see* **phoneme**—but not truly parallel. As normally used, the term refers to different forms with identical functions, such as the /s z əz ən/ of the English plural (*cats, dogs, bushes, oxen*), or the different root forms in *keep/kep-t.*

allophone *see* **phoneme.**

alphabet: a signary for writing language in which each phoneme is represented by a character. Such purity is rarely or never found in nature. There is no conceptual difference between writing /č/ as č or *ch* or *cz*, i.e. with *alpha-*

betic diacritics; but something like Gk ξ = /ks/ is a true departure from the alphabetic principle, as is writing the same sound in more than one way, for example the German phoneme /f/ written *f, ff, v,* and occasionally *ph.* The poor 'fit' between English orthography and the phonology of the language means that the spelling is heavily morphographic, that is, the decision of whether to write /miyt/ as *meet, meat,* or *mete* depends not on phonology but on what morpheme is being represented.

alveolar ridge: a passive articulator, being the more or less palpable shelf behind the upper front teeth on the roof of the mouth, formed by a thickening of the bone around the sockets (*alveolae*) of the teeth. In many languages (including English) a range of speech sounds involve articulation of the apex of the tongue against the alveolar ridge, e.g. [t d n]. (A12)

ambisyllabic *see* **tautosyllabic.**

analogy: short for *analogical change,* a change in pronunciation caused by the influence of one form (or class of forms) on another. (46-55)

anaptyxis: a kind of excrescence consisting of the 'unfolding' of a phone between two originally adjacent phones. Now commonly restricted to syllabics, as in Lat. *pōculum* 'cup' < *pōclom* but originally of any type of sound, as when *prince* is pronounced /prints/, or PIE **srowmos* > OE *stréam. See also* **epenthesis.** (17)

Anatolian *see* **Hittite.**

aniṭ *see* **seṭ.**

antepenult: the third syllable from the end of a word.

anticipatory assimilation/dissimilation: a change in the pronunciation of a segment relative to the phonetic features of some following segment, as in Lat. *penna* 'feather' < **petnā* (assimilation) or **kan-mn̥* > Lat. *carmen* 'song'. Synonymous with *regressive assimilation/dissimilation.* (15)

aorist: a term from Greek grammar (literally 'without boundaries; indefinite') but denoting a range of verb categories widely found in languages. Aoristic verbs refer to actions that do not occupy a span of time, either because of the inherent meaning of the verb (as *find, explode,* or *arrive*) or because an action is named without regard to real-time duration (as in *Fred plays first violin in the civic orchestra*); the beginnings of events (the ingressive aorist, as of Greek); or their end (as the telic aorists of English, e.g. *Fred built the shed*—note that *Fred never finished the shed he built* is incoherent). Pragmatically, aorists very often refer to actions in the past, and have evolved into completed-action preterites in modern Greek; but in the archaic Indo-European languages (including Greek) they are also found with future and iterative force, and form imperatives—not a possibility in the case of a true preterite.

apex: (a) in phonetics, tip of the tongue (A12); (b) in Latin epigraphy, a sort of lopsided circumflex sporadically used in inscriptions to mark long vowels.

aphaeresis: loss of a sound (usually a vowel) from the beginning of a word, as in NE *possum* < *opossum*, NGk *máti* 'eye' < *ommátion*. (18)

apical: in phonetics, articulated with the apex (tip) of the tongue, for example [t̪ t d d̪ n]. (A12)

apicoalveolar: in phonetics, an articulation of the apex of the tongue against the alveolar ridge, as [t d n]. (Usually *alveolar* for short.) (A12)

apicodental: in phonetics, an articulation of the apex of the tongue against the back of the upper incisors, as [t̪ d̪ n̪]. (Usually dental for short.) (A12)

apicodomal *see* **retroflex.**

apocope: loss of a sound from the end of a word, as NE *quick* < OE *cwicu* or It. *legge* 'reads' < *legit* (itself apocopated from **legeti*). (18)

apophony: a synonym of **ablaut.**

approximant: a manner of articulation in which the active and passive articulators approach one another closely but without producing audible turbulence in the airstream. The English vocalic glides [y w ɹ] are approximants, as are German /r/ [ʁ] and French /r/ [ʁ ʁ̥] (in some environments). (A11)

area; areal features *see* **linguistic area.**

Armenian: a branch of Indo-European currently spoken in the Republic of Armenia and parts of Turkey and Iran. It belongs to the satem group but shares many innovations with Greek.

articulation: (a) In the narrow sense, the movements or positions of the active articulators of the oral cavity (lips, tongue) relative to the passive articulators (teeth, roof of the mouth). (b) Broadly, the movement or position of all the organs of speech in producing speech sounds. These consist of four independent mechanisms: airstream, phonational state, oro-nasal state, and articulation in sense (a). (**Appendix** passim)

aspect: a term of varied (and disputed) sense, having to do in general with the nature of a verb action—unique vs iterative/habitual, goal-related ('telic') vs open-ended, finished ('perfective') vs non-finished. Authorities disagree over whether the distinction between statives (*knows*) and eventives (*learns*) qualifies as a question of aspect, similarly such things as the difference between *Fred wrote a letter...*, and *Fred was writing a letter (when...)*.

aspiratae: an obsolete phonetic term for aspirated stops and, loosely—when discussing Grimm's Law—for fricatives. (Taken from Latin grammar, itself apparently a mistranslation of the Greek term *dasús* literally 'rough'—which would be *asper* in Latin—for voiceless aspirated stops.)

aspirated: in phonetics, characterized by a release feature usually entailing a delay before the onset of the following segment and accompanied by a more or less audible turbulence in the flow of air past the point of articulation. (The difference between affricated and aspirated release is mainly a matter of timing.) (33, 58, 125, 135.vii, A7)

assimilation: a change in pronunciation resulting in a net increase in the number of phonetic features shared by two segments, e.g. *pn* > *bn* or *kw* > *kw̥* or *pt* > *tt*. (15)

assisted articulation: several types of articulation require a moving stream of air from the lungs to effect the closure at the point of articulation. Chief among these are a single very brief closure called a *tap*, as in Spanish *pero* or (for many speakers) English *witty;* and the *trill*, which involves several such closures in very rapid succession, which is the normal 'r-sound' of such languages as Italian and Arabic. Very flexible articulators are requisite: practically, only the uvula and the apex of the tongue are involved in such articulations, though a kind of labiodental flap is found in West African languages. (Note: this is a salient natural class of sounds, but there seems to be no standard term for it.) (A11)

asyndetic: without a conjunction, as in the phrases *twenty-three* and *open for breakfast, lunch, dinner;* or *let dry for two, three hours* (= 'two or three'). More commonly, a sequence of conjoined elements such as *morning, noon, and night* is only partially asyndetic.

atonic: of a syllable, not having the word-accent; antonym of *tonic.*

attenuative: of adjectives, a derivation signifying the presence of a trait in a reduced or attenuated degree, as English *biggish, greenish.*

augmentative: a derived noun type referring to large or menacing versions of the type, as in many Italian nouns derived with -*accio* and -*one,* e.g. *frusta* 'whip' *frustone* 'big/long whip'. (Not as commonplace in derivative morphology as diminutives.)

auxiliary: a verb of morphosyntactic rather than lexical function, typically marked for morphology features like tense and voice while the 'main verb' (the element with lexical meaning) is in some absolute form. Languages with elaborate inflectional morphology generally have few auxiliaries. Where the histories of auxiliary verbs are clear, they are usually from ordinary independent verbs or complexes. The modal auxilaries of English (*may, can, must*) were once independent verbs; *have* and *be* still are; and an example of a complex is the dialectal American English future marker *finna* < *fixing to.*

back: (a) of vocalic (open tube) phonetics, a tongue-body-position such that the narrowest part of the vocal tract is between the velum or pharynx and the tongue body. Among symbols for back vocalic sounds are [u ʊ o ɔ a]. (b) The dorsum of the tongue, i.e., the broad and relatively inflexible surface of the tongue behind the apex. (A15 ff)

back formation: a term differently used by different authorities, mainly: (a) the abstraction of an imaginary morphological partial from a form, as *to burgle* from *burglar;* (b) a kind of leveling, namely, the creation of a new 'basic' form from a 'derived' one, as singular *glove* from plural *gloves* or *live* vb. and all its forms on the basis of OE *lifde* [livde], preterite of *libban;* (c) the creation of a simplex from an earlier-formed complex, as *to baby-sit* based on the much earlier *baby-sitter*. (54)

bahuvrīhi: a term from Hindu grammatical theory for a type of adjective compound very common in the older Indo-European languages, as in the numerous Greek formations in *eu-* (*eú-noos* 'well-intentioned') and *polu-* (*polú-thriks* 'with abundant hair'); the word *bahu-vrīhi-* itself is an example, lit. 'having much rice'. Bahuvrīhis in English are practically limited to numbers and body-parts: *lion-heart* 'having the heart of a lion', *nine-finger(s)* 'having (only) nine fingers', *two-bit,* and, with adjectival morphology, *broad-backed, thick-furred.*

Baltic: an Indo-European branch comprising East Baltic (Latvian, Lithuanian), and West Baltic (the extinct Old Prussian).

Balto-Slavic: according to some scholars, a branch of Indo-European which includes the Baltic and Slavic languages. Others regard the two groups as making up separate branches. (The dispute, which has been rancorous at times, probably is beside the point: there are reasons for thinking that Old Church Slavic is a West Baltic language, correlative with Old Prussian.)

Bartholomae's Law: a phonotactic rule of Indic whereby any obstruent cluster including a voiced aspirated (i.e. murmured) stop became voiced aspirated throughout, as [b̤] + [t] > [b̤d̤]. Originally this included sibilants, as [b̤] + [s] > [b̤z̤], (*bh + s* > *bhzh*) but in a subsequent development clusters including murmured sibilants devoiced and deaspirated, so [b̤z̤] > [ps] (*bhzh* > *ps*).

Bernoulli's principle: in fluid mechanics, a theorem relating the movement of a fluid (liquid or gas) to pressure. It follows from the Law of the Conservation of Energy: a stationary fluid has *static energy* (pressure, in effect); a moving fluid has in addition *kinetic energy,* and the sum of the two is constant. The Bernoulli effect is critically important in several major areas of articulatory phonetics. The air moving through the glottis (a tiny aperture compared to the trachea) increases greatly in velocity, and the static energy (pressure) necessarily drops. This drop is large; in the absence of turbulence it is on the order of the inverse of half the square of the difference in velocities. It is this pressure-drop which brings about the (temporary) closing of the glottis which is one of the sequence of events necessary for the production of the human voice—and, analogously, the closing of the air-passage in the embouchure of reed musical instruments. (The Bernoulli effect is also responsible for keeping airplanes in the air—the difference between the speed of the air passing over the humped upper and the flat lower surfaces of the airfoil is what provides the lift; the action of an airplane propeller, which is in effect a rotating wing; and also the action of carburetors and simple atomizers.) (A4)

bilabial: a **point of articulation** involving the lower lip articulating against the upper lip, as [m b p]. (A12)

blending *see* **fusion** *and* **portmanteau**.

borrowing: the imitation or copying (not literally 'borrowing' at all) of a linguistic feature proper to one language or dialect by speakers of another. Words are most commonly borrowed—no lexicon is free of borrowed items —but any component of language may be borrowed. (30, 37, 44, 122, 127, 130)

bound: of a morpheme, never occurring as a whole utterance. Affixes and clitics are bound by definition. The plural suffixes of English and the prefix *un-* are examples of affixes; the genitive marker of English ('apostrophe-*s*') and Lat. *-que* 'and' (e.g. *vēnitque* 'and he came', *bōsque* 'and a cow') are examples of enclitics. Stems are either bound or free. *Cat* /kæt/ is an example of a free stem, cf. pl. /kæts/. *Wolf* n. is a free form but is not a stem (*see* **clitic** for *wolf's*); the plural *wolves* contains the bound stem /wulv-/. The complexes /kæts/ and /wulvz/ are of course themselves free.

branch: a group of languages belonging to a language family which share innovations indicating a period of development later than the Proto-language. Germanic and Indo-Iranian are examples of branches of Indo-European.

breaking: in diachronic phonetics, the evolution of a complex vowel nucleus from a simple one, as in the long mid vowels of Old High German (PGmc *fōt-* 'foot' > OHG *fuozz*) or certain tonic mid vowels in Romance (the higher-mid vowels in French and Italian, the lower ones in Spanish: compare PRom. **fẹnu* 'hay' > Fr. *foin* /fwẽ/, It. *fieno*, but Sp. *heno*, on the one hand; and **sẹpte* 'seven' > Fr. *sept* /sɛt/, It. *sette*, but Sp. *siete*, on the other). Some scholars confine the term to ingliding innovations, but there is no difference between ingliding and the evolution of raising glides on the long vowels of English. *See also* **smoothing**.

breathed: (from *breathe*) an obsolete phonetic term synonymous with voiceless. (A4)

cacuminal: in phonetics, a synonym of retroflex. (A12.6)

case: a morphological marking which indicates how a noun relates to other words in a syntactic structure. Prepositions/postpositions have some of the same functions as cases, and languages with large numbers of cases typically have few prepositions/postpositions, and those with few cases have larger inventories of prepositions/postpositions.

causative: a type of derived verb with the meaning of the base verb plus the meaning 'cause (someone else) to … '. Thus to the root *pat-* 'fly': Vedic *pat-ati* 'flies' vs *pāt-ayati* 'puts to flight'; similarly NE *rise* vs *raise*. Such forms may acquire specific meanings; in many languages with causative paradigms, for example, the form which is componentially 'cause to read' actually means 'teach'.

cavity features: the coordinates of vocalic phonetics, e.g. tongue height and advancement. These details affect the resonance of the vocal tract. (A15, A16)

Celtic: a branch of Indo-European. Gaulish was formerly spoken over a very large area of Europe, though scantiness of linguistic remains leave unclear the relationship between European Gaulish, Galatian (Near Eastern) and Celtiberian (Spain). Present-day languages are Irish (Gaelic, Goidelic) and Welsh (British, Brythonic). Breton, spoken in northwestern France, is the language of Welsh or Cornish-speaking émigrés from southern England. In the pronunciation of the term, at present there is divided usage between initial /s/ and /k/. Both are standard.

central: of vocalic (open tube) phonetics, a tongue-body-position intermediate between front and back. [ə ʌ ɨ ʉ] are some symbols for central vocalic sounds. (Note that the phone [a], which since Bell's time has usually been called central, is in fact back.) (A15)

centum *see* **satem.**

checked: in phonetics a synonym of **closed.**

classical language: an ancient language which is not (and as a rule literally never was) the native vernacular of any speech community, but which is cultivated as a vehicle of learning or other special functions in areas such as law and religion. Examples are Church Latin, Church Slavic, Classical Mongolian, Classical Arabic, and Sanskrit.

clitic: a bound morpheme which is PROSODICALLY bound; that is, it binds not to a stem but to any adjacent form. A clitic which binds to ('leans on') a preceding form is called an *enclitic,* one that binds to a following form is called a *proclitic.* Lat. *-ne* (the question particle) and *-que* 'and' are enclitics. The English genitive marker 'apostrophe-*s*' is an enclitic, not an ending: as a matter of accident it mostly binds to nouns, but doesn't have to: *the man who just called's phone number....* In English and many European languages the definite articles are proclitic.

closed: a syllabic followed by a tautosyllabic consonant is said to be in a closed syllable. Whether a syllable is open or closed is a phonetic matter and cannot be determined from written representations.

coarticulation: the simultaneous articulation of two oral features, such as adding rounding to a dorsal stop ([kʷ] vs [k]), superimposing a high back tongue body on apical articulation ([tᵚ] vs [t]), or any palatalization (q.v.). Some languages have simultaneous occlusions, such as [g͡b] (a voiced stop with closure simultaneously bilabial and dorsal) and [k͡p], its voiceless counterpart; here the two features involved are coequal; the usual terminology implies that in [kʷ], say, the dorsal occlusion is primary and the rounding is something in addition. A glottal occlusion occurring together with a consonantal is sometimes loosely called coarticulated (e.g. the [t̰] at the end of a common pronunciation of *good night*) but this would seem to entail terming all phonational states 'coarticulations', and nasality as well.

code-switching: shifting from one language to another in mid-utterance. Many polyglots do so unselfconsciously and extensively, but the term would also apply to dropping [byɛnãtãdü] *bien entendu* into an English sentence, but not to *ciao* pronounced exactly like *chow*. (That would be simply a borrowing.)

cognate: having the same etymon. Thus OE *mynd* and Lat. *mēns* 'mind' both reflect PIE **mṇtis* (the *ti*-stem nomen actionis of the root **men-*). Commonly also used of partially-agreeing forms: OE *fisc* and Lat. *piscis* 'fish' are said to be cognate, even though the former is an *a*-stem and the Latin word is an *i*-stem, and therefore they can't literally be traced to the same etymon; ditto OIr. *íasc* 'fish' which reflects the full grade **peysk-*. (94-5)

The term is also a noun, thus: 'OE *fisc* and Lat. *piscis* are cognates'.

comparative method: the theory and practice (not really a 'method' at all) of demonstrating that languages are related, by reconstructing features of the putative Proto-language.

compensatory lengthening: a type of diachronic development in which the loss of a segment correlates with an increase in length in some remaining segment. The segment that lengthens is commonly the one that immediately precedes the lost one, but not invariably: PIE **ni-sd-os* 'nest' > Lat. *nīdus;* Gk **thent-s* 'putting' > *thens* > *theis* /tʰēs/. (20)

complementary: mutually-exclusive. In linguistics, most commonly encountered in the phrase *complementary distribution.* Ex.: in English, [ɹ̥] (voiceless [ɹ]) is always found immediately after a voiceless stop at onset of stress, e.g. *cry, pry, try,* and not anywhere else; and [ɹ] is never found in this environment. Put differently, since [ɹ] and [ɹ̥] in English are in complementary distribution, there is something always true of the environment of [ɹ̥] which is never true of the environment of [ɹ].

compound: a word containing two or more otherwise independent elements. How to define a compound as distinct from a phrase is troublesome in detail; but in general, if the notion 'word' is understood to be essentially prosodic, a compound has only one tonic accent subject to whatever the usual accentual restrictions are, relative to the form as a whole and without regard to any traits of the component parts. Lat. *ánimam advértō* 'turn (unfavorable) attention toward' is a phrase; but after univerbation becomes *animadvértō,* with one tonic. This test shows that English street-names with *Street* are compounds but those with *Avenue, Road* and the rest are phrases: compare the prosodics of *Elm Street* vs *Elm Avenue.* In languages with case-marking, there is also the morphological test that only one element in a compound will be marked for case—not an absolute test, of course, cf. NE *birdsnest,* and see **dvandva.**

The other side of the coin is how to classify forms like *lord, lady, nostril, dismal, daisy,* and *fellow,* which are etymologically compounds (e.g. OE *nos-*

þyrl 'nose hole' > NE *nostril*) but which cannot be said to have internal structure in present-day English.

In written English, compounds are treated inconsistently. The approved spelling writes some of them solid (*swordfish*), some with a hyphen (*horse-radish*), some with a space (*crab cake*); and not always consistently (both *horsepower* and *horse power* are endorsed, by different authorities). These purely orthographic questions are without linguistic significance.

A characteristic type of Indo-European verb morphology adds one or more preverbs to a root, and these formations are commonly called compounds: Skt *abhi-gam-* 'approach' (root *gam-* 'go'), Lat. *corrumpō* 'break apart' (*rumpō* 'break'), NE *forswear, repaint, untie.*

Nouns (both substantive and adjective) are the compounds par excellence, and the functional relationships between the ingredients of compound nouns are varied and unpredictable, as may be appreciated from such English forms as *snowman, mailman, eggplant, shellfish, battlefield, countryside, saucepan, fire sale,* and *melt-water.* Many are difficult to explain concisely if they aren't in fact totally opaque: *soap-opera, catwalk, cockpit, letterhead, aftermath, heirloom, goose bumps, honeymoon, boiler-plate* 'fixed text', *blackmail, bootleg, shorthand, weathervane, peacock, cheapskate, scapegoat, threshold, keepsake, flapjack, tadpole, sidekick,* and so on.

The Hindu grammarians developed an extensive terminology for Sanskrit compounds, based on function and derivational relationships. Some of these terms—which exemplify, rather than describe, the compound type in question—have enjoyed a certain currency in European linguistics. *See* **bahuvrīhi, copulative compound, dvandva, karmadhāraya,** and **tatpuruṣa.**

compromise dialect: a uniform regional or national standard speech which results from ironing out various regional and social differences, as when a jumble of immigrant English dialects converged on uniform systems in Australia and (regionally) in North America; similarly Spanish in Central and South America (and among colonists generally) *See* **koinē.** (119)

concord: a morphosyntactic property of some languages, whereby anaphoric pronouns (*he, she, it*), and adjectives in construction with a noun, share one or more of the noun's categories such as gender, number, and case. Thus, in the Latin sentences *Bellus juvenis uxorem amat* 'The handsome young man loves his wife' and *Bellam juvenis uxorem amat* 'The young man loves his pretty wife', the two different forms of the adjectve—*bellus* (masculine singular and nominative) and *bellam* (feminine singular and accusative) —define which words in the sentence make up syntactic constituents.

Concord is also seen in relationships between verbs and nouns. In the Indo-European languages, finite verbs are said to 'agree with' their subjects, i.e., the verb and its subject show concord in the categories of person and number. The verbs of Semitic and Bantu languages show gender concord as well, but those of the Bantu languages are marked for such concord with their OBJECTS as well as for their subjects, and there are up to two dozen genders (concord classes).

Examples from Swahili, with the concord markers in upper-case letters: *ninaKIpenda KIle KItabu* 'I like that book', but *ninaYApenda YAle MAkaša* 'I like those chests' (*ni-* 'I', *-na-* 'present tense', [OBJECT CONCORD MARKER], *-pend-* 'like' *-a* 'indicative').

conjugation: (a) the term for the inflections of verb forms; (b) also, the term for a particular verb form-class, i.e., a suite of cooccurring forms, such as the four regular conjugations of Latin (defined by whether the infinitive is *-āre, -ēre, -ere,* or *-īre*).

consonant: a term in phonology for a class of sounds of mostly consonantal articulation, and characteristically patterning as onsets and codas around syllabics. Vocalic consonants are traditionally known as semivowels (a term with other definitions): [yw], but also including [h] and the type of retroflex or tongue-bunched approximant seen in the English [ɹ] of *rare.* (A6a)

consonantal *see* **vocalic.**

contamination: the influence of the pronunciation of one word on another, in the absence of any etymological connection; but (unlike folk etymology) there is some functional or associational basis, e.g. Late Latin *October* like *September* and *November;* NE *covert* /'kəvərt/ altered to rime with *overt;* the name of the letter J now rimes with the name of the letter K, replacing the (presumed) earlier pronunciation riming with I (a pronunciation still current in parts of Scotland). (51)

continuant: in phonetics, a segment articulated with a passage of air through the vocal tract; that is, all resonants and fricatives. The antonym is *occlusive.* Some schools of phonetics limit the defining flow of air to the oral cavity, and for them, consonantal nasals [m n ñ ŋ] are NON-continuant (but not occlusive). (A21)

contoid: a synonym of consonantal. *See* **vocalic.**

copulative compound (*see* **compound**): compounds that are functionally equivalent to phrases with conjunctions, as *twenty-five = five and twenty.* These were common in Sanskrit and could include any number of members,: *deva-gandharva-mānuṣa-uraga-rakṣas-(ās)* 'gods and Gandharvas and humankind and snakes and demons' (Mahābhārata). (One of the elements, *ura-ga-* 'snake(s)' lit. 'chest-goer(s)', is itself a compound.) In modern European languages the type is rare apart from stray forms (*Schleswig-Holstein*), the numerals, and compounds modifying a noun (*mother-daughter outfits, city-county offices, east-west flights*). *See also* **dvandva.**

coronal: a phonetic feature coined in the 19th cent. as a synonym of *retroflex* (or *cacuminal*) but used since the 1930's to denote the natural class of phones articulated with either the apex or front of the tongue, i.e. the dentals, alveolars, retroflexes (apicodomals), and palatals. (A12)

Crimean Gothic: a Germanic, apparently East Germanic, language attested as spoken by a group living in the Crimea in the 16th century, and therefore the latest-attested East Germanic language. The entire corpus is a short word list and a couple of phrases, all very much damaged in transmission.

daughter language: a later, changed form of an earlier language; hence, commonly, a member of a language family.

deadjectival: any formation derived from an adjective, as in NE *greenish, happily, happiness, redden*. A verb like *to yellow* is deadjectival even though not formed with any overt affix.

declension: the term for the morphological forms assumed by pronouns, nouns, and noun-like words (adjectives, participles, gerunds, and so on).

denominative: any morphological derivative based on a noun, e.g. NE *kingly* or *hateful*, but preeminently applied to verbs derived from nouns, like NE *to skin, to table, to back, to provision*. Many languages have one or more affix forming denominative verbs; examples are NE *beautify, begrime, demonize*.

dental: in phonetics, a shorthand term for apicodental, i.e., a phone articulated by the tip (apex) of the tongue against the upper front teeth. Commonly—and unfortunately—the term is used to denote any apical articulation, whether or not teeth are involved. (A12)

desiderative: in verb morphology, formation whose function is the meaning of the verb plus a wish (on the part of the grammatical subject of the verb, NOT of the speaker) to perform an action or be in a state. Some verbs that are formally desideratives have lexicalized meanings, such as the Sanskrit verb *bhikṣa-* 'beg', which is componentially *bhi-bhg-sa-* 'wish to share' (root *bhag-* 'share').

desinence: literally an ending. In linguistics usually a suffix marking case, number, person. (*Désinence* is the usual French term for ending.)

deverbative: any form derived morphologically from a verb, as such English nomina actionis: *perturbation (perturb), disturbance (disturb), hatred (hate), proof (prove)* or nomina agentis (*painter, writer, printer*). Zero derivation (i.e., function derivation with no formal mark) is found in English, e.g. *love, kiss*. Participles, infinitives, and gerunds should probably be considered deverbatives but usually are not.

diachronic: pertaining to the passage of time. Diachronic linguistics is the study of the features of language as they change (or don't change) through time; its antonym is *synchronic*.

diacritic: a mark or symbol added to a letter to indicate a particular value, e.g. ẹ, ę, ẽ, ě, ē, ĕ, ė, é, ê, è (the letter *e* with various commonly used diacritic marks, indicating some specific different value of the symbol). Letters themselves may be used diacritically: *sh* (English) and *sz* (Polish) differ from *š*

(Lithuanian, Czech, and linguistic usage generally) in technique only: that is, the *h* and *z* are functionally equivalent to ˇ.

dialect: (a) a form of speech only slightly different from another form of speech, in contrast to the degree of difference expected between *different languages;* (b) a form of speech differing by any amount from a *standard language;* (c) a purely conventional term for a form of speech, as the *Chinese dialects* or the *Greek dialects.* There are other uses as well. (112-7)

dialect borrowing: taking over the pronunciation of a word from a closely related form of speech, which usually therefore differs only slightly from the expected form, e.g. NE *vixen* from a southern dialect whose traits include voicing of word-initial fricatives (cf. *fox*); or Lat. *rūfus* 'red' (of hair), showing a Sabellian, probably Oscan, development of intervocalic PIE **dh* (cf. native Latin *ruber* 'red'); or NE *wag(g)on*—a doublet of native *wain*—borrowed from Dutch. (There's no question that English and Dutch, and Latin and Oscan, were different languages and not dialects in any of the usual senses; but *dialect borrowing* is nevertheless the term in such cases.) (44)

dialect chain *see* next.

dialect continuum: related forms of speech spread over a geographical area which differ from one another roughly in proportion to their distance from one another, with few or no major discontinuities ('dialect boundaries'). Also known as a *dialect chain.* Examples are Romance and East Slavic (116, 119)

diction: not a standard term in linguistics; used here (75-80) to refer to a linguistic phenomenon which, despite its importance, has no familiar designation. Diction is the characteristic use of terms in expressions without semantic significance. That is, collocations like *run an errand, pose a question, draw a conclusion, make a face, take a turn, raise an objection, cut a caper, pull a stunt, set an example, strike a balance, lay a claim, commit a crime* and so on, do not reflect (or provide) any semantic properties of the lexical items *run, pose, draw, take, raise, cut, put, set, strike, lay,* and *commit,* which are surrogates for 'make, do' (the WORDS *make, do* are themselves of course employed in diction: *make a bed, do an about-face* are specific, not generic, and arguably even *Do something!* is an example of English diction). Such collocations change; latterly one hears *take a decision* almost as often as *make a decision.* It goes without saying that such details are language-specific: we 'play' a musical instrument in English and German, 'sound' it in French and Italian, 'ring' it in Hindi; and in English-speaking jazz circles, all instruments, pianos and bull-fiddles included, are *blown.*

digraph: any symbol consisting of a combination of two letters; *æ* and *œ* are common digraphs, but so is German *ß* = *ss* and the IPA's ʧ and ʤ, and even arguably & = *et* 'and' and @ = *ad* 'at'.

diminutive: a type of derived noun referring to smaller or younger objects, as in Lat. *fīliolus, -a* for *fīlius, -a* 'son, daughter', German nouns in *-chen* and

-lein. Abundant in some languages, they are rarish in English (*kitchenette;* but may be more productive than normally reckoned, as in *tootsies, booties, panties,* and the numerous hypocoristic forms in /-iy/ as Bobby, Peggy). Such nouns are often as much affectionate as literally diminutive; and some nouns etymologically diminutive may become generic in meaning, like Lat. *oculus* 'eye', NE *pupil* originally 'little doll', German *Mädchen* 'girl'.

diphthong: in phonetics, a syllabic nucleus in which the articulators (tongue and lips) are in movement. Some authorities limit the term to a type of syllabic in which the tongue is in movement for the whole duration of the segment, as in English *how, high.* These are also called *falling diphthongs* (because resonance decreases from the beginning of the nucleus to the end of it). Other authorities include the so-called *rising diphthongs* (from the increase in resonance during the nucleus), that is, nuclei consisting of a period of rapid articulatory movement terminating in a steady state, as in *yacht* /yat/ and *wad* /wad/. (A19-20)

dissimilation: a change in pronunciation in which the phonetic features of a segment become less like the features of some other segment, as in NE *seldom < selden* or Lat. *merīdiēs* 'noon; south' < **medio-diēs.* (16)

dorsal: in phonetics, a segment articulated with the back (dorsum) of the tongue. Includes (listed front to back) *dorso-palatal* as in [ḳ g ɲ], *dorso-velar* [k g ŋ], *postvelar* [q ɢ].

dorso-palatal *see* **dorsal.**

dorso-velar *see* **dorsal.**

dorsum: of the tongue, the upper surface of the main body of the muscle mass. (A12)

doublets: two (or more) words of different form and meaning but traceable to the same etymon, e.g. NE *off* and *of; road* and *raid; covert* and *cover; black* and *Blake; chair* and *cathedra.* Some authorities seem to apply the term mainly to items like the first four examples, where formal similarity is salient and where the different forms are from the same language (though not necessarily the same dialect). Cf. **cognate.**

drift: a concept first formulated by Edward Sapir to explain why, for example, languages like those in the Germanic group, having started to lose post-tonic vowels in Proto-Germanic under certain circumstances, would keep on losing them—long after the community had ramified into very different forms of speech—until there were few post-tonic vowels left. More interestingly, if in fact a language changing through time is flowing, as Sapir put it, 'in a current of its own making', that might also explain why certain innovations would show up seemingly independently in otherwise divergent daughter languages. For example, at more or less the same time, long high vowels diphthongized in diverse Germanic languages (OE *mús* > *mouse,* OHG *mūs* > *Maus*), but long after the languages had become mutually unintelligible (or had anything much in the way of contact). However, the drift theory probably underestimates contact effects; and in murkier situations, it amounts to a restating of the facts (and in somewhat mystical terms), not an explanation of them.

dual *see* **number.**

dvandva (*see* **compound**): a term from Hindu grammatical theory for any copulative compound, but historical linguists sometimes reserve the term for the Indo-European prototype, which was limited to two members, and with the peculiarity that both parts had tonic accent and both parts were fully inflected—but in the DUAL number. For example, Ved. *dyā́vā-pr̥thivī́* 'heaven and earth' looks as though it should mean 'the two heavens and the two earths'. The type everywhere—even in the Rigveda itself—tended toward the more usual type of compound, e.g. with only one inflected member and a single tonic syllable; but in other languages we find relics of the early state of affairs: so OE *áþum-sweoras* (1×, Béowulf) 'son-in-law and father-in-law' is a compound of normal type except for being inflected as a PLURAL.

ejective: a shorthand term for 'stop articulated with egressive laryngeal airstream mechanism'. (Sometimes called 'glottal ejective'.) (A3)

enclitic *see* **clitic.**

ending: a bound morpheme coming last in a morphological complex. In Indo-European languages, endings mark case/number/gender in nouns; in verbs, (a) subject person/number and (b) voice. (Some use *ending* and *suffix* interchangeably.) See also **stem.**

epenthesis: virtually interchangeable with anaptyxis, but the term is sometimes reserved for the apparent metathesis of a glide as seen in Gk *baínō* 'go' < *$g^w anyō$. (17)

etymology: the history of a meaning-bearing form. When a form has no KNOWN etymology, it is conventionally (if inaccurately) said to 'have no etymology'. (93)

etymon: a historical form ancestral to a later form. Commonly reserved for unattested (hypothetical) forms, as in: 'PIE *$penk^we$ 'five' is the etymon of Sanskrit *pañca*, Gk *pénte*, Go. *fimf*, etc.'. But one might also say with propriety that OE *cǽse* is the etymon of NE *cheese*, and that Lat. *cāseus* is the etymon of OE *cǽse*.

eventive: a semantic category of verb: verbs denoting actions, often (but not necessarily) with outcomes. NE examples would be *see, build, grind, explode.* In English, the real-time present of such verbs is expressed in the 'present progressive'.

excrescence: any change in which a phonetic segment appears where none was before, e.g. the *t* in OE *stréam* < PIE *srowmos* 'a flowing'. (17)

extension: in semantic change, a synonym of **widening.** (61-2, 64-6)

factitive: a type of verb formation. Given a noun or adjective of meaning 'X', a factitive verb would have the force 'to make someone (or something) be X', as in *to clean, enrich, dampen, pauperize.*

fall together *see* **syncretism.**

feature *see* **phonetic feature.**

finite: of a verb, in traditional terminology: marked for the category of (subject) person. Cf. **infinitive** and **person.**

folk etymology: a change in pronunciation which alters an inherited form in the image of some nonhistorical derivational connection, as when *wheelbarrow* becomes *wheelbarrel* or MHG *ābentiure* 'adventure' (a courtly borrowing from French) becomes NHG *Abenteuer* verbatim 'evening-hour'. The term is synonymous with *popular etymology.* (53)

fortis: literally 'strong', a phonetic term of imprecise and arbitrary use, contrasting with lenis 'weak'. Vaguely synonymous with *tense.* The Latin terms *fortes* and *lenes* are used as nouns to mean 'fortis/lenis consonants'.

fortition: a phonetic change in which an articulation becomes 'stronger', a term with a variety of more or less imprecise or arbitrary definitions. The antonym of *lenition.* (24)

fossil forms: lexical items, meanings, or bound morphemes which survive in a lexicon but are not found in novel combinations. Thus NE *brook* 'tolerate' occurs only in the expression *to brook no opposition*, and the sense 'rotate' of the verb *throw* survives only in one or two fixed collocations like *to throw a pot* (form clay on a potter's wheel).

A little different is a morphological fossil like NE *was/were*, the only survivor of the once-common Old English alternation between different stems for the singular and plural preterites of verbs (e.g. *ič dranc, wé druncon* 'I drank, we drank'). In *for the nonce*, the *n-* of *nonce* is etymologically the accusative ending of the definite article (OE *þone*), by metanalysis. The 'instrumental *the*' (*the more the merrier*) is a fossil of a fossil, continuing OE *þý*, a form of the definite article ultimately reflecting some otherwise lost case.

free: in morphology, a minimal form occurring as an entire utterance. (Not a very useful definition; more realistically, the antonym of *bound.*)

fricative: in phonetics, a continuant articulation in which the passage of air through a narrow aperture creates turbulence which results in noise (q.v.). *Spirant* is an exact synonym. (A8)

front: of vocalic (open tube) phonetics, a tongue-body-position pushed forward toward the teeth. The action of the jaw in concert with the tongue results in a large number of different degrees of aperture for front vocalics. Symbols for typical front vocalic phones are [iɪeɛæɑüöy]. (22, 28-9; A15)

full grade *see* **ablaut.**

fusion: (a) in diachronic phonology, a sequence of segments turns into a single segment with some of the phonetic properties of the source elements, as when [on] > [õ], or [sw] > [f]. (21-2) *See also* **palatalization.** (b)

In morphology, complexes in which the functional components are not resolvable into formal partials, as Fr. *au* /o/ 'to, the, masc., sg.' or NE *teeth* 'tooth, pl.'. Such formations are sometimes called *portmanteau morphs*. (*See* **agglutinative**.)

gemination (literally 'twinning', a term inspired by the double writing of the letters): the lengthening of a consonant, e.g. PGmc *$satjana^n$ 'to set' > Old Saxon *settian*, or Lat. *legere* 'to gather' > It. *leggere*. (17)

gender: in the grammar of noun phrases, literally the 'class' or 'type' of a noun which determines—or better, is determined by—adjective concord. (The term comes from the Lat. *genera nominis* literally 'kinds of noun'.) For Proto-Indo-European, some evidence points to an aboriginal two-class concord system, conventionally called *neuter* and *common*. Most early Indo-European languages, however, have three, conventionally called *masculine, feminine,* and *neuter* (literally 'neither'). These terms are artificial: all but a very few 'masculine' and 'feminine' nouns name objects, substances, or abstractions; and a few nouns of neuter gender name beings with definite reproductive features, e.g. OE *wíf* 'woman', NHG *Mädchen* 'girl', Lat. *scortum* 'prostitute' (either sex). Since 'grammatical genders' are nothing but concord classes, languages are not limited to two or three; Swahili has six, and other Bantu languages have twelve or more. Many large families of languages, e.g. Uralic, Altaic, and Austronesian, have no concord classes at all.

generalization: (a) a subvariety of leveling, being the spread of a PHRASAL alternant (or its type) beyond its original distribution, for example the displacement of NE *mine* by *my* before vowels, as *my apple, my effort,* or the invention of the prevocalic alternant forms in dialectal French /mwaz twaz/ 'me, you' next to regular /mwa twa/ (patterned on plural /nuz vuz/, the prevocalic forms of /nu vu/ 'us, you'). (47b) (b) In semantic change, a synonym of widening. (61-2)

Germanic: a branch of Indo-European conventionally divided on the basis of shared innovations into three subgroups, West, North, and East. West Germanic includes English, Dutch, and High and Low German; North Germanic comprises the Scandinavian languages (except for Finnish and Lapp, which are not Indo-European languages but belong to the Finno-Ugric family). There are a number of early-attested languages in the branch (Old English, Old Saxon, Old High German, Old Norse/Old Icelandic). The earliest, Gothic, is the principal representative of the extinct East Germanic subgroup.

ghost word: a word listed in dictionaries and glossaries, and perhaps the subject of scholarly discussion, but which is a fabrication or blunder rather than a member of any naturally-occurring lexicon. The exact limits of the term are not settled. For a certainty, it applies to forms, created by whatever blunder, which come to be listed in dictionaries or handbooks, such as *cock* 'the nock of an arrow', in Johnson's dictionary and successors; or *phantomnation,* a misprision of *phantom nation* (equipped with an equally imaginary meaning in the dictionaries of Worcester and Webster, 1864). Less clear is how to classify a word found only in a glossary and therefore possibly coined by its author and existing only in his imagination, such as Cockeram's *basiate* which (he says) means 'to kiss'.

The term is not used of things like typographical or copying errors in texts, like Go. *plapjo* (1×) 'street' probably for **platjo,* nor usually for hapax legomena in glossaries created by copying errors.

Lexical figments probably exist in all scholarly traditions, and a drawback of the cumulative nature of scholarship is that once they are 'established', such errors can be hard to root out. The Oxford English Dictionary (1st ed.) gathered together some hundred or so 'spurious words' on pp. 4093-6, some with discussion of their provenience.

glide: a vocalic segment defined partly by cavity configuration and partly by a movement of the articulators during the segment. Examples of glides in English are the sounds symbolized [y w h ɹ] as in *yacht, watt, hot, rot.* (A21)

gloss: (a) a brief translation of a cited form, as: Gk *khandánō* 'hold'. Glosses are for convenience, and can be traps for the unwary. In the example, for instance, the force of *khandánō* is more exactly 'contain, comprise'; this is a legitimate meaning of *hold* (as in 'the harbor can hold only ten ships'), but that sense of *hold* is unlikely to be the one that first occurs to a reader not already familiar with the Greek word. (97a) (b) A notation in the margin or between the lines of written material, explaining or paraphrasing a difficult or ambiguous word or phrase. Since items accidentally omitted in copying were written the same way, a later copyist might misinterpret a gloss as an omission, resulting in a copying error known as an *incorporated gloss.*

glottal stop: a phonational state consisting of a closure of the glottis. Symbol [ʔ]. *See* **phonation.** (A4, A4a)

glottalic theory: the cover-term for a group of ideas for revising the reconstruction of Proto-Indo-European manners of articulation, for example replacing the terms **d* and **dh* by **t'* (glottal ejective) and **d,* respectively.

glottis: the opening between the vocal folds. (A4)

Gothic *see* **Germanic.**

grade, gradation: systems of morphophonemic alternation are sometimes known as gradation; and even when the system itself is not actually called gradation, the elements of the system may be known as grades. In Proto-Indo-European languages and its daughters, ablaut is only sometimes called vowel gradation but the alternating elements are always known as *e*-grade, *o*-grade (collectively, the full grades), zero grade, and so on. Similarly the consonant gradations of Baltic Finnic languages, e.g. Finnish; cf. the nominative and genitive singularsas follows: *lääkki* 'doctor' *lääkin; pöytä* 'table' *pöydän; kylpy* 'bath' *kylvyn.*

grammar as an abstract noun was once a synonym of what is now known as morphology (thus such odd statements as 'Chinese has no grammar'). Also traditionally used to mean the opinions on usage as propounded by 'grammarians'. In modern parlance, a grammar is the totality of the analyses of the patterns and functions of all linguistic elements in a language—sound system, morphology, diction, syntax, lexicon. The generalizations that make up such a grammar are known as rules. This can easily lead to unfortunate habits of thought, whereby the 'rules of grammar' (or the 'rules of a language') are conceived of as dictating the structure of the language, e.g. that English has no words beginning with /ŋ/ BECAUSE a 'rule' prohibits it.

grammaticization, grammaticalization, and **morphologization** are synonymous terms naming the evolution of a lexical item into a morphosyntactic function marker. Thus *will* in English earlier meant '[would] want to', now it is little but the marker of the future tense. In many cases, such a marker retains its lexical status too, for example *have,* which functions (inter alia) as a marker of the past tense of MAIN verbs after modals (*be born* is a verb that does not occur in the present perfect, thus *She must have been born in Russia* is not an example of the present perfect, and is contradicted by *No she wasn't,* not by **No, she hasn't been*); but *have* also retains its many lexical senses as well.

Another facet of the process is the evolution of free forms into clitics (as in English *'ll, 's,* and *'ve* from *will, is,* and *have*) and affixes from clitics. Some authorities theorize that all affixal material is the result of grammaticalization. Such a history can be defended in some cases: the Latin imperfect stem (*portābā-* 'was carrying') is formed with what is descriptively the affix *-bā-*, which can be explained as an encysted form of the verb 'to be' appended to some verbal derivative, with all of the original relationships formally obscure thanks to the action of sound laws and other forces.

Grammaticalization can be observed in progress and sometimes it can be reconstructed with some confidence, as in the Latin example, but the prehistory of most clitics and affixes is obscure if not totally opaque: the forms to be explained are very short and semantically general, and their historical developments partly outside the actions of known sound laws.

Grassmann's Law (also known as the *dissimilation of aspirates*): a phonotactic rule of both Greek and Indic, whereby a sequence of two aspirated consonants, separated by a vowel, dissimilate: for example, the expected reduplicated stem seen in Gk |thi-thē-mi| 'I put' (root |thē|) is realized as *tí-thē-mi.* Similarly in Indic, |dha-dhā-mi| 'I put' (root |dhā|) is realized as *da-dhā-mi* (p. 24)

Greek: a branch of Indo-European whose earliest-attested texts—bookkeeping records from 1200 BC—are in a dialect known as Mycenaean. The earliest literary monument is the *Iliad*, in a recension dating from ca. 800 BC. in a mainly Ionic dialect but with many stray traits of other dialects.

Grimm's Law: the Proto-Germanic Consonant Shift, whereby: all PIE voiceless stops become fricatives; voiced stops become voiceless; and voiced aspirated stops became voiced fricatives or voiced stops. In synopsis: PIE **t* > PGmc **þ* or **ð*; PIE **d* > PGmc **t*; and PIE **dh* > PGmc **d* or **ð*. (Environment determines which alternative outcome is found.) *See also* **Verner's Law.** (29b, 95)

groove fricative (or groove spirant) *see* **sibilant.**

guṇa: in Hindu grammar, full grade. (Lit. 'inherent nature'.) *See* **ablaut.**

guttural: synonym for dorsal (once common, then obsolete, now once again more commonly encountered).

hapax legomenon (pl. **hapax legomena**; often *hapax* for short, pl. *hapaxes*): a word attested only once. The Greek noun *níps**, *níphos** 'snow(flake)' is known from a single form in a poem by Hesiod, the acc.sg. *nípha*. Many forms known only from glossaries are hapaxes, but then it is often unclear whether the uniqueness is owing to rarity or to an error in transmission. The Greek glossary attributed to Hesychius is largely made up of hapaxes, some of which are transparently garbles, e.g. *tré* 'you' acc.sg., said to be Doric, which is surely *twé* (in Greek letters *τρέ* and *τϝέ*, respectively, the latter using an obsolete letter). The Oxford English Dictionary contains numberless entries like *absonate* 'to avoid' which are known only from word lists whose authors probably coined them and whose occurrence in utterances otherwise is in doubt. In special circumstances, words can become practically instantaneous hapaxes. Alexander Pope coined the word *bemused*, which he intended to mean 'in the thrall of the Muses, preoccupied with artistic (particularly poetic) creation'. He used the word twice, in works published in 1705 and 1735, both times (pace the OED) in this sense. But the 1735 occurrence occurs in a context which seemingly led everyone, not just the editors of the OED, to reinterpret the word to mean 'befuddled, distracted', and that has been its use ever since, leaving Pope's original sense isolated. (The citation in the OED—*A parson sat, be-mused in beer*—may seem clear, but the full context makes clear the intended and quite different sense of the word.)

haplology: loss of a repeated sequence in a word. The repetition is rarely exact; typical is *stĩpi-pendium* 'soldier's pay' > Lat. *stĩpendium*. (pp. 31-2)

heterogloss *see* **isogloss.**

heterosyllabic *see* **tautosyllabic.**

hic-et-nunc (Latin 'here and now'): referring to real present time, that is, an action taking place as the speaker speaks: *Helen is writing a letter*. In many languages a given form is ambiguous: *Helena trinkt Kaffee* in German might be either generic (like English *Helen drinks coffee* (rather than tea)) or hic-et-nunc (i.e., saying what Helena is doing right now. The so-called present tense of English has hic-et-nunc function only in performatives, e.g. *I promise I won't tell him.*)

high: of vocalic (open tube) phonetics, a tongue-body-position which is close to the roof of the mouth. Symbols for typical high vocalics are [iɪɨuüʊɯ yw]. (A15)

Hittite: the best-attested of the languages of the Anatolian group, whose exact relationships to one another and to the usual Indo-European languages is still being discussed. Other languages in the group are Luwian (transmitted in cuneiform and also in a form once misnamed 'Hieroglyphic Hittite'), Lydian, Lycian, and Palaic. *See* **Phrygian.**

homonym, homonymous *see* next.

homophonous: having the same pronunciation, as NE *right* 'not wrong', *right* 'not left', *right* 'due', *right* '90 degrees', *write, rite.* Homophony is also seen in affixes such as Lat. *in-* (the privative prefix, e.g. *infirmus* 'infirm') and *in-* (the ingressive/completive prefix, as in *ingredior* 'walk into'); or the English markers of the past tense (*walked*) and the past participle (*[have] walked*). —The term is synonymous with *homonym(ous),* though some usage authorities urge more or less elaborate systems of classification such as differentiating between homophones which are spelled the same and those which are spelled differently, and other distinctions of no linguistic interest.

homorganic: in phonetics, a term variously used by different authorities. Generally, sounds which share a phonetic feature are said to be homorganic; more particularly the term applies to point of articulation; more particularly still, to adjacent sounds in a sequence. For example, in *untimely,* the last sound of the prefix and the initial sound of the root are homorganic; in *unpleasant* they aren't.

hypercorrection: an altered pronunciation in place of an inherited one perceived as erroneous, as *unwieldly* for *unwieldy; simular* for *similar;* or *intimant* for *intimate.* The phenomenon shades insensibly into folk etymology, spelling pronunciation, contamination, leveling, and slips of the tongue. *See also* **hyperurbanism,** next. (55)

hyperurbanism: a near synonym of hypercorrection specifically involving aiming at (and missing) a supposedly higher or more normative speech style, as *chicking* for *chicken.* (Not to be confused with malapropisms like *punctuation* for *punctuality* or *lurid* for *vivid.*) (55)

hypocoristic: pertaining to the nursery; 'baby-talk'. Hypocorisms (*dad, ma, Billy, Ted, Meg, Libby*) usually belong to an informal register. Some may become standard, however, as *buddy* < *brother;* or Go. *atta,* Ru. *ot'ets* both 'father', or when onomastic hypocorisms like *Jack, Beth* and *Molly* become forms of given names independent of their sources. (38)

imperfect: a tense referring to an anterior (past) action or state which is not specified as having gone to completion or otherwise ceased. English *was writing, was sitting* are imperfects: the time is past, but there is no information in the verb form itself as to whether the action or state is true of the present as well.

impersonal: in morphosyntax, predication marked as third person but in functional fact without agent or instrument. Verbs of weather are typically thus: Lat. *pluit*, NE *it is raining*. Many other kinds of impersonals are found. In Latin, a whole set of (formally stative) impersonals deal with states of mind: *mē piget* 'I'm annoyed', *mē taedet* 'I'm bored', *mē paenitet* 'I repent (of)', *mē libet* 'I like'—literally 'it annoys me, it bores me' and so on.

implosive: (a) Shorthand for 'a sound articulated with ingressive laryngeal airstream', e.g. [ɓ ɗ ɠ ʄ].(A3a) (2) In some phonetic terminology, a consonantal phone in coda: in Fr. *tête* [tɛt] (or [tɛ·t]) 'head', the first [t] is said to be *explosive*, the second *implosive*.

inceptive: a synonym of inchoative and ingressive. *See* **ingressive.**

inchoative: a synonym of ingressive and inceptive. *See* **ingressive.**

Indic: one component of the Indo-Iranian branch; many of the most widely-spoken languages of modern India (Hindi, Marāṭhi, Bengāli, etc.) belong to the Indic family. The term may also be virtually a synonym of Sanskrit.

indicative: a verb category. In complex systems the form for generic assertions, denials, etc. The superordinate category is mood. *See* **modal.**

Indo-Iranian: an Indo-European branch, falling into two well-defined sub-groups (Indic and Iranian) and possibly a third (Dardic).

infinitive: in traditional usage, any verbal element unmarked for person, including gerunds and participles. Now the term is normally limited to a verb form historically (and to some degree syntactically) a nomen actionis, and therefore not marked for person. Infinitives may be marked for such verb categories as tense and voice; but they may have such FUNCTIONS no matter how marked (e.g. the passive force of NE *easy to clean*).

An infinitive par excellence is typically a fixed and more or less predictable component of the verb paradigm; and that may be considered part of its definition (in contrast to, say, the nomen actionis, q.v.). Finnish has four functionally differentiated infinitive formations, and a fifth absolute (the complement of the negative verb) which could be analyzed as such if so wished. Even Latin had two infinitives; one, called by that name, is uninflected (e.g. *dīcere* 'to say'); the other, called the supine, is cognate with some Indic infinitives, and came in two different cases (the accusative, e.g. *dictum* 'to say', which functioned mainly in purpose clauses; and the vestigial 'ablative', so called, as in *mīrābile dictū* 'marvelous to say').

infix: a bound morpheme that interrupts a morpheme. (Cf. prefix and suffix.) In a few language families, like Austronesian, infixes are abundant; in most languages they are rare or nonexistent. English and most modern Indo-European languages do not have any. Proto-Indo-European had one infixing verb stem marker, *-ne- alternating with *-n-. For example, to the root *yewg-/yug- 'link, join; yoke' the present/imperfect finite stems were *yuneg-/yung-, componentially *yu-ne-g- and *yu-n-g-. Crucial is that *yug- is a single element, not a sequence of elements *yu- and *-g-. Two things that are often confused with infixation are (1) sequences of pre- or suffixes: no infixation is involved in NE *hopelessness,* nor in NHG *vorgestellt,* the participle of *vor-stellen* 'introduce'; (2) tmesis: the Cockney embellishment of *absolutely* into *abso-bloody-lutely* does not involve any morphological operation at all; *bloody* (or a less polite intensifier) is not an affix. Affixes by definition are bound, and are attached to stems.

ingressive: (a) In semantics, signifying the onset of an action or state, as NE *redden* or Lat. *rubēscō* both 'become red'. Greek has a class of aorists with ingressive meaning. (b) In phonetics, a segment articulated with the airstream moving into the body, as in [ɓ ɗ ʄ ƥ ƙ] (laryngeal airstream mechanism—called *implosives* for short; A3, A22-3), or the *clicks* (short for ingressive velaric airstream mechanism). Synonyms of (a) are inchoative and inceptive.

innovation: literally 'something new'—i.e., any change in language. For example, the development in Old English of the allophones [s, z] for PGmc */s/: [z] intervocalically and [s] elsewhere. Then, in a later innovation, the resulting [z] and [s] became the phonemes /z/ and /s/ (e.g. *lose* and *loose*). The Old English merging of the three original present plural endings into uniform -*aþ* (so *beraþ* 'we, ye, they carry'), and the subsequent abandonment of the ending altogether, are both innovations.

instrumental: a case whose base meaning is 'means or instrument', as in Skt. *aśvena* 'by means of a horse' (stem *aśva-*), Hitt. *ki-eš-šar-ri-it* 'by hand' (*kessar-* 'hand').

intensive: a secondary type of verb paradigm with the sense of strong, vigorous, or emphatic action, as in Skt. *stanistanīti* 'bellows furiously' (root *stan-*) or the French derivatives in *re-* (*redouter* 'to dread, to fear' cf. *douter* 'to doubt, to suspect').

internal borrowing: a term used by some linguists for the replacement of a lexical item by a word already present in the language, as when in English *deer* (originally 'animal') took over the erstwhile functions of *hind,* or *with* (originally 'against') replaced *mid.* (9)

internal reconstruction: hypotheses about the history of a language framed on the basis of the alternation and distribution of sounds within the synchronic system itself. The reasoning is the same as in the comparative method, but is less powerful and reliable because of the limited nature of the data. (105-11)

intervocalic: occurring between vowels.

IPA: (a) The International Phonetic Alphabet. (b) The International Phonetic Association. (A23-7)

isogloss: the boundary between the geographical areas occupied by different linguistic features, e.g. the areas of the USA where people use *bag* vs. *sack*, or where *vary* and *very* are homophones vs. a minimal pair /væriy/ /veriy/. The term *heterogloss* is nowadays being promoted as a better term for the concept. (116)

Italic: the term for the Indo-European languages of Italy. Scholars differ as to whether Latin-Faliscan and Sabellian (attested mainly as Oscan and Umbrian, and scraps of many other languages in addition) actually make up a branch of Indo-European or whether, like, say, Germanic and Celtic, they are two distinct branches that happen to be geographically adjacent to one another. And some of the ancient languages of Italy are so meagerly attested that little can be guessed except that they are (probably) Indo-European. *See also* **Latin.**

karmadhāraya: a term from Hindu grammatical theory for a type of compound comprising a whole predication, as is seen in English *barkeep, spokeshave, lifeguard,* and *doorstop;* Lat. *armiger* 'squire' (lit. 'arms-carrier'), Gk *khoēphóros* 'libation-bearing'. Forms like *bookkeeper* and OE *brópor-bana* 'slayer of [someone else's] brother' are built with overt nomen agentis markers but probably qualify as karmadhārayas, as does *thanksgiving*. Verb-first predicate compounding of the type *spendthrift, stop-gap, scarecrow,* Fr. *chasseneige* 'snow plow', *porte-couteau* 'knife-rest', are either rare or unknown in the older Indo-European languages.

koinē: literally (in Greek) 'common, shared'. Narrowly, the pan-Hellenic Greek, largely based on Attic-Ionic dialects, whose spread ultimately displaced the multitudinous Greek 'dialects' (115). The term is also used to describe an extreme type of compromise dialect, extreme in the sense that the ingredients are (like the indigenous Greek dialects) structurally diverse. Most loosely, the term is little but a synonym of *lingua franca*, q.v.

labial: in phonetics, any segment whose articulation involves narrowing the aperture between the lips. This may be the point of articulation as in the bilabials [mpbβ], or a coarticulated feature of rounding, as in vocalic phones like [uoüw] or as in consonantals like [k^{w}g^w] or the 'whistled' stops of Twi [t^w]. (A12)

labiodental: in phonetics, any segment whose point of articulation involves the lower lip and the upper front teeth, as [f v p^f]. (A12)

lag assimilation/dissimilation: an increase/decrease in phonetic similarity relative to some preceding segment: Gk *leirion* borrowed into Latin as *līlium* 'lily', Lat. *rārus* 'rare' > It. *rado*. Synonymous with *progressive assimilation/dissimilation*. (16)

language family: two or more different languages that used to be the same language. (1, 94-111)

laryngeal: (a) in phonetics, a term for what are more often nowadays called pharyngeal sounds, that is, speech sounds articulated behind the uvula, such as the Arabic consonants known as ˁayn and ḥa. (b) In Indo-European linguistics, the term of art for a class of consonants of undetermined phonetics, less sonorant than the semivowels but, like them, occurring in both consonantal and syllabic forms. Highly similar things are attested in some Salish languages. (The only true 'laryngeal' would be the glottal stop, q.v., which however is a phonational state, not an articulation.)

lateral: in phonetics, a resonant defined by an articulation in which the oral cavity is largely open but blocked at least as far as the midline, e.g. [l λ]. (133.1, A10)

Latin: a language of the Latin-Faliscan subgroup of the **Italic** branch of Indo-European. In essence it was the language of the city of Rome and environs, and in all probability not the only language spoken even in that small area. Latin is very similar to, but not the same as, Proto-Romance—the source of the Romance languages spoken widely in Europe and the New World. These include French, Italian, Romanian, Spanish, Portuguese, Raeto-Romansch, and many other languages commonly called dialects such as Friulan, Picard, and Provençal (Occitan).

lax *see* **tense.**

lenition: (a) In phonetics, a 'weakening' of articulation, a concept suffering from the same problems of definition as its antonym, *fortition*. (24) (b) In the Celtic languages specifically, phonetic change in postvocalic consonants (*see* the Note on Notation). These changes depend on the conditions present in PREHISTORIC periods, and operate over word-boundaries, resulting in a singular morphosyntax, for example OIr. *a chride* /aχrĭðe/ 'his heart', *a cride* 'her heart', *a gride* 'their heart'. (The possessive pronouns reflect Proto-Celtic **osyo, *osyās, *oysom* respectively, whose different terminations account for the treatment of the initial of *cride* 'heart'.) (24, 37)

leveling: an extremely common type of analogical change that results in, and seems to have the purpose of, simplifying the fit between form and function. It most commonly eliminates or reduces alternation, as when *older* replaced *elder*, but it can be more dramatic, as in the replacement of *kine* by *cows, tithe* by *tenth*. (The earlier replacement of *ky* by *kine* seems to be neither simplification nor its opposite.) When leveling involves the morphosyntax it is often termed *generalization*, q.v. (46-9, 50)

lexical diffusion: the spread of a change in pronunciation from word to word over time. (32)

lexicon: the component of the grammar listing the meaning-bearing forms of a language, including affixes and roots; what else it specifies differs from theory to theory. For example, the information that the past tense of *go* is *went* in English is regarded by some as a lexical matter, in contradistinction to *walk/walked, wait/waited,* etc., which are handled by the morphology.

lingua franca: ('language of the Franks') a Romance-based pidgin once widely used around the Mediterranean and in Africa as an auxiliary language (that is, it has no community of native speakers) for commerce etc. Loosely, any language that serves such a function, whether or not it also is a naturally-occurring form of speech, such as Russian (in the USSR) or English.

liquid: (a) according to some, a consonantal resonant, i.e. [r l m n ŋ] (A6); (b) more narrowly, the natural class of taps, trills (*see* **assisted articulation**), and laterals. (A10-11)

linguistic area: speech communities which are contiguous, geographically, often share structural features (called areal features) which may or may not be inherited from a shared proto-language. The languages in a linguistic area may be and often are from diverse linguistic stocks. It is routine for the phonologies of a geographic region to show broad similarities: for a trivial example, a region of western Europe comprising most of France and Denmark, and parts of adjacent areas where German and Dutch are spoken, have a uvular approximant [ʁ] rather than the earlier apical tap or trill. More strikingly, in the evolution of present-day Finnish (a Finno-Ugric language), Proto-Baltic Finnic sounds were lost if they were not also present in BOTH Proto-Baltic and Proto-Germanic (two Indo-European languages, with very different phonologies). In the Balkan region, Romanian, Greek, Bulgarian, and Albanian have all lost the category verbal infinitive.

loan word *see* **borrowing.**

locative: a case whose basic meaning is 'place where': Lat. *humī* 'on the ground', *rūrī* 'in the country', Skt. *puri* 'in the city'.

loss: the disappearance of anything: a segment or string of segments, e.g. *soft* /sɔft/ + *en* > *soften* /sɔfən/, OE *tó beran(ne)* > *to bear*; a phoneme, e.g. /h/ drops in Late Latin (and all Romance languages). The *beran* example is a case of morphological loss as well, since the *-an(ne)* was specifically the marker of the infinitive. Through time, many words are lost from lexicons, as are many meanings: *sad* used to mean 'heavy', *aggravate* 'to charge with a serious crime', *queen* 'wife', *repugnant* 'contradictory'. Some authorities describe **merger** as a loss. (16b, 18, 29c)

low: of vocalic (open tube) phonetics, a tongue-body-position as much out of the oral cavity as possible. Phonetic symbols for low vocalic phones include [æ ɑ ʌ ɔ]. (A15)

manner of articulation: the nature of the contact or close approach of two articulators, for example stop (complete occlusion), fricative (narrow aperture with turbulence in the air-stream), lateral (midline of the oral cavity blocked). (A21)

mediae: in obsolete phonetic terminology, voiced sounds or, more specifically, voiced stops. (Taken from Latin grammar, itself calqued on the Greek term for voiced stops.)

medial: of a phonetic segment, occurring between two other sounds, i.e., by definition, neither the first nor the last sound of a word.

melioration: a change in meaning in which the connotations or the register of a word improve, i.e. become more positive or less negative. NE *queen* comes from OE *cwén* 'woman; wife'; the Romance source of *brave* (widely borrowed in European languages) originally meant 'brutal, thuggish'. Antonym *pejoration*. (64, 66)

merger: the total loss of a phonological contrast; for example, OE /ü/ and /i/ have indistinguishable reflexes in Modern English; or PIE **l* and **r* fall together in Indo-Iranian. (What might be termed *conditioned merger* is here designated primary split.) (27-8)

metanalysis: an analogical process which moves a morpheme boundary, as when *an eke-name* 'an alias' (lit. 'also-name') > *a nickname* or LLat. *frontispicium* 'that which first meets the eye; the façade of a church' is reinterpreted (in Middle French) by way of folk etymology as *frontis-piece*. (p. 90-1)

metaphony: any phonological alternation, but most commonly a synonym specifically of umlaut and vowel harmony.

metaphor: a figurative use of a word in an implied comparison with the basic meaning, as in *foot* of a mountain or *wing* of a building. Such uses are very commonly lexicalized, that is, they are fixed features of the lexicons of the specific language. (68-74)

metathesis: the transposition of segments as in NE *comfortable* as usually pronounced (/kəmftərbəl/); PIE **spek-* 'look at' > Gk *sképtomai* 'I examine'. (19)

metonymy: a figurative use of a word that is not a metaphor (q.v.). The semantic relationships are diverse—*container for the thing contained, material for product, part for the whole, cause for consequence* and others. The common thread might be thought of as ADJACENCY (in time or function as well as in space). (75-84)

mid: of vocalic (open tube) phonetics, a tongue-body position intermediate between high and low. Symbols for mid vocalic phones include [eɛoə]. (The phone [ɔ], often classed as mid, is in fact low.) (A15)

middle (voice): In Indo-European and several daughter languages, a category of eventive verb signaling some special interest or involvement on the part of the actor in the outcome of the action. Often little more than a reflexive in effect, and often functionally as elusive as the distinction between *I'm going to have some coffee* and *I'm going to have me some coffee* in English.

minimal pair: a pair of words differing in a single segment and of different meaning, as NE *spin* and *skin* (which differ in a single feature, the point of articulation of the voiceless stop). Similarly Lat. *aliō* 'from another' vs *āliō* 'with garlic', or Fr. *fin* /fɛ̃/ 'end' vs *vin* /vɛ̃/ 'wine', where the initial consonants differ in the single feature of voice. (A4)

modal: a loose collection of verb categories conveying degrees of opinion, on the part of the speaker, as to how likely it is that an action will take place (or, in some cases, has taken place). In English these distinctions are handled in various ways: periphrastically (*I suppose*), by sentence modifiers (*presumably*), and by auxiliary verbs (*must, may, might* and the like) but also morphologically to some degree (*What if I called you before I came over?*, where what are formally past tense verbs are used to talk of a conditional future action). (8)

The verb categories optative and subjunctive are modal, but have nonmodal functions too, for example, the use of subjunctive forms in indirect questions in Latin, where 'I already know what he said' is expressed as something that looks like 'I already know what he WOULD HAVE SAID'. Mood and aspect interplay curiously, as in *The cat would sit in her lap for hours,* where *would,* usually a conditional marker, has past-tense habitual (indicative) force.

mood *see* **modal.**

morpheme: a meaning-bearing form. NE *cats* consists of two, /kæt/ (a stem) and /s/ (a bound morpheme meaning 'more than one'). Loosely, *cats* itself is often referred to as a morpheme, i.e., the term is often practically a synonym of *word.*

morphographic: of writing systems, a signary in which the signs represent words, as ⟨6⟩ which represents /siks/ in English, /sei/ in Italian, /kūsi/ in Finnish, and so on; ⟨$⟩ = /dalər(z)/, ⟨&⟩ = /ænd/, and so on. In European writing, morphography is incidental, but some writing systems (cuneiform, Egyptian Hieroglyphics, Chinese) use this principle heavily. None use it exclusively. Different spellings of homophones like *wait* and *weight* in English are a kind of morphography, and the Greek use of letters to write numbers (α' = /hēs/ 'one' etc.) is pure morphography despite the origin of the morphograms, ditto English *lb.* = /pawnd/.

morphologization *see* **grammatic[al]ization.**

morphology: the component of a grammar that describes meaning-bearing forms and their distribution. Linguists have long tried to subdivide morphology into INFLECTIONAL and DERIVATIONAL types, though the distinction is troublesome in detail. Informally, inflection is the kind of morphology that marks nouns for case, number, and gender; verbs for person of subject or object, and for tense and mood. Derivation is salient in turning one part of speech into another, as in *behead* and *whiten* (verbs derived from a noun and an adjective, respectively); but this criterion is not reliable. Infinitives, for example, fit this characterization but usually are not classed as derivation; in *reddish* and *squarish* an adjective is derived from an adjective; similarly noun from noun in *violinist;* but most linguists would not hesitate to call these forms derived. Inflectional morphology usually has fully-predictable semantics, while derivation is often unpredictable in its semantic consequences (cf. *matrimony* and *patrimony*). 'Inflection' can be elusive, however, as in the distinction between the past-tense forms *burnt* and *burned* or *wet* and *wetted;* and in any case, definitions including terms like 'usually' and 'often' are no definition at all. (3-6, 104, 106-8)

morphosyntax: morphology and syntax taken as interactive components in a single system. Thus in Latin, *amātur* 'he is loved' and *amātus est* 'he was loved' are equally passive in force but the relationship between them and the respective actives (*amat, amāvit*) is formally different, one being purely morphological, and the other involving syntax/morphology, a composition of a finite verb (the present tense of the verb 'be') and a past participle.

murmur: a phonational state in which the vocal folds vibrate as in voice but inefficiently and with a relatively large volume of air moving through the glottis. Also known as *breathy voice*. (A4a, A18)

mute: in phonetics, an obsolete synonym of stop. (A7)

narrowing: (a) in semantics, the adding of semantic features, as when Lat. *vīvendium* 'life support, nourishment' > Fr. *viande* 'meat', or OE *hund* 'dog' > *hound* 'hunting dog'. (61, 63) (b) In phonetics, an obsolete term for raising, i.e. increasing the tongue height.

nasal: (a) in phonetics, an articulatory feature defined as a lowered velum such that a resonator—the nasal passages—is added to the vocal tract; consonantal and vocalic phones all may be nasal. The antonym is *oral*. The oro-nasal state is one of the four independent variables in articulatory phonetics. (b) The acoustic trait that follows from (a). (c) A shorthand term for *consonantal nasal,* that is, a phone type with oral occlusion and lowered velum, as [m n ñ ŋ]. (A5)

natural class: in phonetics, any group of phones sharing one or more articulatory feature. In general, the more shared features, the more compact the class: 'all stops' is a class, and a compact one; but 'all voiced stops' is more compact still. (A21)

neuter *see* **gender.**

noise: a term in acoustics for sound made up of random (or nearly random) frequencies. Totally random frequencies make *white noise*. (A8)

nomen actionis literally 'action noun': a noun derived from a verb naming the action of the verb, but commonly used also for an outcome, and so on: *relation/relationship* (*relate*), *confession* (*confess*), *stealth* (*steal*), *proof* (*prove*). (In English some nomina actionis are homophonous with the verb, as *love, turn, set, drop*.)

nomen agentis literally 'agent noun': a noun derived from a verb naming the performer of the action, as in Lat. *āctor* 'one who acts' (*agō*), OE *webba* 'weaver' (*wefan*), NE *singer, painter*. In early Indo-European languages, certain verb compounds had nomen agentis sense without any specific derivational ending: Lat. *auceps* 'fowler' (etymolgically 'bird-catcher'), *avispex/auspex* 'bird-watcher', Ved. *vṛtra-han-* 'slayer of the monster Vṛtra', Gk *androbrŏt-* 'man-eating'. A few such formations are seen in present-day English, as *barkeep, doorstop*.

nonce-word, nonce-form: a word created on the spot. When formed more or less normally (e.g. *treey* 'having trees' or *elephanthood*) such a form usually can't be recognized as absolutely unusual. Less conventional formations are easier to spot: *upping and downing* (of copulatory movement), *me-too-ish* 'imitative', *conversationalizing* 'conducting a conversation'. Many such forms are in fact more or less jocular, e.g. *Professor of Paintology* as an academic with specialized knowledge of coatings. (These examples all from native speakers.) Many standard items of vocabulary probably start out life as a nonce-form (*containerize* for example, *absent* in the sense of 'in the absence of', *factoid*), though it is by definition impossible to be certain about specific instances.

non-past: in the simplest tense systems, the distinction is between past-time events (the preterite tense) and everything else—present (hic-et-nunc), habitual, stative, future. The tense systems of the early Germanic languages were of this type, and robust traces of it are still seen in English, e.g. *The tickets go on sale next Monday* or *When Alice calls, tell her I'm on my way.* (The simple present is optional in many of its occurrences in English, but is required in future temporal clauses.) See **preterite.**

nucleus: in phonetics, roughly, the region of a syllable of highest resonance. In an English word like *part* [pʰaɹt], the [a] is the nucleus of the syllable. In other uses of the term, [aɹ] would be considered the nucleus. (Most attempts to define syllable structures segment by segment are not workable in detail.) (A1)

number: overt morphological indication as to whether a noun, pronoun, or verb refers to one or more than one object. This kind of marking is typical of the Indo-European and Semitic languages and many others, but is not universal. The simplest system is *singular* (one) and *plural* (more than one). In very many languages, including some Semitic and Proto-Indo-European, the system is *singular, dual* (two) and *plural* (more than two). Many languages, Chinese and Japanese e.g., lack the grammatical category of number except in such contrasts as 'I' vs 'we' (which is only secondarily a matter of number in any case).

obstruent: in phonetics, a natural class of oral consonantal phones involving some aggressive interference in the airstream; it comprises the stops, affricates, and fricatives. (A7-8, A21)

occlusion *see* next.

occlusive: in phonetics, a natural class of oral consonantal phones involving the complete blocking of the flow of air in the vocal tract; it comprises the stops, e.g. [p t k], and affricates, e.g. [pᶠ č ǰ]. (A7-8)

open: of a syllabic, not followed by a tautosyllabic consonant. See closed.

optative: a modal (or mood) in Greek and Sanskrit. The Proto-Indo-European optative was probably a derived verb stem (like the desiderative and the causative) but in most Indo-European languages it becomes fully integrated into the verb paradigm. It is the source of what is called the *subjunctive mood* of Latin (and Romance) and the Germanic languages.

oral: a phonetic feature for sounds articulated with the velum up (closed). See nasal. (A5, A21)

oro-nasal *see* nasal.

Oscan *see* Italic.

Osthoff's Law: In Greek and some other Indo-European languages, original long vowels shorten before tautosyllabic resonants but not before intervocalic resonants: PGk *tāns* acc.pl.fem. 'that' > *tans* whence Gk *tās*. (Had the vowel remained long, the result would have been ˣ*tēs*.)

Palaic: an ancient Indo-European language attested in western Anatolia. See Hittite.

palatal: shorthand phonetic terminology for those phones articulated against the hard palate with the front part of the dorsum of the tongue. Examples are the [ñ] (IPA [ɲ]) of Fr. *digne* [diñ] 'worthy' and It. *legno* [leño] 'wood'. (Not to be confused with palatalized, q.v.) (22, A-12.7)

palatalized: of consonantal phones, pronounced with a coarticulated high-front tongue body. Consonantals of all points of articulation so occur. (22)

paradigm: (a) in traditional terminology, a pattern of inflection of verbs, nouns, and so on, especially as presented in table form in a grammar book. (b) More rigorously: an array of forms in a language which are partially alike and partially different in both form and meaning such that the formal partials align with the functional partials.

pejoration: a change in meaning in which the connotations or the register of a word decline, i.e. become more negative or less positive. Lat. *vītiōsus* 'weak' > NE *vicious;* OE *hros* 'steed' (i.e., high register, poetic) > NE *horse* (generic). (64-5)

penetration: an exact synonym of epenthesis. (22)

penult: the next-to-last syllable in a word.

perfect: a verb category. (a) An anterior (past) tense signifying completed action but with the implication of effects or results continuing into the present, as in the distinction in English between *have written* (perfect) vs *wrote* (aorist) and *was writing* (imperfect). (b) In Indo-European linguistics, a FORMAL category which in such daughter languages as Germanic, Latin, Greek, and Sanskrit evolved into an anterior tense, but in the proto-language it seems not to have been a 'perfect' at all but a stative (a force it still has in some verbs in Greek, Latin, and Germanic). *See* **stative.**

person: a discourse category. Intelligible discourse must distinguish between *speaker, spoken-to,* and *other.* To this minimum various languages add further distinctions, as for example *we/us* which means 'speaker together with one or more others' (which may expressly exclude the spoken-to). The traditional terms in European grammar for these categories are *first, second,* and *third person,* respectively. In early Indo-European languages, these discourse categories as they apply to the agent or instrument of an action, or the subject of a state, are obligatorily marked on the finite verb by endings named the same way. Modern Indo-European languages use a mixture of person-marked endings and personal pronouns. In other languages, the persons of OBJECTS are similarly marked; in yet others, neither is, or the marking is optional. In the latter case, person is usually indicated by *personal pronouns. See* **impersonal.**

pharynx: the body cavity between the vocal folds and the root of the tongue. (In anatomy, the pharynx is treated as that segment of the alimentary canal between the esophagus—which is somewhat lower than the larynx—and the mouth.)

phonation: the state of the vocal folds. This is one of the four independent variables in articulation. For general phonetic purposes the principal options are: glottal stop, voice, and voicelessness. More detailed treatments need further distinctions. (A2, A4)

phone: a phonetic segment (q.v.); synonymous with *speech sound.* (A1)

phoneme: an element of phonology very diversely defined. Here it refers to an abstraction consisting of a set of phonetically similar *allophones* in complementary (i.e., mutually-exclusive) distribution. An allophone may be any phonetic feature or combination of features, but most allophones are phonetic segments (phones). In transcription, phonemes are written between virgules: NE /pænt/ *pant* is phonetically [pʰǽ·t] in which the allophones are /p/ = [pʰ], /æ/ = [æ], and /t/ = [t] (or [ʔ] or [tʰ]), whereas the allophone of /n/ before tautosyllabic /t/ in a stressed syllable is not a segment at all, but takes the form of the FEATURES of nasality and length in the preceding syllabic. (Cf. /kæt/ [kʰæt] *cat* in which the [æ] is short and oral.)

phonemic split: a diachronic process in the course of which a phoneme becomes two or more different phonemes. Two kinds are distinguished, primary split and secondary split, q.v. (28-9, 99-100, 110-11)

phonetic feature: any component of articulation or acoustics which is intrinsic to the production (in the case of articulatory phonetics) or identification (in the case of acoustic phonetics) of a describable speech sound. In articulatory phonetics, the features of a segment will specify: the airstream mechanism (initiator and direction of flow), phonational state (voiced, voiceless, etc.), the oro-nasal adjustment (*see* **nasal**), and articulation (point and manner). (**Appendix**, passim)

phonographic: of writing systems, the use of signs to represent sounds or sequences of sounds. The two principal types are alphabets and syllabaries.

phonology: the study of the speech sounds that occur in a particular language and their distribution; that is, whatever the theory (and there are many), the object of study is an abstract, language-specific system of patterns of speech sounds.

phonological change: a diachronic change in the phonology of a language. (3, 12, 13, 25-9)

phonological split = phonemic split.

phonologization = secondary split, *see* **phonemic split.**

phonotactic: pertaining to the SYSTEM of occurring sequences of phonemes in a language. For example, in English, two copies of a given phoneme never occur in sequence except across a morpheme boundary, as in *still-life* or *set-to*. In Italian phonotactics, however, such sequences are virtually unconstrained, so /bello/ 'handsome', /sette/ 'seven', as well as across morpheme boundaires, as in /dimmi/ 'tell me'.

Phrygian: an Indo-European language attested in central Anatolia, but not a member of the Anatolian group (languages related to Hittite); it has a family resemblance to Greek.

place of articulation *see* **point of articulation.**

plain: of articulation, not involving distinctive release or airstream features, as a *plain stop* is a stop not aspirated, not glottalized, not murmured, etc.

plosive: (a) an obsolete synonym of stop. (b) Used by some present-day phoneticians as shorthand for 'stop articulated with egressive pulmonic airstream'. But since the majority of stops in most languages are plosives by this definition, the term is still practically synonymous with the term *stop*. (A7)

plurale tantum: 'plural only'. In languages with overt marking for number, there may be lexical items that have no singular, like English *scissors, dregs,* and *eaves*, Lat. *tenebrae* 'darkness', Gk *erepía* 'ruins'. (Plural: *pluralia tantum*.)

point of articulation: region in the vocal tract where two articulators (tongue, lips, teeth, and so on) touch or form the narrowest point in the vocal tract. An exact synonym is *place of articulation*. (A12, A13)

polysemy: multiple meanings for the same form.

popular etymology *see* **folk etymology.**

portmanteau: (a) a word created by combining elements of two words of similar meaning, e.g. *happenstance* < *happen* + *circumstance*. (Synonyms: *blending* and *telescoping*.) (52) (b) In morphology, fusions are sometimes called *portmanteau morphs*, e.g. *went* = 'go' + 'past', or Lat. *bon-a* (two elements) = 'good' + 'nominative' + 'singular' + 'feminine'.

posttonic: coming after the tonic (accented) syllable.

post-velar *see* **dorsal.**

postvocalic: immediately preceded by a vowel.

prefix: a bound morpheme which precedes the element it binds to, as in *re-paint, pre-judge, un-happy*. Several prefixes may occur in a row, as NE *un-re-painted*, or Lat. *con-com-itāre* 'to accompany', with two copies of the prefix *com-*.

preterite: a tense referring to past action, and synonymous with *past;* the term is particularly common in simple tense systems that lack divisions of 'pastness' such as completed vs non-completed or past vs earlier past. The verb systems of Hittite or the older Germanic languages have preterite/nonpast tense systems.

pretonic: preceding the tonic (accented) syllable. (Context alone is usually the only clue as to whether the term is used to mean 'any preceding' or 'immediately preceding'.)

prevocalic: immediately followed by a vowel.

primary split *see* **phonemic split.**

primitive: (a) An obsolete synonym of *Proto-*, so *Primitive Germanic* and *Proto-Germanic* mean the same thing. (b) *Primitive Irish* is the term for the epigraphic (ogam stones) attestation of Irish, predating Old Irish.

privative: a denominative adjective meaning 'characterized by lacking so-and-so', as *penniless, unpainted*, Lat. *impudēns* 'shameless' (*pudor* 'modesty'), Gk *ádikos* 'unrighteous' (*díkē* 'justice'). Similar-looking deadjectivals, e.g. *unhappy* or *unpopular,* are negatives, not privatives; and verbs like *unseat, untie* are known as reversives.

progressive assimilation/dissimilation: changes in pronunciation such that the phonetics of a segment become more/less like the phonetics of a preceding segment. *See* **lag assimilation/dissimilation.** (15-6)

prothesis: in the evolution of a language the appearance of a new sound at the beginning of a word, as in the Romance development of *e-* before clusters of **s-* plus stop: Spanish *escuela* 'school' < PRom. **skǫla*, Gk *amaldū́nō* 'soften' < PIE **ml̥d-* 'soft(en)'. Adjective *prothetic*. (p. 27)

prosthesis: a variant form of prothesis.

proto-language: a form of speech, usually hypothetical, thought to be the common starting-point for members of a language family. (1, 96-104)

recomposition: a kind of analogical leveling in which a new morphological complex is created to replace a complex whose components have been altered by regular developments, as when NE *housewife* arises alongside the regularly-developed *hussy* /həziy/, or /forhed/ replaces /farəd/ as the normal pronunciation of *forehead*. (50)

reconstruction: the technique(s) of framing hypotheses about features of prehistoric (or otherwise unrecorded) stages of a language. More or less synonymous with *comparative method*. (94-111)

reduplication: a type of morphology in which some or all of the phonemes in the affix are copied from the stem. Thus the description of the affix is a sort of blueprint or pattern rather than a single form or short list of forms. In Indo-European languages, the stem of the perfect and some presents were formed with a consonant-copying reduplicating prefix: e.g., root *men- 'have in mind', perf. *me-mon-e 'has in mind'. In Austronesian languages, reduplication is ubiquitous. (109)

reflex: a sound or form that *reflects* an earlier sound or form is said to be its reflex, as in a sentence like: 'PIE *s is reflected in Latin by a number of different sounds, the most surprising reflex perhaps being Lat. *br* from *sr.'*

reflexive: of morphosyntax, a predication in which the object of a transitive verb is the same as the subject. In some languages this is marked by special syntax or lexicon, as in NE *he cut himself,* or with special verb forms. But in e.g. Old English, where the special forms of Modern English hadn't yet developed (and the third person reflexives of Germanic had been lost), there is no special reflexive morphosyntax: 'him' in 'he cut him' could refer to the speaker or some other male. In some Indo-European languages there is a special reflexive pronoun, as in the French *se.* This however is third-person only, there being no special markers for the other persons (and there is no real need for any; English *myself* etc. is semantic overkill).

In addition, there are idiomatic and other special uses, such as the Romance use of the reflexive to make transitive verbs into intransitives: in Italian, a rock *spezza* 'shatters' a window-pane; the glass itself *si spezza.*

regressive assimilation/dissimilation: changes in pronunciation such that the phonetics of a segment become more/less like the phonetics of a following segment. *See* **anticipatory assimilation/dissimilation.** (15-6)

related languages: members of a language family. (1, 94)

relative chronology: the ordering of two or more innovations in a chronological sequence relative to one another, but without regard to calendric dates. For example, the final consonant of the Arabic article *ʔal* assimilates to following coronal consonants, thus *az zaitūn* 'the olive', *aθ θawr* 'the bull'. In most varieties of Arabic, proto *g > ǰ* (a coronal articulation). Since *ʔal* does not assimilate to this /ǰ/, thus *ʔal ǰillāb* 'the shirt', we infer that the change *g > ǰ* postdated the assimilatory changes affecting *ʔal.* (31, p. 143)

release: the pulling apart of articulators after an occlusion. Since air pressure builds up at a point of occlusion, the audible effect of release can be altered by such variables as how rapidly the organs separate: plain release [t] (or, more explicitly, [t˭]), aspirated [tʰ], or affricated [tˢ]. (A7-8)

resonance: a passive property of vibrating bodies such that (depending on size and other details) certain frequencies are reinforced—resonate—while others are suppressed, or are damped as the term has it. The energy lost from the damped frequencies is added to the reinforced ones. —In the vocal tract, all resonators are chambers (e.g., the nasal passages), or more accurately, the volumes of air in the chambers. (A14, A19)

resonant: any speech sound in which resonance is a prominent defining trait, i.e., nasals, liquids, and all vocalic sounds. (Synonymous with sonorant.) (A21, A4b, A18)

retroflex: (a) an articulatory feature involving the raising of the apex of the tongue; these may be vocalic (as in the English vowel of *bird* [bɚd]) or consonantal (as in (b)). (b) A shorthand way of referring to sounds produced with an apico-domal point of articulation. Symbols standing for such sounds are [ṭḍṇṣ] (= IPA [ʈɖɳʂ]). (A12.6)

rhotacism: any change with [r] as its outcome, but preeminently the Italic change of intervocalic *s* to *r* in ca. 350 BC. (28, 30-1)

rhotic: a term coined by Peter Ladefoged for any sound 'spelled with an *r*-like letter'.

rill: in fricative phonetic terminology, an obsolete synonym of groove. (It is a loan-mistranslation of Ger. *Rille* 'groove'.) (A22)

Romance (languages) *see* **Latin.**

root: a minimal form with lexical meaning. As an analytic concept, it is more useful in some languages than others, thus it is insightful for Arabic, Sanskrit or Indo-European, less so for Greek or Latin, and close to useless for English or French.

rounded: a phonetic feature denoting segments pronounced with the lips close together and more or less projected. In most languages the mid back and high back vocalic phones (glides included) are rounded, the remaining vocalics being unrounded. (A fuller catalogue of lip positions would be *spread, neutral, compressed, rounded,* and *projected.*) (A15)

Sabellian *see* **Italic.**

samprasāraṇa: in Hindu grammatical terminology, zero grade. *See* **ablaut.**

satem and centum languages: Indo-European languages have generally been regarded, albeit not without controversy, as divided into two large subgroups. The basis of the division is innovations involving the reflexes of the reconstructed Proto-Indo-European palatal series of stops. In all satem languages, these are reflected as sibilants (which may undergo further evolution); in the centum languages, they are reflected as stops or the reflexes of stops. The satem languages and branches are Albanian, Armenian, Baltic, Slavic, and Indo-Iranian; the centum languages are Celtic, Germanic, Greek, Latin, and the Tocharians. How to classify some poorly-attested languages of the family is a problem; also (for different reasons) the Anatolian languages. (28)

schwa: in phonetics (a) a reduced vowel (i.e., a vowel shorter and of less distinct phonetics than the typical syllabic), as in the second syllable of English *Helen.* (b) The term for the mid central unrounded syllabic, symbolized [ə], as in English *sofa* [sowfə]; the term often includes all mid central unrounded vowels, such as [ɨ ɜ ʌ]. (c) In Indo-European linguistics, a reconstructed short vowel, *ə, once thought to be the realization of a reduced long vowel, but currently understood to be a syllabic laryngeal (*see* **laryngeal**). (d) Historically, *schwa* is a term in Hebrew phonology for a reduced vowel (Hebr. *š·wa*) alternating with full vowels.

secondary split *see* **phonemic split.**

segment: the minimum unit of speech in articulatory phonetics, consisting of a constellation of phonetic features preceded or followed by a different constellation: the words *snap, laughed,* and *fix* consist of four segments each: [snæp] [læft] [fiks]. Segmentation is an ideal concept, however, with both practical and theoretical ambiguities. (**Appendix** passim, 13-45 passim)

semivowel: (a) a pseudo-phonetic term (of long standing) for a sound which is phonetically vocalic but phonologically a consonant. That is, the concept is the outbirth of a mismatch between phonetic facts and phonological norms. (A6) (b) A loose synonym for glide. (A18) (c) In Indo-European linguistics, a class of twelve reconstructed sounds whose shared characteristic is that they alternate between consonantal function (*y w r l m n) and vocalic function (*i u r̥ l̥ m̥ n̥).

seṭ: literally 'with an -*i*-', a term from Pāṇini's Sanskrit grammar denoting certain roots which consistently took a linking vowel -*i*- between the root and certain affixes beginning with consonants. Roots whose formations lacked such a vowel were designated *aniṭ*, lit. 'without an -*i*-'. This theory, then, is purely descriptive, but current Indo-European theory offers an explanation: it traces the fugitive vowel to proto-consonants, the so-called laryngeals, and the term *seṭ* has been taken over by Indo-Europeanists to refer to PIE roots ending with a laryngeal, like *ǵenH- 'beget' vs roots like *gʷhen- 'strike dead' (cf. the Sanskrit derivatives from these two roots, formed with the same nomen agentis suffix -*tar: jan-i-tar* 'progenitor' vs *han-tar-* 'slayer').

shift: a phonological change which can be stated in terms of one or more natural class features, which therefore applies to several sounds at once, 'all voiced stops become fricatives', e.g. Famous sound shifts are Grimm's Law and the Great English Vowel Shift (in which every long vowel raised one articulatory place except for the already highest vowels, which underwent breaking). The loss of the contrast of vowel length in the early histories of Romance and Slavic probably should be accounted a shift, but rarely is; the development of fricatives out of all aspirated (and some plain) stops in the evolution of Modern Greek is definitely a shift.

Sometimes the term is just a synonym for 'sound change'. (32)

sibilant: a groove fricative or affricate in which the aperture is small and narrow, in comparison with the wide and thin aperture of slit fricatives. The concentration of noise frequencies in sibilants is strong, high in pitch, and compact, i.e., in plain language, a sharp hissing sound. (*Sibilant* is etymologically 'whistling'.) All sibilants are more or less apical. Some authorities use the terms *hissing* and *hushing* for sounds of the [s] vs the [š] types. Symbols standing for typical sibilants (and sibilant affricates) are [s z š ž č ǰ] (= IPA [s z ʃ ʒ tʃ dʒ]). (A8)

Slavic: *see* **Balto-Slavic** for the subgrouping debate. Old Church Slavic, a language a few sound laws away from Proto-Slavic, is the earliest attested language of the family and in interesting ways is a very conservative form of speech. Modern Slavic languages bear roughly the same relationship to Old Church Slavic that the Romance languages bear to Latin. Current Slavic languages are subdivided into West (Polish and Czech, for example); East (Russian and Ukrainian); and South (Bulgarian and Serbo-Croatian, for example, but including Old Church Slavic). *Slavonic* is a synonym for Slavic; *Sclavic* and *Sclavonic* are obsolete synonyms.

slit fricative: a type of fricative articulation in which the aperture is wide and thin, resulting in a diffuse and relatively soft noise. Slit fricatives are formed at all points of articulation. Symbols standing for typical slit fricatives are [f v θ ð χ γ]. *See* **sibilant.** (A8, A13)

smoothing: in diachronic phonology, the evolution of a phonetically simple nucleus from a complex one, as when PGmc. **ay* > OE *á* (PGmc. **stainaz* > *stán* 'stone'). PGmc. **aw* > OHG *ō* before certain consonants (PGmc. **fraws* 'froze' > OHG *frōs*), and there was a wholesale loss of diphthongal phonetics in the history of Latin and its descendants. The history of English includes the wholesale breaking of vowels in various environments and the subsequent smoothing of the results: Lat. *vallum* borrowed as OE *weall* [wæəl·] > NE *wall* [wɔl].

sonant: in phonetics, an obsolete synonym of voiced. (A4)

sonorant: a synonym of resonant. (A21, A4b, A18)

sound law: a statement of diachronic relationship consisting of an input (the starting point), the later development (also called the reflex), and the conditioning factors if any. The inputs and conditions are limited to phonological factors, which include word boundaries (since the word is a prosodic unit). Typical would be: OE *d* > NE ð/V́_r, that is: 'Old English /d/ becomes modern English /ð/ between a stressed vowel and /r/' (e.g., OE *fæder* > NE *father*). Note that a rule like OE *d* > NE *d*/#__, that is: 'Old English *d* remains unchanged in English in initial position', is no less a sound law than a rule which specifies a change. (25, 30)

speech island: a language or group of dialects, by implication of no great geographic extent, surrounded by a different language, as in the German-speaking regions of Hungary and Czechoslovakia, or the Albanian enclaves in Sicily. (118)

spelling pronunciation: a (usually) sporadic change based on a wrong choice among alternatives in an inconsistent spelling system. (43)

spirant *see* **fricative.**

spirantization: a diachronic change whereby an occlusive becomes a fricative, e.g. [t] > [s], or [č] > [š]; or, by stages: [k] > [č] > [š]. (23, 34)

split *see* **phonemic split.**

Sprachbund: a synonym of linguistic area, q.v.

spread *see* **unrounded.**

stative: a type of verb which denotes the state of the subject (rather than an event which the subject initiates or participates in), such as *know, fear, own, be happy, be dead.* As the examples show, states may be either transitive or intransitive. In Proto-Indo-European, what is called the perfect tense seems to have been neither perfect nor a tense but stative, thus **woyd-e* 'knows', **me-mor-e* 'is dead', **me-mon-e* 'has in mind, remembers', **de-dok-e* 'accords with community values'.

stem: a morpheme to which affixes are attached. Some stems are free, like the English verb *(to) house* /hawz/, to which affixes like /əz/ '3sg.pres.', /d/ 'past', /iŋ/ 'gerund' are added without change; some are bound, like the noun stem /hawz-/ which is never found except with the plural suffix, viz., /hawzəz/ *houses* (cf. *house* sg. /haws/). In English, a majority of stems are free; in morphologically elaborate languages like Greek, Latin, and Sanskrit, stems are generally bound.

stop *see* **manner of articulation.** (A7)

subgroup: related languages which share innovations. The term is sometimes used as a synonym of branch, sometimes for subsidiary divisions within a branch.

subjunctive *see* **modal** and **optative.**

substantive: short for *noun substantive,* i.e. a *noun.*

substitution: when a word is borrowed, most sounds in the word are replaced by the more or less different sounds that occur in the phonology of the borrowing language. Where the replacement sound is different from the target sound to some large and noteworthy degree, however, it is sometimes treated as something special, called a substitution. Hawaiian, with its small inventory of obstruents, substitutes /k/ for most target obstruents: *Kana* 'John', *Kalikimaka* 'Christmas', *kauna* 'town'; NE /sæŋfroyd/ for Fr. *sang froid* /sãfrwa/. As the last example hints, substitution is part and parcel of what is commonly called speaking a (foreign) language with a heavy accent, e.g. a francophone's [zis] for NE [ðɪs] *this.* (p. 191)

substratum [language(s)]: the language(s) of a population whose elites speak a different language—the *superstratum* language—which is used also for official purposes. Such situations, which are far from uncommon, are of interest to historical linguists because of the possibility that substratum speakers will effect change in the superstratum language by importing substratum features into it. (37, 122)

suffix: a bound morpheme following a stem, like the English plural markers or Latin verb endings. Suffixes also occur in sequences: NE *childishness* contains two suffixes in a row: /čayld/ plus /iš/ forms a new stem, an adjective, to which de-adjectival suffixes like /nəs/ and /liy/ are added. In some languages many affixes are strung together: e.g. Turkish *gönüllerinizde* 'in your hearts', which is resolved into *gönül-ler-in-iz-de* 'heart-pl.-your-pl.-in'. *See* **agglutinative.**

suppletion: (lit. 'filling out') in morphology, the term for a paradigm's full complement of forms being made up from two or more different stems. The case is clearest when the elements involved are etymologically completely unrelated, as in the personal pronouns of Indo-European (Lat. *ego/ mē* 'I/me', for example), common adjectives (NHG *gut, besser* 'good, better'), or verbs such NE *go/went*, Lat. *sum/fuī* 'am/was', Gk *légō* 'say', aor. *eîpon*. The term is also applied to what appear to be different stems built to the same root, but which are functionally equivalent, as in the Proto-Indo-European interrogative pronoun stems *k^wi-* and *k^we-*. Some paradigms LOOK suppletive but are not, by this definition, because their elements are in fact from the same stems or roots: e.g. OIr. *bé* nom.sg. (archaic) 'woman', *mná* gen.sg., from *g^wenH* and *g^wneH-s,* respectively, a regular paradigm altered by purely regular sound changes.

surd: an obsolete phonetic term for voiceless. (A4)

svarabhakti (or svarabhakti vowel): an anaptyctic vowel or glide. (17)

syllabary: a writing system in which the signs represent a vowel and (usually) one or more preceding or following consonants. The Japanese kanas are syllabaries, in which five signs stand for vowels and the balance are for -c(y)v-, where c = any consonant and v = any vowel, e.g. *-ka-, -ki-, -ku-, -ke-, -ko-, -kya-, -kyu-* etc. In more complex syllabaries, such as the Akkadian, in addition to signs for -v- and -cv- there are signs for -vc- and -cvc-.

syllabic: a sound, usually a resonant and still more usually vocalic, which is the nucleus of a syllable. Framing an accurate and rigorous definition of what makes a segment syllabic has tied linguists in knots for generations; the every-day sense of *vowel* is close enough for most purposes. But the second syllable of NE *button* [bʌtn̩], which is syllabic, does not fit most people's idea of 'vowel'; and *psst* [pst̩] has a non-resonant syllabic, as also seen in a Slurvian pronunciation of English *it's cool* [t⸗şkʰu·wl] in two syllables, or Chinese [şẓ̍ᴵᴵᴵꜜ] 'four'. *See* **nucleus.** (A14)

synaesthesia: sense-transfer (loud colors, sweet sounds). This is the basis for many metaphors, but there is some evidence that a few individuals PHYSIOLOGICALLY sense flavors tactilely, see sounds, and so on. (72)

synchronic: pertaining to a point in time. *Synchronic linguistics* is a synonym for *descriptive linguistics*, that is, the study of linguistic structure as a coherent whole in a given speech community at a given time. Ancient as well as modern languages can be studied thus. The companion term is diachronic linguistics.

syncope: the loss of any medial sound (but often understood to be limited to syllabics). (18)

syncretism: literally 'a falling-together'. (a) In phonology, when two or more sounds become the same sound, e.g. Proto-West Germanic *d*, *t* fall together in word-final position in modern German. (27, 28, 100, 101) (b) The conflation of originally different case functions in one case, as in the syncretism of the prehistorical genitive and ablative cases in the Greek genitive.

syntax: the study of the linguistic meaning of utterances which cannot be found in the words themselves nor in the real-world context (known as *pragmatics*). *Timothy flattered Brad* and *Brad flattered Timothy* consist of identical words but have different meanings, and it is up to an analysis of the syntax to explain why and how.

tantum: (Latin) 'only', as in *plurale tantum* 'plural-only', *futurum tantum* 'future-only'. It is an adverb; the plural of *plurale tantum* is *pluralia tantum*.

tap *see* **assisted articulation.**

tatpuruṣa: a term from Sanskrit grammatical theory for a type of compound in which the first part modifies the second: *blackbird, treehouse, armchair, manpower*. In languages with case-marking apparatus the difference between tatpuruṣa compounds and phrases is obvious. In English there are characteristic prosodic differences, as *bláckbird* (compound) vs *bláck bírd* (phrase), and semantic ones as well (an albino blackbird is not a *black bird* but is still a *blackbird*). The prosodic test shows that names of *streets* in English are tatpuruṣa compounds (*Jóhnson Street, Élm Street*) while all other genres are phrases (*Élm Ávenue, Élm Boúlevard, Élm Dríve*).

tautosyllabic: literally, occurring in the same syllable. The question of practical interest, though, is virtually limited to whether a postvocalic consonant is or is not in the same syllable as the syllabic. In NE *must*, the final /st/ is tautosyllabic with the vowel; in *musty* only the /s/ is, the /t/ being the onset of the second syllable, i.e., /s/ and /t/ are *heterosyllabic*; in *mistake*, both the /s/ and the /t/ are onsets to the second syllable. In English, after a stressed vowel a single intervocalic consonant is *ambisyllabic*, that is, although phonetically short, it is simultaneously the coda of the preceding syllabic and the onset of the following, as in English *fishy, happy, leafy*. In many languages, all syllables are open and so in e.g. Russian, *noša* 'burden' is syllabified ['no-šə], and *nitka* 'thread' is ['ñi-tkə]. *See* **Osthoff's Law.**

telescoping *see* **portmanteau.**

tense: (a) in morphosyntax, a verb category having to do with the relative time when an action takes place. The minimal tense opposition is between *past* and *non-past*, which is the system of the early Germanic languages and Hittite. At the opposite extreme are languages with a dozen or more verb paradigms marked for fine distinctions of temporal remoteness as well as other categories altogether such as whether the effects of a past action are continuing into the present; or for locating the time of actions relative to one another; marking them as instantaneous or continuing, and so on.

(b) In vocalic phonetics, the term for a supposed feature which is more accurately an inventory of features, which may (in a given language) occur singly or together. Thus, in English, the vowels of *read, raid, rowed,* and *rude,* called tense, are in actual phonetic terms comparatively long—a tenseness trait—but also are characterized in several standard dialects by the rising offglides [y] and [w]. For many speakers of English, however, the vowels of *fan* and *fawn* are also tense and, while definitely long, they either have centering offglides or no offglide at all. And in various dialects of English (Irish, for example) if there are offglides on high or mid vocalics they are inglides, as [ɹe·ə̯d] *raid.* Its antonym is *lax.*

(c) The tense/lax terminology is also commonly used nowadays as an undefined and undefinable binary feature used to distinguish pairs of vocalic phones like [i] vs [ɪ], [e] vs [ɛ], [o] vs [ɔ], even when there are no distinguishing traits whatever apart from tongue-height, as in the second syllables of Fr. *poignée* [pwɛñe] 'handle' ([+tense]) and *poignet* [pwɛñɛ] 'wrist' (lax, or rather [−tense]).

tenues: an obsolete term for voiceless; more particularly but not exclusively voiceless stops. (Taken from Latin grammar, itself calqued on the Greek term for plain voiceless stops. The singular is *tenuis.*) (96)

Tocharian: an Indo-European language, or actually two languages, attested in texts of Buddhist scriptures and commentary, found in Chinese Turkestan. The application of this ethnonym to the language is now generally held to be wrong. Toch. A is sometimes known as Turfanian, Toch. B as Kuchean. Though attested late, from ca. 7–8th cent., and in frustratingly lacuna-ridden manuscripts, the languages are of great importance for the reconstruction of Proto-Indo-European.

tonic: characterized by having the main word-stress. Cf. *atonic.*

trill *see* **assisted articulation.**

truncation: loss of one or more segments in phonological or morphological patterns, e.g. NE *comical* /kamǝkǝl/ but the adverb *comically* is /kamǝkliy/, not ˣ/kamǝkǝliy/; or, in French, the deletion of the vowels of *de, le, la* before a word beginning with a vowel: *d'amour, l'amour;* or, in English, the loss of /t/ in *hasten, soften.*

ultima: the last syllable of a word.

Umbrian *see* **Italic.**

umlaut: (a) the common phenomenon of a change in the phonetics of a vowel conditioned by the phonetics of a following vowel, as in Romanian. (b) Commonly used without qualification to refer to any of the numerous such changes in the histories of North and West Germanic languages. (c) Familiarly, the diacritic more formally known as a diaeresis, used to mark (certain) 'umlauted' vowels in modern German, as *ä ö ü*, so that one might say of *Hände* 'hands' misspelled *Hande* that 'the umlaut has been left off'. (15)

underdifferentiation: of phonographic writing systems, a failure to represent all the structural contrasts of the language. In Greek, the two phonemes /a/ and /ā/, likewise /ü/ and /ǖ/ are never differentiated in writing; neither are English /θ/ and /ð/. Differently, phonological contrasts may be sometimes reflected in spelling, and sometimes not; for example vowel length in modern German, or the contrast between /s/ and /z/ in English. (cf. 131.1)

univerbation: the coalescence of a phrase into a single word, as NE *alive* < OE *on life*, NE *maybe*, Fr. *beaucoup* 'much', Sp. *hidalgo* 'nobleman' < *filius de aliquo* 'someone's son', Lat. *rēspūblica* 'civil government' (literally 'the public matter').

unrounded: pronounced with the lips parted or even drawn back (some languages have specifically *spread* vocalic phones). An articulatory feature more pertinent to vocalic phonetics than consonantal, but found in both types. English /š ž č ǰ/, for example, are more or less definitely rounded. *See* **rounded.** (A17)

uvular: articulated in the back of the oral cavity; in the case of trills and taps (*see* **assisted articulation**), the uvula ('grapelet') itself will be an integral articulator, whereas in the case of uvular stops, symbol [q] (or [ḳ]) and [ɢ], the uvula is not in play. (A11)

velar: in phonetics, a segment articulated against the velum (soft palate, but commonly including more or less of the hard palate). Symbols for common dorso-velar sounds include [k g ŋ]. *See* **dorsal.** (A12, A13)

velum: (a) a passive articulator, being the region of the roof of the mouth including, for most speakers, the forward portion of the velum proper (the *soft palate*) and the rear margins of the hard palate. (A12) (b) The same organ, functioning as a valve whose position accounts for the difference between oral (up) and nasal (down) phones. (A2)

Verner's Law: an important condition on Grimm's Law stating that fricatives between resonants in Proto-Germanic become voiced when not preceded by the Proto-Indo-European tonic accent (which is unrelated to the Germanic tonic accent); in all other environments the fricatives remain voiceless. Thus initially and after tonic vowels PGmc *f $þ$ $χ$ $χ^w$ s remain unchanged; after atonic vowels they become *$β$ $ð$ $γ$ $γ^w$ z. Thus: PIE *$préwseti$ 'freezes' > PGmc. *$friusið$; but *$(pe)prusmé$ 'we froze' > *$fruzum$. (29b)

vocal folds: a pair of adjustable membranes housed in the larynx at the top of the trachea (windpipe). In speech acts, they may be brought close together so that air from the lungs moving between them causes them to close and open rapidly, producing a sound called voice; or held apart so that lung air passes silently between them (*see* **voiced** and **voiceless,** *and also* **glottal stop.**) For much of phonetic history, the usual term was *vocal cords.* For some reason there has long been discomfort over the proper term for the anatomical feature in question: over the years various supposedly better terms have been urged, such as *vocal ledges, bands, lips,* and *ligaments.* (A4)

vocalic: a natural class of phones articulated with lung air passing through the mouth and over the center of the tongue, without audible local friction. All other speech-sounds articulated in the mouth are consonantal. (*See* **glottal stop.**) Vocalics include what are commonly known as vowels and semivowels and also [h] and the English retroflex glide *r* [ɪ]. (A21)

vocative: the case used as a form of address, as Lat. *Mārce* 'O Mark', Ved. *pítar* 'O father'.

Even in caseless languages like English, vocative forms are phonetically distinctive: when not the first word in a sentence, they are atonic and in effect parenthetic. Something similar seems to have been true of Proto-Indo-European vocatives.

English also has words like *kiddo* and *ma'm,* which are found only in the vocative; but they are better regarded as forms of address than 'lexical vocatives' or the like.

vocoid: a synonym of vocalic.

voice: (a) in phonetics, *see* **voiced.** (b) In the verb morphosyntax of Indo-European languages, several slenderly-related phenomena are called 'voice'. The most familiar is the distinction in transitive verbs between the *active voice,* where the agent or instrument is the subject of the verb, i.e. is in the nominative case and takes verb agreement; and the *passive voice,* where the undergoer or recipient of an action is the grammatical subject, and the 'logical subject' (that is, the agent or instrument) is either expressed by an oblique construction or is unexpressed altogether.

In Indo-European languages a different category is known as the *middle voice* (or, less happily, the *medio-passive voice*). This seems to have differed from the active voice mainly in the degree of interest or involvement in the outcome of an action on the part of the agent. At times it comes close to a reflexive in force: Skt *yajate* mid. 'performs a rite for oneself' vs *yajati* act. 'performs a rite [for someone else]'.

The full list of relationships between sentential roles (agent, patient, etc.), verb concord, and 'aboutness' in the languages of the world is complex. Note, for example, that in English, transitive stative verbs like *have, own, hate* for some reason do not normally form passives.

voiced: in phonetics, a phonetic feature: segments classified as voiced are pronounced with the vibration of the vocal folds. With very few exceptions, all possible combinations of phonetic features occur concurrently both with and without (voiceless) the vibration of the vocal folds, but the great majority of resonants are voiced. Antonym *voiceless*, next. (A4)

voiceless: a phonetic feature. Segments classified as voiceless are pronounced without the vibration of the vocal folds. Antonym *voiced*. (A4)

vowel: a term in PHONOLOGY (not properly a phonetic notion) for a class of sounds usually characterized by vocalic articulation, but not necessarily. In Serbian and Sanskrit, the vowels include a syllabic trill [r̩]. (A6a)

vowel harmony: the converse of umlaut, i.e. the phonetics of the vowels of suffixes are influenced by the vowels of roots. In Hungarian for example the plural markers of nouns include *-ek, -ak, -ok* depending on the cavity features of the closest preceding vowel: *kez-ek* 'hands', *lov-ok* 'horses'.

vṛddhi *or* **vriddhi** (lit. 'increase, enlargement') in Hindu grammatical terminology, *ā* when it functions as lengthened grade, as *pādam* acc.sg. 'foot' next to *padi* loc.sg. 'on foot', or *drāupada-* 'descendent of Drupada'. *See* **ablaut.**

widening: in semantic change, the loss of semantic features, as when Lat. *oleum* 'olive oil' > 'oil in general'. *See* also **narrowing.** (61-2)

zero derivation: a term used by some scholars to denote derivation (*see* **morphology**) without overt morphological apparatus, as *to tidy* vb. (< adj.; cf. *blacken* < *black*) or the noun *a break* from the verb *to break.*

zero grade *see* **ablaut.**

GLOSSARY OF LINGUISTIC TERMS
IN GERMAN

Terms that are transparent (*Kasus, Optativ, Präsens/Praesens, Reduplikation, Kausativum, femininum*) are not included, nor are words whose linguistic meaning is the same as the ordinary lexical meaning, e.g. *Entwicklung, ererbt, Stammbaum.*

abg. (Altbulgarisch): Old Church Slavic.
Ablautreihe: ablaut 'series'; *see* **Reihe.**
Ableitung: derivation.
Abstufung: gradation.
Abtönung: *o*-grade (*see* ablaut *above*).
ags. (angelsächsisch): Old English.
ahd. (althochdeutsch): Old High German.
ai. (altindisch): Sanskrit.
air. (altirisch): Old Irish.
aisl. (altisländisch): Old Icelandic.
altbulgarisch: Old Church Slavic.
althochdeutsch: Old High German.
altindisch: Sanskrit.
altirisch: Old Irish.
altisländisch: Old Icelandic.
altniederdeutsch: Old Low German.
altnordisch: Old Norse.
altsächsisch: Old Saxon.
an. (altnordisch): Old Norse.
angelsächsisch: Old English.
Anlaut n.: word-initial position; adj. **anlautend:** occurring in word-initial position. Exx. 'Idg. **s* im Anlaut ...' *or* 'Anlautendes idg. **s* ...' = 'PIE **s* in word-initial position'.
as. (altsächsisch): Old Saxon.
Auslaut n.: word-final position; adj. **auslautend:** occurring in word-final position. Exx. 'Idg. **s* im Auslaut ...' *or* 'Auslautendes idg.**s* ...' = 'PIE **s* in word-final position'.
Auslautverhärtung: devoicing in word-final position.
bedingt, Bedingung: conditioned; condition(ing).
betont: accented; tonic.

Betonung: accentuation.

Beugung (or Biegung): inflection.

Bildung: formation, stem; e.g. Perfektbildung 'the formation of the perfect (tense) stem'.

Bindevokal: linking vowel, stem vowel.

Brechung: of vowels, breaking.

Dehnstufe: in ablaut, lengthened grade.

Dehnung: lengthening.

Deklination: declension.

Einzelsprache: individual language (literally), but in different contexts often more accurately 'a language', 'dialect', or 'specific language'. The implied contrast is with language families and branches, such that e.g. after speaking of common (shared) features of the Germanic family/branch one might introduce einzelsprachlich details, that is, details pertaining to the specific languages. *See* voreinzelsprachlich.

Endbetonung: accent on the final syllable.

entsprechen: correspond to.

Entsprechung: correspondence.

Ersatzdehnung: compensatory lengthening.

Fernassimilation, -dissimilation: assimilation/dissimilation at a distance, as Italo-Celtic $*p \ldots k^w$- > $*k^w \ldots k^w$-, NE *seldom* < *seldon*, respectively.

Formenlehre: morphology, more particularly historical morphology.

gemein-: pan-, e.g. *gemein-germanisch* 'pan-Germanic'; adj. shared, common.

Gemination: (of consonants) lengthening.

Genera nominis: *see* Geschlecht.

Genera verbi: *see* Verbalgeschlechter.

Geräuschlaut: obstruent.

Geschlecht: (grammatical) gender.

geschlossen: closed, in phonetics, i.e. a syllabic followed by a tautosyllabic consonant.

Gesetz: law; rule (typically a sound law, e.g. *Verners Gesetz* (or *das Vernersche Gesetz*) 'Verner's Law', *Dehnunggesetz* 'lengthing rule').

Glied: branch; subgroup; subdivision.

gliedern: subdivide.

Gliederung: subgrouping; classification.

grammatischer Wechsel: lit. 'morphological variation', Jacob Grimm's term (but still used) for the alternation of reflexes of PIE voiceless obstruents in the Germanic languages, which Verner's Law (q.v., above) explained.

griechisch: Greek.

Grundsprache: proto-language.

Grundvokal: 'basic' vowel. In the context of Indo-European linguistics, what-

vowel is functionally equivalent to *e*-grade. So the basic vowel of the root 'put' is (in pre-laryngeal terms) *$\bar{e}$*, thus *$dh\bar{e}$*- (= *$dheH_1$*-); that of the root 'see' is *o*, thus *ok^w*- (= *H_3ek^w*-).

Gruppe: a word of vague denotation; in phonology, a 'sequence' of sounds.

Guttural: dorsal; velar.

Halbvokal: semivowel; depending on context, either the glides specifically or all six Indo-European semivowels *y, w, r, l, m, n*.

Hauchlaut: [h].

Hauptsatz: independent clause, adj. **hauptsätzlich.**

Hochstufe: obsolete synonym for full grade (ablaut).

idg. (indogermanisch): Indo-European.

indogermanisch: Indo-European; often Proto-Indo-European.

Inlaut n.: word-medial position; adj. **inlautend:** occurring in medial position. Exx. 'Idg. *s* im Inlaut ...' *or* 'Inlautendes idg. *s* ... ' = 'PIE *s* in medial position'.

keltisch: Celtic.

Konsonantismus: consonant phonology.

kymr. (kymrisch): Welsh.

kymrisch: Welsh.

lateinisch: Latin

Laut: (speech) sound, phone.

Lautgesetz: sound law.

Lautlehre: phonology, more commonly phonological history.

Lautumstellung: metathesis.

Lautverschiebung: sound shift. Specifically, the first Germanic (Grimm's Law) and second (High German) consonant shifts.

Lautwandel: (phonological) alternation.

lett. (lettisch): Latvian.

lettisch: Latvian.

Liquiden: liquids, i.e. laterals and 'rhotics'.

lit. (litauisch): Lithuanian.

litauisch: Lithuanian.

Mediae: voiced stops.

mhd. (mittelhochdeutsch): Middle High German.

Mischform: hybrid form (from contamination, e.g.).

mittelhochdeutsch: Middle High German.

Modus (pl. Modi): (grammatical) mood.

Mundart: dialect.

Muta: stop.

nebeneinander: adjacent; as a noun, adjacency.

Nebensatz: subordinate clause; adj. **nebensätzlich.**

Neubildung: (morphological) innovation; adj. **neugebildet.**

niederdeutsch: Low German.
Nomina: nouns.
Partizip: participle.
polnisch: Polish.
Reduktionsstufe: reduced grade (schwa secundum).
regelmäßig adj. regular; Regelmäßigkeit: 'regularity'.
Reibelaut: fricative.
Reihe: (ablaut) series; used in two distinct senses: (a) the alternating sets themselves (e.g. *e, o, zero;* or *ē, ō,* *ə*); and (b) of such sets in combination with the Indo-European semivowels (e.g. *e, o, zero; ey, oy, i; en, on, ṇ,* and the rest).
Satz: sentence; clause.
sächlich: neuter.
Schleifton: falling ('circumflex') pitch.
Schwund: loss.
Schwundstufe: in ablaut, zero grade (including schwa primum).
schwach: (lit. 'weak') in morphology generally, REGULAR or AGGLUTINATIVE (as in the Germanic dental preterites). As applied to adjective morphology in the Germanic languages, *weak adjectives* are the (pseudo-)*n*-stems that were originally DEFINITE.
Senkung: (of vowels) lowering.
Silbe: syllable.
Silbenschichtung: haplology.
Silbenträger: (of a consonantal) syllabic, phonetically [ṛ ṇ] e.g.; in the customary notation of Indo-European linguistics, *ṛ, *ṇ.
Sonorlaut: resonant phone (all vocalics, and the consonantal nasals and liquids).
Spaltung: (phonemic) split.
Spirant: fricative.
Sproßkonsonant: excrescent consonant.
Sproßvokal: anaptyctic vowel.
Stamm: stem.
Stammbildung: stem-formation.
stark: (lit. 'strong') in morphology generally, irregular or fusional (as in the Germanic ablauting preterites of the *drink, drank* types). As applied to adjective morphology in the Germanic languages, the adjectives formed to various stems which functionally were originally INDEFINITE.
Stimme: voice.
stimmhaft: voiced.
stimmlos: voiceless.
Stoßton: tonic accent, particularly some sort of pitch phonetics contrasting with falling pitch (*Schleifton*).

Stufe: grade, e.g. of ablaut.
Tenues: voiceless (plain) stops.
Tiefstufe: zero grade (ablaut).
Tiefton: secondary accent.
Themavokal: thematic vowel.
Ton: accent; tonic accent.
überliefert: attested; **Überlieferung:** attestation.
unbetont: unaccented; atonic.
unregelmäßig: irregular.
uridg., urindogermanisch: Proto-Indo-European (also a noun).
Ursprache: proto-language.
verallgemeinert: generalized.
Verbalgeschlechter: a calque on *genera verbi:* in verb morphosyntax, the voices.
Verbindung: (consonant) cluster.
Verbum (pl. Verba): depending on context, (a) verb; (b) word.
Verdoppelung: of consonants, lengthening; of syllables, reduplication.
Verhältnis: correspondence.
Verkürzung: (phonetic) shortening.
Verschiebung: (sound) shift.
Verschlußlaut: occlusive; *also specifically* stop.
Verwandschaftsname: kinship term.
Vokal: vowel.
Vokalbestand: inventory of vowel phonemes.
Vokalismus: vowel phonology.
Vollstufe: in ablaut, full (*e,o*) grade.
voreinzelsprachlich: pertaining to proto-languages or pre-languages, most commonly of branches, e.g. features of the Germanic languages which appear to be traceable to Proto-Germanic would be described as *voreinzelsprachlich*, in contradistinction to the *einzelsprachlich* features which arose in the histories of the individual Germanic languages.
Wechsel: variation (*Akzentwechsel* 'variation (or alternation) in accent', e.g.).
Wurzel: root.
Wurzelnomen: root noun.
Wurzelpräsens: root present stem.
Zeitwort: verb.
Zischlaut: sibilant.
Zuwort: adjective.

BIBLIOGRAPHY

Aitchison, Jean. 1991. *Language Change: Progress or Decay?* 2nd ed. Cambridge: Cambridge University Press.

Allen, W. Sidney. 1965. *Vox Latina: a Guide to the Pronunciation of Classical Latin.* Cambridge: Cambridge University Press.

———. 1987. *Vox Graeca: a Guide to the Pronunciation of Classical Greek.* 3rd ed. Cambridge: Cambridge University Press.

Anttila, Raimo. 1988. *Historical and Comparative Linguistics.* Amsterdam: Benjamins.

———, and W.A. Brewer. 1977. *Analogy: a Basic Bibliography.* Amsterdam: Benjamins.

Baldi, Philip, ed. 1991. *Patterns of Change, Change of Patterns: Linguistic Change and Reconstruction Methodology.* Berlin: de Gruyter.

Barber, Elizabeth J. Wayland. 1974. *Archaeological Decipherment; a Handbook.* Princeton: Princeton University Press.

Beekes, Robert S.P. 1995. *Comparative Indo-European Linguistics: An Introduction.* (Transl. of the original edition (1990) in Dutch.) Amsterdam: Benjamins.

Benveniste, Émile. 1954. Problèmes sémantiques de la réconstruction. *Word* 10:251-64.

———. 1973. *Indo-European Language and Society.* (Transl. by Elizabeth Palmer.) London: Faber and Faber.

Birnbaum, Henrik. 1978. *Linguistic Reconstruction: Its Potential and Limitations in New Perspective.* Washington, D.C.: Institute for the Study of Man.

Bloomfield Leonard. 1933. *Language.* New York: Holt, Rinehart and Winston.

Buck, Carl Darling. 1949. *A Dictionary of Selected Synonyms in the Principal Indo-European Languages.* Chicago: University of Chicago Press.

Bynon, Theodora. 1977. *Historical Linguistics.* Cambridge: Cambridge University Press.

Campbell, Lyle. 1999. *Historical Linguistics: an Introduction*. Cambridge: MIT Press.

Chadwick, John. 1963. *The Decipherment of Linear B*. New York: Vintage.

Chambers, J.K., and Peter Trudgill. 1980. *Dialectology*, Cambridge: Cambridge University Press.

Cleator, Philip Ellaby. 1961. *Lost languages*. New York: John Day.

Collinge, N.E. 1985. *The Laws of Indo-European*. Amsterdam: Benjamins.

Coulmas, Florian. 1996. *The Blackwell Encyclopedia of Writing Systems*. Oxford: Blackwell.

Croft, William. 1990. *Typology and Universals*. Cambridge: Cambridge University Press.

Crowley, Terry. 1998. *An Introduction to Historical Linguistics*. 3rd ed. Auckland: Oxford University Press.

Daniels, Peter T., and William Bright, eds. 1996. *The World's Writing Systems*. Oxford: Oxford University Press.

Davis, Garry W., and Gregory K. Iverson, eds. 1992. *Explanation in Historical Linguistics*. Amsterdam: Benjamins.

Diebold, A. Richard Jr. 1960 Determining the center of dispersal of language groups. *International Journal of American Linguistics* 26:1-10.

Dyen, Isidore. 1956. Language distribution and migration theory. *Language* 32:611-26.

Embleton, Sheila. 1986. *Statistics in Historical Linguistics*. Bochum: Brockmeyer.

Esper, Erwin A. 1973. *Analogy and Association in Linguistics and Psychology*. Athens, Ga: University of Georgia Press.

Fisiak, Jacek, ed. 1980. *Historical Morphology*. The Hague: Mouton.

Fox, Anthony. 1995. *Linguistic Reconstruction, an Introduction to Theory and Method*. New York: Oxford University Press.

Friedrich, Johannes. 1966. *Entzifferung Verschollener Schriften und Sprachen*. 2nd corrected edition. Berlin: Springer. (A translation of the first edition (1954) by Frank Gaynor was issued under the title *Extinct Languages*. New York: Philosophical Library.)

Gilman, E. Ward, ed. 1989. *Merriam-Webster's Dictionary of English Usage*. Springfield: Merriam-Webster.

Hall, Robert A. Jr. 1950. The reconstruction of Proto-Romance. *Language* 26:6-27.

Haugen, Einar. 1950. The analysis of linguistic borrowing. *Language* 26:210-31

Hock, Hans Henrich. 1985. Yes Virginia, syntactic reconstruction is possible. *Studies in the Linguistic Sciences* 15:49-60.

———. 1991. *Principles of Historical Linguistics*. 2nd ed. Berlin: Mouton de Gruyter.

———, and Brian D. Joseph. 1996. *Language History, Language Change, and Language Relationship: an Introduction to Historical and Comparative Linguistics*. Berlin: Mouton de Gruyter.

Hoenigswald, Henry. 1950. The principal step in comparative grammar. *Language* 26:359-64.

———. 1960. *Language Change and Reconstruction*. Chicago: University of Chicago Press.

———. 1963. On the history of the comparative method. *Anthropological Linguistics* 5:1-11.

———. 1991. Is the 'comparative' method general or family-specific? In Baldi, 1991, pp. 183-91.

Hopper, Paul, and Elizabeth Traugott. 1993. *Grammaticalization*. Cambridge: Cambridge University Press.

Jeffers, Robert J., and Ilse Lehiste. 1979. *Principles and Methods of Historical Linguistics*. Cambridge: MIT Press.

Jespersen, Otto. 1909. *A Modern English Grammar*. Pt 1. Sounds and Spellings. Copenhagen: Munksgaard.

Joos, Martin. 1967. *The Five Clocks*, with an introduction by Albert Marckwardt. (Originally published in 1962 as *International Journal of American Linguistics* vol. 28 no 5, being publication no. 22 of the Indiana University Research Center in Anthropology, Folklore, and Linguistics.) New York: Harcourt Brace & World.

King, Robert. 1967. Functional load and sound change. *Language* 43:831-52

Ladefoged, Peter. 1975. *A Course in Phonetics*. New York: Harcourt Brace Jovanovich.

Lamb, Sidney M., and E. Douglas Mitchell, eds. 1991. *Sprung from Some Common Source: Investigations into the Prehistory of Languages*. Stanford: Stanford University Press.

Lass, Roger. 1997. *Historical Linguistics and Language Change*. Cambridge Studies in Linguistics 81. Cambridge: Cambridge University Press.

Lehmann, Winfred P. 1992. *Historical Linguistics: an Introduction*. London: Routledge.

————. 1993. *Theoretical Bases of Indo-European Linguistics*. London: Routledge.

Lehmann, Winfred P., and Yakov Malkiel, eds. 1982. *Perspectives on Historical Linguistics*. Amsterdam: Benjamins.

Malkiel, Yakov. 1993. *Etymology*. Cambridge: Cambridge University Press.

Mallory, James. P. 1989. *In Search of the Indo-Europeans*. New York: Thames and Hudson.

Martinet, André. 1960. Function, structure, and sound change. *Word* 8:1-32

————. 1964. *Économie des Changements Phonétiques*. 2nd ed. Bern: Franke.

Matasović, Ranko. 1996. *A Theory of Textual Reconstruction in Indo-European Linguistics*. Schriften über Sprachen und Texte, herausgegeben von Georg Holzer. Bd 2. Frankfurt/Main: Peter Lang.

Matisoff, James A. 1990. On megalocomparison. *Language* 66:106-20.

Meillet, Antoine. 1925. *La Méthode Comparative en Linguistique Historique*. Oslo: Aschehaug. (Available in translation as *The Comparative method in Historical Linguistics*. Paris: Champion.)

————, Marcel Cohen, et al. 1964. *Les Langues du Monde*. Novelle Édition. Paris: Champion.

Miranda, Rocky V. 1975. Internal reconstruction: scope and limits. *Lingua* 26:289-306.

Mühlhäusler, Peter. 1986. *Pidgin and Creole Linguistics.* Oxford: Blackwell.

Nichols, Johanna. 1992. *Linguistic Diversity in Space and Time.* Chicago: University of Chicago Press.

Polomé, Edgar C. 1990. *Research Guide on Language Change.* Berlin: Mouton de Gruyter.

Ringe, Donald A. 1992. On calculating the factor of chance in language comparison. *Transactions of the American Philosophical Society* 82.1. Philadelphia: American Philosophical Society.

————. 1995. 'Nostratic' and the factor of chance. *Diachronica* 12:1:55-74.

Salmons, Joseph C. 1992. A look at the data for a global etymology: **tik* 'finger'. In Davis and Gregory 1992, pp 207-28.

————. 1993. *The Glottalic Theory: Survey and Synthesis.* Washington, D.C.: Institute for the Study of Man.

Sampson, Geoffrey. 1985. *Writing Systems: a Linguistic Introduction.* Stanford: Stanford University Press.

Scherer, Anton. 1968. *Die Urheimat der Indogermanen.* Darmstadt: Wissenschaftliche Buchgesellschaft.

Stern, Gustaf. 1931. *Meaning and Change of Meaning.* Bloomington: Indiana University Press.

Sturtevant, Edgar H. 1940. *The Pronunciation of Greek and Latin.* 2nd ed. Philadelphia: Linguistic Society of America.

Szemerényi. Oswald. 1996. *Introduction to Indo-European Linguistics.* (In effect, the 4th edition of his *Einführung in die Vergleichende Sprachwissenschaft.*) New York: Oxford University Press.

Teschner, Richard V. 1972. *Anglicisms in Spanish. A Cross-Referenced Guide to Previous Findings together with English Lexical Influence on Chicago Mexican Spanish.* University of Wisconsin Dissertation.

Thomason, Sarah Grey. 1976. Analogic change as grammar complication. In: *Current Progress in Historical Linguistics.* Proceedings of the Second International Conference on Historical Linguistics,

Tucson, Arizona January 12–16, 1976, William M. Christie, Jr., ed. Pp 401-9. Amsterdam: North-Holland.

———, and Terrence Kaufman. 1988. *Language Contact, Creolization, and Genetic Linguistics.* Berkeley: University of California Press.

Tuten, Donald N. 1998. *Koineization in Medieval Spanish.* University of Wisconsin Dissertation.

Twaddell, W. Freeman. 1938. A note on Old High German umlaut. *Monatshefte für Deutschen Unterricht* 39:177-81.

Weinreich, Uriel. 1968. *Languages in Contact: Findings and Problems.* The Hague: Mouton.

Williams, Joseph M. 1976. Synaesthetic adjectives: a possible law of semantic change. *Language* 52:461-78.

SUBJECT INDEX

THE NUMBERS REFER TO PAGES

INDEX OF LANGUAGES CITED

THE NUMBERS REFER TO PAGES

This text is set in Stone and Stone Semibold, created in 1987 for Adobe Systems by **Sumner Stone**. He designed a family of three styles (Serif, Sans, and Informal), all three in roman and italic versions, and in three weights. **John Renner** added a matching set of phonetic characters for Stone Serif and Stone Sans.

Stone's large aperture and a colossal x-height call for additional leading for readability. On the other hand, its crisp and supple drafting, together with this x-height, make it remarkably legible, even in smaller type sizes.

The small capitals and text figures are from the URW foundry.

The running heads are set in Copperplate Gothic, cut by **Frederic Goudy** in 1903 for ATF, a face which from its creation has been very widely used, in a bewildering variety of weights, outlines, and profiles.

CURRENT ISSUES IN LINGUISTIC THEORY

E. F. K. Koerner, Editor
Zentrum für Allgemeine Sprachwissenschaft, Typologie
und Universalienforschung, Berlin
efk.koerner@rz.hu-berlin.de

Current Issues in Linguistic Theory (CILT) is a theory-oriented series which welcomes contributions from scholars who have significant proposals to make towards the advancement of our understanding of language, its structure, functioning and development. CILT has been established in order to provide a forum for the presentation and discussion of linguistic opinions of scholars who do not necessarily accept the prevailing mode of thought in linguistic science. It offers an outlet for meaningful contributions to the current linguistic debate, and furnishes the diversity of opinion which a healthy discipline must have. A complete list of titles in this series can be found on the publishers' website, *www.benjamins.com*

254 **BALDI, Philip and Pietro U. DINI (eds.):** Studies in Baltic and Indo-European Linguistics. In honor of William R. Schmalstieg. 2004. xlvi, 302 pp.

253 **CAFFAREL, Alice, J.R. MARTIN and Christian M.I.M. MATTHIESSEN (eds.):** Language Typology. A functional perspective. 2004. xiv, 702 pp.

252 **KAY, Christian J., Carole HOUGH and Irené WOTHERSPOON (eds.):** New Perspectives on English Historical Linguistics. Selected papers from 12 ICEHL, Glasgow, 21–26 August 2002. Volume II: Lexis and Transmission. 2004. xii, 273 pp.

251 **KAY, Christian J., Simon HOROBIN and Jeremy J. SMITH (eds.):** New Perspectives on English Historical Linguistics. Selected papers from 12 ICEHL, Glasgow, 21–26 August 2002. Volume I: Syntax and Morphology. 2004. x, 264 pp.

250 **JENSEN, John T.:** Principles of Generative Phonology. An introduction. 2004. xii, 324 pp.

249 **BOWERN, Claire and Harold KOCH (eds.):** Australian Languages. Classification and the comparative method. 2004. xii, 377 pp. (incl. CD-Rom).

248 **WEIGAND, Edda (ed.):** Emotion in Dialogic Interaction. Advances in the complex. 2004. xii, 284 pp.

247 **PARKINSON, Dilworth B. and Samira FARWANEH (eds.):** Perspectives on Arabic Linguistics XV. Papers from the Fifteenth Annual Symposium on Arabic Linguistics, Salt Lake City 2001. 2003. x, 214 pp.

246 **HOLISKY, Dee Ann and Kevin TUITE (eds.):** Current Trends in Caucasian, East European and Inner Asian Linguistics. Papers in honor of Howard I. Aronson. 2003. xxviii, 426 pp.

245 **QUER, Josep, Jan SCHROTEN, Mauro SCORRETTI, Petra SLEEMAN and Els VERHEUGD (eds.):** Romance Languages and Linguistic Theory 2001. Selected papers from 'Going Romance', Amsterdam, 6–8 December 2001. 2003. viii, 355 pp.

244 **PÉREZ-LEROUX, Ana Teresa and Yves ROBERGE (eds.):** Romance Linguistics. Theory and Acquisition. Selected papers from the 32nd Linguistic Symposium on Romance Languages (LSRL), Toronto, April 2002. 2003. viii, 388 pp.

243 **CUYCKENS, Hubert, Thomas BERG, René DIRVEN and Klaus-Uwe PANTHER (eds.):** Motivation in Language. Studies in honor of Günter Radden. 2003. xxvi, 403 pp.

242 **SEUREN, Pieter A.M. and Gerard KEMPEN (eds.):** Verb Constructions in German and Dutch. 2003. vi, 316 pp.

241 **LECARME, Jacqueline (ed.):** Research in Afroasiatic Grammar II. Selected papers from the Fifth Conference on Afroasiatic Languages, Paris, 2000. 2003. viii, 550 pp.

240 **JANSE, Mark and Sijmen TOL (eds.):** Language Death and Language Maintenance. Theoretical, practical and descriptive approaches. With the assistance of Vincent Hendriks. 2003. xviii, 244 pp.

239 **ANDERSEN, Henning (ed.):** Language Contacts in Prehistory. Studies in Stratigraphy. Papers from the Workshop on Linguistic Stratigraphy and Prehistory at the Fifteenth International Conference on Historical Linguistics, Melbourne, 17 August 2001. 2003. viii, 292 pp.

238 **NÚÑEZ-CEDEÑO, Rafael, Luis LÓPEZ and Richard CAMERON (eds.):** A Romance Perspective on Language Knowledge and Use. Selected papers from the 31st Linguistic Symposium on Romance Languages (LSRL), Chicago, 19–22 April 2001. 2003. xvi, 386 pp.

237 **BLAKE, Barry J. and Kate BURRIDGE (eds.):** Historical Linguistics 2001. Selected papers from the 15th International Conference on Historical Linguistics, Melbourne, 13–17 August 2001. Editorial Assistant: Jo Taylor. 2003. x, 444 pp.

236 **SIMON-VANDENBERGEN, Anne-Marie, Miriam TAVERNIERS and Louise J. RAVELLI (eds.):** Grammatical Metaphor. Views from systemic functional linguistics. 2003. vi, 453 pp.

235 **LINN, Andrew R. and Nicola McLELLAND (eds.):** Standardization. Studies from the Germanic languages. 2002. xii, 258 pp.

234 **WEIJER, Jeroen van de, Vincent J. van HEUVEN and Harry van der HULST (eds.):** The Phonological Spectrum. Volume II: Suprasegmental structure. 2003. x, 264 pp.

233 **WEIJER, Jeroen van de, Vincent J. van HEUVEN and Harry van der HULST (eds.):** The Phonological Spectrum. Volume I: Segmental structure. 2003. x, 308 pp.

232 **BEYSSADE, Claire, Reineke BOK-BENNEMA, Frank DRIJKONINGEN and Paola MONACHESI (eds.):** Romance Languages and Linguistic Theory 2000. Selected papers from 'Going Romance' 2000, Utrecht, 30 November–2 December. 2002. viii, 354 pp.

231 **CRAVENS, Thomas D.:** Comparative Historical Dialectology. Italo-Romance clues to Ibero-Romance sound change. 2002. xii, 163 pp.

230 **PARKINSON, Dilworth B. and Elabbas BENMAMOUN (eds.):** Perspectives on Arabic Linguistics. Papers from the Annual Symposium on Arabic Linguistics. Volume XIII-XIV: Stanford, 1999 and Berkeley, California 2000. 2002. xiv, 250 pp.

229 **NEVIN, Bruce E. and Stephen B. JOHNSON (eds.):** The Legacy of Zellig Harris. Language and information into the 21st century. Volume 2: Mathematics and computability of language. 2002. xx, 312 pp.

228 **NEVIN, Bruce E. (ed.):** The Legacy of Zellig Harris. Language and information into the 21st century. Volume 1: Philosophy of science, syntax and semantics. 2002. xxxvi, 323 pp.

227 **FAVA, Elisabetta (ed.):** Clinical Linguistics. Theory and applications in speech pathology and therapy. 2002. xxiv, 353 pp.

226 **LEVIN, Saul:** Semitic and Indo-European. Volume II: Comparative morphology, syntax and phonetics. 2002. xviii, 592 pp.

225 **SHAHIN, Kimary N.:** Postvelar Harmony. 2003. viii, 344 pp.

224 **FANEGO, Teresa, Belén MÉNDEZ-NAYA and Elena SEOANE (eds.):** Sounds, Words, Texts and Change. Selected papers from 11 ICEHL, Santiago de Compostela, 7–11 September 2000. Volume 2. 2002. x, 310 pp.

223 **FANEGO, Teresa, Javier PÉREZ-GUERRA and María José LÓPEZ-COUSO (eds.):** English Historical Syntax and Morphology. Selected papers from 11 ICEHL, Santiago de Compostela, 7–11 September 2000. Volume 1. 2002. x, 306 pp.

222 **HERSCHENSOHN, Julia, Enrique MALLÉN and Karen ZAGONA (eds.):** Features and Interfaces in Romance. Essays in honor of Heles Contreras. 2001. xiv, 302 pp.

221 **D'HULST, Yves, Johan ROORYCK and Jan SCHROTEN (eds.):** Romance Languages and Linguistic Theory 1999. Selected papers from 'Going Romance' 1999, Leiden, 9–11 December 1999. 2001. viii, 406 pp.

220 **SATTERFIELD, Teresa, Christina M. TORTORA and Diana CRESTI (eds.):** Current Issues in Romance Languages. Selected papers from the 29th Linguistic Symposium on Romance Languages (LSRL), Ann Arbor, 8–11 April 1999. 2002. viii, 412 pp.

219 **ANDERSEN, Henning (ed.):** Actualization. Linguistic Change in Progress. Papers from a workshop held at the 14th International Conference on Historical Linguistics, Vancouver, B.C., 14 August 1999. 2001. vii, 250 pp.

218 **BENDJABALLAH, Sabrina, Wolfgang U. DRESSLER, Oskar E. PFEIFFER and Maria D. VOEIKOVA (eds.):** Morphology 2000. Selected papers from the 9th Morphology Meeting, Vienna, 24–28 February 2000. 2002. viii, 317 pp.

217 **WILTSHIRE, Caroline R. and Joaquim CAMPS (eds.):** Romance Phonology and Variation. Selected papers from the 30th Linguistic Symposium on Romance Languages, Gainesville, Florida, February 2000. 2002. xii, 238 pp.

216 **CAMPS, Joaquim and Caroline R. WILTSHIRE (eds.):** Romance Syntax, Semantics and L2 Acquisition. Selected papers from the 30th Linguistic Symposium on Romance Languages, Gainesville, Florida, February 2000. 2001. xii, 246 pp.

215 **BRINTON, Laurel J. (ed.):** Historical Linguistics 1999. Selected papers from the 14th International Conference on Historical Linguistics, Vancouver, 9–13 August 1999. 2001. xii, 398 pp.

214 **WEIGAND, Edda and Marcelo DASCAL (eds.):** Negotiation and Power in Dialogic Interaction. 2001. viii, 303 pp.

213 **SORNICOLA, Rosanna, Erich POPPE and Ariel SHISHA-HALEVY (eds.):** Stability, Variation and Change of Word-Order Patterns over Time. With the assistance of Paola Como. 2000. xxxii, 323 pp.

212 **REPETTI, Lori (ed.):** Phonological Theory and the Dialects of Italy. 2000. x, 301 pp.

211 **ELŠÍK, Viktor and Yaron MATRAS (eds.):** Grammatical Relations in Romani. The Noun Phrase. with a Foreword by Frans Plank (Universität Konstanz). 2000. x, 244 pp.

210 **DWORKIN, Steven N. and Dieter WANNER (eds.):** New Approaches to Old Problems. Issues in Romance historical linguistics. 2000. xiv, 235 pp.

209 **KING, Ruth:** The Lexical Basis of Grammatical Borrowing. A Prince Edward Island French case study. 2000. xvi, 241 pp.

208 **ROBINSON, Orrin W.:** Whose German? The ach/ich alternation and related phenomena in 'standard' and 'colloquial'. 2001. xii, 178 pp.

207 **SANZ, Montserrat:** Events and Predication. A new approach to syntactic processing in English and Spanish. 2000. xiv, 219 pp.

206 **FAWCETT, Robin P.:** A Theory of Syntax for Systemic Functional Linguistics. 2000. xxiv, 360 pp.

205 **DIRVEN, René, Roslyn M. FRANK and Cornelia ILIE (eds.):** Language and Ideology. Volume 2: descriptive cognitive approaches. 2001. vi, 264 pp.

204 **DIRVEN, René, Bruce HAWKINS and Esra SANDIKCIOGLU (eds.):** Language and Ideology. Volume 1: theoretical cognitive approaches. 2001. vi, 301 pp.

203 **NORRICK, Neal R.:** Conversational Narrative. Storytelling in everyday talk. 2000. xiv, 233 pp.

202 **LECARME, Jacqueline, Jean LOWENSTAMM and Ur SHLONSKY (eds.):** Research in Afroasiatic Grammar. Papers from the Third conference on Afroasiatic Languages, Sophia Antipolis, 1996. 2000. vi, 386 pp.

201 **DRESSLER, Wolfgang U., Oskar E. PFEIFFER, Markus A. PÖCHTRAGER and John R. RENNISON (eds.):** Morphological Analysis in Comparison. 2000. x, 261 pp.

200 **ANTTILA, Raimo:** Greek and Indo-European Etymology in Action. Proto-Indo-European *ag'-. 2000. xii, 314 pp.

199 **PÜTZ, Martin and Marjolijn H. VERSPOOR (eds.):** Explorations in Linguistic Relativity. 2000. xvi, 369 pp.

198 **NIEMEIER, Susanne and René DIRVEN (eds.):** Evidence for Linguistic Relativity. 2000. xxii, 240 pp.

197 **COOPMANS, Peter, Martin EVERAERT and Jane GRIMSHAW (eds.):** Lexical Specification and Insertion. 2000. xviii, 476 pp.

196 **HANNAHS, S.J. and Mike DAVENPORT (eds.):** Issues in Phonological Structure. Papers from an International Workshop. 1999. xii, 268 pp.

195 HERRING, Susan C., Pieter van REENEN and Lene SCHØSLER (eds.): Textual Parameters in Older Languages. 2001. x, 448 pp.

194 COLEMAN, Julie and Christian J. KAY (eds.): Lexicology, Semantics and Lexicography. Selected papers from the Fourth G. L. Brook Symposium, Manchester, August 1998. 2000. xiv, 257 pp.

193 KLAUSENBURGER, Jurgen: Grammaticalization. Studies in Latin and Romance morphosyntax. 2000. xiv, 184 pp.

192 ALEXANDROVA, Galina M. and Olga ARNAUDOVA (eds.): The Minimalist Parameter. Selected papers from the Open Linguistics Forum, Ottawa, 21–23 March 1997. 2001. x, 360 pp.

191 SIHLER, Andrew L.: Language History. An introduction. 2000. xvi, 298 pp.

190 BENMAMOUN, Elabbas (ed.): Perspectives on Arabic Linguistics. Papers from the Annual Symposium on Arabic Linguistics. Volume XII: Urbana-Champaign, Illinois, 1998. 1999. viii, 204 pp.

189 NICOLOV, Nicolas and Ruslan MITKOV (eds.): Recent Advances in Natural Language Processing II. Selected papers from RANLP '97. 2000. xi, 422 pp.

188 SIMMONS, Richard VanNess: Chinese Dialect Classification. A comparative approach to Harngjou, Old Jintarn, and Common Northern Wu. 1999. xviii, 317 pp.

187 FRANCO, Jon, Alazne LANDA and Juan MARTÍN (eds.): Grammatical Analyses in Basque and Romance Linguistics. Papers in honor of Mario Saltarelli. 1999. viii, 306 pp.

186 MIŠESKA TOMIĆ, Olga and Milorad RADOVANOVIĆ (eds.): History and Perspectives of Language Study. Papers in honor of Ranko Bugarski. 2000. xxii, 314 pp.

185 AUTHIER, Jean-Marc, Barbara E. BULLOCK and Lisa A. REED (eds.): Formal Perspectives on Romance Linguistics. Selected papers from the 28th Linguistic Symposium on Romance Languages (LSRL XXVIII), University Park, 16–19 April 1998. 1999. xii, 334 pp.

184 SAGART, Laurent: The Roots of Old Chinese. 1999. xii, 272 pp.

183 CONTINI-MORAVA, Ellen and Yishai TOBIN (eds.): Between Grammar and Lexicon. 2000. xxxii, 365 pp.

182 KENESEI, István (ed.): Crossing Boundaries. Advances in the theory of Central and Eastern European languages. 1999. viii, 302 pp.

181 MOHAMMAD, Mohammad A.: Word Order, Agreement and Pronominalization in Standard and Palestinian Arabic. 2000. xvi, 197 pp.

180 MEREU, Lunella (ed.): Boundaries of Morphology and Syntax. 1999. viii, 314 pp.

179 RINI, Joel: Exploring the Role of Morphology in the Evolution of Spanish. 1999. xvi, 187 pp.

178 FOOLEN, Ad and Frederike van der LEEK (eds.): Constructions in Cognitive Linguistics. Selected papers from the Fifth International Cognitive Linguistics Conference, Amsterdam, 1997. 2000. xvi, 338 pp.

177 CUYCKENS, Hubert and Britta E. ZAWADA (eds.): Polysemy in Cognitive Linguistics. Selected papers from the International Cognitive Linguistics Conference, Amsterdam, 1997. 2001. xxviii, 296 pp.

176 VAN HOEK, Karen, Andrej A. KIBRIK and Leo NOORDMAN (eds.): Discourse Studies in Cognitive Linguistics. Selected papers from the 5th International Cognitive Linguistics Conference, Amsterdam, July 1997. 1999. vi, 187 pp.

175 GIBBS, JR., Raymond W. and Gerard J. STEEN (eds.): Metaphor in Cognitive Linguistics. Selected papers from the 5th International Cognitive Linguistics Conference, Amsterdam, 1997. 1999. viii, 226 pp.

174 HALL, T. Alan and Ursula KLEINHENZ (eds.): Studies on the Phonological Word. 1999. viii, 298 pp.

173 TREVIÑO, Esthela and José LEMA (eds.): Semantic Issues in Romance Syntax. 1999. viii, 309 pp.

172 DIMITROVA-VULCHANOVA, Mila and Lars HELLAN (eds.): Topics in South Slavic Syntax and Semantics. 1999. xxviii, 263 pp.

171 WEIGAND, Edda (ed.): Contrastive Lexical Semantics. 1998. x, 270 pp.

170 LAMB, Sydney M.: Pathways of the Brain. The neurocognitive basis of language. 1999. xii, 418 pp.

169 GHADESSY, Mohsen (ed.): Text and Context in Functional Linguistics. 1999. xviii, 340 pp.

168 RATCLIFFE, Robert R.: The "Broken" Plural Problem in Arabic and Comparative Semitic. Allomorphy and analogy in non-concatenative morphology. 1998. xii, 261 pp.

167 BENMAMOUN, Elabbas, Mushira EID and Niloofar HAERI (eds.): Perspectives on Arabic Linguistics. Papers from the Annual Symposium on Arabic Linguistics. Volume XI: Atlanta, Georgia, 1997. 1998. viii, 231 pp.

166 LEMMENS, Maarten: Lexical Perspectives on Transitivity and Ergativity. Causative constructions in English. 1998. xii, 268 pp.

165 BUBENÍK, Vít: A Historical Syntax of Late Middle Indo-Aryan (Apabhraṃśa). 1998. xxiv, 265 pp.

164 SCHMID, Monika S., Jennifer R. AUSTIN and Dieter STEIN (eds.): Historical Linguistics 1997. Selected papers from the 13th International Conference on Historical Linguistics, Düsseldorf, 10–17 August 1997. 1998. x, 409 pp.

163 LOCKWOOD, David G., Peter H. FRIES and James E. COPELAND (eds.): Functional Approaches to Language, Culture and Cognition. Papers in honor of Sydney M. Lamb. 2000. xxxiv, 656 pp.

162 HOGG, Richard M. and Linda van BERGEN (eds.): Historical Linguistics 1995. Volume 2: Germanic linguistics.. Selected papers from the 12th International Conference on Historical Linguistics, Manchester, August 1995. 1998. x, 365 pp.

161 SMITH, John Charles and Delia BENTLEY (eds.): Historical Linguistics 1995. Volume 1: General issues and non-Germanic Languages.. Selected papers from the 12th International Conference on Historical Linguistics, Manchester, August 1995. 2000. xii, 438 pp.

160 SCHWEGLER, Armin, Bernard TRANEL and Myriam URIBE-ETXEBARRIA (eds.): Romance Linguistics: Theoretical Perspectives. Selected papers from the 27th Linguistic Symposium on Romance Languages (LSRL XXVII), Irvine, 20–22 February, 1997. 1998. vi, 349 pp. + index.

159 JOSEPH, Brian D., Geoffrey C. HORROCKS and Irene PHILIPPAKI-WARBURTON (eds.): Themes in Greek Linguistics II. 1998. x, 335 pp.

158 SÁNCHEZ-MACARRO, Antonia and Ronald CARTER (eds.): Linguistic Choice across Genres. Variation in spoken and written English. 1998. viii, 338 pp.

157 LEMA, José and Esthela TREVIÑO (eds.): Theoretical Analyses on Romance Languages. Selected papers from the 26th Linguistic Symposium on Romance Languages (LSRL XXVI), Mexico City, 28–30 March, 1996. 1998. viii, 380 pp.

156 MATRAS, Yaron, Peter BAKKER and Hristo KYUCHUKOV (eds.): The Typology and Dialectology of Romani. 1997. xxxii, 223 pp.

155 FORGET, Danielle, Paul HIRSCHBÜHLER, France MARTINEAU and María Luisa RIVERO (eds.): Negation and Polarity. Syntax and semantics. Selected papers from the colloquium Negation: Syntax and Semantics. Ottawa, 11–13 May 1995. 1997. viii, 367 pp.

154 SIMON-VANDENBERGEN, Anne-Marie, Kristin DAVIDSE and Dirk NOËL (eds.): Reconnecting Language. Morphology and Syntax in Functional Perspectives. 1997. xiii, 339 pp.

153 EID, Mushira and Robert R. RATCLIFFE (eds.): Perspectives on Arabic Linguistics. Papers from the Annual Symposium on Arabic Linguistics. Volume X: Salt Lake City, 1996. 1997. vii, 296 pp.

152 HIRAGA, Masako K., Christopher SINHA and Sherman WILCOX (eds.): Cultural, Psychological and Typological Issues in Cognitive Linguistics. Selected papers of the bi-annual ICLA meeting in Albuquerque, July 1995. 1999. viii, 338 pp.

151 LIEBERT, Wolf-Andreas, Gisela REDEKER and Linda R. WAUGH (eds.): Discourse and Perspective in Cognitive Linguistics. 1997. xiv, 270 pp.

150 VERSPOOR, Marjolijn H., Kee Dong LEE and Eve SWEETERS (eds.): Lexical and Syntactical Constructions and the Construction of Meaning. Proceedings of the Bi-annual ICLA meeting in Albuquerque, July 1995. 1997. xii, 454 pp.

149 HALL, T. Alan: The Phonology of Coronals. 1997. x, 176 pp.

148 WOLF, George and Nigel LOVE (eds.): Linguistics Inside Out. Roy Harris and his critics. 1997. xxviii, 344 pp.

147 HEWSON, John: The Cognitive System of the French Verb. 1997. xii, 187 pp.

146 HINSKENS, Frans, Roeland van HOUT and W. Leo WETZELS (eds.): Variation, Change, and Phonological Theory. 1997. x, 314 pp.

145 HEWSON, John and Vít BUBENÍK: Tense and Aspect in Indo-European Languages. Theory, typology, diachrony. 1997. xii, 403 pp.

144 SINGH, R.K. (ed.): Trubetzkoy's Orphan. Proceedings of the Montréal Roundtable on "Morphonology: contemporary responses" (Montréal, October 1994). With the collaboration of Richard Desrochers. 1996. xiv, 363 pp.

143 ATHANASIADOU, Angeliki and René DIRVEN (eds.): On Conditionals Again. 1997. viii, 418 pp.

142 SALMONS, Joseph C. and Brian D. JOSEPH (eds.): Nostratic. Sifting the Evidence. 1998. vi, 293 pp.

141 EID, Mushira and Dilworth B. PARKINSON (eds.): Perspectives on Arabic Linguistics. Papers from the Annual Symposium on Arabic Linguistics. Volume IX: Washington D.C., 1995. 1996. xiii, 249 pp.

140 BLACK, James R. and Virginia MOTAPANYANE (eds.): Clitics, Pronouns and Movement. 1997. 375 pp.

139 BLACK, James R. and Virginia MOTAPANYANE (eds.): Microparametric Syntax and Dialect Variation. 1996. xviii, 269 pp.

138 SACKMANN, Robin and Monika BUDDE (eds.): Theoretical Linguistics and Grammatical Description. Papers in honour of Hans-Heinrich Lieb. 1996. x, 375 pp.

137 LIPPI-GREEN, Rosina L. and Joseph C. SALMONS (eds.): Germanic Linguistics. Syntactic and diachronic. 1996. viii, 192 pp.

136 MITKOV, Ruslan and Nicolas NICOLOV (eds.): Recent Advances in Natural Language Processing. Selected Papers from RANLP '95. 1997. xii, 472 pp.

135 BRITTON, Derek (ed.): English Historical Linguistics 1994. Papers from the 8th International Conference on English Historical Linguistics (8 ICEHL, Edinburgh, 19–23 September 1994). 1996. viii, 403 pp.

134 EID, Mushira (ed.): Perspectives on Arabic Linguistics. Papers from the Annual Symposium on Arabic Linguistics. Volume VIII: Amherst, Massachusetts 1994. 1996. vii, 261 pp.

133 ZAGONA, Karen (ed.): Grammatical Theory and Romance Languages. Selected papers from the 25th Linguistic Symposium on Romance Languages (LSRL XXV) Seattle, 2–4 March 1995. 1996. vi, 330 pp.

132 HERSCHENSOHN, Julia: Case Suspension and Binary Complement Structure in French. 1996. xi, 200 pp.

131 HUALDE, José Ignacio, Joseba A. LAKARRA and R.L. TRASK (eds.): Towards a History of the Basque Language. 1996. 365 pp.